D0782739

Bookworm

Conversations with Michael Silverblatt

Edited by Alan Felsenthal

The Song Cave

The Song Cave

www.the-song-cave.com

© Michael Silverblatt, 2023

Cover by Art Spiegelman

Design and layout by Janet Evans-Scanlon

All rights reserved. Printed in the United States of America.

No part of this book may be used or reproduced in any manner whatsoever without written permission except in the case of brief quotations embodied in critical articles and reviews. Members of educational institutions and organizations wishing to photocopy any of the work for classroom use, or authors and publishers who would like to obtain permission for any material in the work, should contact the publisher.

ISBN: 978-1-7372775-8-3

Library of Congress Control Number: 2022951381

FIRST EDITION

Contents

Editor's Note

With over three decades of KCRW's *Bookworm*, how to even begin narrowing down a selection for print? As this book's organizing principle, Michael and I decided to let the voices of the past guide us in our choices—the glorious voices of the dead. We began with our sense of the burden of the past, voices that will never be heard again and that will only be dim intuitions of evidence of what it was like to live in an age defined by its writers.

These conversations present an interviewer who's come fresh from an immersion in the writer's work with no one's point of view but his own. There's no school of thought or theory that these interviews represent. Instead, they encompass the voice of someone who loves to read struggling mightily to keep up with the new work of authors who are constantly emerging, coming to be loved, and who deserve the attention of an informed interviewer.

Michael does it without maps, without predetermined questions. He lets the conversation go where it chooses to go, or wants to go, or needs to go, until it becomes part of the ebb and flow of possibility between two human beings who are generating respect for and interest in one another. He does not regard himself as a literary critic, but rather as a reader, whose charge is to put into words the qualities he loves in what he's read.

Bookworm practices the guest-host relationship as the ancients did—where hospitality was the sacred right of any guest. The show doesn't exist to humiliate or insult writers. It doesn't say that these are the only writers, or even the best writers. These are the writers with whom Michael held a deep kinship and understanding. In many cases, these writers became his close friends beyond the show, and Michael has said that they taught him not only how to read their work but how to live.

Most of these conversations were conducted face-to-face in the studios of KCRW in Santa Monica, California. A few took place over the phone or at the home of the author. The conversation with John Berger is the only one that was not aired on KCRW; it was filmed, thanks to the Lannan Foundation, at Berger's home in France, and can be viewed online (lannan.org).

You can listen to these conversations through KCRW's extensive *Bookworm* archive (kcrw.com). We've tried to stay as close to the audio as possible with these transcripts, and we've noted things that would be obvious to the listener but not the reader.

The history of *Bookworm* is too long and varied to be represented in one volume. May this selection lead you to listen to more shows and to seek out the books that will change your life.

—ALAN FELSENTHAL

John Ashbery

2007: *A Worldly Country*

MS: It's been a great desire of mine to have John Ashbery as my guest on *Bookworm*. I have been reading his poems since I was a student. John Ashbery gave me his book *Three Poems* when it first came out. I've been reading him constantly ever since. He's a connoisseur of wonderlands, if you bear in mind that Wonderland can be chaotic, that what goes on there is often an exchange of incomprehensions, that the people that one meets are often not very nice, that anything can follow and non-sequiturs are the rule. In addition, Wonderland incorporates a good deal of parody, pastiche, extraordinary events that take place at bewildering speeds. I remember when I first read the Alice books, coming across the forest where things lose their names. Alice is pictured in the famous illustration by Tenniel clutching a fawn, not knowing who she is, which is often, for me, the effect, thrilling and bewildering, of Ashbery's poetry. I wanted to begin by asking you if that kind of nonsense and Wonderland itself was important to you?

JA: Well, yes. Certainly *Alice in Wonderland* is one of the first and major books I ever read. It seems very much a reflection of the world that we live in and has a lot to teach us about it, I guess.

MS: I think so, too. I noticed that this new book has epigraphs both from Auden and from Empson. And I know that British poetry has been very important to you. Could you talk about that a bit?

JA: Well, it was, yes. When I was in high school and began reading contemporary poetry and writing it myself, Auden was considered the greatest living poet—in English, at any rate—even more so than Eliot because Eliot was already a historical figure. When I began reading modern poetry, I was as puzzled as everybody else is when they first encounter it.

   Although Auden would not seem to be one of the more fearsome or difficult modern poets, to me he was. I couldn't understand, for instance, how he was allowed to get away with using slang and popular song lyrics and have those at the same time in conjunction with old English forms and archaic language, and all of it mashed together in a slurry that seemed to me something that you weren't allowed to do in poetry. And it was coming to terms with this situation that got me really interested and involved in writing myself and trying to explore the implications of this situation of the *mélange de tout*, a potpourri kind of poetry.

MS: I didn't like him when he became understandable. Did you feel that way?

JA: Well, yes. He hadn't done that when I started reading him. This would have been around 1944 or 1945, and Auden's later poetry hadn't yet come along. What I was reading was what he had written in England before coming to the United States in 1939, as well as the more recent ones, such as *The Sea and the Mirror*, a wonderful version of *The Tempest* that he wrote after getting to America, and *For the Time Being*, a Christmas oratorio. Then *The Age of Anxiety*, which came in 1947, again a kind of dramatic masque, which uses the Icelandic verse form.

MS: The thrill for me was *The Orators* and the play *Paid on Both Sides*.

JA: Yes. Those I think are his greatest works, and he characteristically denied them or denounced them. He did allow *The Orators* to be reprinted finally in the '60s, but with a little introductory note saying that he thought he was insane when he wrote it. The older Auden, who was very commonsensical, no longer believed in poetry with a capital P, as he put it, didn't believe that it should be privileged or funny. I mean, funny peculiar. I still prefer his early work.

MS: When I started reading you, I guess what I liked immediately was that it made the noises of poetry, but it didn't seem like poetry. It seemed almost as if it were an impersonation of poetry by someone who loved it but didn't want to write it as it had been before. Does that make sense?

JA: I think that's a way of putting it, yeah. Also, I think that you can take any line of Auden's poetry of the '30s and early '40s, and no matter what it is, if it's something that's not even a complete sentence, you realize that you're in a poem, that you can relax, that this is a guy who writes poetry. I'm trying to think of an example of a line, for instance. There's one poem that begins: "Consider this and in our time." It doesn't really matter what "this" is. You already know that "this" is going to be poetry.

MS:　It's also aligned to something that I once heard you say. It made me very happy because when I was in school, people liked to take *Self-Portrait in a Convex Mirror* and show you the development of its thought, and I had read that you'd said that it was meant to sound like a lecture that you were at, and that you were falling asleep during, and could barely follow what was being said, except that it was making the noise of a lecture.

JA:　I don't remember saying that, but I can believe that I did. It's the noise of poetry that's important. What the message of the lecture is, is a lot less urgent for me.

MS:　It seems to me, too. This is a funny thing to say, but when I read *Flow Chart*, sometimes I'll read it late at night, the hour is progressing, and it seems to me suddenly I've landed in a place where it makes complete sense and I can't believe that this is happening. I'm almost lit and incandescent with the possibility. Then I'll wake up in the morning to read it again and can't find what it was that I thought was there. I wondered, are you aware of these poems flicking off and on in insignificance?

JA:　Well, I don't know that I am, but this certainly is the way dreams operate in *Alice in Wonderland*. As you said, these truths are somehow much more convincing to me, and I think to a lot of us, than what we are being told we have to understand right now. We're being told that in a dream, too, but we're taking it from the source.

MS:　Yes. I think that we're dreaming all the time.

JA:　I agree.

MS: I forget who it was, but someone said that dreams are like the underground river and that from time to time a fish from that river jumps and appears in daylight and then falls again. But constantly underneath what we think we're thinking, there's something else that's running in parallel and is always the present to us. There's never a moment in which consciousness is single.

JA: Yes. That's mentioned in a novel by the Austrian writer, von Doderer, that there is a constant current in our minds that's flowing according to its own program, and that at any moment one can let down a bucket and pull up some water which is always from the same river, no matter what has happened since the last time we examined it.

MS: There's also a sentence in von Doderer—he's talking about his own career—which goes something like: first you break the windows, then you are the windows.

JA: That's wonderful.

MS: I wondered if you had that sensation because I know you say in one of the early essays that a poet's job is to defy criticism.

JA: Well, I was perhaps going overboard a little when I said that. Perhaps I was stinging from some early critical spankings I had received, but that again is, I guess, one of my ideas that I took from elsewhere. Cocteau said that one should read criticism of oneself very carefully so as to be able to not do all of the things critics tell you that you should do, in fact, to go against them and do the opposite.

MS: But do you have a sense of having become one of the windows that needs to be broken now?

JA: No, I don't, but I wouldn't be at all surprised if that were the case. Time and literary history don't stop. There is always more breaking to be done. I'm reminded in that regard of the very beginning of Gertrude Stein's novel, *The Making of Americans*, and she quotes this anecdote about—you probably could phrase it better than me.

MS: I love it. Let's see if we can do it.

JA: A man was being dragged by his son through his own orchard. When they came to a certain tree, the man yelled, "Stop! I never dragged my own father farther than this tree."

MS: Someone told me that that's actually from Virgil.

JA: I knew it was from somewhere else, but I didn't know where.

MS: It's astonishing. I also wanted to talk to you about something that you said that I think is absolutely thrilling. You were talking about Gertrude Stein, which is why I bring it up. You were talking about her magnificent *Stanzas in Meditation*, and you said, "Yes, there is monotony, but let's remember that water flows monotonously over the falls, generating electrical power." I find that one of the things that people have lost track of is an interest in boredom and monotony.

JA: As long as it's the right kind of monotony. Now, what do I mean by that? Well, I guess the kind that produces electricity, and you have to encounter it first to know whether that's going to be the case.

MS: You're writing about Alfred Chester. You say that at a certain point in literature, it seems that Chester is interested in finding the world still more awful than Jean Genet found it. That somehow the idea that the world is awful is addressed to the reader who's meant to feel guilty for having occasioned this awfulness. It reminded me of that interest in not judging, in being ambivalent, that these poems are not about even the Auden effect of *The Age of Anxiety*. It's not a scold. You're not telling people what to think.

JA: Well, I hope not, and I think not. But, yes, I find in some of those writers and in other ones, say like Céline for instance, there's this hectoring subtext that you are somehow responsible for all of the horrors that I'm dredging up for you to look at.

MS: Let's hear you read from your new book.

JA: This is the title poem, "A Worldly Country." It's rather unusual for me in that it rhymes, although I used to write rhyming poems when I first started writing poetry because I thought it would be hard to do and discovered that it wasn't, so I went on to writing non-rhyming poetry.

A Worldly Country

Not the smoothness, not the insane clocks on the square,
the scent of manure in the municipal parterre,
not the fabrics, the sullen mockery of Tweety Bird,
not the fresh troops that needed freshening up. If it occurred
in real time, it was OK, and if it was time in a novel
that was OK too. From palace and hovel
the great parade flooded avenue and byway
and turnip fields became just another highway.
Leftover bonbons were thrown to the chickens
and geese, who squawked like the very dickens.
There was no peace in the bathroom, none in the china closet
or the banks, where no one came to make a deposit.
In short all hell broke loose that wide afternoon.
By evening all was calm again. A crescent moon
hung in the sky like a parrot on its perch.
Departing guests smiled and called, "See you in church!"
For night, as usual, knew what it was doing,
providing sleep to offset the great ungluing
that tomorrow again would surely bring.
As I gazed at the quiet rubble, one thing
puzzled me: What had happened, and why?
One minute we were up to our necks in rebelliousness,
and the next, peace had subdued the ranks of hellishness.

So often it happens that the time we turn around in
soon becomes the shoal our pathetic skiff will run aground in.
And just as waves are anchored to the bottom of the sea
we must reach the shallows before God cuts us free.

I should do that more often. I think there's a real pleasure in rhyming
things like "highway" and "byway," "chickens" and "dickens."

MS: Well, I remember thinking when some of the rhyming poems started to appear that they were like dum-dum poems. The point was to rhyme dumb, and that the poem gave the impression of an idiot who thought that this is poetry, this is what a poem is supposed to sound like. Do I remember correctly? Is it in the Ella Wheeler Wilcox crazy section in which someone who thinks that poetry is about making majestic statements and rhyming them too, both at the same time?

JA: That's the Calypso section.

MS: It's amazing. It's a kind of making fun, yes, of people who think poetry is this?

JA: Well, more than that, I think it's a redeeming of demotic or disesteemed material and saying, this is poetry, too. Even the little rhymes that occur to us when we're shaving or eating breakfast have a right to exist, just as much as the high flown.

MS: Now is that inclusion of disesteemed material, disowned material, is that part of the democracy of poems?

JA: I think it should be. I've always felt very warmly towards clichés and use them a lot. The reason being that they're the way we talk when we talk to each other and are trying very hard to make ourselves understood and to make people like us or get something that we want. We resort to these age-old, tired expressions, which to me have a holiness about them just because they've been used so much by people to communicate and touch each other. Yes, for a democracy of stylistic elements such as self-conscious, poetical language, crude slang, journalistic prose, textbook boring exposition, I see all these as rolling around with each other and being a medium of communication that is what poetry tries to function as.

MS: Now, you wrote *A Nest of Ninnies* with James Schuyler, and that novel is an amazing anthology of the dead things that people say that are hilarious. I find it impossible to read without laughing out loud. How did you get so good? Did you practice the celebration of the maudlin, that procession of perfectly dumb phrases that everyone says?

JA: We never expected that this work would see the light of day; we wrote it really to amuse each other. I think we were both remembering our lonesome and boring childhoods—both of us in small towns in upstate New York, of course we didn't know each other then—and what our parents would say, what we heard on the radio, in newsreels, funny popular expressions that didn't last very long and that we were preserving in this way.

MS: Sort of like "See you in church," in the poem that you read.

JA: I don't know if anybody still says that.

MS: I doubt it.

JA: Of course, it was said not meaning literally, I'll see you in church, but it was just a way of saying, "So long."

MS: Now, those last two lines of "A Worldly Country," in which God is invoked in a final couplet and anticipating a freedom that comes once you reach the shallows. This poem, in its rhymes at least, is interested in shallowness, a reward almost for the long haul. I was talking to you once on the phone about de Chirico in his late, realistic charcoal sketches, that sense that now it's time to go and do what everyone does. The great experiment is over, and he's just waiting to be taken, it seems to me.

JA: Well, it is an ambiguous deliverance, and I am nothing if not ambiguous, because I feel it's a way of crowding extra meaning into whatever I write. Since God is cutting us free, that's a slightly ominous operation; in fact, operation is, I guess, what it is. What are we being freed from? I guess we're being freed from the depths, which is a good thing, since it means we won't drown, but on the other hand, we're being delivered to the shallows, and maybe that's not such a good thing either, not so good for our heads. I wanted a complicated deliverance at the end of that poem, and that's part of it, I think.

2007: *Haunted House* by Pierre Reverdy, translated by John Ashbery, and *Prose Poems* by Pierre Reverdy, translated by Ron Padgett (RP)

MS: I found that two wonderful poets had done translations of the French poet Pierre Reverdy. Both of these volumes are published by Black Square Editions. They are the prose poems of Pierre Reverdy. I had seen poems by Reverdy in various anthologies and read about Reverdy, but I had not had a sustained experience of the work until I encountered these translations. I became transfixed, fascinated, and I thought it would be wonderful to have the two poets who've done these extraordinary translations with me together. One book is *Prose Poems*, translated by Ron Padgett; the other is a long prose poem called *Haunted House*, and it's translated by John Ashbery. Now, what is known about Reverdy?

JA: Actually, I'm not an authority. He was born in 1889 in Narbonne, in the south of France near the Mediterranean. He went to a lycée, I believe in Toulouse, and then came to Paris around the turn of the century or a little later. He was associated with painters, especially Picasso and Juan Gris, at the time when Picasso was newly embarked in Paris and living in Montmartre. Later, around 1915, he published a review which reproduced art of those artists, and also he published the poetry of the young Surrealists who were about ten years younger than he was. And he was a kind of mentor to them at that time. Later on, in the '20s, after Surrealism was founded—I don't think he ever actually officially belonged to it—he moved away from Paris to the town of Solesmes.

RP: It's near Chartres.

JA: Yeah. In fact, in *Haunted House* there's an allusion to the countryside which is called the Beauce, one of the few specific allusions in the work. I'm not sure why, I believe he converted to Catholicism. Solesmes is renowned for its cathedral choir. I had recordings of it even in the '40s, but I'm not sure if that's the reason that he lived there. I know that he was married, but I don't really know anything about his life.

MS: Well, it's said that no one knows very much about his life, and I wondered why. Was he a very solitary person later on?

JA: I think probably he was. The mere fact that he went to live in this village after the giddy life of Paris in the '20s would seem to indicate that he had a kind of reclusive nature.

MS: Ron Padgett, in his translator's note, mentions that he's been at work, in a sense, on translating these poems for many years. Ron, you mentioned that, despite the rambunctiousness of your own work, the austerity and spookiness of Reverdy appealed to you. When did you first find his work?

RP: I think I first read it when I was in college; at least that's my first recollection of it, in some anthologies. Also, I recall reading some of John Ashbery's translations in *Evergreen Review* in the early '60s, which I thought were very, very good translations. My teacher at the time, Kenneth Koch, also was a big fan of Reverdy's work. All of that funneled me toward him. I was interested in the literature of that whole period in Paris—Apollinaire, Max Jacob, and others. Reverdy interested me because his writing was so unlike mine and yet I liked it so much, and I was perplexed as to why I liked something that was so unlike me. That got me hooked on him. And then, when I went to live in Paris in the middle '60s, I really fell for him there and started dogging his footsteps, although he was dead for five years already. I went and found the building he had lived in and the print shop he had corrected proofs in—that sort of detective work, just for my own pleasure. I got more and more fascinated with him the more I read, partly because he was so stingy with information about his own life. When he first moved to Paris as a young man, he was employed as a proofreader for a large daily newspaper, which required that he work all night. He walked to work all the way from Montmartre down to Montparnasse, and then he walked home at dawn. So he became this sort of nocturnal creature, and that can give rise to all kinds of phantoms.

JA: Actually, he published a magazine called *Nord-Sud* (or North-South), which is the name of the metro line that connects Montmartre with Montparnasse, which, when he had the cash, he must have taken.

MS: Many of these poems are walks by the railroad tracks and seeing the homeless people around the station and a kind of incandescent vision of the solitariness of other people. That sense of a gone one seeing the other loners, unable to interrogate them, but unable to imagine anyone who would dismiss or look down on them.

RP: Yeah, you see the solitary person in the street at night, and you wonder who they are and how they got there. Also, as we said, he lived in Montmartre beginning in 1911, and at that time that was a slightly spooky neighborhood. It wasn't entirely safe; there were a lot of seedy characters on the edges of it. Just walking around at the wrong time of day might get you in trouble. Maybe that contributed to his trepidation of being in the street and wondering who that person coming toward him in the street is.

MS: At the end of this interview, we'll be hearing a section from *Haunted House*, but I thought I'd begin by asking Ron Padgett to read some of the prose poems. Tell us about the book in which these occurred.

RP: Reverdy's first book was called *Poèmes en prose*, just *Prose Poems*. It was published in an edition of one hundred copies in 1915 at the print shop where he did proofreading, and he helped with the printing as well. Six copies of these were special editions. He had two of his friends do handmade covers for six copies. The first three copies were decorated by Juan Gris, and the second three were decorated by Henri Laurent—these very beautiful, you can imagine, priceless objects. Then he dedicated various poems to his friends: Max Jacob, Picasso, Juan Gris, Henri Matisse, Georges Braque, and others. Then the binding of this book took place at Reverdy's apartment. It was bound by his wife and, I think, Henri Laurent's wife, Marthe, and by Georges Braque's wife, Marcelle. The women sat around and did some sewing after this book was printed. Then it was distributed just, you can imagine, one hundred copies to the happy few. Anyway, the couple of excerpts that I'll read are from this first book. I've just picked three here.

At Dawn

In my dream the head of a child was in the center.
　　If the clouds gather on your roof and the rain spares you, will you keep the secret of this double miracle?
　　But no voice calls you. If you get up, barefoot, you'll get sick. Where would you go, anyway, across these ravines of light.
　　The quilts kept the silence. Legs folded under, he walks on his wings and goes out. He was an angel and the whiter morning that was rising.

The Wind and the Spirit

It is an astonishing chimera. The head, higher than this floor, takes up its position between two wires and jams and stays. Nothing moves.
　　The unknown head speaks and I do not understand one word. I hear no sound—down on the ground. I am always on the sidewalk across the way and I look; I look at the words the wind brings, the words it's going to hurl further away. The head speaks and I hear nothing, the wind disperses it all.
　　O great mocking or gloomy wind, I have wished you'd die. And I lost the hat that you have also taken away from me. I have nothing left, but my hate endures, alas, longer than you.

To Each His Own

He hunted the moon, he left the night. One by one the stars fell into a net of running water.

Behind the trembling aspens a strange fisherman watches anxiously with an open eye, the only one, hidden under his big hat, and the line quivers.

Nothing is caught, but he fills his basket with pieces of gold whose glittering is darkened inside the closed hamper.

But someone else was waiting further down the bank. More modest, he was fishing in a mud puddle the rain had left. That water, from the sky, was full of stars.

MS: I find this poet Reverdy, who is new to me from these translations, to be one of the most extraordinary experiences I've had reading poetry recently. Now, *Haunted House* comes to approximately sixty-two pages. It's one long prose poem. John, can you tell me about the tradition it comes from?

JA: Again, I don't know very much about it. Not very much has been written about it, but it obviously has its roots in the work of the writer who called himself the Comte de Lautréamont in the nineteenth century, who wrote a work called *Les Chants de Maldoror* (*The Songs of Maldoror*), which was the work that really inspired the Surrealists fifty years later when they began. It's a sort of mock-epic in a very high-flown but at the same time satirical vein. It's rather cruel and nightmarish but also very lyrical and beautiful.

The other tradition may well have been the prose poems of Max Jacob. I think that he and Reverdy were the two great twentieth-century French poets. The Surrealists were interesting, and they were very good at creating buzz, but their actual poetry I don't think is on the same level as Jacob, who was about ten years older than Reverdy and who was a champion of him. I have the impression that Reverdy really couldn't get along very well by himself. I happen to own a letter from Jacob to André Breton asking for money for Reverdy, saying, "He's in a very bad way. If you know somebody who could raise some cash for him, that would be wonderful."

I don't know whether this letter was ever sent or perhaps it's a copy of one that Jacob did send to Breton. I don't know whether Breton ever replied or did anything for Reverdy. But he did, in the early '30s, I think, in one of the Surrealist magazines—they were always having these questionnaires, especially what ten books would you take to a desert island. And André Breton chose *Haunted House* as one of the books that he would take with him, which I think is rather surprising because by that time Reverdy had already left Paris, apparently converted to Roman Catholicism, and was living in the abbey town of Solesmes near Chartres. And Breton of course was violently anti-Catholic and anti-clerical, as were all of the Surrealists.

MS: But I think that it's completely clear: even Breton with his taste and passion for excommunication could not escape the power of a Reverdy poem like *Haunted House*. It's truly extraordinary. What makes it difficult to translate? I believe this is the first translation of it ever.

JA: Yes, it is, and one thing is that there are many very long sentences with complicated clauses and grammar, not unlike the problems one faces translating Proust. It's very difficult to keep all of those in balance when you're working on them. There were also a few very arcane puns. I had to call for help to some French friends in a few cases. I have translated the poetry before. I love it. I find the poetry, including what Ron just read, to be very different. It's very self-effacing almost, and oblique and occupied with very tiny degrees and differences. Kenneth Koch, who was a great admirer of Reverdy, once said, "He likes to write about very tiny things like the shadow of a pin on an apple."

MS: Also, in the prose poems, there's a profound sense of shame, desiring to go to places where he won't be looked at. There is an almost dread of encounter.

JA: Yeah, I think some of that might be a bit parodic. The great nineteenth-century epic writers like Zola, for instance, I think are in the background there.

MS: I was thinking also of *Gaspard de la Nuit*, that sense of a nighttime vision. Yes, the shame and strange craven dignity are sort of formal.

JA: Wasn't *Gaspard de la Nuit* the basis for Schoenberg's—

MS: *Pierrot lunaire.*

JA: Yes. Therefore, that led into expressionism from the 1830s when it was published. Aloysius Bertrand was the name of the writer of *Gaspard de la Nuit*. Not really known for anything other than that. Although I believe he is credited as being the first to write prose poems.

MS: Yes, I think so. That's what sent me to him. I was fascinated by the sudden evolution of the prose poem—where did it come from? That and Aloysius was a name that I always liked as a child. I'm going to ask John Ashbery to read a section of his translation of *Haunted House*. There's a kind of adventure poem; it's there to some extent in *Hebdomeros* and the first section of Wallace Stevens's "The Comedian as the Letter C." The self seems to go on an exciting and threatening voyage. For readers who don't know this tradition, it's so thrilling because it's aligned to Verne and adventure books and yet crossed with aspects of spiritual questing that make it naked and shocking and thrilling at the same time.

JA: There are a number of themes that occur almost cyclically, in the Wagnerian sense, in this work, one of them being a shipwreck, which is happening in this particular passage:

"In mid-ocean, after one of the most frightful maritime disasters of modern times, the position of the shipwrecked survivor whom a narrow spar allows to float just underwater is singularly critical. How will he manage to go and finish the hand of cards begun at a café on one of the smaller boulevards. Perhaps a shark will soon come and shear off his two legs. What will he do? Viewed from above, or simply from a distance, from the bridge of a comfortable battleship or from an even safer position on terra firma, the ocean's waves are imposing, magnificent to behold; their contemplation raises the immortal soul of man who compares them unfavourably to his perishable casing, but at a considerable distance from the coasts, toward one of those places where, from the height of the crow's nest, one perceives that the horizon has suddenly taken on a circular form as precise as though traced by a full-scale compass, they become terrifying—huge and terrifying. Such is the opinion of the castaway who even goes so far as to add that he finds them vertiginous. Vertigo is swallowed up by the swipe of an albatross's or a seagull's wing between the distance that separates the hollows and the crests of those liquid foothills. The castaway has had about all he can stand; his obvious lack of training begins little by little to aggravate his severe handicap in this endurance test that God has deemed equitable and salutary to send his way. But then too, into what risky adventure did he carelessly plunge? Isn't the weather nicer in that café in the capital, ornamented with luxurious mirrors which make it seem larger? All those sounds of voices in the mirrors, all those reflections of glory in the clouds of smoke; that gale of words which drags the motions of hand and hair towards the revolving doors. Those magnificent poses, in which no line is wasted; those audacious phrases that go flying around the lamps and whose wings will never be censured; that sweetness of living, of wallowing in money, of demanding of others what one can't provide oneself, that ease of daydreaming and forgetting, of shouting for no reason, of singing, of inviting a crowd, of talking at night, of sleeping on emptiness, of emptying the mind, of twisting the heart, of losing at poker, of winning at fear, of laughing in the eyes and the wrinkles of one's best friends, of racing without danger along the tracks of intrepid cities and, above all, that certificate of existence which provides us with the services of our coevals at too modest a price, why did he leave all that for this precarious solitude on the plains of the ocean? Look at him now, beginning to reflect and rest his elbows on his spar with an anxious air. How will he ever finish that card game?"

MS: That's so beautiful.

2009: *The Landscapist* by Pierre Martory, translated by John Ashbery

MS: Today I have the pleasure of talking to John Ashbery, the translator of a volume of Pierre Martory's poetry, *The Landscapist*, published by The

Sheep Meadow Press. It's a dual-language edition in English and French. I encountered Martory's poetry in a little magazine around ten years ago called *o·blēk*, and I found it enchanting. In fact, I couldn't wait to find more. Over the years, there have been chapbooks, then a volume, and now this, *The Landscapist*, is the completest volume of his work to be translated by John Ashbery. Now, it's my belief that among the ways we know and understand a poet is by the work he chooses to translate, and the involvement with Martory's work, as well as with Martory, has been lifelong for Ashbery. In fact, this volume was nominated for the National Book Critics Circle Award as a nominee for poetry, not for translation; that's how good the translations are and how extraordinary the poems are. John Ashbery met Martory in Paris when he first went there on a Fulbright. What year was that, John?

JA: I met him in the spring of 1956.

MS: I'm curious, this is an interview with Ashbery, who is my favorite living poet, and it is as much about your work as about Martory's. What was French poetry for you when you went to Paris in 1956?

JA: Well, actually I arrived in the fall of '55. I really didn't know French very well at that point, so much of it remained totally below my radar. I had read translations of Rimbaud, René Char, Verlaine, et cetera, but I couldn't really read it in the original, and my project, which you had to have in order to get a Fulbright, was to do a sort of an anthology of twentieth-century French poetry in translation. I did that, actually, although I never republished most of the results. As I say, it was still terra incognita mostly for me.

MS: You had a taste for French poetry though. Had you studied it at Harvard?

JA: No, I studied French in high school for about four years. At Harvard, I didn't take any French literature courses, but I read Proust when I was an undergraduate, in English of course, and I was attracted by things French, as so many of us are. I read French fairy tales when I was a child, Perrault and others, and it always seemed as though that was a place of romance and pageantry and all the things one wants.

MS: I'm hoping that listeners will discover a good number of things to read, and I want to mention a very beautiful French fairy tale that you translated in a book called *Wonder Tales*, which Marina Warner edited. Can you then say what you thought French poetry would be before you encountered it?

JA: Well, probably there would be an element of surrealism in it, obviously, because that's where surrealism began, and I had read some Surrealist poetry in translation—André Breton, Paul Éluard. In America and England, there wasn't really any tradition like that, and I was attracted to surrealist painting even when I was taking children's art classes at a local museum and wondered why there couldn't be something like that in poetry. The few attempts in English in the early twentieth century were not really very exciting.

MS: I remember that in the late '60s we were reading *The Banquet Years*, which had very good chapters on Jarry, Apollinaire, and Satie. It made the work irresistible. Dada and surrealism seemed much more fun than what was going on in American poetry, and mysterious and funny as well. I remember that someone got a copy of Erik Satie's play, *Le piège de Méduse*, and started doing an impromptu translation for me. And I was so amused and entertained by it because it had elements of farce and mystery, theft, heist, all of it punctuated by dances by a mechanical monkey, who lurked at the side of the stage and performed certain jigs, tarantellas, extraordinary pieces, all of them less than sixty seconds long, by Satie. That fascination with brevity seems a part of it too. Also, something I know is that Pierre Martory had a fascination with popular song entering poetry. It's there in Apollinaire. Irving Berlin enters some of the songs by Erik Satie. In particular, I think "That Mysterious Rag" is part of his ballet *Parade*. All these things make it seem almost like, with its interest in music hall and burlesque, something that would be beloved by Americans. Why do you suppose that there wasn't—and, until you, isn't really—an American tradition derived from French poetry?

JA: I don't know really. Of course, Frank O'Hara is certainly another person who would be influenced by those things. And it was he who first turned me on to the music of Satie, for example. There wasn't very much recorded back in the days when I first met him, which was in 1949. He could play the piano, and he also wrote music himself, and he would play pieces by Satie so that I could get an idea of what they were like.

MS: Now, you speak in the introduction to *The Landscapist* of Martory's fondness for the novels of Raymond Queneau—or you suspect there's a fondness for Queneau—which you speak of as a palliative for the overly existential novels of Camus and Sartre. And there is in the work, rather than angst, the thing that Satie loved: melancholy. And it seems to me that he's a great and beautiful practitioner of a comic melancholy, which stems, in many cases, from childhood. I want you to read his mother poem, and we'll talk from there.

JA: Yes, I left the title in French, "Ma Chandelle est morte," which is a line from the famous nursery rhyme "Au clair de la lune (mon ami Pierrot)." It means "my candle is dead" or "my candle has gone out."

Ma Chandelle est morte

My mother's bedroom has flowered wallpaper
Wallpaper with paper flowers
My mother will abort a black and red prince
A gnome with a harelip
A thousand blue and yellow stripes delight my wakings
I remain the handsomest the wisest
I remain the best of my mother's sons
And my mother with her profile drawn on the wall
Has gone out early to drink absinthe
Or buy bread or wash my underpants
Or sell my underpants and hers to no one
Mouse with red cheese time is passing
Mouse my gray sister you speak with your nails

A hole hides a trap
An evening hides a day
A morning is never anything but a tired evening
Of this day too much like the day beyond the window.

MS: Was that an early poem by Pierre Martory?

JA: Most of them don't have dates. I think that probably dates from the early 1950s, before I knew him.

MS: Now, tell me, where and how did you meet?

JA: We met in a café at Saint-Germain-des-Prés. We were introduced by a literary critic who was rather well known at the time, who I had met a few weeks before.

MS: Who was that?

JA: His name was Henri Hell.

MS: A French literary critic?

JA: Yes.

MS: You'll pardon me, but when I look at the pictures—there are two in the book—he's adorable and looks so charming. In your introduction, you mention that the poet Ann Lauterbach, who'd met him, had found him as if he were literally a spellcaster. I sense that this is true from a little piece that Dara Wier wrote about one of his poems in a collection about over-looked poems. Can you describe the spell that he cast?

JA: Well, I'm not sure he was aware of it. He was extremely shy, among other things, but also he could be very impertinent on short notice. Part of his charm, certainly for his American friends, of which he had quite a few, was his accented English, which was slightly German. He learned German in school before he learned English, so his French had a slightly German, in fact, slightly Yiddish accent. He also used German constructions in English, which came out very charmingly.

MS: Now, I hear that, at this time, you write back to friends in America about the number of movies you're seeing and how the movement of movie images should influence poetry and is fantastic to the poetry. Did you go to the movies with him? Were you at his side?

JA: Yes, we went, often several times a week, usually to American movies in the original language at the big movie houses on the Champs-Élysées, mainly because I was homesick for America and Pierre just liked any American movie. I remember we saw—I don't know why it comes back to me—*The Revolt of Mamie Stover* with Jane Russell. I turned around at some point and noticed, sitting behind me, the famous movie actor Jean Marais, who was Jean Cocteau's lover and starred in his films. It seems strange that all of us should be there for Jane Russell.

MS: It seems to me that everything becomes, in some way, strange for you there in Paris, that the language is not American, that you're writing poems in French and translating them into English as if your own language were a foreign language. Seeing American films, and not only American films, but I've got the sense that he liked American musicals. You mentioned that he saw *Reveille with Beverly* in Morocco. And I know that you once told me about how much you liked *The Great Gildersleeve*. It must have been a very interesting form of Americanism there in Paris, learning and writing French poetry to do an anthology. You were editing, what I still take to be one of the best literary magazines and art magazines that ever existed, *Art and Literature*, with some of the most fantastic translations—the first translation of Bachelard, I think, the first translation of a section of de Chirico's novel *Hebdomeros*—many of these translations by you. It seems like a very fertile period, and yet you say in this introduction that you rarely spoke to one another about your work. I'm very curious about this. Would you say you shared a sensibility rather than talking about poetry itself?

JA: Yes, I think that's it. I still don't talk about poetry with my friends, or with anybody really, if I can avoid it, which I can't always do. On the other hand, there certainly was discussion of things poetic among us. In fact, Pierre did some early translations of poems of mine when we first met, and my French wasn't good enough at that point to translate him or even to really judge the quality of his work. That only came a few years later. It took me quite a long time really to get fluent in French.

MS: You lived with him for around ten years?

JA: Yes. Well, from the spring of '56, shortly after we first met, until the fall of '65, when I moved back to America. We didn't always live together, there were periods when we lived apart, but mostly we did.

MS: Now, I'm very interested, at a certain point in his life, after publishing one novel and having the second rejected, and a third that he was asked to change the ending of—and decided that he would not publish rather than changing the ending—he does not publish in France. The work is secret and rarely shared. It's not just your translations: you are creating Pierre Martory as a poet.

JA: Well, possibly, yes.

MS: For a public. This has been an act of creation that's gone on for many years. Before I knew you, I would see these translations and wonder sometimes if Martory existed. He seemed too good to be true. Now we have a really beautiful, full-length book. I want to hear a poem that I think is extraordinarily beautiful, nonsensical, and haunting called "Litanies."

JA: Litanies

May it please the shower of gold to cover me for I am cold from soft metal
May it please the shower of gold to cover me for I am cold from soft metal

May it please the shower of water to cover me for I have faith of
metamorphosis
May it please the shower of water to cover me for I have faith of
metamorphosis

May it please the harsh idea to nourish me for I thirst after my false loves
May it please the harsh idea to nourish me for I thirst after my false loves

May it please the afternoon to suffice me for I've had too much of my
dark days
May it please the afternoon to suffice me for I've had too much of my
dark days

May it please the near here to open for me for I've knocked at its door
in vain
May it please the near here to open for me for I've knocked at its door
in vain

May it please the calm sea to swell for I've trapped too many sea-lice
May it please the calm sea to swell for I've trapped too many sea-lice

May it please the incarnate soul to show itself for I have believed in the
incarnate soul
May it please the incarnate soul to show itself for I have believed in the
incarnate soul

May it please the closed fist to show itself for I've drawn the rusty blade
May it please the closed fist to show itself for I've drawn the rusty blade

May it please the lover the loved to lie to itself for I've known the weight
of the lie
May it please the lover the loved to lie to itself for I've known the weight
of the lie

May it please the man in tears to bruise himself I've howled the cry of
    my dreams

May it please the man in tears to bruise himself I've howled the cry of
    my dreams

MS: That seems to me to be a particularly beautiful, exquisite, and sad poem. And yet it still partakes of what I call an overtone of nonsense because of the religious litany sense. There's something of "You Are Old, Father William." Suddenly something is being stood on its head, and the impulse to prayer is turning into something personal and entirely heartbroken.

JA: He claimed not to be religious, but I've wondered at that line: "May it please the incarnate soul to show itself for I have believed in the incarnate soul." I never really believed that he had abandoned the Roman Catholic religion that he grew up with, although he insisted that he had.

MS: Now, I'm curious, you have a long poem called "Litany." Does it bear relation to the religious aspect of litany? In a sense, this poem does. At any rate, its beauty convinces one that he hasn't abandoned the possibility that a litany, that a prayer, that repetition offers. I'm wondering that about your own work, if you don't mind answering.

JA: I think it's a sheer coincidence the titles are the same. I'm not sure I had read this poem at the time I wrote my poem, because a lot of these poems I found in his papers after his death.

MS: The impulse to write something called "Litany," in what way might it be a religious impulse?

JA: Well, I'm an occasional churchgoer and have been exposed to the "Great Litany" in Episcopal service. Then there's of course the other meaning of litany, some tiresome list. This litany of complaints, for instance. I think I meant both of those things.

MS: We're in your room here in Hudson, New York. There are pictures of Pierre around that you've shown me. Do you find yourself missing him a great deal?

JA: Yes, I do, actually. I think about him a lot. I wish that his life had been happier because I don't think it was. I tried to make it as happy as possible. I discovered several years ago now an unfinished memoir that he wrote, only about ten pages long, which I'm intending to translate at some point. He had scribbled the title on top, *Ne m'oublie pas*—don't forget me. So I've been trying to take that seriously.

2010: *Planisphere*

MS: John Ashbery is one of my favorite guests because it's easy to say he's one of my two or three very favorite living poets. To me, John Ashbery has been an education, in every way, in what poetry can do. First of all, John, what is a planisphere?

JA: It's a flat rendering of a hemisphere shape, such as a map of the globe, one-half of our terrestrial globe, for instance. It's mentioned in a poem by Andrew Marvell, which has always been part of my consciousness: something about our love should be compressed into a planisphere. I don't remember what the rest of it is. A poem is really a flat rendering of feelings or experiences. That might be one reason for justifying it. I also just like the sound of the word.

MS: Words appear in your poems and reappear. I noticed, for instance, in this book, one poem mentions "sticker shock," and then a later one has "Sticker Shock" as a title. These repetitions that occur, are they accidental or just luck of the draw?

JA: That one was. I didn't realize, in fact, that there had been a repetition. Contemporary jargon is very much constantly shifting around in my brain. Then words like "sticker shock" and "aha moment," which also appears in one of the poems, get used along with more highfalutin words like "planisphere."

MS: I wanted, first of all, to hear the poem "Episode." The first of two poems called "Episode."

JA: Yes, there are two called "Episode," and that actually was not accidental. I knew that there were two. I liked that, calling them "Episode 1" and "Episode 2."

Episode

In old days, when they tried to figure out
how to write the sweetest melodies, they fell
on a bed, chewed the pillow. A moon rankled
in the crevices of a shutter. In 1935
the skirts were long and flared slightly,
suitably. Hats shaded part of the face.
Lipstick was fudgy and encouraging. There was
music in the names of the years. 1937
was welcoming too, though one bit one's lip
preparing for the pain that was sure to come.

"That must be awful." I was hoping you could
imagine it. Yet I will be articulate
again and articulate what we knew anyway
of what the lurching moon had taught us,
seeking music where there's something dumb being said.

And if it comes back to being all alone
at the starting gate, so be it. We hadn't wanted
this fuss, these extras. We were calm
under an appearance of turmoil, and so we remain

even today, an unwanted inspiration
to those who come immediately after
as well as those who came before, lots of them,
stretching back into times of discussion.
I told you so, we can handle it, hand on
the stick shift headed into a billboard
labeled Tomorrow, the adventures of new music,
melismas shrouding the past and the passing days.

MS: In the poem, you mentioned being an unwanted inspiration to those who come immediately after as well as to those who came before. *Publishers Weekly* commented, I think perceptively, that they thought that you had now come to the point of being influenced by younger poets whom you've influenced. Do you think that's the case?

JA: Oh, yes, definitely. I read the work of young poets a great deal. Since I have been a teacher, or was for a number of years, I obviously had to since I was teaching poetry-writing courses. I've always tried to avoid the cliché "I learn from my students," which a lot of professors use, but it's true in my case. I learned from some of them, anyway. I often find the work of young poets who have absorbed my work and were influenced by it and then threw it off, wanting to break away and write something new. That, of course, influences me all over again. I can make the same effort to break away from myself, once I read them.

MS: I was talking to Howard Stokar, Charles Wuorinen's partner. He quoted you as saying something that fascinated me. I don't necessarily want to know what you meant, but what you might have meant. He said that you said that language sometimes gets in the way of the poetry.

JA: I don't remember saying that. I can't really imagine what I meant, although it's a fascinating statement, and I intend to ponder it and find out what it was I may have meant, if I said it.

MS: You see, it would be fairly easy for me to imagine you or any number of other poets saying that the meaning sometimes gets in the way of the poetry, but the language getting in the way of the poetry seemed a new realm to me and kind of exciting.

JA: Well, I suppose once we got rid of the meaning, then it's time to start getting rid of language. Why I am interested in such things is a different question, which I at the moment can't think of an answer to. I suppose new kinds of poetry are always exciting if they open up new areas in that sense.

MS: I've often thought when reading you that there's a quality of language, like language when a child discovers it before it becomes useful.

JA: Yeah.

MS: When it can be something that's played with and put down. Parents might clap their hands out of delight about what a child has said but not meant. I think that your poetry does that on occasion. There is a sense of equipment being there, games and toys. I remember that there were all sorts of things I played with as a child that were abettors or tools for making language, like rebus games and things like that, that were more fun when they retained their mystery, their possibility. I suddenly thought, "Well, no critic wants to talk about this, but the idea of language before it has gotten serious and useful seems to me to be a poet's language."

JA: I suddenly remembered—I'm pretty sure it's a passage from Kafka's diaries where he describes being very young, maybe two years old, and hearing what he thinks is someone, perhaps his mother, saying, "I am reveling in the grass." I think I'm remembering that correctly. At the same time, that made me remember an early memory of being in a school where I went to kindergarten and coming to the top of the stairs and saying, "I regret these stairs." Of course, I didn't know what regret meant, but it seemed very profound. In fact, I think it was. I did regret those stairs.

MS: Let's hear another poem. I'm crazy about the one called "Upstate Dancers."

JA: Upstate Dancers

The plants grow in proscribed wonder
at having accomplished this feat,
at least this far. Ivy, calceolaria,
don't have that much to think about—
any and all distractions welcome.

As one would spear a fish
the next layer becomes rudely evident.
"All of us here"—including me out—
are eager to know your plans
and to help in any way we could.

Sometimes a stench decides everything.
We're all better at some things.
It doesn't matter that your soles have patches,
that your big toe wiggles appreciatively.
Some of us are going to mind more than others.

Upstate dancers don't dance much
anymore. The trolley lines sped through,
shucks, an empire ago. Fishing lures
were coated with a sandy surface—makes 'em
more attractive I believe. So why did
it happen with an echo? We thought we
had taken it into account. Turns out we were wrong.

MS: What were you thinking about when you wrote that one?

JA: I have no idea. I usually don't, as a matter of fact.

MS: Do you know what they are?

JA: The poems?

MS: Yes.

JA: No.

MS: It's a pleasure to me that you don't. Do you know then when it's completed or when you've gotten it right or when it's not working? What are the criteria?

JA: They're highly subjective. I know when they don't work and when I don't want to use them, when I want to reject or recycle, but I really don't recycle very much. I'd rather start over from zero. I don't know, a kind of mechanism clicks off or on when I feel I've finished a poem. That's enough for me.

MS: *Planisphere* immediately, even before you know what it means, suggests a metaphysical poem. The finding of the exact phrase and that sense of the beautiful in the arcane, combining with the typical and culture-worn. Yes, everyone will say, "Well, that's what Ashbery does." But it seems that here in the title poem, it's almost effortless. Let's hear "Planisphere."

JA: Planisphere

"Mysterious barricades…"

Maybe I should footnote that—it's a harpsichord work by Couperin, an eighteenth-century French composer, *Les Barricades Mystérieuses*. There's always been a great deal of speculation as to what exactly that means. Could it mean perhaps a young woman's maidenhead? That's been one explanation offered. If that's unfamiliar to you, it would be unfamiliar to many people. It's always hard to know how rarefied one's allusions ought to be before one reins them in. On the other hand, I don't think it really makes very much difference. You can read that and not know what it referred to and still take account of it in the poem, I guess.

"Mysterious barricades, a headrest (of sorts),
boarded the train at Shinjuku junction…"

MS: What is Shinjuku junction?

JA: That is a subway stop in Tokyo, I believe. I actually didn't check it, but I was in Tokyo a couple of times, and I think I passed through there.

"…to the palpable consternation of
certain other rubberneckers already installed
in the observation car of their dreams. 'It's so peaceful
on my pallet. I could just *live* here.'
In a second the deadbeat returned with lunch tokens.
It had been meant to be sublime, but hell was
what it more specifically resembled. Remember
to hold the course and take two of everything. That way
if we make journey's end before the tracks expire
we'll have been found living in it—the deep magenta
sunset I mean.

There is nothing like putting off a journey
until the next convenient interruption swamps
onlookers and ticket holders alike. We all more or less
resembled one another, until that fatal day in 1861
when the walkways fell off the mountains and the spruces
spruced down. I mean it was unimaginable in a way.
You'll have to install a park with chairs and restrooms
for the weary and a simple but firm visitors' code
for it to be given out in your name and become a boon
to limp multitudes who thought you were somebody else
or didn't know what it was you did. But we'll stay clean,

by God, and when the tide of misinformation reaches
the first terrace, we'll know what to do: yell our heads off
and admit to no mistakes.

The land stretched away like jelly into a confused cleft.
All was yapping, the race having ended
before we arrived, with mixed results.
Nobody knew what they owed or how much credit
had been advanced, being incapable of niceties like buzzing
and herding fleas till the next shipment of analgesics arrived.
It was like forming signals out of loam when you were young
and too discouraged to care very much
about aftershocks or where the die ended up.
It was too smoky in the little kitchen garden or *potager*
to pay much mind to the rabbits and their plankton
dispensary. Something had been launched. We knew that."

MS: Now, you'll allow me to kvell over the plankton dispensary. There are
certain phrases that appear in this book; jelly is mentioned several times,
but my favorite is the jelly farm. Someone told me that Knott's Berry Farm
and Smucker's were both jelly farms, but it doesn't matter to me. Tell me
how things like that come to you. Spontaneously? Do you have them before the poem? Can you do that for me?

JA: Well, mostly they occur to me while I'm writing. I maybe will start off
with a few phrases or images in mind and proceed to write from them
to see where it takes me. In the course of doing that, other things will
happen, like the plankton dispensary. I sort of apologize for that because
everybody knows that rabbits don't eat plankton, so why would they want
a plankton dispensary. On the other hand, it just seemed right, so I wasn't
going to do anything about it. I was going to leave it in place. I guess I've
reached a point where there are things in my work that I can't defend, but
I'm not going to worry too much about it.

MS: That's what seems to me to be so wonderful. At first, I didn't know what to do with your poems at all except to reread them. They were so mystifying to me. I reread them for years without understanding that I already understood them. Or that whatever understanding by and large was required had been internalized. That I now took pleasure in these sentences and lines of poetry, the like of which I couldn't find anywhere else. Then I grew to love and look forward to them as a favorite thing. Almost like something giving me the delight that certain toys did, but there were no longer toys like that. For me, although the poems are not trying to do anything, force any recognitions—they're somewhat diffident often—they nevertheless seem to me to be therefore still more amusing and more delightful. I guess I've grown up with you and been there while poetry, to the extent that it's changed, has changed because of these things. This is turning into a very long-sentence tribute. To seemingly know of someone who never took orders, who did it—what do they say, "I did it my way"—and never had the felt obligation to surrender to anything but one's own strange impulse. It seems marvelous and exemplary to me.

JA: Thank you, that's wonderful. I always hoped that what I was writing would connect with the reader, but it took a long time for that to happen. When I first began reading modern poetry, I thought, "Well, this is wonderful, it's so strange and hard to read. I'd like to write that way myself. I'm pretty strange. I'll just put it in poetry, and people will like it." After it was published, I realized that it was really too strange, that I had somehow gone beyond the pale. For a number of years, really, I didn't have much of an audience, and people thought I was being willfully obscure, which is not really what I was intending. At the same time, I guess I didn't want to take the steps to be totally unobscure either. So I kept on, even during periods when I thought I would maybe stop writing poetry since it was just annoying people, and I should maybe find some other means of expression, like needlepoint or something. After that, it dawned on me that this was what I like to do, so I was going to do it. If nobody else liked it, well, that's too bad, I didn't mean for that to be, but my own pleasure was what I should be thinking about at this point. Eventually, it seems to have connected with people such as yourself.

MS: Let's end with a short poem. I'm very fond of "Zero Percentage."

JA: Zero Percentage

So call it untitled, but
don't imagine you'll be let off the hook:
The title will find it as surely
as a heat-seeking missile locks on
an asteroid. Down below, armies
and oceans of taxis will squawk unfeelingly.
The title always wins.

MS: Now, can I ask you? Is it a play on winning the title?

JA: Oh, I hadn't thought of that. Undoubtedly I meant that, but I don't remember.

John Berger

2001

MS: I'm in John Berger's kitchen, which is an unusual place for me to find my-self because Berger is one of the first people I started reading when I got to college. His book G had just come out. It was the first book I ever received for free in the mail from a publisher, and because it was followed almost immediately by a hugely different book, I said, "This is very interesting. G, a novel of Don Giovanni full of Kierkegaard and Mozart." Yes?

JB: Absolutely, yes, yes.

MS: Yes, yes, but this is a novel of a seducer, and it's followed by novels by the storyteller, and I was very, very interested in that moment that took you essentially from being a person who plots the G person, the seductive person, the writer of seduction and trickery, to a writer of a much simpler, storytelling kind. What were you thinking of when you began G? Be-cause it seems to be a place that you did not go back to.

JB: Well, Michael, before I answer that, I would like to say this. If we're in this conversation as equals, it seems to me that this should be clear: you're an incredible expert—but I don't like the word expert—inhabitant, hunter about books, about written text, about mad literature that you cross and live in and relate to what is outside that forest, which is life. I have a feel-ing you began with books. I'm the opposite. In fact, I don't know so much about literature, and I don't know so much about books, and I'm not a very verbal person. I think quite a lot about some things about life, but usually in a very inarticulate way. And then I try to come with that onto the page. So this seems to me a very interesting situation between us because one of us is going from page to life and the other is trying to go from life to page, and maybe that's—

MS: Maybe there's an intersection.

JB: Maybe, therefore, there's an intersection.

MS: You see, I was very shy as a child, and books told me about the world, and I depended on my writers to be worldly. *G* is, in a sense, a very worldly book, yes?

JB: When you say that, you mean you read books in a way so that they could help you to live?

MS: So that they would tell me how others have lived. I'm sure you do this too. Sometimes you reach a line in literature that's so beautiful that you start to cry because *this* is it.

JB: Yes.

MS: I read Peter Handke's play *Kaspar* and Kaspar, the wild child's first sentence was, "I want to be someone like someone else once was." This was an experience where I said, "I understand. I want to be someone the way somebody else once was." And I found these lines possibilities for life in books.

JB: Yes, so something that people don't talk about very much, and of course it has actually changed a great deal because of the new media and television, but until fifty years ago, it seems to me there was another function about books, a way more superficial but at the same time very important function, which is that when you were young, in reading books, you also learned how to behave in certain situations.

MS: I know what you mean, but I think I learned how not to behave. The people around were so busy behaving that I went to a book. In other words, in one of your most recent books, *To the Wedding*, the characters turn up the music very loudly, and it's said that they are trying to keep the din of the world away from them. I used books the way you might use music to make a very, very noisy world for me to live in, and what I loved when I read Berger was to enter in particular the world of the village. It was a world I had not dreamed of. And before that was the world of *G*, a world of cunning, a world of subterfuge, a world of sexuality, a world of, dare I say so, the erotic aggression of Don Giovanni. These were all possibilities that a boy growing up in a house in a suburb with parents who didn't read and no readers around, you looked to the people who were worldly. I heard you first. I was using my eyes, but I heard the words, and I was always very taken by the naturalness with which, even when the novels are wittier, as in the case of *G*, the words always seemed to speak out loud and to be very present. The page makes language present in your work, I think.

JB: Michael, can we just go back one moment? Because when I said that books, stories that you read on the page, perhaps show you how to behave, you took it to mean how to behave well, how to be polite, how to behave conventionally. But it seems to me that it is much, much deeper than that.

        When you are eleven, or even when you're seventeen, and suddenly you find yourself for the first time facing a woman who has just lost her man—he has just died ten minutes before—how to behave is not a question then of manners. Or maybe you find yourself alone with a dead animal or you find yourself frightened on a river or something. Books and stories can also help us to know how to carry ourselves, what stance to take in front of situations. It's at that level that I meant it because, of course, I agree with you that the books that mean most to me are the books that teach us subversion—subversion in face of the world as it is—books that suggest the honor of an alternative.

MS: I'm interested because you mentioned in a story called "Passeur," the smuggler, that an early teacher told you, "if you must cry, cry afterwards—and cry among the people who love you." I think it's what you're talking about when you say what if you're with a dead animal? How do you respond as a surviving person rather than a shirker and a crier, yes?

JB: Yes, yes, and that man really existed. It's not a fiction.

MS: It didn't sound like fiction.

JB: He was really called Ken. But I'll tell you something very strange. Okay, how did that story come about? I really was in Krakow, Poland. I was in this market, and suddenly, incredibly strongly, he was there. Although it was—how long ago?—forty years since I'd seen him. And, of course, I thought about him from time to time but not daily, or weekly even, although I knew I had enormous debt towards him. But this is what I want to say, which is interesting because I thought about him and remembered. Then I sat down and took a piece of paper, and like that I drew a portrait of him—without thinking really—and it was an incredible likeness. It surprised me, not when I was doing it, but afterwards.

I was looking at it; it was him. I think that is very interesting because it tells us something about the way memory works and the way that what is absent is present. There's a wonderful letter by Rilke to the painter Balthus when Balthus was a kid. You probably know it; you remember it. Balthus has just lost a pet animal, it has died or something like that, and Rilke says to him—I'm paraphrasing badly—but he says, "Loss has a very strange and not contradictory relationship with the opposite of loss, which is possession." In fact, when we lose something or somebody, if that thing that we have lost is important, we begin to possess it internally more strongly than when we "possessed it externally." This story about the drawing is somewhere connected with that.

MS: Yes, but I think that for you it does begin with loss. Loss and ghosts both. Lost ways of life, lost ways of thinking about survivors, who survive not in life but survive in a way of life, in a continued idea about life. So that loss is one of your main subjects in fiction.

JB: Well, you can see better than I what are my subjects. As I say, the writer is never quite sure. What I would say, if that is true, I would say firmly that it is not a loss or sense of loss that has anything to do with nostalgia. In a very curious way, it is a sense of loss directed towards the future.

MS: Tell me more about that.

JB: I don't know. I can't tell you more about that.

MS: You're not an easy one. [*both laugh*]

JB: Well, okay, first of all, writers are benevolent—or sometimes not—thieves. They're always stealing. I'm stealing now because what I'm going to tell you, as though I've just thought of it, is not true. In actual fact, a friend of mine, a doctor in London, she wrote me this last week. We were having a correspondence about the Fayum portraits. They're the Egyptian portraits painted by Greek Egyptian painters, which were then placed on the graves of the dead or the sarcophagi of mummies. These are extraordinary portraits. There are certain paintings by Goya that have the same kind of expression. Anyway, the point is that people posed for these portraits knowing that the portraits were going to be there to represent their presence after they were dead. Often they were still young and in good health. They were sitting there and saying, "Here I am," but in a certain sense the painter was the painter of death. They were also aware of what they would be afterwards.

At the same time, these paintings, seen by others, would represent the past when the painted person was still alive, so that in these incredibly simply painted and observed heads you have three times coexisting: past, present, and future. Then, what my friend the doctor said was, "and maybe that also happens when you have really great performances in the theater. There is the coexistence simultaneously of past, present, and future."

MS: That's very interesting. Do you think about novels in that way?

JB: Tell me more.

MS: A meeting point of the past, the present, and the future. In *To the Wedding*, for instance, the characters seem to be destined, hurtled toward a wedding, the way a river is hurtled through a landscape, the way the father is hurtling on his motorcycle. There is a huge sense of futurity, and yet this is not preparation for a bridal wedding, this is the world in which there is AIDS and death and a decision to commit to not the boisterousness of a wedding but the boisterousness of a wedding despite the fact. So there's a sense of what a wedding was in the past, what a wedding can be now, what a wedding will be in the future. The novel seems to stand at a point at which it's projecting its action across past, present, and future, yeah?

JB: Yes. I have difficulty, I have difficulty really in talking in an intelligible way about time, about, anyway, linear time because somewhere deeply—I am not sure whether to say in my imagination or in my soul—somewhere deeply it seems to me that all instants coexist. If you ask me about writing stories or novels, the aim is not necessarily what I achieve—God almighty!—but the aim is that every incident, every word, every silence, above all every silence, in that story coexists, is instantaneous in the same instant. This is the sense of urgency that I have when trying to write, and it's also actually something that I feel when I'm not writing and not thinking about writing and when I'm living. That I can describe but I can't explain. And then when we start talking about the past or the present or the future, suddenly I feel that we are a tram on rails, whereas before we were bounding like hares.

MS: It's interesting because *urgency* is one of your constant words, as is *confidence*. The first time I see them together is in that cubism essay, "The Moment of Cubism," when you speak about the urgency of the movement and the confidence of the movement. And it occurs in your fiction, it occurs everywhere. These seem to be the primary virtues for you, for an artist.

JB: Yes, but isn't that quite lived? By which, I mean, if you are in an urgent situation, which may inevitably mean also a somewhat dangerous situation, and if you know—coming back to what we were saying—if you know how you want to face that, how to behave, at that moment you experience a confidence that is incomparable and that you can find under no other circumstances. When things are easy and there's no urgency, there is no confidence as strong as that one.

MS: It's interesting that you say so because I have to tell you that the qualities that I relish most in your fiction are qualities of tenderness, quietness. It's almost the opposite of urgency. It's a quality of wisdom that I find there. It's very understated. The narrative voice is almost *sotto voce* as if this voice, which is speaking now, has never not been speaking. The stories that were always being told are always being told and told in this way. Yes, there's a change of time. Always the stories are fresh, and yet always the stories are ancient and refer to values and honor that are somehow maintained against many different odds.

When I read them, I often find myself crying because they return me to a kind of peacefulness that isn't very common in my life, that I look for in fiction now. I think that fiction is one of the places where we go for silence, a worded silence, words that amount to or return to silence. And the best fiction maybe even aspires to a kind of muteness.

JB: Yes, I agree with both those things, the silence and the muteness. Yes, and also that silence, isn't there in it an extraordinary sense of being inside? That is to say, inside without what normally accompanies the notion or the experience of being inside, which is a sense of containment. There is no containment, and yet one is inside an interior, inside. And I reject totally the very, very shortsighted Freudian explanation that this is simply a desire to return to the womb.

MS: No, what I think—I didn't understand it until I got here, to this place— but you see, I think that what happens on the pages of these books is that they aspire to the quietness of this environment. And that really, you found yourself something I could not have known until I got here because I've always lived in cities. This work is full of the divisions between country and city and the reason why the country is, to some extent, disappearing as people move to the city. I think that what you have is around you. I'm looking out of a window, and I'm looking at something that comes as close to looking eternal as I know how to see, these mountains.

Many writers who are writing in an environment in which there's a lot of activity, a lot of action, they're keeping things rolling. "Keep it moving, keep it jumping," is the motto of the fiction. This is a fiction— I'm only sitting here understanding this by being across from the window and across from you—this is a fiction of slowing down. This is a fiction of finding the rhythms that are more natural to eternity than to excitement.

JB: I don't know.

MS: Why not?

JB: Yeah, why not?

MS: Why not, why don't you?

JB: [*long pause*] It doesn't—I see what you mean. Of course, it's very perceptive what you say, and I can put myself very easily in your skin and see it like that and—

MS: No, no, let's skip perceptive. I know that you ride motorcycles; I know, therefore, that you like speed. I know that what I'm saying about slowing things down couldn't possibly be entirely correct because you wouldn't be a motorcycle guy if that were true. And yet I'm saying with the conviction of someone who has just read and reread the bulk of your work that what I see throughout the work is a growing education in tenderness, in slowness, in eternal values, in what is *conserved* in a life. I think that the essence of the conservation instinct is in a ghost story. Whether it's a ghost story in which you see your teacher, you conserve your past, or a ghost story like the one in *Pig Earth*, in which we hear three lives of a woman who is a ghost being narrated, more remarkably, by a man who is a ghost as well.

What has become more baffling, more eerie, more displaced and lost than these incredibly vivid figures who are living a phantasmal, erotic life before you on the page in a situation that doesn't exist? There are no more characters in this story. We don't know it, but everyone in the story is dead. The story is silence enunciating itself. A once-upon-a-time action is cleared out of the living spaces, and now we are reencountering story in the air itself. I think this is closer to what I'm trying to say.

JB: Yes, tenderness is—I suppose first of all one has to begin with the fact, which everybody has always known until recently, that life is full of pain. Not only pain, but it has a lot of pain. Tenderness is in part a response to that, but it is also something else. It seems to me that it is a refusal to judge. It seems to me that actions have to be judged with incredible vigor and all the time declared. There is so much that has to be judged, so much that has to be denounced, and also so much that has to be praised, but not people. I do not think we have the right of any final judgment of anybody.

Tenderness is, in a way, an expression of that refusal to judge. It is also something that exists completely apart from so-called intellectual development and also apart from given cultures. There are so many modes of tenderness, from the powerless to the erotic, for example. And this is perhaps connected to the other thing you were saying. You were talking about ghosts and the past. Okay, I would put this differently because it seems to me, and has really almost always seemed to me, that the dead are present. Actually, we live with the dead. This is, of course, something that in our instant culture, this moment in a large part of the world, is ignored, dismissed totally, but this living with the dead is maybe the first thing which distinguishes man, man as a species. It is, perhaps, what makes man a human.

If I feel this way intensely, I would give—and I have always done—maybe two explanations. One was—wrong tense—*is* my father, who was in the First World War, infantry officer four years in the trenches, wounded but survived for four years. Very, very few infantry officers survive that long. While I could talk about him, that's not really important. I sensed his experience from the time I was very young. It was not something he talked about. Sometimes I would hear his nightmares. But it deeply marked me. If you like, I can just read you a poem I wrote, which is about that.

MS: I would love that.

JB: It's called "Self-portrait," as to say, self-portrait of me:

Self-portrait 1914-18

It seems now that I was so near to that war.
I was born eight years after it ended
When the General Strike had been defeated.

Yet I was born by Very Light and shrapnel
On duck boards
Among limbs without bodies.

I was born of the look of the dead
Swaddled in mustard gas
And fed in a dugout.

I was the groundless hope of survival
With mud between finger and thumb
Born near Abbeville.

I lived the first year of my life
Between the leaves of a pocket bible
Stuffed in a khaki haversack.

I lived the second year of my life
With three photos of a woman
Kept in a standard issue army paybook.

In the third year of my life
At 11am on November 11th 1918
I became all that was conceivable.

Before I could see
Before I could cry out
Before I could go hungry

I was the world fit for heroes to live in.

Then, when I came here, twenty-five or more years ago, to live among mountain peasants, this was an extraordinary confirmation of what I'm talking about, because for them it is a completely accepted fact that they live with the dead. The dead are here. And they will be the dead, and the dead in a certain sense are there to help them die. I would put it in terms of the presence of the dead, rather than the past, which always implies, or often implies, a kind of nostalgia. Or if not a nostalgia, a conservatism in a global sense.

Because if I could just go on for one moment, and if we come back to the tenderness now, it seems to me that one of the essential elements in tenderness is that it is a free act, a gratuitous act. It has an enormous amount to do with liberty, with freedom, because one chooses to be tender. And in a certain sense, in the face of so often what is surrounding us, it is an almost defiant act of freedom.

Then, if we just go back one moment more to something else you said, because it connects, you asked me about motorbikes and riding at high speed. One of the things about riding bikes is not really to do with speed. It is a very intense experience, I think, both psychic and physical, of freedom. It isn't actually getting to the traffic lights, the top, and then being the first off. [*laughter*] I mean, there is that. But the real freedom is something different. It is when riding a bike, you observe, you observe, you observe everything all the time, and then you make a decision. The consequences of that decision come almost immediately. At the same time, you have very little protection, physical protection, against them, so that between decision and consequence, they're not absolutely instantaneous, but they are like that. You decide something and it happens, for good or bad.

Whereas, in the rest of life, inevitably the time is more delayed or there are many, many more constricting considerations or factors. There is more friction, if you wish, between decision and consequence. That is, in a very lived sense, something which seems to me to touch not necessarily the essence but something very deep about what I mean by freedom. And that freedom is nothing to do with that kind of power or speed or whatever. I mean, it is to do almost with its opposite. It is the free choice, in some way, by gesture or glance or action of tenderness.

MS: Well, this, if I can improvise here, reminds me very much of what Kleist says about marionettes when he says that they are—

JB: Yes, but you say it, say it, say it.

MS: Well, he is considering the great marionette theaters, and he tells us essentially that the human being, in his eye, aspires to the role of the marionette, not declines from it. He says we should experience a state in which we are dependent on our strings to show in relation what our souls are, not our humanity. So it sounds as if the way you're talking about the motorcycle is that it becomes a vehicle for the operation of the soul, yes? In a way? Because what Kleist is trying to say is that our freedom is exceedingly limited, and when we think we're exhibiting it, we're frequently only showing our bondage. But our true freedom is the ability to move within a sphere that has nothing to do with will, that has entirely to do, I would think, with what you're calling the consequence of a decision. A consequence that arrives immediately upon the decision, just like the puppet whose arm goes up when the spring goes up. The body that swerves when you decide to turn this way instead of that, and you had better incline because otherwise you'll throw yourself. You live in your own consequence, and that becomes freedom, yeah?

JB: Mm–hmm.

MS: This is really one of the central texts of Romanticism. It is that asking at every moment: Can the soul rise from the human and display itself?

JB: Yes, yes. Novalis.

MS: Yes, Novalis as well, absolutely, yes. You see, one of the reasons that I love reading your essays is because every time I turn around, you are citing—now you say to me that you're a person who went from the world to books, but somehow or other we've shared certain crucial texts over the years. One is Hugo von Hofmannsthal, one is Apollinaire, and also Leopardi. Whenever I'm reading Berger, I have a belief that the real books are not the books that people know about. For some reason, either they're not taught or they're not translated or they're not translated well enough, and so people are living in the absence of the food they need, the literary food that you would need in order to *feel* life.

I've always thought that what literature was to you was the expression of certain ideas that would make it possible to feel more deeply.

JB: Ideas, ideas, or something else.

MS: What I mean by ideas is an older, Greeker thing. I mean image.

JB: Yes, yes, okay. Yeah, okay. Of course, we're talking up to now quite a lot about all the motivations of writing, biographically or autobiographically. In my experience, there is also actually another kind of writing, which is to do with the world, to do with something happening. It can be something quite private and small, or it can be something huge and global. When witnessing that, reacting to it—and I do react and think very quickly. That is true. It is no credit to me, this is my metabolism. Anyway, reacting to that, there is then the *obligation* to write. This *has* to be said, not really by me, doesn't matter who says it, but it has to be said because it is needed. This needs to be read at this moment. In some ways, if one talks of oneself as a storyteller—often, often I have the feeling that the role of the storyteller is misunderstood because storytellers don't invent stories. The story is found or is told or is somewhere there, and then you take it and you write it or you tell it and it goes elsewhere. You have delivered it, yes?

MS: Yes.

JB: Yes, and in the same way, this other kind of writing has to respond to what is happening because it needs to be read. I mean, in a sense, once more, you are simply a channel for that to which you make yourself open. That's another kind of writing. Sometimes this can simply be because you've suddenly found an unknown painter or an unknown poet who you think is really incredible, and you can't stay silent about it. Or it can be that it is now absolutely necessary to speak out, everybody, in the loudest possible way, against this monstrously proposed war against Iraq.

That kind of writing has always occupied more of my time than I would wish, but we haven't chosen the world into which we have been thrown. We have to try to make sense of it.

MS: Now, I'm interested here because yesterday, last night, we were speaking a bit, and several times you said, "This is a story that happened yesterday." And I'm very interested in this phrase, because someone else might say,

"This is something that happened yesterday." What is a story that happened yesterday?

JB: What is the difference between a happening and a story?

MS: Something that comes to you as a story, and that is very interesting to me because I think it's a crucial thing that happens to writers, that a story happens rather than an event.

JB: Well, I suppose the first thing to say, which is very clear when you think about it—but most people, maybe when you hear the story, you don't think about this—is that all stories begin with their end. I mean, until there is an end—

MS: It hasn't been a story.

JB: It isn't the story.

MS: Yes, yes.

JB: I mean, the end isn't necessarily definitive, it may simply be the laugh line of a joke, but it is the end, yes? Then what else is it about a story? In some kind of way, isn't it to do with the fact that the events related form a kind of, one could say, magnetic field, or one could say constellation, with a certain symmetry. In that magnetic field, in that constellation—this is ideal, what I'm saying now—every word in that story is made fresh or is, shall we say, clean. Arguments cannot do that. I mean, written arguments cannot do that so much. Poetry is the supreme example of that, when the poem is written really well. Stories also do that, and it is so, so, so, so important today because we are surrounded by words that have been hijacked, made utterly filthy, contradicting their own sense, words with which people deceive themselves to commit evil acts, words which actually lead to evil. There is no other kind of evil, because evil works with words.

What else do I mean by a story? You tell me what stories mean to you. You, the reader, tell me.

MS: Well, when I was given only yesterday "Passeur" to read, I thought, well isn't this interesting. We are in a Polish square in Krakow, a story happened yesterday: I thought I saw the ghost of my teacher in a square, in Poland. Now, stories are made in part of mystery. Nothing in this story, and it's almost thrilling, is going to tell us why we see him in Poland at that point. He dies in New Zealand, in fact. We've never had anything in the story that brought us to Poland, but this square is a situation of a dream. And like a dream, everything that happens in it happens in the past, the present, and future. When I read *Pig Earth*, I first encountered someone who doesn't know how to sell and therefore sits at the side of the market, not raising her voice and maybe not selling anything. Similarly, in this Polish market, this contemporary market, there are these women yet again, eternally present as in a dream. They are the ones who sit but don't sell. The John character approaches one of them, thinks that she is selling something that looks like chess pieces. It turns out to be cheese. He buys three pieces. If they were chess pieces, maybe only one. There is mystery, magic, and repetition. That is necessary, it seems to me, to a story.

JB: Yes.

MS: The sense that you are hearing voices that you have already heard from somewhere else. In other words, creeping up through your books, every time I read a new story now, there are echoes from the other stories that say to me, "This is a story by John Berger." The world of the other stories is creeping in through the cracks of this story so that there is a hugeness in the world. Then, for me, this is almost—well, I'm very charmed by it—but more and more in the stories there will be a John or Jean. Your name will proliferate, and yet these are not egotistical fictions. I'm very interested in the ghostly presence of the writer in the form, almost as if the story is whispering your name, whispering versions of your name: Jean, John. It's very funny to me. Sometimes they're male, sometimes they're female. The presence of the writer is there, but not there as an ego gesture. It is there the way anything else would be there in a dream, as an internal gesture.

He must be there. How could you have a dream without a dreamer? The question is who is the dreamer who dreams the dream? I think that when I read a story by John Berger, part of what I'm trying to learn is who is the dreamer who is dreaming this dream? He's come to a village. There are all sorts of rules in *Pig Earth*: rules about how to handle animals, rules about how to court, rules about how to marry. Part of this story is, how does John Berger fit into this world? He's come as a stranger, but is he a stranger? Look at how intimately he's writing this story; how could he be a stranger? And yet how can he be intimate with it? It's a totally anomalous and alien world.

Now, you have to understand, I think of your fiction, especially your later fiction, as a kind of miracle. I don't think as many people as will know this miracle know it yet. Part of what I like in talking to you, is that I suspect that people will have to find out about this miracle, because I don't think it is in any other writer. I think that you have mastered not only a world that you've made yours, but a world that your relation to is mysterious. That the world invokes you as much as you invoke the world.

JB: Michael, maybe I'll just read you a short poem because we were talking about language and to whom it belongs. And so, this is a little poem called "Words":

The tongue
   is the spine's first leaf
forests of language surround it

Like a mole
   the tongue
burrows through the earth of speech

Like a bird
   the tongue
flies in arcs of the written word

The tongue is tethered and alone in its mouth

Also, I wanted to tell you a story, not that happened yesterday. It seems to me something we refer to, but is worth bringing out, is the thing about surprise. It seems to me that actually, exactly the art of storytelling is the art of reinventing or reliving or finding for the first time surprises. I mean, the fuse never catches light in the story unless there is surprise, not only for the reader but for the storyteller. It's not a surprise that the storyteller creates, it's a surprise that life offers. I mean, because there's the garden out there, you were looking through that window, and there's the garden. Through that window there are some blackcurrant bushes, and every year, in late June, July, we collect all those blackcurrants. We make a kind of cordial, which is very good, much better than what you can buy.

I was collecting them, hands in the leaves, and your hands get wonderfully blueberry colored. One of the things about blackcurrants and especially the leaves is this very, very strong, heady smell that they have. It's an absolutely unique smell. Even when you approach the bush you have it, and when you touch the leaves it becomes stronger. I was picking these berries, putting them into a pail, and then I noticed right away that on the leaves there were tiny, living, little white snails, about the size of my little fingernail, white pearly silver. There were many of them on the leaves because obviously they adore eating those. In picking the berries, by accident sometimes I would take a leaf or a snail, which I would throw out so that after half an hour, this bucket was there and it was near full with blackcurrants.

Then I saw two or three snails who had fallen there amongst the blackcurrants. The thought crossed my mind that maybe in a bucket of blackcurrants there is a snail scene of paradise. Then I thought, "Huh, okay I've finished things." So I looked at one, picked one up, and I thought, "Yeah, okay, I'll do a drawing. I'd like to draw these snails." I went to get some paper, and I put the snails on the table outside in the garden. The incredible tension of those spirals is absolutely extraordinary. It's something that Leonardo knew about. Well, I'm no Leonardo, but I began drawing. Because they were there on the table—I mean, I knew I wasn't drawing a person or a dog or bird in the sky—so I took my time. But very quickly, after about a minute, I saw that these snails were in fact moving, moving all the while. I would look, and it had already moved. The angle of the shell had shifted as its weight on its body had shifted, and then its body would begin to move.

I went on like that, but suddenly I realized that they moved really at an extraordinary speed. I concentrated on two others, and there was a third one a little farther along. I spent just a few minutes with the two, and the other one had actually got to the edge of the table. So, nothing, just a story about the surprise of observing with what speed, when you're really watching them, snails move.

MS: Well, this reminds me of, and even my description of, what I find in your stories. In the book that was published in Britain as *The White Bird*, but in America as *The Sense of Sight*, there is almost a climax, a culmination to these essays. It's almost as if they're not exactly narrative but what Laura Riding called a "progress of" essays. Toward the end, you have the essay on Leopardi, followed by, I think, what is really a connecting essay, "The Production of the World." What you, in essence, say is that what the artist makes is the production of the world, that the artist is engaged in the process of the production of the world. It's almost as if this is what a snail does when it moves in front of an artist's eyes. He's adding to the production of the artist's sight, which then in the form of a drawing and narration adds to the production of the world.

In other words, if we were to create a new theory of production and mass production, we would say that every movement in the world has a countermovement in the eye and that this leads to a picture or a story if the person seeing happens to be an artist. There's another thing that I think of in what you're telling me, and I hadn't thought about it in your work before, although now it seems very obvious. People used to ask Dr. William Carlos Williams why he didn't move away from Paterson. He would say, "Who will record the language of Polish grandmothers?"

JB: Beautiful, beautiful.

MS: I think that what I was describing as the world inventing you as you invent it in these stories, which might be a Calvino idea or a Saul Steinberg idea, is really that sense that the world is constantly in production and that we, in our motion through it, are part of the production of the world.

JB: Yes, I would formulate it like that exactly.

MS: I don't know of another writer whose sense of living is that living adds to living. It's almost as if you need a Kantian term to define this almost inspired sense that what we are and that how we move adds to the universe of the universe.

JB: Maybe, I'm not sure, but maybe visual artists are more aware of this than writers. It seems to me it's possible. Why? Well, that's complicated, and I'm not sure that I can answer it. In fact, that article, "The Production of the World," the starting point is van Gogh, I think, isn't it?

MS: That's right. And no one has before seen the world at its axis. What he does in decomposing these objects is add to the store of what we know of these objects and what we mean when we say "an object in the world." This is a very profound thing, I think. Gertrude Stein says in *The Making of Americans*, "And everyone is imagining some such thing." Whether we know it or not, when we look at a painting, when we read a story, when we progress through the itemization of the world's detail, we are producing world. And everyone is imagining some such thing, whether they know it or not, the thing that makes living bearable, as opposed to the pain you're talking about or the pain you talk about that Leopardi feels, that he is adding to the world itself, in his perception.

JB: Yes, yeah. I don't know why I want to say this. It is really a question. But according to their physical conditions and circumstances, people are obliged or become accustomed to a certain time perspective, yes? If you have less than two dollars a day to live, like two-thirds of the world, your time perspective is, for one thing, quite short.

No, not a perspective of your whole life and death, but I mean the time in which your imagination and your energy and your observation is operating. People with more privilege and more comfort and more relative security have another. I think that this time perspective has a great influence on observation, observation of the world.

I don't mean an artist's observation, I mean people, kids, everyone. And I am not sure, I am not sure how it works, but it seems to me to be something quite important. I think there is a kind of paradox in it because I think that one might suppose that those with, by necessity, very short-term time scale think that their imaginations are more limited. But I suspect it is the opposite.

I don't really know why I say that. I will go back to something else you said, which is perhaps related to that. Quite a long time ago now—was it the past century?—you asked me, "So you wrote *G*, and then you started a writing trilogy or stories about mountain peasants, and it was a big change. How did it happen?"

It is true, and this is perhaps related to what I was just saying because after I finished *G*, which took me a long time, six years, somewhere I said to myself, "You know what you are doing with narrative now. Yeah, you have mastered it."

MS: I like this. No, no, I think it's very important for a writer to be able to say that.

JB: Yes, but wait, because then, I mean a couple of years later, I was here. Four years later I was here. And I didn't actually come here to think about writing about mountain peasants. Finally, I became involved with how badly we talk. I just came to love some of the men and women who had spent their lives here, what they had learned from the past, and what they were surviving with. And then I wondered—no, the stories asked to be written.

The stories were mixtures always of fiction and truth, which is such a stupid distinction. The stories asked to be written. I discovered that everything that I had learned writing *G* was useless. This concerned everything. It concerned the rhythm of a story. It concerned the grammatical construction of a sentence. It concerned the unsaid, what is left blank. *All* had to be changed.

To give you one very simple example. In the conversation and the thinking of urban people of a certain formal education, the word *but* is really quite important. She is beautiful *but* drives a Jaguar. Well, that's not a very good example, but let's stay with it because it is amusing. In the talking that goes on in peasants' heads, the word *but* is extremely rare. It is usually *and* because they are used to living with contradiction.

We nourished our pigs, we loved them, not *but* we ate them, *and* we ate them. You can multiply that a thousand times because this different use of language has to do with a different attitude towards duration. Yeah, that's all I can say.

MS: I loved G when I read it, but when I read *Pig Earth*, I felt the sentences breathing. One of my teachers was René Girard. He wrote a book called *Deceit, Desire and the Novel*, a lot of it having to do with Stendhal, and there is a lot of Stendhal in G—

JB: Well observed. Yes.

MS: But it *is* the mind of deceit, desire, triangulation, constant calculation. It's almost as if another career could have branched from it. It's the kind of book that Ivy Compton Burnett would have written twenty of, each one more complicated than the last. Then you get *Pig Earth*. I said, "Oh, look at this." Anything can be a story. The slightest emotion can make a story.

This is someone who has decided: this is my decision. I have decided that this is someone who decided that the plots of the world, the world and its plots, were not wonderful. The world of deviousness and deviation compared deviousness to surprise. How natural surprise is, and how decadent the devious is. To some extent this is a novel of someone who is saying, "I will lead a decadent life or I must start afresh." And he starts afresh.

We get *Pig Earth*, which is full of air and mystery. It is almost written by someone who is taking a completely different breath, starting a completely different life. It has what we were talking about before, the air of freedom in it. Yes, a reader is going to have to make adjustments immediately. There is going to be no tolerance for sentimentality about the slaughter of animals. There is going to be no fakery about people's sexual hunger, and that hunger is not going to be manipulated by stratagem. It is going to be openly asserted and found.

Sontag is right when she says there had to be, after D. H. Lawrence, someone who was alert to the sexuality of the world. When you describe the parsley of a woman's thighs, this is a free and dewy world again. Not a world that's being transected by schemes.

I thought, "Oh my goodness, how does a writer begin an invention like this?" In its way, it's like what happens to Beckett after he finishes writing those novels and starts writing those plays. A whole new world is entered. As you suggested, it is syntax, but it is vision too and a different sense of what the satisfactions of life entail.

JB: Well, then I ask you another question, because you see what's on the pages I have written more clearly than I do. What about when I leave the peasants and return to writing about more urban life, like *To the Wedding* or *Lilac and Flag* or *King*? What happens then?

MS: When I get to *Lilac and Flag* in the trilogy, I am returning to the city with a terrible sense of loathing, desperation, and deprivation. It's as if what you've brilliantly said is, "Who, given the suffering of these peasants, would not want to see it come to an end?" And yet, if it comes to an end in the city, where everyone is losing identity, their tradition, their ancestors, their ghosts and their stories—it's as if the writing is like a potato peeler, and it's stripping me bare, because I *know* what the previous books had given me.

It is what happens when suddenly, during the tumult in *To the Wedding*, we learn that the young woman has AIDS. We've wondered why has this cook, with his strange menu of mussels, been in this novel? He seems random, but he is the entry of something other than love in the world. He is about to be jailed. He disappears in the novel. She goes to prison, and she tells him, "I could kill you. I could kill you. You've ended my life."

We see that between the world of the continuous ending of the life of the peasant and the abrupt ending of the life through AIDS, a city-bred disease, a disease bred by repetition and lust and loss, you are giving us irreducible alternatives. Neither one is possible, and yet the strength of this work is to see and embody both of them. That is how I would answer you. How would you answer my answer?

JB: I would answer with a story.

MS: Okay.

JB: Just after I had written *Lilac and Flag*, I was reading in French prisons to prisoners, which is a very humbling experience. It is voluntary and obviously it is not a compelled reading. Anyway, in French prisons, you either read to ten or thirty, and then guards are there, of course, all the time. Their attention of listening is mind-blowing.

I mean, they are wonderful publics, really wonderful and attentive, and they give you an enormous energy. It is incredible what can happen in a theater, but it is not comparable to this. Actually, this attention is almost chilling. It is so intense. Then sometimes there is discussion and talk, and they ask questions.

The story I really wanted to tell you was just on the side of that. This was a prison in Poitiers. High security and enormous procedures to get in, and the prison authorities don't really like these readings. Anyway, there they didn't.

There was a man who was about forty, wearing a very smart T-shirt. He obviously thought that we needed welcoming. He came in. We were already sitting. He came over and said, "Make yourselves at home. Please feel at home here." We began reading, and a couple of hours later when it was over, he said, "I am sure we will meet again at some place."

The point about this story is that it's about the place where things happen and the word *home* and the word *meeting* and the curious laws of hospitality, even under conditions like that.

This question of hospitality seems to me also to have a lot to do with storytelling. It is a question of hospitality to the reader. Hospitality has nothing to do with being polite or being frightened of being offensive or all those things like that. No, hospitality is a question of allowing a space in the story for the reader to take her or his place. Then that place has to be such that naturally there is the possibility of the reader participating, actually participating in the telling of the story.

Finally, at its most extreme, this comes to that line, which I will misquote, but it is the end of one of the marvelous Borges poems: the reader who has read this poem has written it.

MS: It reminds me of one of the stories in *Into Their Labours*, a really passionate story. As I was reading it, I thought this must have been an annunciatory story, one that tells the writer that he is on the right path. It is a story called "An Independent Woman." It is a story about hospitality, and there is a certain point in it where, for the woman, Catherine, the pipe that takes water from the spring to her house has gotten blocked.

She doesn't want to be dependent on anyone and has been going to the spring and bringing the water back to the house. But this will not do. It's getting to be winter, and everything is going to freeze, and she will slip. We know already about her that she is willing to die. Once when she was sick, the doctor said it was pleurisy, and rather than letting her brother and her neighbor take care of her, she at first stays very aloof. And finally she lets them cup her.

There is an extraordinary image when they put the cups to the skin, the flesh of the back rising like bread into the cup, but it is also a preparation because she is going to make pastry. She is not just going to make pastry in the story. She is going to make twenty-five pastries because she is aware that her brother and this neighbor are doing something extraordinary and spending two—and it is going to go into three—days helping her unblock and locate even the pipe.

She makes twenty-five pastries, and I thought about this when you talked about the reader entering and starting to tell the story. I said to myself, "Oh that's enough pastry. That's enough for me there, too. What a good number of pastries to make."

JB: This is wonderful.

MS: Yes, yes, because it is more than enough. It is more than enough for even the telling of the story to fulfill the reader's hunger. Do you know what

I mean about that magic where you enter the story, and you are feeling the cold, and you are feeling the digging, and then the hostess in the story brings twenty-five pastries and—apple *gnôle*, is it?

JB: *Gnôle.* Yes, with alcohol.

MS: *Gnôle.* You see, I am practically dazed because she is coming out to *me* at that point in the story to say, "Stop working. I am not going to let you work anymore. You must sit down and have some pastry." Well, they have already in the story given us this image of bread and baking and pastry as being part of a cure.

It's the loss of the brother and the connection—looking for the connection for fresh water to come back to the house. The brother has buried the pipe a meter deep. Couldn't he have been less a perfectionist, they say. It is always about, as you go through this story, reconnecting to the rightness underlying things. The brother has been killed, and they would be just as happy to insult Matthew. But instead the pipeline goes directly across the field. There is this burst of mud and shit, and then the water becomes silvery in her house. And it is as if the story reaches its connection in every way imaginable. I love the way this works. It is a whole process of making a connection to the past but, most important, exactly what you are saying: hospitality and community.

It begins with the three of them. One says, when the pastry comes out, "Do you remember we used to stay up late at night on Christmas Eve eating this pastry?" Immediately a past is invoked for them all that she has been wise enough to invoke by making the pastry. I can't tell you how much I love this story. Was it one of the breakthrough stories for you in *Pig Earth*?

JB: First, just in brackets, something you said. Hospitality as a principle always implies more than enough. That's its sign in a strange way, even if it is only a question of words. Is that story a breakthrough story? I don't know. Yes, I think so. It is one of the stories in that book which is the least transformed.

It really is a portrait of Mary Raymond, whom I loved. I really did. I can hardly think of the story, really, because as soon as you start talking about it or if I reread it, I just see her. Yeah, I see her, hear her voice. And then a very strange thing, because—how to say this?—when she died, it must now be about twenty years ago, life here, her house, the immediate surroundings, but above all the life in this village, has changed enormously.

When I was writing that story and the other stories, I knew this transformation was taking place. I also knew it was a transformation taking place all over the world: the elimination of subsistence peasants because the new world economy had no place for them. And at that time people would say to me, "Okay, okay, but I mean this is nostalgia, and you just, you retired from the world."

Now we begin to see more and more the crisis of this is provoking a global crisis of nourishment—ecological and economic. This is an absolutely fundamental problem and the whole of Salgado's *Exodus*, for example, is actually about the same thing. I was sort of aware of that in a way, but I wasn't aware of the speed of the transformation that would happen here.

This is what I want to say. When I go to that house now, which has been rebuilt, where the goats were is now a pantry, and where her bed was is a computer. Suddenly—how to say this?—I do not know where I am, and I find myself as though I am now in another century, which at that time was not really imaginable.

I described this very badly, but it is as though I have to stop because it is one of the loops of time I find very, very hard to talk about. It is very difficult for me to find the continuity between what I experienced then and what I am living now. The difficulty of this is really disturbing and confusing, as though the ground is taken from under my feet, *but* having said that, the story avoids this, and the story contains the continuity which even I, who wrote it, can't have.

MS: That's right, that's right, it is the pipe. It is what underlies and finally re-connects that gives that sense that what has been had can be had again.

JB: Yes, exactly, Michael, yeah.

MS: I am trying to remember an English novel set in something called Satis House. It may even be a Dickens novel. It is the idea of having enough and more than enough. It's an ironic title. It was always taught to me this was the place, although it was called the house of a novel, the house of enough, the house of sating, that there was never enough. And many people say that this is the ultimate story of the British novel: the house that seems to be Satis House that does not offer any comfort.

JB: Yeah, there is a—

MS: It's Victorian.

JB: Yes, yes, yes, yes. No, I can't find it either, but we can both smell it.

MS: I see these stories as being very much in contrast to the British novel. The British novel for me is always saying, "Never enough. You never have enough. Need more. Not enough. Even the good one has to come and learn to be a bad one if there is to be enough." And there is an endless seduction of the characters until they form—it is almost as if when you read a Jane Austen novel, as great as the Jane Austen novel is, by the end of it they have become the British Empire.

JB: [*laughter*]

MS: Yes, they have to become the whole, they have to replicate the whole social system, and this will allow the novel to end. It is not really marriage, it's government.

JB: Very good. Yes.

MS: Now you go, yes.

JB: No, no, you.

MS: I am interested because you mentioned hospitality, and you were talking about the prison and about reading there with Nella Bielski, with whom you wrote *Goya's Last Portrait* and several other plays as well.

JB: Yeah, we wrote the play about the gulag, *A Question of Geography.*

MS: I wanted to ask you about collaboration, because it seems to me that throughout your career you have been involved in projects and collaborations with the BBC and even in novel-writing with photographers. Collaboration seems very much of an essence, and in a sense, these stories are your collaborations with this community.

JB: No novel. I think it would be very hard to collaborate on a novel. For scenarios or for theater, yes, because after all what is theater? It is interchange, it is dialogue, and so the idea of collaboration, of exchange in the working method is not very contradictory to what the substance or the form of the thing would be.

About collaboration, I could tell you about how we worked, Nella and I, but maybe the first thing to say is what I think is a golden rule. When you are collaborating—and this was also true, for example, with the photographer Jean Mohr, because these books we really made together, including the layout—the one temptation which must be avoided is to trade with each other. That is to say, "You don't maybe like this red, but I do." "Okay, well I will give you this red, and when we come here to this being like a lemon, you remember the red?"

MS: Give me the lemon.

JB: Give me the lemon, yes. This is absolutely fatal. One must oppose. When one is opposed, one must oppose and oppose. It is not always easy, and it could lead to considerable conflicts, even to hurt sometimes, but I think it is necessary. What happens with a bit of luck—and if the angels are not too far away—is that this is the prelude to assured discovery, which neither of you have thought of, suddenly occurring. That third one is usually correct.

This I think is very, very interesting, and one can talk about that in other ways, you know. A long time ago, I used to lecture about painting to railway workers who really hadn't seen much painting, hadn't been to museums and so on. What was always interesting is that when they were looking at an image and they had some problem with something in it, the way the problem was posed or formulated or the conclusions drawn were, in my opinion, often forced, but nearly always it actually did concern a problematic point or area.

Opinions are often wrong, but the attention of a point which produces conflict or opinions is nearly always a weak one. If we come back to collaboration, that is why when one is collaborating one must be not brutal, not at all, but one must not make concessions, because it is unworthy of both of you.

MS: This leads me to many interesting questions, and I want to combine several things we are talking about. You were talking about those loops of time in which something disappears and one can no longer remember how that something got lost or how it seems to have gotten lost so quickly or so easily. Now, in my life nowadays, I find myself asking, where did all the people I loved who read books all the time, where did they go? How did we lose it?

How did we lose this beautiful thing in which we wouldn't talk about ourselves? We would talk about stories and tears and beautiful things and what it was like last night when I was reading this book. I thought about the first time I ever saw that: it was in a collaboration, it was in *Let Us Now Praise Famous Men* by James Agee and Walker Evans. I think about it a lot because one of my teachers, Dwight McDonald, was Agee's executor.

There is a section called "How We Got Caught," in which voice after voice tries to recreate the process by which their lives were taken away and a fake, a sharecropper, a desolate existence replaced. In your book it is that wonderful, magnificent man who knows the value of money who says, "Yes, they sell us the tractor, but then there are the other machines. We are misusing our tractor if we don't have the other machines. They will lend us money to buy those other machines, and then we will owe the money too, and we will have to work for them in order to pay them the money we owe them to use the machine to help the tractor." It is that sense of someone having that moment of knowing how we got caught. Otherwise something disappears in the logic of capitalism, and you find yourself not loving your life anymore and not knowing how you got caught.

I think it happens to us as beings in culture as well. We are losing our literature, we are losing our ability to communicate amongst ourselves about our own heritage, that we have been dispossessed, and that if we ever lose that string of logic, how were we caught, there is no return. You see that this is the terrible thing because I, like you, get accused at times of that terrible word, conservatism. I want to say the desire to conserve literature is not the same as political conservatism. This is a misuse of language.

JB: Yes, yes, I don't add because I entirely agree with you, entirely.

MS: But how did we come to these paths, do you think? Because it happened just as you were saying. Who would have thought it could happen so quickly? Who would have thought it would happen so completely? Who would have thought it could happen here? The whole series of questions you invoke about your village has occurred to culture itself all over the world in what feels like the blink of an eye.

JB: I often find myself in the role of consoling, and I think the gesture, the will to console, is a very arrogant one. I don't like it. I don't think it has anything to do with giving, which is different. I hesitate to say this because I don't want to console you. Listening to you, I agree with what you say, but somewhere I think that maybe we need to look at it, not really differently, but from a slightly different angle because a potentiality can continue to exist while apparently invisible for a period, and perhaps for a longer period than we imagine.

I mean, if we look at the television almost anywhere in the world now, not all the time but most of the time, we see the shit that they deliver. But if you wake up in the middle of the night and listen to the radio stations that go on all night, sometimes playing music, quite often talking, suddenly—and there are people listening all night—you hear a different tonality.

You hear a different way of communication, which is not shit, and which is connected with the past and connected with another future, as opposed to the instant future of the moment. It happens on radio, and more and more people listen to radio: quite a lot more artists who once thought about television now think about radio. Okay, that's one little sign that I am talking about.

The other thing is that, from time to time, two or three times a year at least, or perhaps more, there are films that come, usually low-budget films, which completely break with what is now the big-budget so-called Hollywoodian—but that is an injustice to early Hollywood—crap that we get. These films evoke, surprising everybody, including the producers. And there is a distribution system which works against these films and so and so on. I mean no idealism. Nevertheless, these films provoke an extensive response, which is quite surprising. For example, there is now showing in France an Iranian film which is simply called *Ten*, a film shot in secret, in which six women just talk in a car as they are driving and driving through Tehran. They just talk about their lives. And it is the most boring film, cinematographically, that you can imagine, the most boring film that has ever been made. And then you start listening, and you stop thinking whether it is boring or not, and you go on and on and on—and it is an extraordinary film. And this film, at least in France, is in many, many cinemas, thousands of people are watching it. Yes, there was a potentiality of acceptance of this film, very difficult to predict before you see it.

Okay, I mentioned that film, but I could mention others. It is more difficult with books because we never know. About films, we can see, we can more or less follow their reception. I mean, what actually happens to somebody when they go to pick up a paperback or steal one? And what happens when they read it? We don't know.

Also the resisting, which I do think is very important. Under the influence of the market and of productivity, which affects even publishing, because now a bestseller is not allowed to finance a book that is likely to sell less. We won't discuss *Harry Potter* for the moment, but we have a tendency like the managers to quantify results. That is to say, how many people read a book? How many people take in something on the radio or whatever? How many people see a play?

That, in a certain sense, is false because we are dealing with the immeasurable. One of the reasons, in brackets, why agriculture, nonindustrial agriculture, resists and is absolutely incommensurate with purely market values, for the same reason, is this: suppose reading a book really influences the reader. That's to say, really changes some small thing. Something that even from the outside will not necessarily be visible to people who know that person. That change, that slight alteration, changes and alters other opinions that person will form, modifies other actions in relation to other people. Those modified actions in relation to other people may somewhat modify the person to whom they are done.

One is involved in something which is not limitless in the sense that it is infinitely huge, but which is also not possible to put a limit to, in quantities. So you change one small thing, you repair one small thing, and it is very difficult to measure the consequences of that because one thing leads to another. One reparation, perhaps, leads to a thousand.

MS: I tend to think that you live certainly closer than I do to the home of "How We Got Caught." You see, I think it became attractive for intellectual people, so called, to agree that humanism is dead. I think they didn't get enough of a rise out of the death of the author, so they tried the death of the human on us.

I think that we have been reeling in the consequence of this announcement of the death of the human, more terrible, I think, in its effect than the announcement of the death of God. See, I am very struck because when I read your books, even *King*, they are very hopeful. They are humanist books.

Transgressive and despairing literature has become a kind of prototype. I never thought, for instance, that the novels of Georges Bataille should be outlawed, but I never thought that they would be a prototype for modern thought. I wanted to talk to you about that, the way in which somehow what used to be called the project of humanism got displaced in our time by a project almost literally of anti-humanism.

"We don't like this book. It is too generous. It is too good natured. It is too old fashioned in its sentiments." I think that something horrifying has followed in its wake, and I wondered what you think.

JB: Maybe one has to look at the concept or the category of humanism because it is relatively recent, really comes from the Enlightenment, and it was a proposal about the future. It was in a certain sense a utopian proposal. Before that there were still human values, and in the notion of humanism, with its utopian proposal, the notion of tragedy began to be eliminated.

MS: An interesting point.

JB: Instead of tragedy there was catastrophe or accidents or wickedness, but the notion of tragedy weakened. The notion of tragedy is profoundly human. This humanism that you are talking about seems to me to have a much longer duration than we perhaps assume.

You know, recently I was in this cave, the Chauvet Cave, discovered five or six years ago to contain perhaps the earliest Paleolithic paintings in the world.

MS: You got to go in.

JB: Yeah, I got to go in. That is a story I can't tell you on camera, but I got there.

MS: That's amazing.

JB: An incredible privilege. You see these paintings. I can show you drawings I made of those paintings.

MS: Oh my God, I am thinking of Lascaux and—

JB: These are 15,000 years older than Lascaux. And you see the sensitivity.

MS: Who did you bribe?

JB: You see the sensibility that drew that horse's nostril and mouth, or the weight of the forepaw of that bear, done in charcoal. And in places it looks as though it was done really yesterday.

The blackness of the charcoal is still as fresh as if it was done yesterday, and on the floor there are these grains of charcoal that fell from the stick they were drawing with.

MS: Oh wow.

JB: I am trying to just draw it for myself on a piece of paper, total silence and the darkness, and suddenly you begin to have the feeling that your hand is almost touching the hand that made it. You also become aware that the sensibility of the hand that made that is exactly the same as ours. You also become aware of the fact that maybe earlier ones will be discovered. 30,000 years ago. And this was a tradition that lasted for 20,000 years after that. And it didn't begin clumsily. It began with this incredible mastery.

Well, isn't it reasonable to claim that humanism is already there 30,000 years ago? I wanted to relativize maybe the finality of the dark crap age in which we live. Also, in that age, as I said before, there are potentialities both taken creatively and received.

In the literary pages of the literary journals they talk about the end of humanism. But travel in a bus going from Poland to the Ukraine with people travelling with a few things to sell. See how they behave, and it is a long way from those literary pages.

There is something which is ridiculous to give the name of humanism to, exactly, but there is a sense of warmth and of suspicion. Of course, of course, of course, of course, never idealize. But a sense of the potentiality and the possibility of sharing and sometimes consoling one another, which is to me much more pleasant actually, more to do with what is happening today, than the incredibly elaborate arguments of the death of humanism.

MS: Your mentioning of the caves is very moving to me because it goes back to what you said about what you believe about fiction, that all time takes place simultaneously. The past, present, and future are overlaid upon one another, and they all represent potentialities. And it connects to the great works of modernism, whether you are talking about James Joyce or talking about Picasso and the sudden intrusion into the world of *Les Demoiselles d'Avignon* of the tribal face mask, that what we have are missing time loops that feel like loss but may not—I am now thinking in the course of assembling this conversation—be actually lost.

JB: Yes.

MS: Yes.

JB: Yes, and always with a reminder that bad news is a very good seller. Because we are so incredibly misinformed. Now I am talking about important political issues, but that's another thing when we talk about disinformation and the management.

MS: It goes without saying—

JB: Of course, of course, it is another subject, extremely important. But actually, we are incredibly badly informed about what people do. Every night we learn about a new sniper or new pedophile or whatever, yes?

MS: Yes.

JB: We begin to have the sense that in the world village in which we live this is all that is happening, but it is just necessary to go to where people are and where they are living closely together, and you see something different. It seems to me it is very, very important to do, and it is very hard, but one must be aware of this misinformation because it is not a question.

It also touches this thing about people always asking, because it comes to the same thing, are you optimistic or are you pessimistic? Which seems to me to be the most stupid question ever asked because obviously everybody is both all the time. And anyway, it completely misunderstands the nature of despair and of hope because hope by its nature is not necessarily optimistic.

I mean hope is something which is held *despite* the circumstances. That is what makes it hope. What is thought of as despair is then turned into its adjective, *desperate*, which in our culture now only means dangerous—incredible, incredible elision of senses. In despair there is quite often at least a search for dignity.

All the time, we have to undo the conceptual and verbal knots with which we are bound and which then affect our own energy and our capacity to believe that it is worth doing this.

MS: Well, you said you weren't going to console me. You have managed. Thank you.

Octavia Butler

2004: *Kindred*

MS: I'm happy to have as my guest, Octavia Butler. And this is a special occasion. It's the twenty-fifth anniversary of the publication of her book that first came out in 1979—*Kindred*. It's a remarkable book, really a breathtaking book. It was recently adopted in that program to have cities adopt books. Rochester read *Kindred*, as I understand it, just as Los Angeles read *Fahrenheit 451*. And, first of all, it interested me, in citing that fact, that both of these books adopted by cities are considered to be science fiction, although their writers have some amount of—what would you say?

OB: Well, *Kindred* really isn't science fiction, just because there's no science in it. I don't know how people feel about *Fahrenheit 451*, but it kind of fits into science fiction in the same way that my book *Parable of the Sower* does: it's not so much the science, it's the future, looking into the future. But *Kindred* is definitely not. Just because I was called a science fiction writer, it gets called science fiction.

MS: That's right. But had you any desire to be called that?

OB: I didn't mind. When I was finally getting published back in the '70s, I was so happy to be published you could have called me almost anything. My first three books were with the science fiction side of Doubleday publishers, and on each cover it said science fiction. Now, they were kind of throwaways, because Doubleday had an agreement, a subscription agreement with schools and libraries, and they knew they were gonna sell a certain number of books no matter what. So they could take a chance on unknown people like me and sell a certain number of books with no real publicity effort. And then the books would die. And mine all made paperback, but for very small sums, and they died there, too. And I had the impression that I was throwing away books. That, at some point, you know, that had to stop, because I was still working at some of the jobs that my character has in *Kindred*. Still doing those horrible little jobs at that time, trying to support myself and write books.

MS:	The equivalent now of phone rooms, say, or, um—

OB:	Oh, I did that. [*laughter*]

MS:	Now what interests me here is—because not only have I read the book, I've read a lot of writing about the book—that the character first appears in her room without an arm, cut from the elbow down. And for some reason, people find this still very strange. And yet it occurred to me clearly that she, coming back from the South, from antebellum, slavery, Maryland, a place where we've seen a man's ears cut off—

OB:	Among other things.

MS:	Yes. Among other things, yes. Her arm is missing because she's a writer. That's what she wants to be. And she's being deprived in some metaphorical way of the power of telling this story, and that her life as a writer depends upon her finding the ability to say it.

OB:	That works. But the truth is, what I was thinking about—and I should tell people that *Kindred* is the story of a modern-day Black woman who goes back in time to the antebellum South and who has to struggle to survive slavery. Now, her last trip back, she knows it's her last trip back because the person who's been calling her back she eventually has to kill. And the reason that I had for her arm being stuck in the wall, the way it was, it's the arm that he was holding. And it stuck there because she couldn't really come back from that experience whole, unmarked, and say, "Boy, glad that's over," and get on with her life. That experience marked her as slavery marked Black people in this country. And that was what I was thinking about.

MS:	Because what I've read in these books has been that not only are these heroes and heroines seeking to define themselves in relation to their heritage, but they're seeking to define themselves as writers—that writing is enormously—

OB: They are. These two people.

MS: Yes. And that when people talk about identity in this book, it's not just racial identity or sexual identity, it's the identity, the right to write. And it seems to me as important in your books as any other act of definition. What was writing to you and reading when you were young?

OB: Well, I began writing when I was ten years old and realized I liked it. And then when my mother spotted me writing and asked what I was doing, I told her I was writing a story. I'd been telling myself stories for years. She said just casually, "Oh, maybe you'll be a writer." And that was my first inkling that there was such a thing as a writer, that people could actually get paid for writing. And all of a sudden things looked a lot brighter because it was something I could do to earn a living that I actually liked. It really rescued me. It gave me a reason to, I guess, to stay in school, to endure the fact that I was painfully shy and had no social life. It just really became my life. So I guess you could say it's been my profession and my religion.

MS: Now, I'm curious, one of the reasons that I know, when I'm reading *Kindred*, that I'm in good hands, is that on around, say, page forty, or maybe even later, it's not until then, when a temporary boss sees Dana—do you say Dah-na or Day-na?

OB: Her name is Edana, but I realize people are going to call her Dana because her actual name only comes up once or twice.

MS: Right. This boss sees Dana with her husband-to-be, Kevin, at a lunch counter. He knows that they're both going to write, and he says they're going to write pornography. And then he says—

OB: I don't think that was a boss. That was a wino—[*laughter*]

MS: But he's on the job too, isn't he?

OB: Yeah. But she works out of a temporary agency that she refers to—before she finds out what the word really means—as a slave market. And I used to work out of a temporary blue-collar agency. And some of the people, a lot of the people who show up for work in those places are winos because they can do a day's work, get some money, and go out and have more than they should to drink, and then come back when they need some more money.

MS: He says that they're going to write together pornography, and that it's going to be chocolate and vanilla pornography. And that's the first time the reader knows that this man that Dana lives with is a white man.

OB: You didn't see it when she came back and was horrified and didn't want him to touch her?

MS: Well, I—

OB: She came back from one of her time trips.

MS: Well, but given what happens on those time trips, being horrified at being touched seemed to me to be a reasonable response universally. And so I thought that it was actually a touch of real narrative brilliance that we don't exactly know that until it's been really kind of obliquely introduced. What were the tools for your research? Because you are trying to create the conditions of slavery as a realistic enterprise. That's not science fiction. And yet these are, for the readers, the strangest and most horrifying things encountered in *Kindred*.

OB: There were different branches of research. The first was, of course, I went off to the library, because that was always what I did when I was gonna be working on a new book. And I went to the history room. This is the old LA public library, before they modified it. And I went to the history room, and I really didn't find that much that was useful. For one thing, my character was gonna be going to Maryland, to the eastern shore of Maryland. It's a small state, and I found some things that were useful, but I didn't really know how to research a historical novel. I didn't know how to find the little things, what foods people were going to be eating, what furniture might be in their house, how they did the usual domestic chores that everyone had to do. I had to find out things like that. And one of my problems was finding out how they did the laundry, and I hunted and hunted in the library, was out of the history room fairly quickly and over into social science, reading slave narratives and that kind of thing. And finally I found out that, no, they probably didn't use washboards or go to the river and beat their laundry on a rock. They were much more likely to use big iron kettles, where they heated the water, and then they used lye soap, of course. And they would beat the clothes with big wooden paddles. And it was like making yourself a human washing machine, in a way: hard physical work, especially in a place that's already hot. Just imagine a job like that in August. And I was so happy that I'd found out. I went home, and my mother phoned. We generally talked to each other every day, and she phoned and asked what I had been up to. I told her, and she said, "Oh, yes, I can recall my own mother doing the laundry that way." I hadn't realized how near history was.

My grandmother was born in the late 1800s, 1890-something. She didn't really know her birthdate because her mother died giving birth to her, and she was in the care of people who really didn't care. So she had a hard life right from the beginning. And I only knew her for a short time during my life because when I was ten she died. But there were other older people in my family that I realized I should talk to. And I did do a little bit of that, family research. So I did library research and I did family research. I also went to Maryland. I had very little money because I sold *Survivor*, my third novel, before it should have been sold. It really wasn't ready. But I sold it and used the money to take a Greyhound bus to Maryland, three and a half days on the bus nonstop.

One day, I came back to the bus station. My feet were hurting. I was tired. I came back to the bus station, and I was gonna have two hours to wait before the bus to Baltimore was going to go. And I sat there and wrote what turned out to be the first and last chapter of the novel. Now, I didn't realize that's what it was, but I guess, in a way, that's where my mind was, just from walking the roads and kind of taking the place in.

MS: Now, what fascinates me is, I did not know your work, because, I confess, unless someone explains to me that a work of science fiction or mystery is special, I stay away. You know, it's almost as if I depend upon friends to pass me the valuable books in these fields. Because I tend to think that, unless the book is special, I might not like it. But your work comes to me, in fact, via writing about it that's been done over the last ten to fifteen years. You've become a writer who is talked about when people are writing about gender studies, about queer theory, about, of course, ethnicity and identity. So that always the inner subject of your work—which is what, eventually, the critics found—or the critics who were writing about the other books that I cared most about—it was through them that I began to hear that these books were not your run-of-the-mill books. And indeed they aren't. I mean, it seems to me that they're literature, you know.

OB: Thank you. And, by the way, *Kindred* was published as a mainstream book, originally. And then Beacon, of course, they never went on about science fiction. So it was probably more accessible than the others. What I do is kind of open to interpretation. Sometimes it is science fiction, as with *Lilith's Brood*—my three novels *Dawn*, *Adulthood Rites*, and *Imago* combined into one. But a book like the one you have there, *Parable of the Sower*, is no more science fiction than, say, *The Handmaid's Tale*. So it's just a matter of people wanting me to be one thing and one thing only.

MS: Now it seems to me that in the histories of oppression, there are several kinds of oppression. And there's the oppression that a writer faces as being stigmatized as a certain kind of writer. No one called Margaret Atwood's *The Handmaid's Tale* science fiction because they'd read *Surfacing*, say, or *The Edible Woman*. But if you start out—

OB: Yes.

MS: —in science fiction, the likelihood is that you're going to remain there. Now, you have done, it seems to me, quite a few things in order not to remain there, including being published by a small press, Four Walls Eight Windows.

OB: Yes. Which became, well, the part of it that I wound up with was Seven Stories Press.

MS: I want to venture something that I don't think has been sufficiently acknowledged. And I think it's one of the difficulties of literature in America. I would venture to guess—in fact, I'd go further—I would bet that if the books continued to be published by Warner with the science fiction covers and the tendency to be paperback-only editions, that what happened several years later, the genius award from the MacArthur Foundation, might not have happened.

OB: Might not have, might not have.

MS: Now, again, the image of the science fiction writer is of someone who, well, hyperbolically, writes thirty books in his or her first two or three years of writing—

OB: Definitely hyperbole. [*laughter*]

MS: But you write a book around every five or six years.

OB: When I began writing, I turned out a book a year because I had all these ideas, and they'd been seething around in my mind since I was twelve. After a while, I told the stories that had been living in my head for so long, and then I began to write much more slowly.

MS: It seems to me, certainly from *Kindred* on, that novel after novel handles material that the writer has had to first prepare herself to handle. That there's a pain, an explosiveness, a searing quality to the acknowledgments of the errors of patriarchy, not on an ideological level, but on the level of the body and the spirit and the emotions. That the novels are an agreement between the writer and her story, to enter the story deeply and fully in a way that someone less engaged or, in a way, someone less antisocial than you—

OB: I don't see myself as antisocial but asocial. I feel that if I am not in the book, as I write it, if I'm not living in it, no one else will. I can't invite people in if I'm not there myself. And that's important to me. There are a lot of what I think of as cold books that are good books, but they don't engage you except intellectually. And I do want to reach people on more levels than that.

MS: Well, I think that you reach people intellectually because you reach people on more levels than that. There's a scene in *Kindred*, for instance, that I didn't expect to find in the book at all. Edana—

OB: Dana, you can call her Dana, sure.

MS: —okay, is speaking to Alice. There is a young white master, Rufus, the son of the owner of the plantation, not a very impressive plantation, who has fallen in love—

OB: With Alice.

MS: Obsessively, with Alice, a free Black woman. He is perhaps able to fall in love with Alice because he has met Dana, who has come to him through time. She is his instance of a Black woman who saves his life. She might as well be, if we were giving it names, his guardian angel. And so it is not unusual for him.

OB: She certainly doesn't want to be and doesn't feel herself qualified to be.

MS: Exactly. And not only that, Alice doesn't want Rufus.

OB: No, she has another man in mind.

MS: And here we find this woman—a realistic woman, a woman who's living in 1976, in Los Angeles—who's sitting with Alice, giving her her options. You can run away and get beaten, worse, or die. You can give yourself to him voluntarily, so called—

OB: Maybe have a little bit of control.

MS: —or you can give yourself to him against your will completely. And, you know, what we're seeing is a Black woman apprising a Black woman of a really ugly reality.

OB: Yeah. And it wasn't a reality that Alice was unaware of. It's just having someone put it into words. I have been criticized for that because people seem to think that my character is pushing Alice into this relationship, when the truth is, there's no way my character could rescue Alice from this relationship. And all she's really doing is saying, here are your options. They're not nice options, but here they are.

MS: At the moment—very significantly, it seems to me—Alice is in the process of making Dana a dress. Dana has arrived in—

OB: Pants.

MS: In pants, in jeans.

OB: In other words, men's clothes.

MS: Men's clothes, and everyone notices. It's the first thing they notice about her, even before they notice that she's Black. This woman in pants is here, traipsing around the antebellum countryside. And Alice has to decide whether to burn the dress. "You know, you do what you want," says Dana. "This is what I have to tell you. I'm not really giving a brief for Rufus's case, although I know him. I'm stating your own case as accurately as I can. Now, the reality is here."

OB: Actually, she does try to help her to get away, originally, but that doesn't work out.

MS: That's right. So what I would say is that what makes these novels unusual is their willingness to brave what would become, subsequently, political incorrectness of a real, real sort, to tell the truth. That you are so deeply inside the narrative that other people's objections about what a role model would do are irrelevant, as opposed to the truth of the situation.

OB: They would be irrelevant to Alice's situation, too, of course.

MS: But I think they're irrelevant to you as a writer, too.

OB: I wanted Dana to be pretty straightforward. As a matter of fact, most of my characters are, especially if they're first-person characters, very straightforward people. And I wanted her to be able to face the truth, even if she didn't like it. And of course she doesn't like it, but there it is.

MS: Now, why do you suppose it is? I mean, other of your books have celebrated a twenty-fifth anniversary—

OB: And more.

MS: And more. Yes. And this was not a bestselling book when it came out.

OB: But it's been a good perennial seller. When Beacon picked it up—and I've forgotten what year that was, but it was some time ago—it kept selling. And Beacon did some good publicity work on it. So they've done a good job keeping it alive. And it has been accepted, as you mentioned, in Rochester. I was there for about eight days speaking every day about *Kindred* to everybody from the junior high school to the old people's home. And that was an experience.

MS: Exactly. When a city adopts a book, again, this has got to be a milestone in a writer's life. It may not be in yours—

OB: It was lovely. Yes, it was lovely.

MS: But does it change the way you regard yourself?

OB: No. No. I spend most of my time in a room with a bunch of books and a computer. That's what I did twenty years ago, except not the computer, but the typewriter. And that's what I do now. So no, most of my regard for myself comes out of the work that I do. Not the work that I did twenty-five years ago or thirty years ago, but the work that I'm doing now.

2006: *Fledgling*

MS: The last time you were here, Octavia, was for the anniversary of *Kindred*. That was my introduction to your work, and I was so startled by it. And you told me that you were really at sixes and sevens about beginning a new novel because you had to find something that would interest you to write all the way through. What was the seedling of *Fledgling*?

OB: Well, first of all, a monstrous writer's block, I'm sorry to say. I had written the two *Parable* books, and I had a third in mind that was not going to be a *Parable* book, but that would be related. And I couldn't write it. And I was just having more and more trouble trying but not writing it. And, as I tell people when I give talks about *Fledgling*, trees died, but nothing good came of it. And I tried writing other books, as well, and nothing came of it. But as it happened, I'm in too many book clubs—not the kind of book clubs where people get together and talk about their favorite book for that month, but the kind of book club that sends you books if you don't return the postcard. And I don't know whether I didn't return the postcard, or I may have written the wrong number on the postcard. At any rate, I got sent a vampire novel. Now, I've read a few vampire novels before—of course everybody reads *Dracula*, I guess, and I read some Anne Rice novels, and one or two others, but I hadn't really been interested. Now, all of a sudden, I read this vampire novel, and it was really bad, but I finished it. Now I read slowly enough so that that's a problem if a book is really bad, and this one had no research done—it should've been researched, and the person had not troubled to do that. And I thought, well, why did I want to finish it? Why did it grab me the way it did? And finally I went out and bought a number of other paperback vampire novels, and read them, and the first thing I learned was that vampire novels can be pretty much anything. I mean, I found some that were mysteries, some that were science fiction, some that were history novels with a vampire, some that were humor, some that were romances. And that was delightful, too, because it meant I wasn't going to be stuck with one model of vampire. And at that point I hadn't thought it through, but as I read through these things, I realized, I want to write one. They're fun. And I wound up writing *Fledgling*, I guess for that reason. I was looking for something to bring the fun back into my writing.

MS: But where do you suppose stories of vampires come from?

OB: I think a lot of it comes out of a need to explain supernatural or seemingly supernatural events. Someone asked me that yesterday, and I said it could be a matter of premature burial, you know, that some poor soul was buried alive and maybe went mad on account of it and managed to get out of the grave and scared the heck out of everybody. It could've been; who knows. But there are, in different cultures, so many different kinds of vampires. I once wrote a book called *Wild Seed*, about—I guess you could call him a soul vampire. He was a person who transmigrated, and every time he took a new body, the person who had been in that body died. But that was a little bit more supernatural than I wanted to get in *Fledgling*. The vampires in *Fledgling* are another species. They're a kind of parallel species that's grown up alongside humanity. They don't have magical powers; they can't turn you into a vampire by biting you, which both I and my character thought was a very odd notion. They need human beings emotionally and physically—they need the blood.

MS: What I found fascinating is that this narrator, Shori, wakes up in the dark. She doesn't know her name, she doesn't know who she is, she doesn't know what's happened to her. She does feel scars, wounds, burns, all over her body. And we're coming to consciousness along with her. Everything we come to know about who she is we come to know—

OB: Through her.

MS: Through her and with her. And so it's really a coming to consciousness book. She's learning about her background and her generations as we do. And so much of what happens in this book is about the creation of a very strong character.

OB: She has to recreate herself, yes. The idea that you could lose that much of yourself. She's actually a fifty-three-year-old being, who looks like a ten- or an eleven-year-old girl, so her appearance is very deceptive.

MS: Now Shori comes to discover that she is the sole survivor of her generation of mothers.

OB: Well, not of her generation so much as of her female family. Her elder mothers, grandmothers, her mothers, her sisters. All dead. These people live sexually separate, so her fathers are over here with her brothers and her grandfathers and all that, however many generations there may be. And the mothers are here. And it's their way of living. I mean, they're not doing it for the purpose of being different. They're doing it because it works for them.

MS: Now, we learn as we discover that her mothers have already been destroyed, and we will witness with her the fact that her father, who has rescued her in a sense, and is about to give her a context—

OB: A home, yes.

MS: His community is destroyed as well. And so she's very aware that she is adrift in the world in a highly codified society, unaware of their rules and rituals, and that she has to learn them. How does anyone go about doing this in a culture?

OB: I think it would be so difficult, and I think that's why I had to write it the way I did. With us looking out of Shori's eyes, because otherwise we'd know too much, and we might not empathize with her the way I wanted people to. She has to remake herself, and sometimes, even without amnesia, we have to remake ourselves. I was interested in that. I was interested in trying to understand just how much the character has lost. So every now and then, I wound up restating it and realizing she's lost her whole education, for instance. Through a good part of the book, she's never met a female member of her own species. So she's lost that knowledge. She doesn't really know how to cope with how to look after her symbionts, the human family that she acquires.

MS:	Well that's the first startling thing. Within a few pages, she has instinctually bitten a man who's picked her up to rescue her. And he's in ecstasy. And the first thing we learn that differentiates the Ina—as she comes to know, that's her species—from what we hear about from vampire books, is that the people she bites are delighted to be bitten. Especially as she licks the wound, her saliva seems to contain—

OB:	It is addictive, it gives them a lot of pleasure, yes.

MS:	So we're watching something very different. We're not watching the growth and spoiling of human society by vampires. We're watching the creation of interbreeds, people who come to live—

OB:	It's not exactly interbreeding, though, because they can't. But it's genetic engineering, a little bit of blending. There's a word for it that, of course, won't come to me right now, but she has had, from a different species, from humanity, a little bit of a genetic transplant, I guess I'd say. And she is the first of her species to have a twenty-four-hour life. I mean, she can be fully awake and alert during the day, which is what her grandmothers who did this were trying to arrange, that she could do this. It makes her different in a way that even more sets her apart from her people. Even when she finally reconnects with some of them, she's not quite like them.

MS:	That was the place, as she comes to suspect that the people who've destroyed the two sides of her family are themselves Ina, that I began to think of the ways in which this novel becomes political, and thought, of course, about Yugoslavia and the creation of differences among people who are in fact very, very similar and need to embrace.

OB: I don't think I could write a wholly apolitical novel. She is—well, some people find her a treasure because she can pass on the genetic gifts that she's been given, even though her grandmothers are dead and their research is burned. Their work is just gonna have to be duplicated by other people. It's not secret or anything, so that is possible. But right now, she's the only one. She had a brother who was a partial success, but he's dead. She has this to deal with. She has to learn to be an Ina, but she isn't quite Ina. So as I said before, she's in a very strange place.

MS: What again caught my eye is you begin to wonder here, given that generations of vampires and generations of vampire stories have kept the vampire as a liability. Travel is difficult because when the sun comes out, they're weakened. There are all kinds of—

OB: She isn't bothered by the sun, actually. By the way, I suppose I should say the secret of her success is melanin. So she is the first Black vampire.

MS: Now, eventually, those of her own species who've destroyed her families are essentially accused of racism.

OB: In a way, yes. It's a strange kind of racism, but what they're doing is looking at human beings and saying, "Oh, these people are the lowest of the low among humans, what do you want to bring them into our people for?"

MS: There's a council of justice, in which the essentially racist family is brought by the other families. They're capable, the other families, depending on how old they are, of detecting lies. And so these people are lying in a court of justice in front of families and friends, knowing they can be detected.

OB: Well the older ones are hoping that they can't be. The oldest, in particular, is over 500 years old and hoping that he can get away with it.

MS: Because I wondered whether this was not, in fact, a secret at the heart of racism itself. That people who know that they are about to be judged—they understand the whole system that would judge them—find not that they are justifying their feelings, they take refuge in concealment. And what fascinated me about that whole section of the book, the climax of the book, is the degree to which logic itself of every kind is subverted. They can be seen into. They are lying to families and friends. They've destroyed their own future.

OB: That's the other thing. Not everyone sitting there at the table wants to see. Some people agree with them. So there's that. And also, I don't know whether I got this in or not, but there is this notion that they would feel, if they can't have this gift, why should anyone else have it? So there's that, too.

MS: Now, to the extent that these books become parables, and that we're witnessing the education of a woman being brought back to consciousness, what has Shori learned from this, that these people exist?

OB: The first thing she's learned is to trust herself. She has reason to worry that she could be a danger to her own symbionts. And she learns that that's not true, she can restrain herself and she doesn't have this to worry about. With the other, she has learned, really, I think, that she can trust her people a little more than she thought. They do come to the right decision. It was hard to understand what the right decision would be. Because here are people who have no prisons. And they have odd ways of taking care of problems. I think I was also responding, not so much that Shori was, but I was responding to the idea that our justice system isn't about justice. It's about who's gonna win. And that's terrible because it means that people will often win when they shouldn't.

MS: So, for me, the book seemed to be about a conflict between those instinctual hatreds and loves, on the one hand, and the traditions that are handed down to us that teach us about our moralities and make us make other choices.

OB: I think, and this sounds way off side, but I was raised Baptist, strict Baptist: no makeup, no swearing, and all that. And I went away from most of that, but what it did do was give me a conscience. Early, early on, a conscience. And for that I'm extremely grateful, because I've seen what people can wind up as if they don't have one. And it's not something they can be given later in life. They can learn the rules, but they're just rules, and rules can be considered to be made to be broken. Shori learned early on that she didn't really want to hurt people. She was very, very capable of hurting people. But it wasn't something she wanted to do. And I think investigating that part of her life, she's just learning that she doesn't have to. And worrying that maybe Wright, her first, is correct in that she took away his choices. She worries about this. She likes the idea that she can hear her symbionts talking about her, and they do basically seem to care about her and like her, and this is important. So Shori has a conscience, however many rules she may not have kept or remembered.

MS: Now, on the other side, there are parts of the council of families who do feel—when they're pressed against the wall, they'll say it—that she's a mongrel, a hybrid.

OB: There are people who feel that way. Even some who agree that she's been severely wronged do feel this way.

MS: And that's what makes for the complexity of the book. What is it that Shori knows, even though she's amnesiac, that they have forgotten?

OB: "Knows" is probably the wrong word.

MS: Intuits? Feels?

OB: Feels, feels. I've met people who don't have a conscience. They're frightening because there isn't really anything to keep them from doing terrible things. I remember someone saying that's why we have religion, so that people will be afraid something will happen to them. It doesn't really work really well. It just seems to me important that you learn early that other people can feel pain just as you can, for instance, that other people have wishes and desires just as you do, and feel it as opposed to simply being told, here are the rules. And this is what Shori has done. Some of them may have lived too long. They have ceased to believe that the rules apply to them, and all they ever really learned was rules. So that may be part of the problem. It was an interesting thing to think about because it forced me to think about the way I was raised. And my mother thought she was teaching me that if I didn't behave in certain ways I'd go to hell. And what she was really teaching me was what I said: other people have feelings, feel pain, have needs. And it was part of me by the time—oh goodness, by the time I was six or seven I was very much aware of it. And I had a relative who wasn't. And he was kind of a gentle sociopath. Not someone who's gonna hit you on the head and make off with your wallet, but in gentler ways might do you a lot of harm. And just the comparison. Writers mine their lives. We go back, and we dig around, and we find all these things that help us understand our characters. And I think that's a lot of what I was doing with Shori and some of the other characters.

MS: Now I have a final question. Throughout your work, it seems that you take great care to not let complex moral issues be simply settled, even when we would like them to be. How do you maintain that moral complexity?

OB: It is complex. Morality is complex. Stories about the good guys and the bad guys don't interest me. Nothing is that simple. And I guess that's really the answer. People are fascinating because they're not simple, and my characters have to be people. Even if they're very odd people, they have to be people. So I think that's what matters to me. If they don't come across to me as people, they don't interest me.

Joan Didion

1996: *The Last Thing He Wanted*

MS: I once found a sentence in *The Journal of Jules Renard* in which he says that, no matter how much care one takes to write as little as possible, there will always be someone who has not read everything you have written.

I've noticed that somehow or other I've read everything you've written, but even people I know who don't read have too. There's a way in which these works enter the popular imagination, even though I don't think they're necessarily understood once they've entered.

I wanted to talk about the newest novel, *The Last Thing He Wanted,* and talk about some of its tones and themes. I thought that I would start with the title.

JD: It just came to me when I started. When you start a novel you never know where it's going to go and you're just working in the dark. I thought I would write a novel in the form of a biography of a figure in Washington who had had some role in events that we would learn about in the course of doing this. I abandoned this, but when I went back to start it again I found in my notes, in all caps, this one phrase: "THE LAST THING HE WANTED." I thought, "That has to be the title." Then you had to figure out who "he" was.

MS: Exactly. That's what interested me, because it sets out a series of resonances in which, like some kind of odd sounding device, the title blinks off and on. *The Last Thing He Wanted* could be, in fact, the last thing that he wanted, desired, this particular woman. Or it could be read in the sense of, "the last thing I wanted was the last thing that I wanted in a million years." It goes back and forth between dread and desire. Then the "he" seems to be this woman's father. The last thing "he" wanted was a million bucks. She feels tender toward him because her husband has dealt in units of 100 million, so it's almost a sentimental desire to get into this life, her father wanting a million.

Of course, the last thing "he" wanted was his daughter's death. There's this strange space that the title starts to occupy. Then you notice how odd it is that the book is narrated by one woman about another, that both of these women tend to disappear in a way.

JD: And the two men are the stronger.

MS: And the two men are strong.

JD: Stronger characters, yeah.

MS: Or given pride of title?

JD: Yes. You can't start anything without leaving its traces on what you've finally done, no matter how many times you've changed it or thrown that out. No mark you make on paper once you've started something is not going to have some shadow in the final thing. The title is the strength of that one character, the man from Washington. Those are probably shadows—what do they call it when they look for bomb traces?—trace residue of that first attempt, when the book was going to be a biography of that character, Treat Morrison.

     The other, the father, comes across very strong to me because I wanted him in the novel. He was a character I wanted to deal with there. The notion that he would be in the novel as Elena's father came later.

MS: Can you describe him before he was Elena's father?

JD: His name was Dick McMahon, and he made deals. When I say he made deals, he made little deals, very small-timey. He could get guns. He could get stuff. He provided things for all kinds of those semi-illegal enterprises that go on, on the domestic underside of our foreign adventures. Actually, if you've read any of the reports, after the Kennedy assassination, of the congressional hearings, there were an awful lot of characters like that who cropped up who weren't by any means necessarily involved in the Kennedy assassination but had somehow passed through the life of somebody involved. I mean, somebody Jack Ruby knew, or somebody so-and-so knew, or somebody who had once met Lee Harvey Oswald.

They were all these kinds of Dick McMahon characters, these small dealers in stuff. They could line up anything you wanted basically in the middle of the night, on a small basis. They weren't dealing around the world, just locally.

MS: I noticed that Dick McMahon has a noticeably different kind of name, say from Treat Morrison, the man in Washington, or Wynn Janklow. I thought how funny it is to have this book in which the men are named Wynn and Treat.

JD: Yes.

MS: I thought to myself, how can it be that these book reviewers don't even seem to notice the tone being given to the naming of these characters, to having a woman named McMahon. Gee whiz, it's not as if you're asking anyone to scale Hyperion's heights to see that one. You think to yourself, the book is finding a way for a woman to try and adapt to all these fields of desire circumscribed by improbably named men.

JD: Well, you never know what you're putting into a book. You never think of things like names. You just know when you have the right one. I knew all along that her last name would be McMahon, but I had real trouble with her first name. I was never very happy with it. One thing that I knew, that I was fixed on, was that her father would call her Ally or Ellie. It would seem to suggest that her name would be obviously a diminutive of an A or an E name. But I couldn't get the right one. Allison was too fancy. Elaine was not quite right for this character or this family. Elena didn't quite have total resonance for me, but I went with it eventually. Then you get stuck with it.

MS: Is that why her name changes? You just said that whatever you put on paper leaves its trace element in the book. As a reader, I think *Play It as It Lays* is a book that defines its title: by the time you finish reading it, you know what *Play It as It Lays* means. Here, too, the title ignites a certain set of resonances that won't get answered until the end of the book. Then you begin to see the book as existing within a field defined by the title. Do you know what I mean?

JD: But you don't know what that field is when you start writing it. You just have this big vacuum. Actually, I did know the title of *Play It as It Lays* before I started. I knew the title of this one very early on, too. *Democracy* I didn't call that, I called it *Angel Visits* for a long time.

MS: *Angel Visits?*

JD: I read someplace that an angel visit was a Victorian term for a pleasant visit of short duration. When I started *Democracy*, I had thought it was all going to take place at a family occasion in Honolulu. An American family in Honolulu who had been there since before statehood and had made a lot of money. A lot of the family dynamic would become clear in the course of the novel. *Angel Visits* seemed right because essentially anybody's life on earth is an angel visit, right? I guess, if you think of it that way.

Certainly in the life of a family, members come, they are born and they die, but the family had gone on. Then it stopped being that. I stopped calling it *Angel Visits*, and for a while I called it *Pacific Distances*, since everybody seemed to be at a distance from everybody else. Actually, "Pacific distances" was a phrase in our house because distances in the Pacific are so much more. If you've just been traveling in the rest of the world and suddenly you have to fly from Honolulu to Melbourne or to Sydney, you have no concept of how long that takes. You can hear it, but until you are doing it—people in the Pacific think of a ten-hour flight as nothing. A ten-hour flight is—

MS: Par for the course.

JD: Yeah. I finished the book, and John said, "Why don't you call it *Democracy*?" That sounded better. By then I was thinking about the fall of Saigon. As I said, you never know what the field is when you start out. It's as if you're operating in a dream and the dream is unfolding around you.

MS: And yet there's a certain kind of dream it is. It seems to me, at least in the last three novels, that although I might not know what to call this kind of dream, it's a dream that Joseph Conrad dreamed also—about guilt and imperialism and the beauty of the natural world being despoiled by the mere act of living in it. A certain distance from the story is required, so a narrator must narrate about still another narrator.

JD: Well, I have to say that before I started each of these I reread *Victory*, which of course has a narrator who tells a story that has been told. It's a third-hand story. The person who told him was not even present for these events. That distance from the story was very exciting to me somehow: it's a way of controlling the story. A lot of Conrad is very exciting to me: the whole landscape, the physical settings. *Victory* opens with the picture of Axel Heyst on the dock there. You're just there.

MS: To mention, in Conrad, the way in which the things are simultaneously funny and ominous. In *The Secret Agent*, the player piano that erupts into song. This strange trade office in *Heart of Darkness*, with two women who are not businesswomen at all. They're knitting. They're the Fates, but only Conrad would dare to make something as exciting and funny and frightening.

JD: The relationship between Axel Heyst and Lena, which we are never close to, is very, very romantic in some way. I see, as I talk to you, that it basically was the beginning of the dream of what happens to Elena in this book. It's a very similar kind of romance. That was the germ of it.

MS: Well, the project, if it can be called that, of the novel at that time seems very reanimated by your work. By that I mean that Conrad, Ford Madox Ford, even Kipling, and certainly James are examining point-of-view in the most relentless way imaginable. To understand these books, really, you have to consider who has said what to whom, when, and what they knew when they were told. What did the teller know?

JD: What does the teller know? I mean, that is the great question in *The Good Soldier*. Who is that teller? You never look at it straight in *The Good Soldier*. Those writers *were* doing that. That was a huge preoccupation of James's, wasn't it?

MS: Enormous. Enormous. It's very interesting to me because I feel that, although your novels have been caught in the fever of public moments and tend to be celebrated, they are classical in this way of investigating what a novel can do in the process of what it does do, which is to tell.

JD: I wonder if that particular group of people at that particular time, if in a way they were the first people to really use the novel to try to get close to human personality, human character. Because to some extent before that novels had been—

MS: Adventures.

JD: Adventures. They had been picaresque tales, or pictures of a society, even, with amusing accounts of how people rose from one class to another or amusing accounts of how they fell in a fixed class structure. Maybe it's that as fixed class structure started to fall apart at a certain point late in the nineteenth century, that's what threw up this group of novelists to look at personality.

There's a dedication that Joyce Carol Oates put in the beginning of one of her novels. I think it was *Do with Me What You Will*, but the dedication was: "For all of us who pursue the shifting phantasmagoria of personality." That seemed very moving to me.

MS: I'm glad that you bring up that book in particular.

JD: *Do with Me What You Will*. It's a fantastic book.

MS: A fantastic book.

JD: A lot of Joyce Carol affects me this way, unlike anybody except Dreiser, really. You become part of the novel. You are in the novel for the length of time you're reading it. I happened to be reading it when we were living in Malibu. We had to go to dinner up the beach. I can remember dragging myself away from the book to get dressed to go to dinner. When we got to dinner and I was sitting—this was dinner at the beach, you know—I'm sitting, and I have a drink, and suddenly I look at what I'm wearing. I have dressed myself for this evening at the beach in a beige velvet skirt that happens to be lined with pale blue satin and has a pale blue satin sash. I don't even know from what corner of my closet I had dragged this, but, as if I was still in the dream, I had dressed myself as the wife of a trial lawyer because of course it's about the wife of a trial lawyer.

MS: What becomes so interesting to me in that book—several of Joyce's books from that period do this—because she is exploring identity, she puts at the center a woman who has become a blank. If I remember correctly, that woman has been kidnapped by her father from the schoolyard.

JD: Right.

MS: One day he disappears and never comes out of a movie theater.

JD: Before that they were living there and hiding there, a horrendous hiding experience.

MS: All I can remember is that she eats raw spaghetti, and she comes out looking very thin and beautiful as a model. This is the last time you get a shred of personality from her. For the rest of time, she is looking for herself in the mirror. She's having autoscopic hallucinations; the self is vanishing on her left and right. I think that for you, too, the self is examined from the perspective of its potential vanishing or absence. Does that have any resonance for you?

JD: Yeah, well, I guess all of it has some. I mean, if you have any sense of mortality, the actual vanishing of self, if it is that easy, then where is the self?

MS: It's only easy in art.

JD: Well, no, it's easy in life. Suddenly, you go across the street, you could die. People die in ways in which they might not have expected when they got up that morning. I think if you were a fearful child of no faith, you maybe grew up with an uncertain sense of your own survival, of your own personality in the world.

MS: I've often thought—and perhaps this is a thoroughly ungentlemanly thing—that, again and again in the Joyce Carol Oates novels, there is almost an obligation, a duty, to reinvent the abusive father. And once he is there, the book can be written because it has a center of fascination and gravity. Do you have anything to say about the elements of a writer's work that must be repeated from book to book? They seem to be sine qua nons for the imagination. Their values may differ, their meanings from novel to novel, but, almost talismanic, certain elements need to be aligned for an imaginative act to occur.

JD: Certainly I see when I'm finished with something that it has parallels or that here are certain elements I've used before. Actually, I try not to think about it too much because I'm afraid if I analyze it too much, they'll go away and my ability to do it again will vanish.

MS: But they can't go away.

JD: It's such a chancy thing, getting up in the morning and doing it.

MS: If nothing one has ever done in one's life has been able to move these things a fraction of an inch, intellection seems least capable.

JD: You're probably right. But one thing I do know is that my interest in writing about something that doesn't take place in very warm weather is low. There has always been a woman in my books who is in some sort of extreme circumstance, some sort of distress. That is what happens. At the end of each of them, it seems to me, although not to every reader, that she emerges dead or alive, stronger, having become in the course of the book more honest, having shed certain delusions. Those are the things that I do see repeated in my own work. I'm just trying to think whether there was an abusive father in *We Were the Mulvaneys*, but I can't remember.

MS: He's sometimes young. Sometimes a character goes on a date with him. But there'll always be something that reveals in fact that he's the father. If he comes for a date, it will turn out that his luxurious hair is, in fact, a toupee. There's always some sign that the father is showing up again. Here he is.

I wanted to talk about a sense I have that the novel, when it's truly being written and found, contains no excess, no moment that does not have implicit within it an underlying possibility of revelation or significance. For me to say that your novels strike me this way is not to say that you've sat down and deduced beforehand the significance of a moment. Rather, it is to say that an instinct is keeping you there.

JD: It's very mysterious. You simply start, and you feel if things aren't happening. If it isn't getting to the right place you want, you know it's not working. So you try to come at it from another way. You can't plan.

I once had a terrible argument. I was teaching one semester at Berkeley in 1975, and I was invited to dinner one night by the chairman of the department. People were having a very spirited argument. They were in the process of basically putting down Scott Fitzgerald on the basis, which was self-evident to them, that he was a terrible novelist because *The Last Tycoon* was so terrible. And I said, "Well, *The Last Tycoon* was an unfinished book." And they said, "No, no, no, but we have the notes. We have certainly at least a third of the novel, and we have the notes for the rest of it." I said, "We really can't judge on the basis of a third of a novel and notes for the rest of it." But it was their conviction that basically every word you put down was written in stone, and every note you made was a cogent note for the completion of a work, which, of course, it isn't. What you do by the time you finish it is that maybe you have used all those notes and all those words, but you have played them. I mean, you have made them work somehow. You've made everything the work, or you have failed.

MS: Well, it's so interesting that you say this, because it strikes me that this is essentially the difference between a crossword puzzle and a crystal. And anyone who would want to read a crossword puzzle—[*laughter*]. I mean, I can contemplate the formation of a crystal. And the crystal didn't want to be a crystal—

JD: No.

MS: It is the result of the process of natural symmetries and forkings—

JD: And compression, yes. One of the things I wanted in this novel was for all that to show because it has a plot, and I hadn't done conventional plots before. The plot is like the plot of a thriller, so it's a demanding kind of plot in plot terms. But when you do that, you cannot have any missteps, you cannot have any waste, even things that you might have buried in another kind of novel. I can think of a lot of stuff, for example, in *Democracy*, which didn't have to be there, necessarily. I could have done without it. Any novel is going to have stuff that you could do without, but if you force yourself to play it out, it's going to be more interesting. And that's really what I was trying to do with this.

By playing it out I mean, if you think of starting a novel as laying out cards on a table, then you have to play each of those cards: they might not be the best cards, they might not take you automatically. But if you force yourself to play them, you have engaged in a kind of cognitive activity which is going to take you a little further than you forced yourself to focus on to think about what is going on here. It's just a way of disciplining yourself, which is the only way of doing it that interests me.

MS: As I watched the narrator following Elena, I sensed that what goes on step by step, outside of the obligations that a thriller forces on a writer, was that at each moment the narrator is discovering something that might have happened to her happening to Elena.

JD: That's interesting.

MS: Elena is married to a wealthy man, and at one point Elena even thinks of herself, when she discovers she has cancer, as giving up her life—as did the heroine of the Greek tragedy *Alcestis*, as she mentioned—for him. They both have daughters at the same school, and interestingly enough, although this narrator is a reporter, it's Elena who is speaking to them on career day about reporting. Elena is someone who eventually does, in a sense, give up her life for a set of unwieldy plans that her father has constructed—another possibility for this narrator. What are the ways in which a woman can be destroyed? And this, it seems to me, accounts for the gaze of the narrator on this heroine.

JD: I think there probably is, which I hadn't realized, a kind of twinship between them.

MS: They are virtually doubles.

JD: Yes. Their children went to school together. Yes, they go to the same parties.

MS: Yes, and they've switched careers in certain ways, along certain lines together. It's almost as if this were in the very most implicit way a cautionary tale for this narrator. What might have happened had I done *x*.

JD: Don't you think all novels are cautionary tales for the writer?

MS: I think that's one of the things that keeps them on track.

JD: They are things you fear. They are almost like talismans you put out there. Basically, if you tell a story, you will diffuse it.

MS: Yes. There's a poem by John Ashbery called "Saying It to Keep It from Happening."

JD: That's it. Yes. During the course of the summer, I was interviewed a couple of times in New York about this book for magazines, and a lot of the people who interviewed me said they could not seem to understand how the main characters in all my books always play out some sort of dramatic, unhappy situation or get divorces while I, on the other hand, have been married for thirty-two years. How could this be? I always say, you're not writing about yourself necessarily. But also there is this thing: it is a cautionary tale. You do tell the story so that it won't be.

MS: Sometimes you're reading something, and you see a word you don't know, and you ask, "Why don't I know it?" And it's because it's some word that you needed to know. And I found this word—no one can tell me that difficult criticism is useless, because it gave me this word—*apotropaic*.

JD: What does it mean?

MS: A spell to ward off a spell.

JD: That's a perfect word.

MS: Yes, it's a perfect word for what a novelist does. In a sense, a novel is a spell to ward off the spell of the culture in which it registers its protest. You see exactly that this is an act of counteracting magic.

JD: Which is I guess why people do write novels. It is a form of practicing magic.

MS: Yes, it seems to me that these books are written each time with the writer intuiting or believing in the end of a way of life that has been important to her. This novel recounts that ending in a way that saves it for the next generation.

I thought I would ask you, on the wake of that oddness, to read us the opening section of *The Last Thing He Wanted*.

JD: Alright, I will. Chapter one.

"Some real things have happened lately. For a while we felt rich and then we didn't. For a while we thought time was money, find the time and the money comes with it. Make money for example by flying the Concorde. Moving fast. Get the big suite, the multi-line telephones, get room service on one, get the valet on two, premium service, out by nine back by one. Download all data. Uplink Prague, get some conference calls going. Sell Allied Signal, buy Cypress Minerals, work the management plays. Plug into this news cycle, get the wires raw, nod out on the noise. *Get me audio*, someone was always saying in the nod where we were. *Agence Presse is moving this story.* Somewhere in the nod we were dropping cargo. Somewhere in the nod we were losing infrastructure, losing redundant systems, losing specific gravity. Weightlessness seemed at the time a safer mode. Weightlessness seemed at the time the mode in which we could beat both the clock and affect itself, but I see now that it was not. I see now the clock was ticking. I see now that we were experiencing not weightlessness but what is interestingly described on page 1513 of the *Merck Manual* (Fifteenth Edition) as a sustained reactive depression, a bereavement reaction to the leaving of familiar environments. I see now that the environment we were leaving was that of feeling rich. I see now that there will be no Resolution Trust to do the workout on this particular default, but I did not see it then.

Not that I shouldn't have.

There were hints all along, clues we should have registered, processed, sifted for their application to the general condition. Try the day we noticed that the banks had called in the paper on all the malls, try the day we noticed that somebody had called in the paper on all the banks. Try the day we noticed that when we pressed 800 to do some business in Los Angeles or New York we were no longer talking to Los Angeles or New York but to Orlando or Tucson or Greensboro, North Carolina. Try the day we noticed (this will touch a nerve with frequent fliers) the new necessity for changes of equipment at Denver, Raleigh-Durham, St. Louis. Try, as long as we were changing equipment in St. Louis, the unfinished but already bankrupt Gateway Airport Tower there, its boutiques boarded up, its oyster bar shuttered, no more terrycloth robes in the empty cabanas and no more amenity kits in the not quite terrazzo bathrooms: this should have alerted us, should have been processed, but we were moving fast. We were traveling light. We were younger. So was she."

MS: I am moved to mention, hearing you read that, at the beginning it sounds a bit like the formula of the witches in *Macbeth*.

JD: It does, doesn't it? It has that kind of rhythm, doesn't it? The beginning of this was something I felt very strongly had to be there. At different points after I had finished it, when it was going through the editorial process, people would bring up maybe dropping the beginning. I had myself thought repeatedly of dropping that chapter and just starting with the action. I was working on a computer: I would take it off, and by the end of the day, I would put it back on again. It just seemed to have to be there, and I was never too sure why. But it is that kind of incantation which kind of controls the thing.

MS: Talk about working spells.

JD: Yeah.

MS: The second thing it reminds me of is, that in the back of my mind, I sense the almost constant presence of work like T. S. Eliot's. The sense of this being the distillate of the dying culture, that the work needs to be pared until what you have stands for the horrible thing that's left. Does *The Waste Land* matter to you?

JD: Eliot and Hemingway were the two people that I read over and over and over again when I was really young, when I was twelve. I taught myself to type by typing out Hemingway stories. I wasn't trying to learn the rhythm of the sentences—although I was, I think, because I could have typed something else—but you could see how they worked if you typed them out again and again. I didn't teach myself touch typing, I just taught myself to type very fast with two fingers. Of course, it is impossible to read it that much without memorizing it. A lot of fragments of Eliot.

MS: "J. Alfred Prufrock" is in here.

JD: Prufrock, yes. There's one line from "Four Quartets" that I've followed my whole life. It's in my mind almost all the time: "at the still point of the turning world." That is a line that has the same kind of resonance for me as has the rich form of liturgy: "As it was in the beginning, is now or ever shall be, world without end. Amen." Eliot's rhythms are just so much a part of my own rhythms, obviously, because there they were overshadowing everything else around them at the time.

MS: I try and chronicle moments in history of these developments, so for me it seems that there is a natural line from James to Eliot and also from James to Hemingway. But to speak about Eliot for a moment, his influence is, of course, enormous. I think that when he mourns, "I can connect / Nothing with nothing," it's not an accident that that becomes an exhalation in Donald Barthelme: "I can connect nothing with nothing, watch me do it!" The gravity has been lost.

In *The Waste Land*, Eliot seems a spectator to a series of really devastating losses. In Joan Didion, the losses seem to be being reported from the center of the devastation spot. But he was still capable of finding a ladder.

JD: Yes. I don't know if that's a difference in the time. All of what was happening to the culture when he was writing was less well known. It was less part of the given. So it may be that he truly thought it was possible—think is too strong a verb, you don't think through these things—that he truly stood apart from what he was observing. In a world as small as the one we know we live in now, none of us can any longer think that we stand apart.

MS: Because I do think that those invocations at the beginning of the books and some of their running lines are part of the Eliot tradition. There is a point at which things, and the desire to attempt to maintain them, become almost like jingles or lines of faith. Some people read these things as the implicit of movie montage, of ghostly voices re-intoning things from the past of the novel, but I tend to see it more as—

JD: A kind of prayer.

MS: Yeah.

JD: I think the first novel when I started doing this was *A Book of Common Prayer*. I called it that after I saw what it was. It didn't have a title when I was working on it. When I looked at it after, I saw that it was full of the liturgical phrasing. Not too many people made that connection, I have to say. People really did not know why that book was called *A Book of Common Prayer*. And yet there it was: all the phrasing was liturgical.

MS: You share with me the sense that people no longer know how to read novels. Well, to some extent, I hope to provide a reminder sometimes here with this show. But what does that do to the desire to write them?

JD: You still keep doing it because you feel more and more marginalized. At the time I was growing up, or the time I was in school, among people I knew, novels were at the very center of our lives—living things. They still are in my life and your life, but this is not as widely shared. At the age when most people I knew wanted to write, they now want to write screenplays. I have no idea why, because it's not like writing. It's like doing something else.

MS: Oh Joan, I wish that I thought, too, that the same people who used to want to write novels are the people who are now writing screenplays, because in that case we would be getting better screenplays.

JD: Well, that's true. [*laughter*] But this inability to read novels. I don't know when that was lost. It's very recent. It seems to me that in the '60s people could still read novels, people could still pick up Saul Bellow and know what he was doing, not treat every novel as if it was a nonfiction account of what the author believed.

MS: The eeriest part of this tendency, or this sudden amnesia, is that it is not a new generation who does not know how a novel works. It is people that used to know.

JD: People who used to know, I know.

MS: Isn't it odd? As if some lake had evaporated inside them.

JD: I know. Do you think that it has to do—I mean, I just wonder if we ever fully evaluated the effect of television storytelling on the mind. Because television storytelling is very linear, and it's basically based on confrontation. If you ever sit in a room where television is being watched, without watching it, you will suddenly become aware that you've been hearing shouting. Everybody is always shouting at everybody else, which I always thought had a deleterious effect on manners, on people's ability to deal with each other at a civil level. But I think that linear kind of storytelling may also have atrophied. To what extent do we know? Watching things is an act that has a profound effect on brain activity, and it may change the way you perceive or think about things.

MS: I have a terrible fear that, in addition to the kinds of stories being told, and the sounds of the telling, that this constant registration of light—

JD: That's interesting.

MS: This registering of meaning in flickers. I hate to try and say something foolish about the relationship of that to one's ability to assemble deeper or inner meaning, but there is something that has happened.

JD: It is a different experience, yeah.

2001: *Political Fictions*

MS: As I was rereading the essays in *Political Fictions* and some of the earlier novels, I came to see that Joan Didion, both in her essays and in her novels, has been effectively examining the same problem, which is that when you create a narrative, you create an expectation of stories that take over, that the details are what's preferable, in a sense, to story. It's only by almost parsing the details out of the story that one can return to a sense of truth.

JD: Return to a sense of the actual thing that's going on, because we super-impose a story on what we see. When you think of a dream you had, you always remember a story that's much stronger than the dream itself. I think a lot of what we experience, we superimpose a story on.

MS: I found myself describing, yesterday, your most recent novel, *The Last Thing He Wanted*, as being the process not of losing a needle in a haystack or of looking for a needle in a haystack, but the miracle of finding a needle in a haystack.

By the time you really understand the book is working, you're aware that you have to handle that book with jeweler's calipers, that the pieces have become so small. And the more you read it, the narrower the micro-seconds of chronology have become, and the more you come to under-stand has been simultaneous in it.

It seems like the analysis is very similar to the way these essays are built, almost as if what happens is the research is gathered, placed side by side, and when you've seen enough things by enough reporters, you know those are the lies and that those are the things that need to be—

JD: To be opened up.

MS: Yes, exactly. What would you say the narrative of the most recent election is at its most basic?

JD: I would say it was about how the political process has been tending, at least over the past twelve years, toward disenfranchising America, toward disenfranchising the actual electorate. Every time I did one of these pieces, I would come to that conclusion. It would take great labor, once again, because it was always coming out from a different angle, to find the path, and then I would find it led to the same place.

MS: I've been thinking about, as I think is inevitable, the recent hijackings and wondering if the immediate rush to create these events as part of a holy war of sorts, a religious war, is part of the narrative you're talking about.

JD: Yeah, I think there are a lot of narratives that we have seen in play since that. We've heard a lot about, "We did it before and we can do it again," and Pearl Harbor, et cetera. Over the past several years, there has grown a popular romance about World War II and that generation.

I've actually heard kids say on television, "Now we have our chance." Well, you know, I don't know what exactly they're talking about. They have told themselves a story about a moment of glory that is going to come.

MS: In the final essay in *After Henry*, the story about the rape of the jogger in Central Park, you make a distinction between the narrative of "the problem of the city is crime" and the actual narrative, which is that the problems of New York City are based on a series of easements and—

JD: It's based on greed. Yeah.

MS: Manipulations that make a popular narrative, like a jogger raped at night, a suitable replacement.

JD: It's a fairy tale, yeah, that covers the actual.

MS: It seems to me that here, too, this desire immediately to move away from the political situation to the idea of a holy war—

JD: Or a crusade, on our part. That word was used, I think.

MS: I think we'll be hearing it more and more. Has it always been, do you think, or at least as long as you've been analyzing, the case that there is a space between the popular story and the actual?

JD: I think that it has been there. I think that, in some ways, the political class has gotten better at it. Polling has gotten much more refined in the past dozen years. You can really cut bits of gathered information a million different ways in a microsecond because of technology, which makes the whole thing move faster. It has a momentum of its own now.

I don't know that it is going to stop unless a whole lot of people stand up and say, "Stop!"

MS: I thought that the effort of the political class is to conceal the details in the popular story. But the effort of the novelist and the essayist is to return actualities to the reader so that, if not reprocessed, at least the insistence with which they've been soldered into resolution can be dismantled again.

I noticed that in the introduction to *Political Fictions*, there is a set of notes that you took on the process of going to the first primary—I believe it was Jesse Jackson's—and being at first told that you were in the wrong place and going through a succession of wrong and righter places appears in the novel, more or less verbatim.

JD: You're right, in *The Last Thing He Wanted*.

MS: I wondered about the relation between the notes that go for fiction and the notes that go for nonfiction.

JD: You see, when I wrote about the '88 campaign, I had a whole set of notes that I made when I was doing the research. I had sixty to eighty pages of single-spaced notes. I just typed as I went along. Of course, I used very little of it.

When I was doing *The Last Thing He Wanted*, it struck me that that particular moment was something humiliating in a way, that it would reveal something. To put Elena in that moment would reveal something about her.

MS: But do you have a sense that it's a different process?

JD: It's not a different process.

MS: That's what I think, that it's not a different process and that its goals are the same, too. Only it's very hard for a novelist to simultaneously construct a story and reveal its counter-story. Life does that for you in the essays. The novelist has to, in a sense, be writing two books.

JD: You are. I can't explain what is different about writing a novel, but that's probably as close as I could get. Nothing is quite as straightforward. There's a reason why I always read *The Good Soldier* before I start. There's a reason that it has an unreliable narrator. Well, we're all unreliable narrators, even those of us who are telling a straight story.

MS: It seems to have moved further in these last two books—not unreliable narrators, but unreliable narratives. The narrative itself—

JD: Is deceptive.

MS: It seems to me to be the most recent development, not only in the political scene, but in fiction as well, that it would be almost old-fashioned now to create a narrative structured around one liar when it seems as if the culture structures stories so that, will you, nill you, you are telling a lie unless you've set yourself the goal of not doing so, and even then.

JD: Even then, who can know? *The Last Thing He Wanted*, on one level, is about the unreliability of narrative. It actually has probably the strongest narrative I ever wrote—the most straight-lined.

MS: Eventually, once it's placed together. You once said in an interview that the last sentence of a story should, if it's working, make you want to read the story again. That worked three times for me in *The Last Thing He Wanted*.

   The last thing I wanted was to enter that world again, and yet I did it like someone walking through a revolving door over and over and over again.

JD: When I was in San Francisco, I walked over to Grace Cathedral, and there were people walking. There's a labyrinth there, you know? There were people walking it, and that was what that novel was. It was like walking the labyrinth.

MS: You once also said, in that very bright interview with Linda Kuehl, that writing a novel is a hostile act, and it seems to me that these essays are as well. Part of the hostility in creating a book that I had to go through, wanted to go through, three times in order to completely inhabit its intricacies is that I feel, as I read the essays—I who have, perhaps, a radio announcer's tendency to general statements—my sentences become demystified. There are so many words in quotes that I want to swear I'll never use again. I'll never be guilty of *that* solecism. The work seems to make the reader, who gives way to it, more and more self-conscious about what lying is. It seems to be designed to do that, to purify the person who's willing to surrender to the book's hostility.

JD: It's kind of a sermon. It's very didactic.

MS: In what way?

JD: It's an exhortation. It's, "Look at this! Take it apart! What are they really saying?" It's, "Read!" I don't mean "read"; everybody reads. A lot of people seem to have stopped reading critically.

MS: It starts from the very beginning. You say that friends and people who knew you would begin by saying, "Gee, Joan. I didn't know that you were a politics junkie." And even hearing that, repeatedly, caused you to realize they actually think the only people interested in politics—

JD: Are the professionals.

MS: Yes.

JD: No one else. That it is not legible to anyone outside and shouldn't be; that it is correctly understood only by its professionals.

MS: And then, given the metaphor, if you are a junkie, you're already addicted enough to want more of things as they are. The process seems like having to put on a set of ears so finely tuned that anything said reveals the hidden sequestering of political culture into a private sector where the people who participate are, in fact, surprised or even bothered by an interest from a common citizen.

JD: Their idea of a response from a citizen is an email that has been sent to them because some interest group has urged its members to send an email to their congressmen. To people in the political class, that is an acceptable contact with the electorate.

MS: And better, an email that's been prewritten, which they only have to address.

JD: Yeah.

MS: Now, if it has reached the point, as you suggest, that the reporters are part of the story they're telling, that they're acquiesced to it, and that they don't report that they've brought in a camel to pose with Bush in the Middle East—

JD: Well, the *LA Times* did report that.

MS: The whole process of misrepresentation now includes the press.

JD: They are present, and they know what the situation actually is, but they don't actually write it down very much of the time.

MS: Right.

JD: They don't write it down. There are a couple of reasons they don't. I suppose the harsher reason is that they would lose access, and if they lose access they can't cover the beat, right? That's one reason, but the other reason is that they come into reporting with an idea that to form any kind of opinion shows bias: it's not fair or impartial. When, in fact, all that is required to be impartial is to come into the situation with an open mind. There is nothing in the journalistic code that prevents you from actually noticing that somebody is saying the exact opposite of what he or she said yesterday and maybe making a comment on that. Or that somebody is doing an event that is meant for the camera. But there seems to be an aversion to rendering judgment.

MS: Given this, is there any way out, or is it all labyrinth?

JD: I always think there is some way out. I always think there is going to be some kind of wake-up call. If enough people notice, enough people say, "That's not what you said yesterday," or, "Why is that camel in the shot?" maybe we can get past this.

There ought to be a way of talking directly. Some people have talked directly to the electorate. I know someone who had run for office, been a senator, and had run for president, who told me once that when he went "off message," as they say, when he said what was really on his mind, that his handlers were desperately upset and, in fact, it seemed to confuse everyone around him. It's just not really done at the moment, but it certainly could be.

MS: In your most recent books, as opposed to the kind of anomy and passivity that reviewers used to write about in your characters, something else has taken its place. As I read an essay of yours, it's as if I become a character in a Joan Didion book, as if the information given me at first makes me feel helpless but then makes me feel angry. That's the beginning of the break in passivity.

It seems what's happened in the work is that the corrective to anomy is a more and more precise analytic mind. What it discovers, that mind, may be so disturbing that at first immobility might be a response, but the corrective to immobility, too, is further research. Has that helped you as a writer?

JD: Yeah, it has. You always doubt that you are going to be able to finish anything, but I have more trust that if I stay with it, it's going to go somewhere, which I didn't really used to have. It's a whole different process than the way I used to write.

A lot of it, I think I told you once, came when I started using a computer, because the DOS was so unforgiving. People were always telling me, when I was in high school, that if I would stop failing geometry, geometry would give me logic, right? Geometry never did give me logic because I could always find another way to solve the problem that wasn't the correct way, right? But there's no way you can solve DOS, except its way. Everything about it was logical, which actually affected the way I thought, in an odd way.

MS: I wondered, too, because if you compare, say, *The White Album* with *Political Fictions*, there's a steelier, finer mind at work. But the people being considered by that mind have also removed themselves from the kind of hysteria that was being looked at in *The White Album*.

This seems to me to be a change in time, but it also seems to be the result, almost, of something cultural as well. These people in *Political Fictions* don't seem as frightened as the people in *The White Album*, perhaps because of psychoactive drugs. I began to think, "Has this been a bleaching of hysteria, since the drugs take care of that with panic?"

JD: Well, I think that the people I'm looking at in *Political Fictions* are public people, so you're looking at their public faces to the world. They know how to do that. They know how to pull their faces together most of the time.

There is always, once in a while, somebody fascinating who doesn't know how to pull his face together. Most of the time, they do. The people I was looking at in *The White Album* were private people, by and large, or accidentally public people.

MS: But I think of all these handlers, for instance, and their snap judgments, and their knowing what they want, what's necessary, and not being confused by an appeal to pity or honesty. They know what being on point means, though something else may be more interesting, some more human statement. It seemed to me as if, "Oh my. These people go home to their pills."

JD: Maybe so. [*laughter*]

MS: I'm curious if you will say what you're working on now.

JD: I sort of have been messing around with something, but I'm not sure whether it'll work or not. It's a sort of extended reflection about California as an idea. I'm not sure where it's going. I would really like to finish it by the spring, but I'm not sure that I will, or finish it at all.

2003: *Where I Was From*

MS: Now, I haven't heard this said before, but as I was reading *Where I Was From*, I thought that it was a joining of two parts of your career. The first five books seem to be the books of despair and connectionlessness. And the next books seem to be very analytic, almost as if the mind has taken responsibility for and control of itself and wants to go deeply into a subject.

JD: That change certainly happened. There just came a moment when all I wanted to do was analyze. Before, I was unsure about what I wanted to do. I wanted to put together sentences, I wanted to express things, but it was a very unformed way of thinking. The change came—part of it was getting older—and this sounds silly, but I began using a computer. I was using an old-fashioned DOS computer—forget Windows. The logic of it was so novel and so overwhelmingly convincing to me that I became a little more logical, myself. I was forced to. This book was almost like opening a vein. And I don't mean it in a painful way, but I just wrote down anything I happened to be—I just let my mind go.

MS: Well, it seems to go between the bewildered style and the analytic style, the two offering correctives to one another as if somehow or other California, the subject of the book—which is part memoir, part essay, part literary criticism, part many things—is being spared finally by a certain kind of uncertainty. Not by exactly idealism or generosity, but an uncertainty as to whether the things being said about California are true merely of California or of America as a whole, or of maybe human nature.

JD: Maybe human nature, yes. The whole California story, as it was told to me, had to do with the difficulty of getting here. And once you got here you were redeemed. Nobody ever talked about what you were redeemed for. Survival, getting through the mountains before the snow fell, was the big, big value, and if you had managed that, then you were home free, as it were. As I started thinking about it, and as I passed beyond not thinking about it into some kind of adult life, survival as an answer in itself began to seem a more and more doubtful value. Survival by itself leaves you aware. California had always celebrated the act of survival, and, in some ways, I think we were left with no other, with no higher value.

MS: You quote Josiah Royce as one who seems simultaneously to see a huge mistake having been made and to see a Golden Age.

JD: He was so wishful. His history of California wasn't a history of California; it was really about the California idea. At the time he wrote that—I think it was published in 1886—nobody has made more damning indictments of the California character, and yet in seconds he would segue into an assurance that we had passed all of that behind us, put all of that behind us and become a community. Well, I don't think we're a community yet, in a lot of ways.

MS: By what standards would community be evaluated?

JD: A sense of responsibility toward others. A sense of connectedness. In this book, I was talking about the lust to incarcerate and to build prisons. Somehow by accident, through that, I got into what had been, since the mid-nineteenth century, an equally strong lust to institutionalize. Among the first real institutions in the state were insane asylums, to which people were committed basically for life, and the treatment was minimal. People were committed for quite casual reasons. I remember one woman in San Francisco was committed because her sister testified to the examining board that she had lost interest in crocheting.

MS: In that chapter, what we watch is the alternation among an attention focused on prisons, schools, and institutions for the insane. And you suggest that the building of prisons is not a change from the building of state universities or of insane asylums.

JD: I think it's a change from the building of state universities but not from insane asylums.

MS: Nevertheless, there has been a focus on building institutions in which to put people you don't know what to do with.

JD: And also there's been very low tolerance for minor annoyance. You know, the person who steals the bottle of Snapple now, if that's his third strike, he goes away, right? The person who loses interest in crocheting in the nineteenth century went away.

MS: You mention, I believe, your grandfather, who spoke about seeing danger, a rattlesnake, and the obligation to kill it as being the code of the West. And although you cite through the book a couple of examples—you do not kill a rattlesnake in a cemetery, and your mother doesn't kill a copperhead near a baby's crib—I think of these essays as killing rattlesnakes, a kind of service for the next person to come along, clearing the poisonous, the striking, the hidden.

JD: I like that idea. I would really be proud to do that.

MS: These essays have been interested in exposing the secret. The newest one I've seen notices that Mr. Bush using the phrase "wonderworking power" is signaling those people who know the hymn "There Is Power in the Blood (of the Lamb)," and there's a kind of secret communication going on, a code that, if not broken, remains inviolate. And it seems to me that these essays are attempts to expose the second agenda to people who would rather be too idealistic than believe that there is a second agenda.

JD: I think my whole impulse is to try to wake people, try to make them see things a little differently. That's putting a good face on it. Make them see it the way I do.

MS: The last time we spoke, we were talking about the title *The Last Thing He Wanted* and the ways in which that title rounds on itself. Here, *Where I Was From* has that problematic *was*.

JD: It does, yeah, and it came to me as the right title and the title I wanted. John, my husband, immediately said to me, "Well, don't you mean—it should be *Where I Am From*, or are you trying to say here that you aren't from California anymore?" I said, "No, I'm not trying to say that." We got into this sort of back and forth about it, and finally I was forced to think it through, and it occurred to me that the reason *Where I Was From* seemed right to me was it was not about the actual geographical place where I was from. It was about the complex of confusions and misunderstandings that I'd had about that place, about my place in it, and about its place in America. It was about a state of mind, or an enchantment, and that was where I was from.

MS: So that place, it's not just that it doesn't exist anymore, it may never have existed?

JD: May never have existed, yes. And yet, for me, as surely as anything, it did exist.

MS: Why was it so powerful in the formation of solace? When people start to talk about the American dream, I think, well, a dream is something you wake up from. But how did it have such a purchase?

JD: I don't know how it did. It was the central story of my childhood. It was the story that, as a family, was seen to give us value. It was everything we were. The cover of the book, which shows the Southern Pacific snow breaker, the big circular plow coming through Emigrant Gap in the Donner Pass. When I first saw the photograph, it almost brought me to tears because it carried an idea of the Donner party and then the engine of progress moving through. The image of the train, the locomotive, is very similar to Frank Norris's *The Octopus*. This story was, for me, a kind of poetry, where you didn't pin it, you didn't analyze it, you just heard the music.

MS: I want to go back to the sense of there being two parts of the career, because I want to talk to you about your own sense of the reception of this work. As you know, I'm an enormous admirer of *The Last Thing He Wanted*. It was almost as if when you were Mad Cassandra, critics were very happy to welcome you into the ranks, I think, because they liked a woman to be mad, you know? It was the old idea that a woman shouldn't say certain things, and so the confidences of bewilderment finally were acceptable. They were almost like giving in.

I never saw a book as powerful as *The Last Thing He Wanted* turned against by so many men. It was almost as if they were saying, "Where is that woman who used to beguile us with her uncertainty, her despair, her alienatedness?" And I think this book, *Where I Was From*, has gotten some of the old kind of reviews because that old figure who doesn't know, who hasn't reached a final conclusion, reemerges in it, and people feel comfortable with her.

JD: Nobody likes a know-it-all. I haven't attempted to analyze it, but I have been surprised at the generally positive reception this book got. The reason it surprised me was I thought it was an extremely difficult book to actually put together, to see as a whole. I don't mean it was difficult for me to put it together, but it's like being handed somebody's dream or somebody's unprocessed thought. It was more like a poem than it was a book, as I thought of it. Or it was a piece of music. Every time somebody handed me jacket copy, all I could think was, "Oh, no!" I couldn't see any way to describe this book.

MS: Well, I remember that when we spoke of it when it was being written, you weren't sure that it would be finished.

JD: That's right.

MS: And I see it as a book that begins again and again. It starts as a sort of memoir but then becomes an essay, and then it traces derivations and roots in history and literature. There is almost a sense that whatever angle the subject is approached from, it won't yield.

JD:	It won't yield the answer. I think as I got close to the end of it, I had no intention of going back to the personal. But it seemed at that time the right thing to do, and I'm not sure even what that meant. It was maybe like Norris, in the final pages of *The Octopus*, when he starts to represent the octopus as nature itself, not the Southern Pacific Railroad. It's that kind of late discovery, where suddenly what I'd been talking about all along was trying to come to terms with life and death and lack of faith.

MS:	Over the years of reading your work, I'd often wondered how it was that you had available to you this family letter or diary, that it hadn't been lost or misplaced. Not only hadn't it been lost or misplaced, but you tell us where it was in the house in Pacific Palisades, where it is in the apartment in New York. And suddenly I realized something. The inheritance from the mother is no longer a keepsake or a souvenir, or even something that says, "Look, we've survived." Suddenly the inheritance is being looked at as evidence, and it's not, it seems to me, just the computer that gives that sense of order and logic to the work. It's somehow the discovery that what you've inherited is no longer sentimental. It is the—what do they call it in the court when they call in something to be put on display relevant to the case?

JD:	It's tagged as exhibit.

MS:	Exhibit, yes. Suddenly these things have become exhibits, and the female presence of the person who maintains the continuity, that idea, has become the person who keeps the records. She may not know what the records are for, but she has the instinct to maintain them. In the very final sections of the book I found this incredible sense of a woman handing something on without knowing the meaning. The daughter experiencing this as an old kind of handing on, what you give that made its way through the snow, through the Donner Pass, through the trip west. And I thought I'd ask you to read the final section of the book because I find it extremely complicated, complex, and moving.

JD:	"When my father died I kept moving. When my mother died I could not. The last time I saw her was eight weeks before she died. She had been in the hospital, my brother and I had gotten her home, we had arranged for oxygen and shifts of nurses, we had filled the prescriptions for morphine and Ativan. On the morning Quintana and I," Quintana is my daughter, "were to leave for New York, my mother insisted that we bring her a painted metal box that sat on a small table in her bedroom, a box in which she kept papers she thought might have importance, for example a copy of the deed to a gold mine in El Dorado County that she and her sister had inherited from their father and no longer owned. My brother said that she did not need the box, that he had already extracted any still operable papers and put them in safekeeping. She was insistent. She wanted the metal box. Quintana brought the box and set it on the bed. From it my mother took two pieces of silver flatware, a small ladle and a small serving spoon, each wrapped in smooth scraps of used tissue paper. She gave the serving spoon to Quintana and the ladle to me. I protested: she had already given me all her silver, I had ladles, she had given me ladles. 'Not this one,' she said. She pointed out the curve of the handle. It seemed that she had what she called 'a special feeling' for the way the handle curved on this particular ladle. It seemed that she found this ladle so satisfying to touch that she had set it aside, kept it. I said that since it gave her pleasure she should continue to keep it. '*Take* it,' she said, her voice urgent. 'I don't want it lost.' I was still pretending that she would get through the Sierra before the snows fell. She was not."

MS: You say of her that she wanted to be stern, a word that used to be synonymous with our word now, *parenting*.

JD: Yes.

MS: And the images that we get of her when your father was in the war, staying at a hotel near the base, and washing the shared tub out with Pine—

JD: Pine disinfectant, yes.

MS: —every night before she bathed you. This figure who is taking a ladle from a metal box: it is both part of her and something beyond that, a kind of stern tenderness that seems extremely, almost touchingly ambiguous. You know, who can explain the curve of a handle?

JD: Yes, and yet the curves of handles were the language we had talked all of our lives. We would talk about things like that and they meant something else. With my father we would talk about, you know, zoning, and it meant something else. It meant things we liked, like the rivers, but essentially you talked in these codes.

MS: Codes. Tell me a little bit more.

JD: Codes? Well, we just didn't talk to each other very directly. I think this is one of the things that is odd to me in this book, which is very directly written. Some reviewers have complained that it didn't reveal very much of myself, but I don't know how much more there is to reveal. This seemed pretty direct, and I'm not usually very direct. The grammar is much more direct. The sentence structure is much more direct. It's much simpler. It's not complicated. It's a much more open book than I've ever really allowed myself to write.

MS: And yet the codes are embedded in it, not quite deciphered? Or for someone else to decipher?

JD: No, the codes were between my mother and father and me. I don't use the codes here. I actually say things pretty forthrightly.

MS: Do you have the feeling of having betrayed them?

JD: No, I don't. I don't have a feeling of having betrayed them. At the same time, I probably would not have written the book before my mother died. Not because we ever would have had a disagreement about it, but it would have given a public aspect to a life that wasn't public.

2006: *The Year of Magical Thinking*

MS: A terribly sad event was the provocation of this book, and your life has been dealing with other sad events about which I don't know how to speak, and we'll speak about the book itself.

Now, you say, as a writer, that knowing what people would do is like breathing to you. And also you've gone to a file called "The Effect of the Change" that you started to write, I guess only days after John Gregory Dunne had died.

JD: Right, it was called "Notes on Change." Well, I wasn't thinking about keeping a file, I was just making a note. It's like a reflex for a writer to write things down because that's how you understand them. This was something that happened that I didn't understand at all.

MS: It becomes the refrain in this book. You look at it again in May, and then again in October when you start to write the book, and the book, in a sense, becomes organized around the refrain.

JD: Right. And the refrain was, "Life changes fast. Life changes in the instant. You sit down to dinner and life as you know it ends. The question of self-pity." The whole book became an exploration of those disjointed words. I didn't set out to write a book. In October, I had tentatively gone back to work. The chronology was: John died on December 30, 2003. And Quintana, our daughter, was in the hospital. She was in the hospital off and on until mid-July. Once she was out, I did a piece that I had promised to do for *The New York Review* on the campaign.

And then I sat down to just collect my notes from this kind of disastrous series of events that was pretty much filling my mind. It was certainly front and center. And when I started doing the notes, I realized, after about three days, that I was thinking about how to organize them, which wasn't my intention. My intention had been to just type the notes for whatever reason. But if you're thinking how to organize them, you're thinking about writing a book. It seemed to me that the only possible way to organize them was to keep repeating the same scenes. It was a way of replicating the exact experience. When something like this happens, you just keep obsessing on it. You see the same scene running over and over and over again. Sometimes it has new details, sometimes it has fewer details. So that was the general idea. Everything repeated itself.

MS: Now, you talk about the famous sentence in your first article from *Life* magazine that announced that you were in Hawaii in lieu of filing for divorce—a kind of sentence that shook everyone who read it and, I think, shakes them still. You knew then that you would be living a life in public as a writer, and that has been part of your subject.

JD: Right.

MS: And I wondered whether that has had a cost.

JD: I think any life led in public costs you something. On the other hand, it's certainly part of being a writer because you're living a life in public whether or not you're ever seen in public. Your innermost thoughts are in public. They're out there. So that's what makes writing a kind of breathtakingly daring act for someone who is essentially shy, which I was as a child.

MS: It seems astonishing to me, but did you feel then that to write this book, if you wrote at all, would be obligatory?

JD: It was obligatory. It was obligatory for a whole series of reasons. One was that it was the only way I was going to understand it and come to terms with what had happened. Because that's just the way I work. That's the way my mind works. I don't actually register anything I think about until I've written it down. The other thing was it was obligatory since this was the thing that was on my mind. What was I going to do? It would be dishonest to sit down and write something else.

At the time that John died, I had a contract to do a book about the Kobe Bryant case. Well, I wasn't going to go back to the Kobe Bryant case.

That wasn't on my mind at all. At that point in my life, that would have been a very destructively dishonest thing to do. It would have been just shutting out the reality of what had happened. There is a sense in which, for any kind of writer, like any kind of actor, it's about putting it out there on the line for the audience. It's a performance. So you have to do that.

MS: The show must go on?

JD: It's like an aerialist. If you don't do it, you're going to get scared and never do it again.

MS: Wow. I'm sure that you were using, to write this book, every bit of craft at your disposal, because it is what, like an aerialist, you had to rely on. But it struck me while reading it that it was bringing aspects of your writing together, perhaps for the first time. There's the Joan Didion, who, in *The Last Thing He Wanted*, is reconstructing an event moment by moment in order to solve, to some extent, a criminal story, to figure out what happened during a vacant three minutes of time. And there's the vortex kind of time that appeared in *Play It as It Lays* and other books, time that ripples outward from a central moment so that you can barely see what you're trying to think about because of the string of associations. And seeing that specificity played against that rippling effect seemed truly astonishing to me.

JD: I didn't even think I was writing this book. My intention was just to make it artless. I didn't want style to get in the way of the directness of it. So I thought I wasn't writing it. And then I realized an excerpt of it was going to be published in a magazine. And the magazine, in the normal course of things, copyedited it. When I saw the copy edit, I realized that I had to naturally take the copyediting out and restore it to the way I'd written it. But it was the first time I realized that, in fact, I had written the book. There was quite a lot of craft in it, although I hadn't planned it. I guess you can devote craft just as arduously to making something look artless as you can to making it look crafted.

MS: You mention at the beginning of the book that you wanted none of the impenetrability that had come to characterize your later work. What do you mean by impenetrability though?

JD: If something is about to be revealed, then generally my instinct is to move away from it and not quite reveal it. This was a case in which I was going to reveal something over and over and over again until you couldn't look away from it. It was just a whole different experience. The writing of it was a different experience.

MS: And in avoiding impenetrability, did you feel yourself developing new techniques?

JD: Well, no, because I thought of this as a kind of one-time technique. For example, there are no transitions. It's like a stream of consciousness. Any thought that came to mind I put down. Now, quite often, if the thought was wrong or obtrusive, I would take it out that night when I went over the pages, so it wasn't totally unedited. It wasn't totally straight as it came out of my mind, but it certainly was to a greater degree than most things I write.

MS: There's so much in this book, so much more that stands revealed. There's a place where you say that those people who used to ask John Gregory Dunne and you if you two were competitive, there's something they don't know about marriage. In the book, so much stands for so much more. It's such an extraordinary compacting of a forty-year marriage. It stands not only in the literature of grief but in the literature of marriage. And I wondered, that always seemed to me a very private thing.

JD: I hadn't intended to write about the marriage at all. I don't mean that I had decided not to. I just mean that I thought I was going to write something about grief. I was going through grief as I was writing it, and one of the things you have to do in the course of mourning is confront all of those memories that keep coming at you. For the first six months after John died, I had been unable to go through that, to face those things, because

I couldn't afford to, because Quintana needed me. All my adrenaline was going toward keeping totally away from any memory that might upset me. So at the point when I began writing a book, I realized that those things were coming back to mind, so I had to write them down.

MS: Now, magical thinking. The first time I became aware of what you felt about it was in an article about South America. You commented about magical realism, that you felt the political devastations in that continent had been so enormous that magical realism was a childlike response to a reality that could not be confronted. And I think you've never liked magical thinking.

JD: Well, I certainly didn't dream that I would ever engage in it, but I certainly did.

MS: What is it?

JD: As anthropologists use it, it's the belief that you can control events through certain rituals or invocations or actions which are entirely superstitious in nature. For example, if you make a sacrifice, crops will come in. In my case, I realized I was engaging in it when I couldn't give away some of John's clothes because I thought he was going to need them. If I gave them away, he wouldn't come back. Then I realized that I was thinking he would come back. I was thinking I could control events which I couldn't. No one can. That was the big lesson.

MS: Is writing an attempt to control events somehow?

JD: Of course writing is an attempt to control events. You can write yourself a pretty controlled little world.

MS: Was it possible then to keep on writing?

JD: Well, I had to. I didn't know any other way to organize the world. It's probably a folly to think you can organize the world, too. It's like imagining that you have control over it. To the extent that I could come to terms with it at all, it was going to be through writing it down.

MS: It has always seemed to me true that the women who I think of immediately when I think of your work have to learn somehow *not* to organize their lives. That lesson that Maria learns—that nothing applies—seems to be a defense against organization.

JD: But they have to learn it over and over again. And I had never really learned it.

MS: Knew it but not learned it?

JD: Right.

MS: It does seem that this book has all kinds of abilities to order within it. Was that because it had become a literary project? And literary projects, if not life, *can* be organized?

JD: I think that's right. If I could organize the book, I could perilously organize my life, right? Or I could impose that order; I could borrow that order for my life. It was very important to me, for example, the ending of the book. I couldn't get that right because the traditional ending for this kind of book is some kind of resolution, right? But I hadn't come to any kind of resolution. The situation, as far as I was concerned, was not resolved. The first time I finished it, there was this kind of false resolution in the last twenty pages. They were a mess. Then I set it aside for a couple of weeks after I had more or less finished it. I'd finished it with this false ending on the 30th or 31st of December that year, which had been my intention—to do it all within the span of the year. I put it aside for a few weeks and then rewrote it. And I found a way not to resolve it but to somehow live with the lack of resolution, which was useful to me.

MS: This is Joan Didion reading from the concluding chapter of *The Year of Magical Thinking*:

JD: "I realize as I write this that I do not want to finish this account.

Nor did I want to finish the year.

The craziness is receding but no clarity is taking its place.

I look for resolution and find none.

I did not want to finish the year because I know that as the days pass, as January becomes February and February becomes summer, certain things will happen. My image of John at the instant of his death will become less immediate, less raw. It will become something that happened in another year. My sense of John himself, John alive, will become more remote, even 'mudgy,' softened, transmuted into whatever best serves my life without him. In fact this is already beginning to happen. All year I have been keeping time by last year's calendar: what were we doing on this day last year, where did we have dinner, is it the day a year ago we flew to Honolulu after Quintana's wedding, is it the day a year ago we flew back from Paris, *is it the day*. I realized today for the first time that my memory of this day a year ago is a memory that does not involve John. This day a year ago was December 31, 2003. John did not see this day a year ago. John was dead.

I was crossing Lexington Avenue when this occurred to me.

I know why we try to keep the dead alive: we try to keep them alive in order to keep them with us.

I also know that if we are to live ourselves there comes a point at which we must relinquish the dead, let them go, keep them dead.

Let them become the photograph on the table.

Let them become the name on the trust accounts.

Let go of them in the water.

Knowing this does not make it any easier to let go of him in the water.

In fact the apprehension that our life together will decreasingly be the center of my every day seemed today on Lexington Avenue so distinct a betrayal that I lost all sense of oncoming traffic.

I think about leaving the lei at St. John the Divine.

A souvenir of the Christmas in Honolulu when we filled the screen with blue.

During the years when people still left Honolulu on the Matson Lines the custom at the moment of departure was to throw leis on the water, a promise the traveler would return. The leis would get caught in the wake and go bruised and brown, the way the gardenias in the pool filter at the house in Brentwood Park had gone bruised and brown.

The other morning when I woke I tried to remember the arrangement of the rooms in the house in Brentwood Park. I imagined myself walking through the rooms, first on the ground floor and then on the second. Later in the day I realized that I had forgotten one.

The lei I left at St. John the Divine would have gone brown by now.

Leis go brown, tectonic plates shift, deep currents move, islands vanish, rooms get forgotten.

I flew into Indonesia and Malaysia and Singapore with John, in 1979 and 1980.

Some of the islands that were there then would now be gone, just shallows.

I think about swimming with him into the cave at Portuguese Bend, about the swell of clear water, the way it changed, the swiftness and power it gained as it narrowed through the rocks at the base of the point. The tide had to be just right. We had to be in the water at the very moment the tide was right. We could only have done this a half dozen times at most during the two years we lived there but it is what I remember. Each time we did it I was afraid of missing the swell, hanging back, timing it wrong. John never was. You had to feel the swell change. You had to go with the change. He told me that. No eye is on the sparrow but he did tell me that."

MS: It's extraordinarily beautiful. It really is.

JD: Thank you.

MS: You say that his last present to you was saying, after he'd reread a section of *A Book of Common Prayer*, that you couldn't tell him anymore that you weren't a good writer.

JD: Yeah. He'd read it during a snowstorm. We were stuck in it, having dinner at home, and we were sitting by the fire. And he read this passage out loud. It was three weeks before he died.

MS: I wondered, given that you're a very good writer, what does it take, after you've lost the person who can tell you that you are, for you to know that?

JD: The first thing I wrote after John died was a piece for *The New York Review* on the campaign, and I found it very hard, even though I have an editor I trust implicitly at *The New York Review*, Robert Silvers. I knew he would not let me fall off the branch, right? But I still felt it was very hard to do without John. The only other thing I've done since John died is this book. And I had a strong feeling that it would be okay, that he would think it was okay.

MS: Has this told you, this experience with *The Year of Magical Thinking*, that you can write another book?

JD: Yes, it probably has told me I can write another book, because I did it this time.

MS: Do you want to?

JD: I suppose I will. I don't know what it will be, but yes.

MS: Because those of us who have been given instruction in endurance from you by reading you—like me—need it.

JD: Well, good.

2011: Bookworm Book Club—*Play It as It Lays*

MS: Hello and welcome to the first ever conversation for the Bookworm Book Club. As you all know, you've voted—I'm telling Joan Didion, though—to read *Play It as It Lays* for our first book. Joan has agreed to look back at this book and answer some of the questions you turned in to me and some of my own, as well. If I am nervous, please pardon me: I've never done this before.

This is, in a way, a breakthrough book. It defines what will be the Joan Didion novel: written in pieces, atomized, becoming fugal, mosaic. When you look back at it, what did it feel like to evolve your own kind of novel and come out with it?

JD: My first novel was very traditional.

MS: It's a conventional novel.

JD: It's a conventional novel, and I had not intended for it to be. I just didn't know how to do what I had in mind. What I had in mind was shattering time. The time sequence was to be shattered, but I simply had no knowledge of how to make that work, so the manuscript was a mess. I had a very small advance on it. The publisher hired an editor, and the editor suggested basically making it conventional. That isn't what she said, but—

MS: This was *Run River*?

JD: This was *Run River*. Then I was determined with the second novel, which was *Play It as It Lays*, to have it my way. It took me a long time, actually, to find that tone. Then suddenly I found it. It was irresistible to write once I found the tone.

MS: That opening sentence has become one of the famous opening sentences in American literature. What did it mean to you?

JD: As a child, I had done a little theater in Sacramento. I grew up in Sacramento. They had a little theater group, and I had played the children in many plays, including Babette in *Watch on the Rhine*. One of the characters in *Watch on the Rhine*, in Babette's hearing says, "The Renaissance man is a man who wants to know what makes Iago evil." That's where it came from.

MS: Amazing. Oh my God. It's like the Joseph Conrad quote at the beginning of *Democracy*. Has anyone ever—

JD: No, there'd be no reason.

MS: Thank you so much. That's amazing. From *Watch on the Rhine*?

JD: *Watch on the Rhine*.

MS: That's Lillian Hellman.

JD: Yes.

MS: Joan, thank you so. I feel like running out of the studio and announcing it to scholars around the country.

JD: Once I had, "The Renaissance man is a man who wants to know what makes Iago evil." Then Mrs. Burstein in the artichoke garden just flowed right in.

MS: The snake?

JD: The snake, yeah.

MS: The snake has always made direct sense to me. The snake isn't responsible for its poison and wouldn't ask about it either. It's perfectly natural. But I'd always wondered where you got "what makes Iago evil." Because, "The other people ask. I never ask," has become like a refrain in your work. "This is what other people do. I don't think that way." It is to let us know that there's a very strong sense of difference between Joan Didion and what other people think. Had that been a childhood impulse?

JD: That had been a childhood impulse, yes. I was determined to be different. Ask my mother.

MS: I wish I could. That must have been an extraordinary thing because I think about all the things you tell us about your childhood and also about Quintana's childhood, which leads to that sense in the book that the child there is an invisible Quintana. Is that the case, or would you not say so?

JD: The child in *Play It as It Lays*?

MS: The offstage child, Kate.

JD: Yes, she was, I think. Yes. I'm trying to think of the time frame. Quintana was just a baby when I was doing *Play It as It Lays*. By the time I finished it, she was clearly talking and all of that, but she was a baby when I was doing that.

MS: She called it "mommy's snake book."

JD: She called it "mommy's snake book" because it had a snake on the cover.

MS: Were you aware of what an evil book it was? Do you think of it as an evil book?

JD: I thought of it as an evil book. In fact, it made me terribly unhappy during the period I was writing it. I didn't realize I was being made unhappy by what I was writing, but suddenly I realized that life had lifted and it was because I had finished the book.

MS: On the website, one of our book club readers confides that she was a woman married to a director in Hollywood during the '70s and says that, because of the shock of being treated the way she was treated, she felt grateful to the book for catching that moment.

First of all, when I read *Play It as It Lays*, I thought, "Joan Didion never expected to be a Hollywood writer." In part, there must be a certain shock because, even though New York may be just as bad in its own ways, certainly the fantasies we have about being a writer, a novelist, being respected in that way were far different from the ways you get treated on a movie. Did that give rise to the novel? Had you been writing for Hollywood yet?

JD: No, but I knew people who worked in the business. I can remember very clearly having a sense about Maria. I was in Las Vegas for reasons that escape me now, and I heard an actress, someone I didn't even know, but she was a beginning actress. She was not terribly established. She was being paged in a casino. Watching her cross the casino to answer the page, she was wearing, I remember, a halter dress, a white silk halter dress. You had a real sense of potential degradation.

MS: Everyone surely already knew that Hollywood was Babylon. It had been called this, it was no news. Did it strike you? Because when this book came out, it was as if people were responding to a clarion call. "Oh, Hollywood is this den of iniquity."

JD: Right, "Hollywood is a bad place."

MS: It wasn't anything that you had discovered, but somehow the book reawakened this idea.

JD: I think people were responding to those short sentences.

MS: Yeah, and the sense that Hollywood was the viper at the heart of the American bosom. It was thought in many senses to be—and many of the readers here are asking questions that I wouldn't really dare ask—based on figures in Hollywood, whereas it seems to me to be variations—

JD: Variations on figures in Hollywood, exactly. It was not based on anyone specific.

MS: Frighteningly, the story is always the same: the head of the studio's daughter, the director's unsuccessful starlet wife, the loss of identity.
     You've spoken of Maria as being strong and enjoyable to write. Now, as a reader, I'm destroyed by the end of the book, by her and her observations. Why strong?

JD: I don't know. She just seemed to me to be a strong character.

MS: As in emotional strength?

JD: Emotional strength, survival, the ability to survive.

MS: She's still waiting at the end of the book. You've said about books that when you finish them you should want to begin them immediately again—and there she is in the mental hospital, dreading, fending off, and sometimes passively receiving visitors. When does she get out, Joan?

JD: I don't know. I haven't taken her out yet.

MS: I've always wondered. Did you want her back? Because we see a lot of these people now, and they are survivors of something truly awful. I would say it is that moment when movies started to look like art and actresses and directors no longer knew what to make of themselves or how. That's destructive in a way. You've said that one of the desperations of filmmaking is people thinking too much that they're artists.

JD: That they're artists, yes. Yes, indeed.

MS: Given that that doesn't happen very much now, which is worse, terrible movies or movies that think they're art?

JD: Movies that think they're art.

MS: That's worse?

JD: We can all live through a terrible movie.

MS: That's very interesting to me. One question from our readers begins with flattery. Since I think that writers deserve flattery myself, and I'm unwilling to stop giving it, here it is: "I believe Ms. Didion belongs among the great pantheon of American dream writers. There are a few women on that list (e.g., Willa Cather and Toni Morrison). The American dream has been variously defined since James Truslow Adams wrote about it in *Epic of America*, 1931. When she wrote *Play It as It Lays*, was Ms. Didion conscious of writing an American dream novel? Does she believe *Play It as It Lays* has become more significant over time, and why? What does it tell us about our identity and authenticity as individuals or as a nation?" That's a big amount to cover.

JD: That's a big question.

MS: Let's talk about the American dream.

JD: I hadn't thought of it as an American dream novel. That's an interesting take on it.

MS: I'm interested in the mention of Willa Cather. That's wonderful.

JD: Wonderful.

MS: Do you identify with Willa Cather as a writer?

JD: No, I haven't.

MS: Do you like her?

JD: Yes.

MS: I do, very much. It seems like it's the Midwestern thing that you talk about when you say that the Okie voice traveled and was the voice of the Central Valley: pioneer spirit and also indomitableness, saying that you won't give up, you won't stop. You seem to have made that decision over and over and over again, even now, being willing after so many deaths to go on tour, to answer questions about an old novel. Can you speak about that pioneer spirit?

JD: I sometimes feel in myself that I don't have it as strongly as I used to. I think all of us, as we get older, become more doubtful about aspects of our personality that we once thought were fixed. What we learn as we get older is that nothing is fixed. Nothing is forever.

MS: I'm fascinated because, if anything, I think of the characters in your early essays as presenting vulnerability and weakness as a badge and that, if anything, I think of you in later books, especially *After Henry* and *Political Fictions*, as being very strong and steel-trap minded.

JD: No, not at all.

MS: Really?

JD: No. The closest I got to a change to steel-trap mind was when I started using a computer. I used a DOS operating system. DOS was so logical that it made me fantasize that I had a steel-trap mind.

MS: It's interesting. I once said to Alice Adams that it seemed she was very wise about relationships. She said, "Don't be fooled. I know nothing about them. I write about them because they scare me so. You want someone who's wise about relationships? Talk to Diane Johnson. We all write about the thing that scares us most. Terrorism scares Diane. All kinds of systems—hospitals, spies—scare Diane. You want to know what someone is scared of? It's what they write about."

JD: Did you ever read that wonderful book of Diane's about the hospital?

MS: It's amazing.

JD: Isn't it amazing?

MS: It's amazing. I think that she is an amazing and virtually overlooked writer. Her most recent book, which is set in the Near East, is *Lulu in Marrakech*.

JD: They're totally original, those books.

MS: Just thrilling. I'm curious: The fear that you begin with, is it because you need instability to dare a novel?

JD: You do need instability to dare a novel. I think I said once that once you put down a few lines in a novel, you're stuck. Those are the terms of the novel. You're going to have to go with them. They're very scary. It's a scary, tense period when you're putting down those lines because your instinct is to take them out immediately, and then you don't get anywhere.

MS: That novel, *Play It as It Lays*, did you begin with your beginning, or did you discover it later?

JD: I began by writing. For a while it was a New York novel. It took place in New York, weirdly enough. Then it was taking place in California and largely in the desert. Maria driving, the freeway, was the first thing I wrote. Then I decided not to make that the beginning, to hold that off and begin with three voices. It was a primitive way of introducing the characters.

MS: From the very beginning, that language of gambling plays into the book. Who taught it to you?

JD: I used to watch my father play craps.

MS: It's a craps term, "play it as it lays"?

JD: Yeah.

MS: What does it mean? Because one of the commentators said, "It's craps," and everyone else said, "No, no, no. It's poker."

JD: No, it's craps. "As it lays" means that the action is closed. Now you're going to have to play out the roll.

MS: Whereas you would be able to pick one die up and roll it again.

JD: Right.

MS: I see. Where did you play craps?

JD: My father would play craps any place he could. I would watch him, but I never learned how to play. I've never been able to master any game because I forget the rules. I myself didn't play craps, but I had read a book by one of the Harrahs in which, by way of explaining about his third wife or his fourth wife or his something, he kept saying, "It goes as it lays." I became interested in this phrase.

MS: I became fascinated when I was reading *The Year of Magical Thinking*. I started saying, "Pasadena."

JD: Pasadena?

MS: Yes. You mentioned that you and John Gregory, when you were receiving a pitch to write a screen project, in order to indicate what you were thinking you would say, "Pasadena," meaning that you had to get to Pasadena, and they wouldn't know that you were taking a pass on it. It's become part of my language. When it's time to leave a party, I'll say, "Pasadena."

It seems as if there are code words and phrases that you enjoyed inventing that go through the whole of your work. I wondered about that. As a writer, do they enter? How frequently are we witnessing a private joke between husband and wife, between father and daughter?

JD: I wonder. I don't know myself because we don't know our own jokes.

MS: Because "Pasadena" is great. I think that one of the things that makes you have such a great ear for dialogue is that it is always spun from common phrases, phrases from craps, a way of telling your husband, "Hey, it's time to leave. This producer doesn't have anything for us." It is so enjoyable to read that and also to know that your family spoke in that kind of deflecting, "Not saying I didn't like it, just saying it was interesting." Deflection is the method of these books. Do you think so?

JD: Yes, of course it is. Deflection is the method of everything.

MS: I was wondering about that, because as I read *Play It as It Lays*, I think a lot about *The Sun Also Rises*. I think of the way in which there are loads of characters being named, and they're all offstage.

JD: They're all offstage, and you don't know very much about them.

MS: Yes, and yet they seem so interesting.

JD: So interesting, but I'm not clear on who they are.

MS: I started to chart *Play It as It Lays*. "This man was in New York. He was in theater. She becomes interested in film acting, and her second man wants to be a film director. Now the third man is a writer director." We barely know, until very much later in the book, that her husband knows of the affair and knows who she's likely pregnant by, but the wife still doesn't know. And he says so: "I know, but she doesn't know."

It's so interesting to see how the background goes through this book almost as in a Hemingway novel. Characters that we barely meet or meet for only a scene. Everyone thinks it's the short sentences of Hemingway, but I think it's also that way of building the back plot.

JD: Of introducing people as they walk past, instead of as they sit down and stay.

MS: That means that anything that can be background notes can be used in the novel.

JD: Can be used, yeah.

MS: Scenes that were once foreground can become background.

JD: They have to.

MS: Is the initial plan of writing a novel doing those foreground scenes and realizing that they can only be referred to and not used? Do you actually write them?

JD: Sometimes I write them, but usually they're just in my mind.

MS: I thought it was fascinating, because then Carter says directly to Maria that she only talks to men that she's slept with. Sure enough, you begin to notice that this is—

JD: A pattern.

MS: —a pattern and a log of her background. It has been in each city and in her childhood as well. Maybe it's not the man she slept with, but the man her mother slept with that she can speak to. These things become almost diabolical when you start to see them and wonder how much a writer has known the character. Do you see it as you write?

JD: You see it as you write, I think. I do. It doesn't exist until you've written it.

MS: Wow. One of my readers in the club wrote, "Though it wasn't immediately apparent to me, it occurred to me a few weeks after finishing the book that one could make a good argument for the novel itself having a serpentine or snakelike structure. Was this by design or just how it turned out?"

JD: It was not by design.

MS: Isn't that wonderful, though?

JD: Yes, it is wonderful.

MS: What does a writer make of the things that people think afterwards?

JD: I'm always fascinated by them because, as I said earlier, I think that there's a collaboration between reader and writer, which contributes a great deal to the work.

MS: You said to Linda Kuehl that so much of Maria was spent at parties reacting to people's bad behavior that you had to put her on stage more or less alone, and that that's how the abortion entered the book. And you went back and laid it in like a sleeve. It seems that so much of the book, the dream of the broken plumbing, is built—

JD: Around the abortion.

MS: I wondered about that. How does that work? Do you jump up and cry, "Eureka!"? Does it come usually from a practical consideration? "Gee, I've got to get her by herself where she's responding to something happening to her."

JD: Definitely, you see those empty spots, those spots where something isn't working, and then you have to devise a way to fill them in, fill in the emptiness.

MS: That can become—

JD: A thing in itself.

MS: A thing in itself. It's the process of free association? You had the snake already on page one.

JD: I don't think I put the snake on page one immediately. You fill it in. You fill stuff in.

MS: That becomes, in a novel that's in small pieces like this, part of the act of reading too. You start to put it together and rearrange the chapters chronologically.

JD: Right.

MS: And rearrange these men. What does Ivan come back for? What does he think he's going to see? He knows that she's left her husband. Does he want her, or does he want money? He's usually wanted money in the past, but seems to be making a play for her now that he knows that Carter is out of the picture. It's so interesting to try to build these offstage moments.

JD: The whole thing is offstage, of course. The whole of that novel is offstage.

MS: Tell me more about that.

JD: It was a way of writing a novel that interested me, to make it all offstage.

MS: Told about or remembered—

JD: Told about.

MS: —but not seen.

JD: Not seen, so you're never exactly sure what's going on.

MS: That's so wonderful, because it's almost as if the novel devises its rules. When she says, "I won't go to that party," it's a way of ensuring that the scene will be offstage and that she'll read about it in *Variety* and find out that her agent has been there or BZ has been there, even though he said he wasn't going to go. That's so interesting, Joan. I'm curious. This is my final question. When you look at or think about it now, do you look at it at all? What do you think of it now?

JD: I haven't read that novel in a while, a very long while, actually. I'm not sure what I would make of it if I read it now. When I last read it, I was startled by how familiar it was to me. Well, of course it was familiar.

MS: Do you ever wish that you had the opportunity—

JD: To rewrite?

MS: —to redo?

JD: I wished that desperately with my first novel, which did not come out the way I wanted it. This one, I thought, came out the way I wanted it on its own terms, so I didn't want to redo this one. No, I didn't want to redo it, and particularly when I remembered how not happy I had been writing it.

MS: Writing is rarely a happy experience for you. Has there been a happy book?

JD: I'm sure there's been a happy book. There must have been a happy book. Actually, my Iran-Contra book was a happy experience.

2013: *Blue Nights*

MS: People who know the sound of my voice know that my voice is full of the awe that I feel to be in the presence of a writer I truly admire. Her new book is called *Blue Nights,* and I thought we would begin by hearing its opening section.

JD: *"In certain latitudes there comes a span of time approaching and following the summer solstice, some weeks in all, when the twilights turn long and blue. This period of the blue nights does not occur in subtropical California, where I lived for much of the time I will be talking about here and where the end of daylight is fast and lost in the blaze of the dropping sun, but it does occur in New York, where I now live. You notice it first as April ends and May begins, a change in the season, not exactly a warming—in fact not at all a warming—yet suddenly summer seems near, a possibility, even a promise. You pass a window, you walk to Central Park, you find yourself swimming in the color blue: the actual light is blue, and over the course of an hour or so this blue deepens, becomes more intense even as it darkens and fades, approximates finally the blue of the glass on a clear day at Chartres, or that of the Cerenkov radiation thrown off by the fuel rods in the pools of nuclear reactors. The French called this time of day 'l'heure bleue.' To the English it was 'the gloaming.' The very word 'gloaming' reverberates, echoes—the gloaming, the glimmer, the glitter, the glisten, the glamour—carrying in its consonants the images of houses shuttering, gardens darkening, grass-lined rivers slipping through the shadows. During the blue nights you think the end of day will never come. As the blue nights draw to a close (and they will, and they do) you experience an actual chill, an apprehension of illness, at the moment you first notice: the blue light is going, the days are already shortening, the summer is gone. This book is called 'Blue Nights' because at the time I began it I found my mind turning increasingly to illness, to the end of promise, the dwindling of the days, the inevitability of the fading, the dying of the brightness. Blue nights are the opposite of the dying of the brightness, but they are also its warning."*

MS: This is a memoir at first concerned with the death of your daughter, Quintana Roo, and following *The Year of Magical Thinking*. Did you think you would be writing such a book?

JD: No, I had no idea. I had some idea that I would write a book about having children, and then as I got deeper into it, or as I began to write it, I realized that it wasn't about having children in the abstract, it was about my child. And that led to thoughts of death because she had died. Thoughts of death led to the blue nights, and the minute I thought of the blue nights, I knew what the book was about. It was about aging and death, which was certainly on my mind.

MS: As you read the book you discover that the subject is one that really hasn't been broached in literature before. There have been people who want to help you age or even want to help you die.

JD: But the assumption is that you don't have to.

MS: Yes, and that a work of literature, by and large, doesn't take it up. It's almost as if writers avoid that.

JD: Right.

MS: Tolstoy does it in *The Death of Ivan Ilyich*, but by and large writers don't like to come to the final moment.

JD: No one likes to come to the final moment.

MS: So when I reach the last twenty or so pages I say, "Oh my! We're going to go as far to the edge in this book as it's possible to go."

JD: I'm so glad you thought that.

MS: It's a stunning thing. I think that it can only be put along with *King Lear* and some of the other works of approaching madness or approaching the end.

JD: Well, you know, I didn't think I would finish this book. I kept thinking I would set it aside, I would abandon it. I've abandoned books before, and this one seemed eminently a candidate for being abandoned because I wasn't having a good time with it. Well, naturally I wasn't having a good time with it when I look back on it. It was not a good-time book.

MS: How did you find yourself able to complete it?

JD: Well, I just decided I had to. Then suddenly I found a rhythm. Sometimes you just make a stab in the dark and exhibit some blind faith that it will take you home.

MS: Now, you had said, in what's become a famous interview for *The Paris Review*, that once you've written the first couple of pages, a book is doomed to the terms you've created.

JD: You've got to use the terms. Yeah.

MS: What seemed to happen in this book, to me for the first time, was that the terms of the book—

JD: Were loose.

MS: Were loose and opened. There seemed to be a point at which the fragments, the bits of mosaic, the special sentences made room for new ones, and the book took on—well, as I thought of it—it went from the fugue state of grief to a fugue itself. It became a piece of music.

JD: It seemed like music to me as I got into it. I can't explain it, but it was definitely more like music than anything I'd ever written.

MS: It seemed as if the balance came from the beauty of the repetition of lines against the simple direness of the facts of the hospital and the doctors. Suddenly the short lines, the single lines became a balance between structure and desperation. The book took a special form of completion. I don't think I've heard it before, even in your work.

JD: Well, it really finished itself. I mean, it took itself home in a way that I couldn't do.

MS: Do you know when you get there?

JD: Do you know when you're home?

MS: Yes.

JD: Yes.

MS: How?

JD: It just feels right. It feels as if you don't have to do any more.

MS: Now, it seems to me that in this book you rip open really incredible wounds. You open the possibility that you haven't been a good mother. I think most parents would rather die.

JD: I think most parents feel, though, that they haven't been good parents. Whether they admit it or not. Most people don't admit most stuff.

MS: Why is that possible for you?

JD: Why is it possible? It's necessary for me to admit the absolute worst that I can imagine.

MS: It brought to mind—I'm a close reader and rereader of your work—some things that you had said in your essay "On Keeping a Notebook." You had said, "Although I have felt compelled to write things down since I was five years old, I doubt that my daughter ever will, for she is a singularly blessed and accepting child, delighted with life exactly as life presents itself to her, unafraid to go to sleep and unafraid to wake up."

For someone to have been able once to have said that to be facing these facts now seems an incredible act of opening up to the possibilities of life at its worst.

JD: That's where it led me, yes. When it started leading me there was when I kept thinking, "You don't have to finish this. You can abandon this book. You can set it aside."

MS: There was the question of whether it was your story to tell.

JD: Always there is. I mean, if you're writing about another person, especially another person in your family, to whom you owe some special loyalty, yes, it's a huge question whether it's your story to tell, and I felt very strongly that certain aspects of this story were not mine to tell. So I kept pushing them off and fighting and trying not to tell them. Then I realized you had to.

MS: That might be part of the tension of the book, because so famously with your first book, *Slouching Toward Bethlehem*, you say that a writer is always selling someone out. The impulse not to, because, in this case, it's your daughter, must create a really—

JD: A tension.

MS: —terrible tug.

JD: Yeah. It did. So I kept doing what I thought of as rambling, but the rambling actually kept leading me back to the same place.

MS: You go to the Greek tragedians, to the idea that it is a tragedy to outlive one's children, to live through the death of one's children. Does that give you perspective?

JD: The idea of the tragedy?

MS: Yes.

JD: Yes it does, because it has been with me since early childhood. The first things I read really were the Greeks.

MS: Do you feel as if you or your family have flown against the gods?

JD: No, I never felt that. I don't think of Greek tragedy as going against the gods. That would be approaching feeling sorry for yourself, which is a form of hubris all by itself, which we have to avoid.

MS: How do you avoid feeling sorry for yourself?

JD: Because it's been on my mind as something to avoid forever. So it's just something I try to do.

MS: Were you taught it?

JD: I was taught about its value.

MS: I remember one of the most startling things I've ever read anywhere is in one of your essays in which you were told to consider, instead of crying, putting a paper bag on your head.

JD: Yes.

MS: You say, "It was useful."

JD: Yes.

MS: It's kind of amazing at a time when feeling sorry—as a nation, as a culture, as an individual, as a people—seems to be the national mood.

JD: Well, if you could find yourself feeling better just by putting a bag on your head, you would do it.

MS: Does it work? Does it still work?

JD: It does. Just like this. It cuts off oxygen. It does something physiological that works.

MS: Wow.

JD: It was explained to me actually, how valuable this would be.

MS: That it was an alternative also to taking a cold shower.

JD: Right. It's much more effective than a cold shower and more available.

MS: For my listeners, I asked Joan if she would do us the favor of reading from what I think of as the final fugue of the book. Some of the references in it will pass you by, but I think it is the definition of what turns this book into music. This is Joan Didion reading from the end of *Blue Nights*.

JD: "Whole days now spent on this one question, this question with no possible answer: *who do I want notified in case of emergency?*

I think it over. I do not want even to consider 'in case of emergency.'

Emergency, I continue to believe, is what happens to someone else.

I say that I continue to believe this even as I know that I do not.

I mean, think back: what about that business with the folding metal chair in the rehearsal room on West Forty-second Street? What exactly was I afraid of there? What did I fear in that rehearsal room if not an 'emergency'? Or what about walking home after an early dinner on Third Avenue and waking up in a pool of blood on my own bedroom floor? Might not waking up in a pool of blood on my own bedroom floor qualify as an 'emergency'?

All right. Accepted. 'In case of emergency' could apply.

Who to notify. I try harder.

Still, no name comes to mind.

I could give the name of my brother, but my brother lives three thousand miles from what might be defined in New York as an emergency. I could give Griffin's name, but Griffin is shooting a picture. Griffin is on location. Griffin is sitting in the dining room of one or another Hilton Inn—a few too many people at the table, a little too much noise—and Griffin is not picking up his cell. I could give the names of whichever close friend in New York comes first to mind, but the close friend in New York who comes first to mind is actually, on reflection, not even in New York, out of town, out of the country, away, certainly unreachable in the best case, possibly unwilling in the worst.

As I consider the word 'unwilling' my lagging cognition kicks in.

The familiar phrase 'need to know' surfaces.

The phrase 'need to know' has been the problem all along.

Only one person needs to know.

She is of course the one person who needs to know.

Let me just be in the ground.

Let me just be in the ground and go to sleep.

I imagine telling her.

I am able to imagine telling her because I still see her.

Hello, Mommies.

The same way I still see her weeding the clay court on Franklin Avenue.

The same way I still see her sitting on the bare floor crooning back to the eight-track.

Do you wanna dance. I wanna dance.

The same way I still see the stephanotis in her braid, the same way I still see the plumeria tattoo through her bridal veil. The same way I still see the bright-red soles on her shoes as she kneels at the altar. The same way I still see her, in the darkened upstairs cabin on the evening Pan Am from Honolulu to LAX, inventing the unforeseen uptick in Bunny Rabbit's fortunes.

I know that I can no longer reach her.

I know that, should I try to reach her—should I take her hand as if she were again sitting next to me in the upstairs cabin on the evening Pan Am from Honolulu to LAX, should I lull her to sleep against my shoulder, should I sing her the song about Daddy gone to get the rabbit skin to wrap his baby bunny in—she will fade from my touch.

Vanish.

Pass into nothingness: the Keats line that frightened her.

Fade as the blue nights fade, go as the brightness goes.

Go back into the blue.

I myself placed her ashes in the wall.

I myself saw the cathedral doors locked at six.

I know what it is I am now experiencing.

I know what the frailty is, I know what the fear is.

The fear is not for what is lost.

What is lost is already in the wall.

What is lost is already behind the locked doors.

The fear is for what is still to be lost.

You may see nothing still to be lost.

Yet there is no day in her life on which I do not see her."

MS: Now, I think you discovered that construction out of single sentences—some people called it a mosaic, though it now seems more musical than visual—in *Play It as It Lays*. It was truly a breakthrough, and here it comes to a kind of a culmination.

You've done this thing that seems to be the most demanding or difficult thing in your style. It's absolutely quintessential: a Didion page becomes recognizable because of the presence of single sentences and strong repetitions. Here it is. And it's as if you are speaking in these final pages, almost from beyond life, from beyond the grave, in a state of recognition. Only this process of breaking things down into single sentences, it's not just poetry, it's syllogism. It's logic.

JD: It is logic, isn't it?

MS: Yeah.

JD: Yeah.

MS: It seems to lead you to a place from which there is no consolation, but consolation is no longer necessary.

JD: Well, consolation is necessary of course, always, in our real life, but you do reach a place where consolation doesn't matter if everything is going well when you're working on something.

MS: I think part of what makes it so effective on the page is that the reader is being addressed so directly, is so directly present to a process of thought. Yet you're not here. I can't reach out and touch Joan Didion and say, "Oh, I'm so sorry," or, "I don't know how it will be okay, but it will be."

So, the page, in bringing the reader so close, there's also an acknowledgment that there's a closeness that can't be achieved with the reader. That we've come to a witness of grief that no camera could give us access to, that only prose can give us. Yet we're cut off from it. And when a book ends this way, that feeling of being ripped apart.

JD: Don't you think that the experience of someone you know dying is exactly that? You're separated from them. It's the separation that makes it unsupportable.

MS: Yes, but Joan, who ever before has said, "The thing I fear is no longer that she'll die but that I won't remember her, that I won't be seeing her and thinking of her every day"? And then, on that recognition, which, you know, perhaps so much thought and grief expends itself on, the book ends.

JD: It had to end there. There was no place to go.

MS: Yes, it is clear that Joan Didion is feeling very deeply and yet using the equipment of a master dramatist. Did that experience, writing the play of *The Year of Magical Thinking*, help you in some sense?

JD: I think it helped me become more open, and it was valuable in about a million different ways. One thing it made me understand, which I had never really fully understood before, was that there is a true collaboration between the audience and the playwright or the writer. There is a true collaboration obviously between any writer and any reader.

MS: When you say collaboration, that's what the reading felt like. That I no longer needed to go through certain steps. I'd been inculcated.

JD: You could follow it. You could track it.

MS: I could follow it. There was an instruction process.

JD: Yeah.

MS: Or, like the recitation of a poem that you've come to know, maybe you don't understand the poem, but you know the rhythms that are involved here, and you complete them for yourself.

JD: That's perfect.

MS: That's what poetry does.

JD: Yeah.

MS: That, I think, is what you've wanted your prose to do from almost the beginning.

JD: I did. I mean, consciously even, but I didn't know how to get there. Gradually, I've learned how to get there.

MS: What a price.

JD: Yeah.

Carlos Fuentes

1994: *The Buried Mirror*

MS: My guest today, and it's a great honor to have him here in the studio, is Carlos Fuentes, the author most recently of *The Buried Mirror: Reflections on Spain and the New World*, as well as many novels. Among them my very favorite is *Terra Nostra*. There is also *The Death of Artemio Cruz*; the very remarkable novella, *Aura*, which is a ghost story; and more recently *The Campaign, Constancia and Other Stories for Virgins, Christopher Unborn*; and now a history of Spain and the New World.

I wanted to start and let listeners get an idea of the wealth of material and information in this book. When I opened it and saw that you began with the bull of the bullfight, went to the bull of *Guernica*, and then brought in the Minotaur, I thought, well, now we enter Greek culture. This is a new way of writing history, a fantasia of interconnection. How did it come about?

CF: Don't forget the bull of the Osborne Brandy, which you see in all the highways and cityscapes of Spain. That big black bull presiding. I think that when you say fantasia, there is an element of dream in the book, in the sense, again, that it's a book I have dreamed about. Because imagine if we all had the right, the possibility to tell our personal history in terms of our culture, in terms of the culture we have lived, or the cultures we have been swimming in, our amniotic liquid, as it were. Well, this is this book. Thanks to the television series, but going well beyond it, I thought, "What an extraordinary opportunity! It should be inscribed in the rights of man to sit down and write your personal history of your culture or cultures." This is what I attempted to do, really.

MS: This is like your Altamira bull in the cave of history.

CF: Yes. But there's not only a bull, there is a hand in the cave of Spain, which I found extraordinary, the imprint of the human hand, which is so visibly there after thirty, forty thousand years.

MS: It's amazing to think of those paintings on the cave vanishing with oxygen.

CF: When people breathe at the bulls, they disintegrate them. We are plastic mythological heroes who arrive and vanquish the bull through our breathing.

MS: It's interesting to think of breathing being a kind of erasure—if the world were a text.

CF: I'm glad you bring up the image of the bull because I've always said that this book ranges visually, pictorially from the caves of Altamira to the graffiti in East Los Angeles. That is the span of this culture. I try to make it instantaneous. We're always fighting as writers against the sequential nature of writing. It is our fate. You cannot avoid it, except some great poets for being able to present the writing simultaneously, but normally, especially if you're writing prose, you have to follow a sequence, a linear sequence. To challenge that sequence, to defeat it somehow is the constant challenge, I think, of the writer on the page. Again, here, dealing with these subjects I had to follow a linear sequence, but at the same time I was trying to violate it constantly in order to make the past present, in order to give everything the quality of the present, which I think is where history happens, where things happen, always in the present.

MS: It seems to me that just as the South American and Latin American novelists have reinvented the novel, this is a kind of reinvention of history. I'm thinking in particular of Eduardo Galeano's books that are very interested in finding a cluster of images rather than one moment. As Pound said, all time is simultaneous. It seems to me a history of all culture has to be told to tell of any culture.

CF: I think that is so, exactly what you say, because there is no real past except in our memory today. The way that memory functions and recreates and imagines and dreams is the true past. I think there is no future, really, except our desire. And the capacity and strength of our passion, our desire is what makes the future. Now, both now. I think that, nevertheless, this book comes from a long tradition of the Hispanic world, which is the reflection on the culture, the self-reflection, the exercise of self-awareness, which you find in so many writers of Spain and Spanish America. I feel very close to Unamuno in many of the things I'm doing and his concept of intra-history, not a meta-history or a really objective history—which he knows, I know, and you know does not exist—but an intra-history in which all the threads, all the elements of the past are becoming present, and we're constantly choosing and giving life to that past, being very conscious that there is no living present with a dead past.

MS: I'm always interested when people bring up other writers to make sure that my listeners know them. This is Miguel de Unamuno, both a novelist and a philosopher—primarily a philosopher. We have him, fortunately, nearly all of him, in English in the Bollingen editions. If a listener were to want to read your favorite Unamuno, where would he start?

CF: I think you would start with *Tragic Sense of Life (Del sentimiento trágico de la vida)*, because I think Unamuno opened my eyes in the sense of revealing that the great tragedy of modernity, of the modern world, was the absence of tragedy.

MS: Yes. The humanization of art seems to be part of that subject. I had not been familiar with Unamuno's fiction until recently, and it's brilliant.

CF: Oh, it's brilliant. He was a great innovator, a great experiment with a novel called *Fog (Niebla)*. It's a novel that is actually making itself as it is told. It is conscious that it is a novel being written as the events are told and lived. Perhaps they live even more intensely because they are conscious of their fictional quality. But this is a great invention of Cervantes, of course, to make the characters realize that they are inside a novel, which is what happens with *Don Quixote*.

MS: What makes me most happy about *Don Quixote* is when we hear reports that there are other people now pretending to be Don Quixote and he may meet imposters. This happens in Book II.

CF: He may meet imposters, or he may read apocryphal versions. Like the Avellaneda book cashing in on the popularity of the book.

MS: That thrills me.

CF: Oh, it's a thrilling event in world literature. I don't think it happens before Cervantes that the character knows he is the character of a book. And he goes to a printing press! He's the first character in the novel who goes to the place where his book is being produced, is becoming a commercial object that will be read by thousands of people. They know all about us. They said, "You know they tell everything we've said. Something that was reserved for God in ancient times now becomes available to the common reader."

MS: Doesn't he also attend a puppet show of his own life?

CF: No, no. The puppet show is a tale in which the Moors have captured the Princess Melisendra.

MS: Oh, that's right!

CF: And he takes out his sword and attacks the puppet theater and destroys it because for Don Quixote there is no boundary between fiction and reality.

MS: To speak about the nonexistent boundary between fiction and reality, this book is called *The Buried Mirror*, and it suggests that in a dark and hidden and underground way, the history of Mexico repeats the history of Spain and that the history of Mexico reflects the history of the United States in different variants. You also talk about "the buried mirror" as being the one that guides the spirit in the afterworld. I guess it's a double question: one, the relation of history-telling to history as it occurs; and two, you've recently been rewriting history in the form of the novel, *The Campaign*, as has Mario Vargas Llosa. This is another buried mirror, and I'd wondered if you'd talk a bit about it.

CF: Yes. Well, I don't think there is any such thing as history as it happened. History is always history as it is told. History is a narrative. History is a memory. I think there's a Ray Bradbury story where a man walks down Olvera Street and enters a strange little Mexican movie house and finds the most glorious Roman epic battle with the Carthaginians taking place and stays there, stunned. This Mexican cinematographer has discovered a way of photographing the past. So this gringo goes in and says, "There's money in this! Let's put music to it, and let's edit it." All those things. It's all very successful. You can see the real Cleopatra, and everybody wonders, "Who did this? How wonderful! What a production!" Until he gets to contemporary history, and then they're promptly shot. The political forces take over and shoot these guys. You cannot enter the inner sanctum of contemporary politics in any way.

MS: That's one way of ending an illusion. The historical novels that you've been writing, there are more of them. Susan Sontag has just written a novel of—

CF: Yes, I know. Happens in Venice, I'm told.

MS: Naples.

CF: Naples, yes.

MS: It's quite amazing. I'm reading the manuscript now and it's an astonishing book.

CF: Oh, I'm yearning to read that.

MS: It's an amazing book. Can you speak a bit about the relation between the history of fiction and the fiction of history?

CF: I think there is a novel of time and a time of the novel. All novels have a time, but not all times have a novel. I think that's an interesting distinction because the novel is a historical product of a certain age. Alright, that's interesting. But what is really interesting is the capacity of the novel to invent time, to create time. There is no novel without history, in this sense. Every single novel creates its history, creates its time. Borges has been especially good at talking about this and making us realize that the time of a novel is the time of the reading of the novel, so that the first time you read *Don Quixote* or *The Trial*, that is when the novel is really beginning. It is its present. It is starting then. Its history is starting then. This is the history I'm interested in.

I wrote *Terra Nostra* to show myself and, hopefully, the reader that there was another history of Spain I could tell. I could invent that history of Spain and make it as viable as the so-called real history, which I wanted to cast into doubt. I think any book, any novel, because it deals inevitably with time, because it is a historical narrative in this sense of creating a time for the reader, it immediately creates another history in the sense that it betrays the official history. The official version of history is always betrayed by a novel, unless it's a very bad novel, of course.

MS: Herodotus gives us characters. We live in a certain historical world populated by people we feel that historians have invented. In *The Buried Mirror*, you too have created a whole cast—I especially love the description of the Spanish kings. They were living and vibrant and often funny to me. What is the historian's morality in creating characters for figures of history?

CF: I know that I'm always attacked by professional historians. They would like to see an objective history and a serious history. No, I think history sometimes can be a riot. In *Terra Nostra* I really imagined Oliver Hardy and Stan Laurel throwing pies at themselves in the Escorial and desacralizing it in a way. I think this right that a novelist takes upon himself or herself is extraordinarily important, as I say, to break down the necessity that official history has of consecrating itself and imposing itself on the subjects and of legitimizing power. I think a novel constantly breaks this up.

MS: It's interesting because in the underground of *The Hydra Head*, there is *The Maltese Falcon*. It's very nice in that book to discover characters who are all character actors who have made their way into the dark corridors of Mexican oil politics from the equally dark corridors of Raymond Chandler and Dashiell Hammett.

CF: That, I think, is the real history, you see, that kind of contact. We were talking about Don Quixote and how he realizes that he is a character in the book. For example, I love an idea of García Márquez's when he says, "We're not really writing individual novels in Latin America. We are writing an enormous novel with one chapter by you, another by me, another by Cortázar, another by Carpentier, another by Vargas Llosa, et cetera." I love the fact that, in many of our novels, like in a deck of cards, when you shuffle the cards, suddenly pieces of another novel appear. I lost a character in *The Death of Artemio Cruz*, a certain Colonel Gavilán who helps Artemio Cruz hide from forces and saves his life. Suddenly, he reappeared in *One Hundred Years of Solitude*. He'd been exiled and appeared there. In *The Campaign*, at the end of the book, the printer, who is the narrator of the story, tells about a manuscript that arrived from Colombia in 1821 when Bolivar was alive, telling about the sad death of Bolivar and how he lost his illusions. He said, "No, no, no. It's too down. It's too pessimistic. I won't publish it." It's *The General in His Labyrinth*. We're constantly getting this kind of creation of another reality because, after all, what are we proposing when we speak of history in the novel or when we write a novel? Forget history, forget everything. We're proposing that what is imaginary is real, that the imagination is a reality.

MS: In a book like *Tres Tristes Tigres*, also, language becomes a simultaneous moment: everything happens at once, within a single word. It's a technique, of course, inherited from *Finnegans Wake*. Which leads me to the question: *Finnegans Wake* was meant to be a kind of universal book of all cultures. You've spoken of the importance of there being international culture, not particular culture. That's a theme within this book. I wondered if you could address that as a novelist.

CF: I think we have finally reached the dream that Goethe had of the *Weltliteratur*, because, yes, one can say the novel is in crisis. "The novel is dead," was the news I received when I started writing. First thing I was told was the novel is dead. Ha ha. Today, I think what you have is an extraordinary group of fiction writers throughout the world writing in many languages, belonging to many nations, but finally transcending the nationality and even the language. I think that it is the quality of the imagination that really imposes itself, finally. I don't think anybody reads Milan Kundera because he's Czech or Günter Grass because he's German or because they write in those languages, but because of the quality of their imagination. This is creating a new kind of geography of the novel that is constantly transcending the old boundaries. In many senses, you see, not only in the sense of nationality, but also in the sense of, when you read a book like *Aspects of the Novel* by E. M. Forster, it seems so absolutely narrow and old-fashioned.

MS: Yes, isn't it amazing—

CF: A well-rounded story with credible characters, psychological depth. We're talking here, Michael, you and I, about novels where the protagonists are whole cultures, civilizations, historical times, languages. Many, many other things that were kept out of this very narrow conception of the realistic novel.

MS: They had that similar book, *The Great Tradition* by F. R. Leavis, and this meant that the novel had been taken from Dickens to George Eliot and deposited at D. H. Lawrence. I always used to feel, "No, this is so unfair." The greatness of the novel includes Canetti, and includes so much unreality and past reality and re-digestion of fantasy.

CF: And the fantastic dimension of the great realistic writers. Balzac! Can you understand the realism of Balzac without all the supernatural fantastic novels of Balzac? Where would Dickens be if he had simply chronicled the life of London without these incredibly fantastic images of night and death and corruption?

MS: Ghosts and goblins.

CF: And ghosts. My God! It is what gives the novel its life, those novels.

MS: I always wanted to ask a writer who writes in Spanish this question. Recently, almost as much as this poker-faced naturalism that they call minimalism has spread across America, there's a make-believe magic realism. It's as if American writers reading you and García Márquez and others feel jealous. They want magic realism too. I'm thinking, for instance, of a book like *A Winter's Tale* by Mark Helprin, where the technique seems stolen. It seems culturally inappropriate. North America does not seem a place where there are flying horses. Do you feel that this is another kind of imperialism?

CF: I don't know, because the concept of magical realism was first used by Alejo Carpentier, the Cuban novelist. For him, it was very clearly a way of giving a charter of identity, if you wish, in Latin America to something he had lived very deeply, which was the surrealist time in Paris in the 1920s and 1930s. I don't think Carpentier wanted to be called a surrealist. He wanted to call himself a magical realist, but he had a point because he was saying all these things that the Europeans have to invent, we give naturally.

MS: It's very funny. You put me in mind of one of my favorite sentences about Picasso. It was, "Picasso was a naturalist with very good eyes."

CF: That is it. That is it. Absolutely. Finally, what we can understand as magical realism has become the province of one writer only. His name is Gabriel García Márquez. He's the only one who can write about women flying off to the sky with their laundry. I don't think this can be repeated. I certainly don't do that. I don't write magical realism. I don't know what to call it, but it is not that.

MS: It's very interesting because history, I guess, creates itself out of fiction, and so now, as Borges says that he invented his precursors, there is also—because, I think, of García Márquez—an interest in Bruno Schulz, the great Polish writer whose images have that in common. I think that what

García Márquez has made us aware of is that there was always, throughout literature, a very old man with enormous wings. It just took a Márquez to shine a light in that direction.

CF: Absolutely right. I don't think now you can repeat the experience of Gar-cía Márquez. I find it very, very difficult.

MS: I think it's true, and I think that is the problem with some of the North American writers who've imported these techniques.

CF: Imagine trying to be a comedian with a bowler hat, a cane, big floppy shoes, a cutaway, and a small Hitler mustache. You can't do it.

MS: Unfortunately, maybe now, enough time has gone by. Maybe you could. If anything, in this culture, I would very much like it if there were silent comedians again.

CF: Yes, but not that one. You can't use those props again. I won't mention any names, but there are so many imitators of García Márquez. They're terrible. They're really very bad.

MS: It's like writing by menu, by recipe. I'm curious here. In the way that most of the Russian writers spent time in Paris, Paris did become a center for Spanish and Latin and South American writers. Cortázar lived there for many years, and it makes me wonder. I think that right now, there really isn't a modern novel in France. You can't think of French fiction with any particular delight at this moment.

CF: You can think of individual writers, of course. You can think of Claude Simon.

MS: Yes, Claude Simon is very great.

CF: Michel Tournier, but he is a German writer who writes in French, I think. No, there isn't that. But, again, I think we've stopped thinking about national boundaries. We think more of individual writers.

MS: Is it possible that the novel went traveling from Paris to South America?

CF: France dominated the popular culture of the nineteenth century the same way that the United States has dominated the popular culture of the twentieth century. Everybody wanted to imitate France, Paris. Today, everybody wants to imitate the North Americans. I find that very normal. It leads to funny things. You know that Guatemala City called itself the "Paris of Central America" during the nineteenth century with the hope, obviously, that someday, Paris would call itself the "Guatemala City of Europe."

MS: I wanted to ask you—and this is a dangerous question to ask as a final question—but it was always said to me when I was in school that the reason why suddenly the South American novels were being published in America was that the translations were being funded by the CIA. Do you believe this to be true?

CF: No, not at all. I don't see Gregory Rabassa as a translator or Knopf or Random House or Farrar, Straus being financed by the CIA. It was paid by the publishers, and they took a great risk in doing so.

MS: We're very grateful to them because right now, for instance, Africa is just beginning to creep back into the American consciousness of the novel, and to think that we have whole continents of writing that we don't know.

CF: Well, Asia is very unknown. Chinese literature is unknown still, I think.

MS: It's just beginning to be known. I think that history is a history of consciousness and perception. Do you know what I mean? The cultural transmogrification.

CF: I'm always delighted there are things we don't know, because I have always been convinced that a writer really writes about what he doesn't know. I don't like writing about what I already know. I want to surprise myself by writing about what I ignore, and then the discovery of what I ignore is where I think one really starts writing interesting things.

1994: *The Orange Tree*

MS: This new collection of linked novellas is called *The Orange Tree*. I congratulate you for having written a book entirely narrated by the dead and the nonexistent. It's very much a ghostly book.

CF: Yes, it is forms of discovering how we perceive life from death. What happens to us when we die, how conceivably we could look upon life from the other shore.

MS: It seems as if, as a result, the world here has become something of a necropolis with, nevertheless, a living orange tree at its center. What does the tree signify for you?

CF: I think very obviously it signifies nature and the fact that it survives us, that it goes on, that it witnesses our follies, our historical madness and survives. Yet what I imply in the last story, the Christopher Columbus story, "The Two Americas," is that for the first time in history, we might deny nature its privileges and take her to the grave with us through nuclear holocaust, through ecocide. We could conceivably be the first generation that achieves this monumental apocalypse.

MS: It's very rare for a quote on the back of a book to be significant to a book. But it seems to me, in this case, Guy Davenport's quote is very significant to this particular book. Davenport says, "In all his books, Fuentes draws tight a tense conjunction of opposites: the sensuously beautiful and the horrifyingly ugly, innocence and evil, past and present, the familiar and the strange, nature and culture." In this book, all sorts of twins recur. There are, as the story says, two Americas, there are two sons of Hernando Cortés who speak a story together. There are two translators, and a story called "The Two Shores," another called "The Two Numantias." This book seems to have at its core an interest in envy and resentment. I wondered if you could speak about that.

CF: One way of looking at the world is in a binary fashion, the world of opposing forces, opposing doubles. I think the commentary by Davenport, who is a great writer and a great critic—*rara avis*, in that sense—is very, very correct. It's almost as though Davenport had forecast this book, *The Orange Tree*. In "The Two Numantias," I go back to one of the first philosophical preoccupations, which is the difficulty in conceiving the relation between body and soul, between flesh and the spirit. It is something that has preoccupied humankind from the very beginning.

The very first philosophers immediately speak of this. Are we one? Are we two? Is our flesh one thing and our soul another? Why do we die because our body ceases to function? Where does our soul go? It has been a constant preoccupation, this binary construction of ourselves and therefore of the world. The story of "The Two Numantias," I think, dramatizes this in the decision by the Roman general, Scipio, of defeating Numantia, the last Iberian stronghold to hold out against the Roman troops, by duplicating Numantia, by creating a perimeter that exactly duplicates the area of the city.

What the city sees in this mirror of itself is a barren no man's land. It is almost an invitation to suicide, an invitation to surrender. At the same time, it is reflecting the divided nature of the man who ordered this, who is Scipio, a Roman general who is a part of a famous military family, yet he is an adopted son. He knows he is a stranger to that family, a divided child taken into that family. Also, he is a military man who is an intellectual, who was the founder of the first intellectual circle of Republican Rome with men like the historian Polybius or the playwright Terence sitting around the orange tree in his courtyard and creating a rhetoric for Imperial Rome, for its future.

This is a dramatic event, I think, in all people's lives. This idea of division, the possibility of duality, of being separated from ourselves. I wanted to dramatize it in order to go forward in my own conception—which is underlying the whole book—a question about what is reality. Is it the purely subjective? Is it the purely individual? Or is it the purely objective, the material world? Both exist, but I do not understand the existence of either the purely subjective world or of the purely objective material world without something I would call the collective individuality. That is the place where my person meets my culture, where it shakes hands with my culture. That would be the synthesis of these constant polarities in the book. The attempt to reach the moment where my individuality becomes part of a wider consciousness, a wider experience of a cultural experience. If I reach it or not, if my characters reach it or not, is open to question, of course.

MS: In the first story, "The Two Shores," there's an almost astonishing finale in which Spain is being colonized by Mexican and South American explorers.

CF: Indians.

MS: Yes, but led as well by a Spaniard who's come to Mexico and whose friend has had his face tattooed, has married an Indian woman, has children with blonde hair but very dark features. It's almost as if suddenly there's a reciprocal world going on. This production of almost, in this book, Disneylands—dis-populated projections of a nonexistent reciprocal culture, of a cross-pollination that simultaneously becomes, as the book continues, quite empty, a ghost town, a town in which a rhetoric is created but it doesn't correspond to a place.

CF: Yes, I think you're absolutely right. I hadn't calculated that it was a Disneyland world. Of course, if we come to the last story, which is that of a Christopher Columbus who keeps mum about his discovery for 500 years and is living in an archipelago called Antilia, which appears and disappears constantly.

MS: Like Brigadoon.

CF: Like Brigadoon. He believes he is in Japan, and finally he is discovered by the Japanese and a consortium that creates a resort in this island called Paradise Incorporated, which is pure Disneyland, of course. It's a purely ersatz civilization. It is a struggle also between ersatz plastic civilizations, commercial civilizations, and cultures that have a deeper meaning in the lives and thoughts and desires and memories of the people who live it. And isn't that what we are living today? This tremendous struggle that is going on between what we have decided to call the global village, with its purely economic values, and the local village, with its loyalty to hearth and to the past and memory and the language.

It's spilling over also into a kind of barbarism. We're caught between two terrible worlds and have yet to construct not the plastic world of the global village or what can be at times the murderous world of the local village, but a civilization that will give room for us all, that will accept us all in our diversity. Is that possible? It's a question.

MS: One would hope so. But, at least in this set of novellas, Columbus becomes a character who's telling us the truth about himself—he announces that he's a Sephardic Jew who is not Italian at all, left Spain during the Inquisition, prays to Spain, the mother—and yet although he is revealing himself, he's being turned by the consortium that owns Paradise Inc. into the equivalent of an audio-animatron. Someone who, even if he elects at this point to tell us the truth, it can only come out in a mechanical, unattended mumble.

CF: Yes, he is transformed into a freak, as it were, by the commercial interests that take over the Antilles. He is given Banana Republic clothes and paraded along with naked slave girls, Indian slave girls, and all of this. It's a kind of carnival that is created. Yet I insist that behind both the comic events of the book and the desolation that you rightfully find in the book, the ghost-like emptiness—that can occur. My question is nevertheless that the play on the second opportunity for history is a serious play. That is, trying to say we must give history a second opportunity in order to reveal all that has been forgotten, in order to recover all that has been marginalized.

MS: In its way, the most human, sensual memories are round, they are of the breast. In this book, the breast becomes, for Columbus, his original vision of a potentially round world, not an apple, we learn, but a pear. The pear being like a breast with its nipple. It seems as if the way of returning to history is through a recognition of more basic needs.

CF: I would say so. First of all, I would like to remark that what you have just quoted is one of the few instances in that novella in which I quote Columbus. It is Columbus himself, in his diary, writing of his conception of the world as a pear and as his mother's breast and talking about his childhood and how he enjoyed his mother's breast. He talks about all this. There is in him that sensuality of the roundness which permits me to circulate amongst different sensualities in the book, in order to try to give sensuality to the idea that all occurs in the present, that sensuality is an act of the present in which the past and the future occur.

I don't think that the past and the future as such exist. I think you and I exist in this moment, and we are remembering, and that is the only past we have. In this precise moment, we're also desiring, and that is the only future we have. I would also like to place the stories in the sensuality that drives towards a conception, a more global conception, a rounded conception of the living moment in which we are, and all it contains.

MS: In *The Orange Tree*, language itself is seen as the product of a sensual act. It's something that is learned by its translators by sucking—from the breast, elsewhere as well. It's as if love itself is a communication of language almost inadvertently in this book.

CF: I think the erotic is the supreme way of communicating. We are these strange animals that make love facing each other, seeing our faces. I think it was Burt Lancaster who said that. [*laughter*] In the film where a band comes into Mexico to save Claudia Cardinale from the clutches of a Mexican bandit played by Jack Palance. You remember the title of that?

MS: No, no, I will never know.

CF: Lancaster wonders why human beings, a man and a woman, are the only animals that make love looking at their faces—almost as if they needed to speak to each other in the moment. The fact is, that we do speak to each other when we make love, we do give a vocabulary to our eroticism, to our sensuality. From there to writing novels and poems, it's a very short step, Michael, a very short step.

MS: It's funny that you bring up an actor because one of the scariest stories in this book—scary because so depersonalized and so caught in an airless nimbus of manufactured space—is one called "Apollo and the Whores," in which an actor—who is, comically, the first American actor to win an Oscar for his performance in a foreign film—narrates from beyond the grave the evening that leads to his suicide, a sort of Billy Wilder situation. I sensed in this book a progression toward the posthuman, with Columbus being the final avatar of this world in which someone becomes a spokesperson for something he no longer represents. I also sensed that the actor in this story, in some peculiar way, is an evolution or heir of the narrator in the first story. He seems to be some reincarnated and still more fallen version of a lost translator.

CF: He says so. Vince Valera, the actor in the story, says so. He says he discovers two things when he dies. One is that the privilege of the dead is to read the minds of the living. So that he has died in this ecstasy of making love with seven women at the same time. What a way to go! He discovers as he goes from the little death, *la petite mort*, to the big death, that there is a privilege in dying in that you can read the minds of the living, so that these women he made cartoons of—the seven girls and their madam—he calls them Snow White and the seven dwarfs. He calls them Sneezy and Dopey and Doc. When he dies, he's able to see in their minds and see the deaths they have in their minds and realize what their real names are. They're not called Doc, she's called María de la Gracia. She's not called Sneezy, she's called Soledad.

As they see him dead, they think of a death, and he sees what deaths they are thinking of. In this way, he's able, he says, to individualize them, to de-Mexicanize them, to de-third-worldize them, to enter into their lives. The other privilege of death, he discovers as an actor, is that he is able, when he is buried under the orange tree—presumably planted by Cortés in the coast of Acapulco almost 500 years ago—that he is capable of acting out all the roles of the other novellas. That he can become the Roman general, Scipio. He can become Cortés. He can become the sons of Cortés. He can become Columbus. He says, "I can become this because it is a part of an incessant movement of conquest and counter-conquest and discovery and decadence and apogee acted out by the movement of peoples, the migrants, their hopes. The hopes for freedom, for justice of so many peoples." He is a part of that world. He is a Sephardic Jew expelled from Spain. It all comes together in that story, which I think is the key story.

MS: The pivot.

CF: It is the pivot because it holds everything together. You know, it's based on a real event and a real person.

MS: Tell me.

CF: The actor, Steve Cochran, who played secondary roles in many films. He was in *Wonder Man* with Danny Kaye. He was in *A Song Is Born*. He seemed to play second fiddle to Danny Kaye and lose the girl to him, if you could believe it. He was in *White Heat* with Jimmy Cagney. Always playing the role of secondary hoods. Then Antonioni gave him a great opportunity, a magnificent film called *Il Grido*. It's a black-and-white Antonioni film in which Cochran suddenly, for no reason at all, there is no explanation, leaves his wife, his home, everything he has, and only takes his little girl by the hand, the nine-year-old girl, and goes out into the fog and the humidity of the River Po and the Milanese countryside in the winter. He just has to leave, but he has to take something that he loves with him, and that is his little girl. It's a very moving, powerful, emotional film which Cochran made. Then his career declined. He went to Acapulco. He rented a yacht, took these girls with him. The yacht was found drifting in front of the coast of El Salvador five days later with Cochran dead on the ship. It's based on that incident.

MS: As a postmodern text, *The Orange Tree* seems to go very far in a direction that, at least for me, in your work, is begun by *Aura*, toward ghostliness and toward the experience of life seen retroactively as existential, but not lived existentially in the present moment. I know that this is a very cold world, a very cold vision. How does one return from it to a simpler human sense, or can one?

CF: Or can one? Indeed. I have a deep sense in my writing, and it is something I share very much with Milan Kundera, we've talked a lot about this and shared this view of the death, not of the novel but of the information a novel can give about living characters in order to make them believable, and present them with a whole set of identity cards, as it were, so that you will know exactly who David Copperfield is, or who Madame Bovary is. All the information is there. But this information becomes useless in a world where no one knows what their identity is. It becomes fake to give this kind of identity that was so abundant, so rich in a Balzac or Dickens or even Dostoevsky novel, to the modern man as imagined by Kafka and by Beckett. K, of course, for a very good reason, has only an initial. For a very good reason, Samsa wakes up one morning and finds out that he is a beetle. What do we do with a beetle? Do we squash the beetle? Do we trample it to death? Or do we look for a new construction of the human personality by what Novalis would call "the figure." He doesn't say it in that sense, but it's almost what Henry James is talking about, "The Figure in the Carpet." The discovery of this unsuspected shape.

MS: The internal pattern.

CF: Yes, and which I have practiced notably in *Terra Nostra*. I wanted very much to give the idea not of characters—because there are characters in *Terra Nostra* that are powerful like the king of Spain. There he is. He has a genealogy behind him and he has papers demonstrating who he is. But constantly his destiny is being decided by three young men thrown on a beach in the Cantabrian Sea and with no sign of identity except a purple cross between the shoulder blades. In this book also, I'm groping towards that idea of a figure that is a character discovered in the moment of his greatest weakness. A character discovered in the moment in which he or she is constituting themselves. This sometimes can be very spooky, or it can give a sense of death or of ghostliness. And yet, it is the moment of the inception of life, which must be ghostly, which must be, I'm sure, very, very proximate to death—the moment in which we are conceived or in which we conceive something in our minds. I would like to see in this book not the establishment of perfectly rounded, traditional, psychological social characters, but the searching, the groping for what I call figures. Cortázar called it figures, Kundera calls it figures. It is this groping of, if you wish to call it, the postmodernist world, or anyway, a world that refuses to believe with Beckett that I do not exist. The fact is self-evident, as he says in one of his plays.

MS: Yet it does give the feeling, these novels, not of the death of the novel, not of the death of the author, but of the death of the human figure. That the human figure is replaced by a series of resonances, impositions, corporations, structures, and the whole having the effect, as here, of a voiceover. Every Martin will have a second Martin to speak. There will be, finally, nothing but the dispersion of atoms. I guess, because others have had such bravura comic elements, this book seemed, like Nabokov's *Transparent Things*, to be the interpenetration of ghostlinesses, of ascending anonymities.

CF: It could be anonymity that is ascending towards a new kind of personality. I insist very much in this, that probably we could be witnessing the birth of something new. It is so proximate to the death of something old that we cannot very well distinguish the tomb from the womb, as it were, to use a Joycean expression. We are groping towards a new kind of consciousness, a new kind that has to take risks, besides. It has to take the risk of apocalypse, the risk of extermination because we have seen it in our times, because we know this is inscribed in history. That this possibility is not something made up in one's mind, that historical violence is a very real thing. When you can kill six million Jews in a few years in Europe, what we're talking about is very serious. This possibility of going from the realm of existence to the realm of nonexistence in history is something that can be very real. I'm not shying away from this possibility of anonymity, as you call it, or ghostliness, but which is also perhaps a rite of passage. It is also perhaps groping for something new, for something different. It is a refusal to stay with all the categories that have led us to some of the worst crimes and disasters in all the history of humankind.

2006: *The Eagle's Throne*

MS: Now, to talk about the classic books that Fuentes has written, including *The Death of Artemio Cruz*, *The Good Conscience*, *Aura*, *Distant Relations*, *Terra Nostra*, *The Old Gringo*, is to talk about some of the most significant literature of the century. The new book is, I would say, after *The Hydra Head*, the political novel, the novel about politics. Although it is written in letters among some twenty-five or so people, it is, I think, a vessel in which ideas—particularly satirical ideas about politics—can be expressed, anatomized. It's a consideration of what the political network means in life, in politics, in psychology, and in love. I wanted to ask you, first of all—is this a satire?

CF: It is, indeed. You hit the nail on the head. I had the purpose of writing a satire, an almost Swiftian satire, well knowing that there is little place for tenderness or love or other things that I associate with the novel but that satire excludes. It becomes very trenchant. It has to be very direct and even bitter at times. Not generous at all. It is not a generous book in any sense, because I don't think politicians, by and large, deserve any generosity. They deserve satire at the end of the road.

MS: Now, this book seems to learn much from Roman history. Perhaps because that is the empire whose decline and fall we know best, having been recorded by the best historians, and then later again by the best historians.

I wonder, though, do you see in the contemporary world an analog to the Roman Empire?

CF: Oh, absolutely. It's your own empire, of course. When I consider the declarations of people like Bush and Condoleezza Rice when they went to war against Iraq. Bush saying, "The United States is the only possibility of human happiness and democracy in the world." Condoleezza Rice saying, "You're with us or against us. We're in the good fight against evil." This good and evil, Manichaean thing that is sometimes the undoing of the United States. The great arrogance that was shown there is an imperial arrogance. Thankfully, you have a democracy, and nobody lasts more than four or eight years, so you can correct course. And I think you must. The great imperial arrogance I saw in this presidency is a harbinger of decadence. When you think you are so secure, so sure, you're masters of the world—you're losing the grasp of the world.

MS: Now, *The Eagle's Throne* is a book that takes place in the year 2020. In that year—shudder to think—Condoleezza Rice is the president of the United States, and Mexico is in a situation in which their president—some of these letter writers know that he is mortally ill. Others plan his displacement by less natural means, and they are, all of them, looking for one who will be the interim president after his death, and more importantly too, who will be elected in the new election year. They are, these characters, planning a good deal ahead in the history of their country. All of them seem to be aware that Mexican politics involves a mixture of sophisticated intrigue on the one hand and barbarity on the other, and that the successful intrigant will be capable of modulating sophistication and violence in an unusually dexterous way.

CF: The novel happens in 2020, and Condoleezza Rice is president of the United States. The novel—that should give us a hint—is an attempt at exorcism. But my experience as a writer shows me that exorcism turns into prophecy very quickly. If you try to get rid of something, you'll only forecast it, at the end. When I started writing this book, the PRI was in power in Mexico. The Party of Revolutionary Institutions that ruled Mexico for seventy-five years was the umbrella party of all the revolutionary factions of the Mexican Revolution. Founded in 1929, it ended in the year 2000—a long reign, in which the primal question was: Who is to succeed the incumbent? A very curious situation, Michael, because the president of Mexico was an all-powerful figure for six years. And then, he went home and nobody spoke about him again. He had the great power of choosing his successor, hand-picking his successor, who is immensely grateful to him until the day that successor *became* head of state, president, and then, immediately, he attacked the former president, he banished him from public life in the expectancy that the same thing would happen to him in six years.

Now that system is over. So I had a problem there. I can't invoke the PRI system anymore, so I projected the novel to a future where Mexico is a democracy, and the in-fighting amongst the cabinet, as happens here, is for the post of candidate of a party—but not, assuredly, of president of Mexico, as happened in the past. So it's even nastier. This is like *The West Wing* with a lot of venom. You have no saintly President Bartlet. Everybody is a Machiavellian schemer. It's almost a guidebook for internal politics, I think, of almost any nation. It's quite universal.

MS: In fact, it's modeled on *The Prince*, on Machiavelli—

CF: Absolutely.

MS: —that, finally, there is a sense that Rome gives way to other things Italian and that these instructions to the prince about how to manipulate power become the instructions of your central, may I say, woman of the letters, María del Rosario Galván. She has had many protégés. She finds politics itself so sexual that she can hold them off in their desire to join her in bed until they will realize that the "long" orgasm has been the manipulation of political power.

She has had many on her string. In fact, almost all the men in the book regard her as an intimate confidante. Therefore, of course, the surprises in the book come from the things that she does not know about herself; that this woman, who has ruled out the possibility of being surprised, is going to be surprised again and again as the book reaches its climax. Now, tell me, I guess Madame de Staël, to some extent, George Sand—has there ever been such a woman?

CF: Well, she's in the model for my book, Choderlos de Laclos's *Les Liaisons dangereuses*. I've thought a lot about—what's the name of the woman, Madame—

MS: Merteuil, yes.

CF: I thought a lot about her when thinking of María del Rosario, of course. The Choderlos character is basically a sexual manipulator, a manipulator of passions, whereas María del Rosario combines passion with politics. Therefore, it is the pitfall because she thinks she can manipulate passions, but passions outrun her. They outrun us all, is what I'm trying to say. We cannot govern our passions one hundred percent. That is the failing and probably the humanity of the character María del Rosario.

MS: It seems to me, though, that in *Les Liaisons dangereuses*, the central subject is the instruction of and the spoiling of innocence. Now, politics is a world from which innocence very quickly departs. We're talking about the manipulation of people who are, to their own knowledge, not innocent, and these characters are searching to make one another naïve. In other words, they are looking for the blind spot, always. They are, in a sense, modeling themselves fantastically on one another. In the second part of the novel, a whole new cast of characters spring up who are modeled on our first cast. There's another woman who has the exact same methods and strategies of instruction, and in fact the exact same protégé. She is trying to be a still better intriguer. She winds up at the bottom of the ocean. Tell me, how does one succeed in this world?

CF: In this case, as you very wisely point out, by imitation. By continuing the Machiavellian process of politics, by making it hereditary. There is in Mexico, particularly in Mexican politics, a strong sense of the hereditary. We were once called the hereditary revolutionary republic. The PRI inherited power from one president to another. We have been inheriting power in a process that goes back to the Aztec emperors, to Mocte-zuma. Cortés replaces Moctezuma, and he inherits the power of the Aztec emperor, the viceroys. We have seldom had a democratic experience in Mexico. It has been inheritance of power from one to the other. And that happens here in this novel. There is a democracy in Mexico, but the characters are quite oblivious to the fact that there is a civil society, and that there are the workings of democracy. They're working in a closed palatial situation. They're within the walls of the fortress, of the palace, and there they can do their intrigues. And once the open air hits them, then the intrigue is over. There is no possibility. They're open to democratic will, to democratic change.

So, it is my point in answering you, they must keep the customs of the realm. "This is the way power has worked, so why will it not work for me? Oh, I'm younger and coming up, instead of that old bitch who's now in power," et cetera. That is the reason. It's a very—how would I call it—a novel where air is missing. It becomes so closed in, in the intrigues and labyrinths of the palace, that you yearn for fresh air, which is what she does at the end from Chapultepec Park. She goes up to the park, to the castle, looks at the city, looks at the valley, and tries to recapture some of her breathing space, some of her humanity, and realizes she cannot. She has to go back to the drudge of politics.

MS: In this realm of imitation, we are also in a novel by Carlos Fuentes, which means, in turn, that the eternal return will be in play as well. Like *Aura*, the ghosts of the past—the mythologies of ancient gods, ancient sacrifices, ancient accommodations with the goddesses of the earth, of nature—are going to be at play, too. One feels, in unusual ways, that this novel, with all of its controlled human manipulations, is encased in the universal truths of eternal recurrence, yes?

CF: Yes, also in the sense that modern Mexicans would like to suppress part of our past, if they consider it barbaric or superstitious. They forget an essential fact about Mexicans. You can be the president of Mexico, you can be the richest businessman in Mexico, the most popular singer, the bestselling author, whatever you want, and you cannot compete with a million people going on their knees to the Basilica of Guadalupe every year. You cannot compete with the pervasive presence of a Christianity that is more than a religion, it is a sacrality. A harking back to the ancient gods, when everything was sacred, when the parrot was sacred, when the wind was sacred, when the cactus was sacred, everything was sacred for the Indian world. The Catholic religion brought all this together in the figure of the bleeding Christ and his suffering mother. And these became the symbols that united the dispersion of sacrality in the natural world.

It's something you cannot beat in Mexico. You can have anti-religious laws, you can have a civil society, whatever you wish, but finally, you have this extraordinary event of a million people going on their knees to see the Virgin of Guadalupe. When you ask Mexicans, "What do you believe in," the majority will say, "The Virgin of Guadalupe and nobody else," not the president, not a political party, not an artist, nobody. It is this extraordinary sense of the sacred that is one of the distinguishing traits of my country.

MS: In *The Eagle's Throne*, the character who appears to be the young prince being instructed by virtually everyone—

CF: Called Nicolás.

MS: —Nicolás, exactly. Discovering his lineage will be part of the concern of this novel. Sometimes he seems to be Mexican, sometimes he seems to be from Marseille. Sometimes he's of American parentage, but we discover, ultimately, that he's the son of a general who has had an affair with the cast-off daughter of an industrialist family. And as a result, he is, in fact, a relative of the woman at the center of the novel. It can be said that I am giving things away. On the other hand, I would prefer to open subjects. This novel seems to suggest that all of these factions are, at bottom, in fact, related.

CF: It's an incestuous affair, Michael. Politics is a very incestuous thing, and this novel is based on that. You think of the character, Nicolás, and you start thinking, "Well, he is far away from this reality we are talking about."

Marseille and Barcelona and the border with the United States, he seems to come from all parts of the world. He's a species unto himself of so many strains. And finally, it comes down—no, it's a family affair. It's really incestuous, over and over again.

MS: One of the reasons why these factions cannot disentangle is, in fact, they are related to one another as much as the nine evil sons are to the head of the cartel. And in fact, throughout the novel, everyone, no matter what they do, has to make a pact with one local lord or another. Everyone has to agree. We'll do, if you will, what we need to, but we won't disturb you. We'll be in the foreground, you will quietly drug deal in the background. And nothing, ultimately, will change the desperate realities of the state, except the names of the people in the slots in the cabinet.

CF: Right. This is true, and it is accentuated by the fact that the PRI ruled Mexico with a strong hand, and sort of kept local politics under its fist. People knew that they depended on the president of the republic for their post, for their money, for their businesses, for everything. Now, in a post-PRI Mexico, in which each entity of the federal republic that is Mexico achieves some kind of autonomy, you have a situation in Tabasco; a different one in San Luis Potosí; you have regional bosses, regional chieftains, as it were, of local tribes, that wrest power from Mexico City, from the president and his office. So there's much more intrigue going on, much more catering to the local bosses, the local chieftains. And therefore, the multiplicity of ambitions, the multiplicity of deals, the multiplicity of shady and shadier characters, is more abundant even than in the past. Is this the price of democracy? Maybe it is. You have to deal here with political bosses in Chicago and this and that daily. Democracy is a dirty business, in a way; at least, a messy business, huh? I think that in the future, Mexico will go through this process in which the central authority that has been there since Moctezuma and the Aztec emperors is going to dwindle away into multiple local authorities.

Which is what gives the novel its action, finally. I couldn't write a novel, like Asturias's *El Señor Presidente*, or García Márquez's *The Autumn of the Patriarch*, because that central figure here is deliberately disappearing. He is sick. He is dying. He is no longer *el señor presidente* with all the powers in the world. The powers are dispersed. Is this good? Is this bad? Is this democratic? Is that the price of democracy? Well, that's the question that hangs over the novel.

MS: It leads to, though, the profound question, not just of this novel, but of *the* novel. As I was reading, I realized that much, much, much of what I know about the world comes from reading fiction, *The Red and the Black*, *The Leopard*, di Lampedusa's great novel—

CF: *The Count of Monte Cristo*, in this case—

MS: *The Man in the Iron Mask*. What is the consequence of learning about the world from fiction?

CF: It is a great, great consequence that you learn about yourself as perhaps through no other medium—which is not disparaging music or painting or film or anything. No, it is that when you are reading a book, you're confronted with the copper of daily life, which is language, which is words. Suddenly, you realize that these words which you use every day to say hello, and to fight, or argue, or be kind, or make love, are not copper. They are gold. They become gold in the process of a narrative. Balzac or Stendhal were writing of no other thing, in a way, than the social and political situation of post-Napoleonic France. But they go beyond that. Tolstoy's *War and Peace* is not really about the Napoleonic invasion of Russia. It is about you and me, and about the things that you, Michael, or I, Carlos, do not know about one another.

The things we are finding out when we are reading a novel, say: "My God, this is myself. This is part of my life. This is who I am, and I didn't know it. I didn't realize it until this mirror was presented to me by Balzac or Charles Dickens or whoever." It's a way of completing the world that is so essential. It's not a frivolous matter; it is not a secondary matter. It is an essential matter to understand yourself—your total self, or your better self, or your more complete self—through the reading of a great novel.

MS: Finally, the book ends in the words of a speechless character, an autistic child now in his 30s or 40s. He is a figure who permanently has no voice. He's the child of the woman who is the central amorist intriguist, with her primary protégé. And they have abandoned this child, who is speaking—yearning—for the presence of visitors, who his memory dimly intuits. He no longer even has nurses taking care of him. He is an autistic, speaking into a void of feeling that will never be satisfied. What does he represent?

CF: Let me tell you a curious story. The origin of this novel in its present form was due to a dinner conversation at William Styron's house on Martha's Vineyard. García Márquez was there, with then-president Clinton, who talked about literature, asked us what our favorite novel was. Each one said, and I mentioned Faulkner. He went into this Faulknerian territory which he knows very well. He's a very good reader. He's a very cultivated man. Then there came a moment when he recited Benji's monologue from *The Sound and the Fury*. García Márquez and I were absolutely amazed that an American president could quote Faulkner at length. We went to Bill's—

MS: I'm amazed too. I have to say, and delighted, yes.

CF: —we went to the library, and read them. I said, "My God, he repeated it verbatim. He knows it by heart." Which is extraordinary. In that meeting, he asked me what I was writing, and I said, "I'm trying to write a political novel about the fact, you know, that Mexico has no vice president. So if the president dies in office, what happens?" I think that brought the novel into focus, and being with an American president who knew Faulkner led me to the end of the novel, because, of course, it's an homage to Faulkner, also. That last chapter recalls *The Sound and the Fury*, and the great admiration we have in Latin America for William Faulkner, who is probably our favorite American author. If it was true that Latin America began south of the Mason-Dixon Line, he's already a Latin American writer.

MS: But given that the book is, in some sense, symbolical as well, what is this autistic child?

CF: This autistic child is all that is not in the rest of the novel. All that is missing in the novel is there in the final chapter.

MS: So, it's that world that politics doesn't touch, can't speak about.

CF: Exactly.

MS: It's the voice of the voiceless. What, in other words, I guess, when we elect representatives, this finale is about what they don't represent.

CF: That's right. It is the voice of the voiceless. It is the voice that is missing from the public debate, from the cackle, and the sound and fury—precisely—of daily life and daily politics.

2011: *Destiny and Desire* (Part One)

MS: To talk to Carlos Fuentes is to speak with one of the most glorious and noble writers in the world. I'm not going to speak myself; I'm going to let the novelist and critic Paul West speak for me in this quote: "Carlos Fuentes is a man of parts with many roles. The versatility which is the hallmark of his excellence applies to him as a fiction-writer, too. There is Fuentes the discreet implier, concerned with special and not always definable states of mind as in *Aura* and *Distant Relations*. There is Fuentes the voluminous, wide-handed visionary, for whom nothing is too small, too big, to go into his homage to the planet, *Terra Nostra*. There is the severely moving Fuentes of *The Death of Artemio Cruz*, who masters the forlorn, the poignant, with impetuous vivacity. There is the Fuentes whose work in process happens to be narrated by a fetus…" And now, Michael Silverblatt speaking, there is the Fuentes of *Destiny and Desire*, a novel narrated by a severed head. In this way, the severed head is, well, a fortune teller. Magicians worked with brazen heads who told the truth, but also we're dealing with the assassinations in Mexico, where, as in this novel, the severed head says that he's the thousandth this month, the first in the last three and a half hours. He's floating in the Pacific, telling us his story before he drowns. And what is he foretelling?

CF: This severed head is not severed by crime but by ambition. He is severed by a woman who wants to get all the heirs of the millionaire, Max Monroy, out of the way, so as to be the sole heiress: one of the oldest stories in the world. That is why he dies. Not part of organized crime, although she uses criminals—it is part of organized ambition, and what drives her to eliminate all the people who would come between her and the great fortune of Max Monroy. Max Monroy has one of his sons in jail, the other two he ignores. He visits his wife, who's a madwoman in the lunatic asylum, et cetera.

MS: In other words, it's a Fuentes novel. [*laughter*]

CF: Of course, it is. Very good, Michael. Very good. There you are. [*laughter*]

MS: I would say the best of many. It's my favorite. I've read them all in these recent years. In particular, it's my favorite because it describes a condition that obtains in the modern world, in which both government and business are turning to crime. That crime becomes the face that government and business present to the world. This seems to be a tragedy, not only of literature but of—

CF: It's the tragedy of a world that is ending, Michael. I think the world we are living in is coming to an end. We don't know what will follow, but something is coming.

MS: In this book, *Destiny and Desire*, there are two friends, nearly brothers, who go to work, one in government, one in business, both of them guided by boundless ambition. One capable of being instructed. He's taught Spinoza, he's taught moderation by an early teacher. The other, really the government, the politician, much more darkly corrupt. The book wants to say, ultimately, the sky meets the sea. Oppositions are one—are these two men, this Cain and Abel, are they in fact the same?

CF: They're not the same. They are part of the same world. They're a divided self, if you wish, but they're the oldest story of the world. They're Cain and Abel, you've just said it. One usually goes to the Bible or a Greek tragedy and epic to find the models for modern writing. I went to Cain and Abel because there was a basic wrenching of the soul there, a separation of brotherhood, separation of the first family of all. They go in different paths. One kills the other. He is an intermediary for the death of Abel, is Cain, but the destiny of Cain is no better than that of Abel, finally. Yes, you're right. It's an old fable in a modern setting, and it is told by a man whose head is floating in the sea, but it says, "Wait a moment, I still have something to tell you." That tale takes 500 pages: quite a head, quite a tongue, quite a memory, because it's his last chance. If he doesn't talk then he'll never talk again; he'll be washed away and forgotten completely. He's already separated from his body.

MS: Now, Carlos, this book seems to work through a series of camouflages, of red herrings, because although these brothers are Cain and Abel, their names in English would be Joshua and Jericho. They wear disguises, and disguises are essential to this novel, in which—true to the tradition of the novel—everyone is ultimately related, just as we are all children of Adam and Eve.

CF: Well, it's a human comedy. It's Balzac. It's the same way the characters reappear and all of them keep coming up. You can't separate them from the totality of the human comedy. I am very Balzacian in nature. When I read Balzac at twenty-one in Paris, I discovered a world. I've tried to keep close to the Balzacian spirit of telling the same novel with different titles, but it's only one novel and characters reappear. Now some characters of past novels reappear in this one. Basically, it's a novel that does inhabit a scenery—contemporary Mexico, the Mexico of today—but always with this mythological bottom of the sea, which is strangely common to all men, belongs to us all. Then you surface, and there are differences, but basically we have a few well-worn myths. They serve us well. We repeat them. They're part of our soul.

MS: In other words, in our depths, we have this myth that binds us. It's only on the surface that our story changes.

CF: The surfaces change a lot, but the deepest pit of the ocean is common to us all.

MS: Not only are there stories that recur, every story in the world circulates so that the story of Adam and Eve begins in Sumer. All of our stories are global.

CF: They're all global. That is what we have taken some time to discover. I feel that the American readership and critics have more or less cut themselves off from what is happening in the rest of the world. It was not so when I started publishing with Farrar, Straus. You published Celan, Mauriac, and Moravia: a lot of foreign writers. This is less so today, and I'm afraid of that. It worries me that there should be this reduced relationship of one of the principal world literatures, which is there in the United States, with the rest of the world. We should try to reconnect through people like you, Michael. I think it's a duty to reconnect the United States with the literature of the world.

MS: *Destiny and Desire* is set in Mexico City. Mexico City is, after all, one of the world's centers of culture. Mexico has a vast culture. The novel is there to show us how many forms, and at how many places, the culture joins the global ocean.

CF: You know, Mexico is one of the oldest cultures, or *the* oldest culture in the Americas, the oldest surviving culture. The oldest city of the Americas, in that sense, is Mexico City: Tenochtitlan, the Aztec city, which was a great metropolis of more than 300,000 people in 1519 when the Spaniards, when Hernan Cortés, arrived. So it has this vast memory of a huge past, which goes on developing. It is the space, the locale of the novel—in the same way that Dublin is the locale for Joyce, or Paris is the locale for Balzac—but it's only part of the story. What comes after the location of the story is what is really interesting. I'm not writing a tourist guide of

Mexico City. Balzac is not writing a tourist guide of Paris. We're doing a basic space, a settlement which every writer needs. Unless you do science fiction, you need a real city, real place, real people, and then you go off and tell a story in literary terms. You forget where you are in a way and you start developing what is not there, which is the story and the characters.

MS: What I love in a Fuentes novel is that there will be characters of action, but, as well, there are philosophers who narrate what it is to think about the subject of the novel you're reading. There are writers as well. One of these characters sits in the courtyard, typing love letters for those without Spanish. Now, let's bear in mind, around twenty percent of the population of Mexico does not speak Spanish. How do they read your work? How do they discover your work?

CF: They don't. Literature in Mexico is read by a minority. A book of mine, if it sells 50,000 copies, is a huge success. There are a few cases, like García Márquez, who can sell hundreds of thousands of books. But a book like *Destiny and Desire* has sold about 50,000 copies in Mexico—it's a huge success, but no more than that. Let's say that each book is bought by one person and read by four, optimistically. That'll give you 200,000 people in a population of 110 million. So it's a small readership, but it tends to filter down and affect people in other indirect ways. Which is the marvel of literature, that the act of a minority—a book, a novel—should finally filter down into the sensibility of the majority. Which is what happens with great novels, or interesting novels.

In any case, that is my case. I feel that I would write anyway for one reader. I don't care. It is the joy of writing that really impels me to write. I have a great joy of sitting every morning and writing the book. Then, if it is published and if I get one reader, it would be enough. If it gets 50,000 readers multiplied by four, that's wonderful. It filters down in ways I never suspect to persons I never knew existed that come up to me and say, "Your character so and so," or, "You said so and so." How did it get there? It is a mystery. I think every writer knows that and is not satisfied with the statistics of a novel but with the influence of the novel. There are books that are not read in their lifetime. Stendhal comes to mind as a great example of a writer who was not read for almost one hundred years. After his death, Henri Martineau rediscovered Stendhal in the 1920s. He came back to life as a classic. That happens, you know.

MS: But how do we feel sure that what today may be an elite will be the future of the literary? Can we be sure?

CF: We don't know. We have to work out of darkness and ignorance, doing what we feel we must do, what we're sure we must do, even if we have no readers at the moment—maybe someday we will, maybe someday we won't. But that is not the question. The question is the great joy of writing, of creativity, and of addressing yourself to an audience you don't know. Finally, I get to see—thanks to you and coming to California and giving lectures—some of the faces of an audience that otherwise I would not know. I know it's there, and I write because they are there, even if I don't know them. There's a give-and-take between the unknown and the writer, which is very mysterious and very good for writing.

MS: Tell me, in this book, *Destiny and Desire*, the women characters seem extraordinary to me. In particular, two. A mother who speaks from beyond the grave and is a kind of prophet. She is a very powerful mother. And another powerful woman, who is the mistress of the head of business. She is the one who is darkly exterminating her rivals because she wants to inherit everything. She's a kind of Lilith figure but very pragmatic. Why these extraordinary women?

CF: I think Mexico is a country of extraordinary women—I know a lot of them—because it is a country that has the seal of machismo. Mexico is supposed to be a country where the values of the man are superior to those of the woman. Therefore, we have extraordinary women because they have to fight against the commonplace—Mexico is a macho country. You know the actress Maria Félix represented that role. She was there to be a central figure of a woman, like Barbara Stanwyck in your movies. Whatever happens, she is the mistress of the movie, even if she's subjected to men. In the final film she made, she is a cowgirl, an old cowgirl. She's still the central figure. She dominates the figure. That comes from cultures that are very male-oriented. You have to have women who oppose that and who affirm themselves more than they would in a country like France or England, let's say.

MS: *Destiny and Desire*—a novel set in Mexico City, in which all of mythology and philosophy, everything available, takes place. Now, in this Mexico City, the presiding philosopher is Machiavelli. Can you tell me why?

CF: I think he's the presiding philosopher of the world. I compare the three great thinkers who make their appearance almost at the same time, with fifteen years difference: you have Thomas More's *Utopia*, Erasmus and *In Praise of Folly*, and Machiavelli and *The Prince*. Now, who is actually present in the politics of the world? It is Machiavelli. You can have desire to have a utopia as More's, or you can sit back and be ironical as Erasmus does in *In Praise of Folly*, but in practical life, it is the triumph of Machiavelli. Machiavelli runs the world from his Florentine grave. As I put him here, he says, "What the hell? I'm always presented as a political philosopher. I loved women, I loved song, I loved disguises, I loved men. I loved the humanity of the world and not only the mind of the world." Yet he always is accepted for us as the great political philosopher.

MS: Yet, you see, Machiavelli, read in every humanities course worldwide, has become the prophet of the global yearning, politically, for the expedient. In *Destiny and Desire* he is, unfortunately, the reality of what is being presented as Mexican business and Mexican politics today. Here we have the worst—as, for many people, the sexual guide is Sade. You've had to write a book in which the worst prevails. What is that like for the writer?

CF: Well, first, there are no happy novels. Happy-ending novels are very rare. One would be probably *The Idiot*, and the others would be *Don Quixote* and *The Pickwick Papers*—I can think of no other. Generally, novels are to remind people that things turn out badly. This country we're in, your country, the United States of America, which has been the land of opportunity, freedom, and the pursuit of happiness, is also a land where you can't find almost a single positive writer. They're all very negative, from Poe right down to Jonathan Franzen. They're all saying this is terrible. We live in a terrible world. I think it's only probably Mark Twain who loves the Mississippi and all that. The rest are extremely critical writers.

MS: Mark Twain knows we live in a terrible world. From beyond the grave, he has his devils warning us about what we're making.

CF: Took one hundred years.

MS: Yes. Before we allowed it to be published, yes. Literature is about how things go wrong. How does a writer who is, as you've said, the bird that bears bad news, the little bird that has a dark truth, how does the writer live in possession of this knowledge?

CF: He writes the book, there's no other way. You can't be as pessimistic in real life as you are in a book, you concentrate that. Dostoevsky was an example of a man who was almost as difficult as his books, the sense of unhappiness. But generally, you know, Tolstoy was a great patriarch, and even Balzac had a great jolly time eating and drinking. You concentrate what you feel that is not being said, Michael. The things that are not being said by your society is what you put into a novel. The novel is the other face, the other coin of a society that loves to praise itself, to say how wonderful I am. I remember my wife was once interviewing Carlos Andrés Pérez, the former president of Venezuela. And she asked him, "What do you think of this guide for political leaders, which is Machiavelli's *The Prince*?" He said, "I don't read *The Prince*, I read *The Little Prince*, which is a better guide."

MS: Don't we need both? Carlos, you wake up in the morning and you write. Having made notes the night before, the dreams you have influence your notes, and you write them down so that the books are widely known, as in the quote by Paul West, for taking many strange and remarkable turns, and for containing multitudes: multitudes of thought, multitudes of dreams, of parodies, of genres. Do you ultimately know what the novel you've completed is?

CF: Of course not. First, I know what I want to write in the evening. I go to sleep, I get up, and I write something that is what I thought, but something new at the same time, something I had not thought of, comes from dreams or madness or inherited—I don't know what. But it appears there, and I write. I'll say, "I had never thought of this. Where did it come from?" It's very mysterious. Then you die and you leave a book that will be subject to interpretation. In life itself, I always let the reader have the last word. These are open books; the final pages are open to the reader for him to continue the novel. I can't write without knowing that there's a reader who will continue the book, who will not end the book, but continue it and pass it on to another and another and another. That is for me the great satisfaction and beauty of writing.

MS: Now, sometimes your novels—I'll follow them—and it will take the third reading before I understand, because—

CF: And you're Michael!

MS: I'm Michael, yes. I'm fascinated. I loved *Distant Relations*. That was a book in which surrealism was claimed for Spanish literature, not for French literature. And by the end, there is a surrealist phantasmagoria, as there is in *Destiny and Desire*—where what we feel we know, the solid ground, leaves from beneath us, and we have to subject ourselves to a kind of visionary condition that the novel brings without interpreting for us. I'm very interested in this.

CF: Well, you're the destiny and the desire of the novel. [*laughter*] This is what I attempt to do. The novel is in your hands and your imagination, and your puzzle, in your dreams. It does not belong to me anymore. I seldom reread myself—sometimes I have to for the purposes of translation; I don't like it. I leave a book and say, "Now it does not belong to me, it belongs to the readers of the book." They make what they want of it. This has to do with what you just said. I cannot work otherwise than by giving you, the reader, you, Michael, that freedom.

MS: Yes, but how do you surrender Carlos? Carlos has his ideas. It seems as if the books enter a phase where they're not being guided.

CF: Yes, I forget the novel is a work of freedom. Because, contrary to what happens in private or public life—especially in public life—everybody has a right to say what he has to say or what she has to say. This, for me, is very important. I am not in favor of this or that character. I'm not blaming any character for what he or she says. You mentioned Asunta Jordán: I don't agree with her as much as I do with the other forlorn young woman, Lucha Zapata, in the book. But I'm letting them both have their say. They're both going to say what they have to say and tell us who they are. There's no other way of writing novels. You have to accept the reasons of your enemy—even in a novel—of those who don't think like you. You can blame them in a newspaper op-ed piece, but you cannot in a novel. The novel is a moral place, in the sense that it permits everyone to have his say or her say. It does permit it. We do hear it in a way that we know is not the personal thinking of Dostoevsky, or Tolstoy, or William Faulkner.

MS: Thank you, Carlos, for joining me.

CF: Great to be with you always, Michael. Whether it be in the high mountains of the Sierras or on the coast, always a pleasure.

2011: *Destiny and Desire* (Part Two)

MS: Often in Latin America, the great political and cultural thinkers aren't journalists, they're novelists. Carlos Fuentes, whose work is required reading in Mexico's schools, is that kind of novelist. Last week, we discussed his most recent work, *Destiny and Desire*. Today, we focus on what drives culture in general, and, in particular, where it's headed in Mexico, a country that finds itself in turbulent times. Now, Carlos, you have taken as your central place Mexico City, much as Joyce took Dublin, much as Balzac took Paris. Take me to Mexico: What is the state of culture that you perceive?

CF: Mexico—and, I would generalize, Latin America—has a thriving culture, a continuity of culture, in comparison with a dearth of politics and economics. The political life is way, way, way behind the cultural life of the country. Mexico has had an uninterrupted culture since the time of the Nahuatl, or Aztec, regime, before the conquest. Then they became a Spanish colony, an independent country, and the culture has had no breaks.

There've been a lot of political breaks in Mexico, there've been revolutions, there've been disasters; all kinds of things have interrupted the political and economic life, but nothing has been able to interrupt the cultural life. I could say this of the rest of Latin America as well. That is our greatest strength. Our greatest challenge is to bring the political life to the level of the cultural life. I know it's very difficult, but it's a challenge we have: Why do we have such a great culture and such mediocre politics?

MS: Now, I'm curious. In Mexico, there are great traditions of the high arts, the *bellas artes*, as well as the folkloric arts. Where and how do they meet? Do they meet?

CF: Yes, they meet constantly, because there is a continuum in which the so-called popular culture meets the higher culture. We have a great bolero writer, Agustín Lara, who is hummed all over the world, and even when people don't know their names, they're humming Agustín Lara tunes. And these tunes are set to a language that derives from the Symbolist poets of the turn of the century, poets nobody reads anymore like Luis Urbina and Amado Nervo. They're at the back of the bolero and the other musical forms that are so popular. So there was a communication between the cultures, which gave a lot from the so-called popular culture to the culture of the elites. Then it comes back also. What is written by the elites is turned back to the culture of the masses that start saying things and repeating things that were really created at the most elite level of the culture. This means that there is a livelihood to the culture, a continuity of the culture that would not be there if you didn't have the two factors intermingling.

MS: Yes. I notice that in *The Mandarin* and the remarkable works of Borges, he's also gifted about telling us about the tango and about the gangster traditions of Buenos Aires, that in South America and Latin America, hand-in-hand, the high and the low, need to consider one another. It seems to me that García Márquez is one of the great instances of the joining of local folklore with the highest mechanics, architecture of what the novel is capable.

CF: I think that's right. I think you could say that of almost any great writer. I think that we'll be mentioning Balzac, we'll be mentioning Faulkner. In Faulkner the whole culture of the South is there, the idiom of the South, the rhythms of the South are there, with what Allen Tate called Dixie Gongorism—a very high sense of literature that comes from Góngora. Who reads Góngora in this world except for a few crazy Latin Americans and Spaniards? So to have a Dixie Gongorism—which is, at the same time, deeply rooted in the plantations, the slave culture, the Black culture, the property culture, the culture of power and dominion in the southern United States—gives you novels like *Absalom, Absalom!* and *The Sound and the Fury.*

MS: Well, I've been talking to a Spanish-speaking novelist, born in Mexico, living in Texas, who tells me that now we will have the novel of the drug culture and the music of the drug culture as well—but there will still be a culture that we endlessly generate, one another, the high and the low.

CF: Yes. I think that is absolutely true, that we're constantly affecting each other, from the low to the middle to the high and back. It's a round trip. That is why culture is vital: because it does not exclude, it includes. Even the worst features of society are presented in a culture. I don't think that culture shies away from any manifestation, any aspect of itself, finally, because it is itself.

MS: Carlos, do you expect a return of the high, at any time, of the high culture?

CF: I think it's there. I think that when I was a young man in your country, opera was a thing of fun. The Marx brothers at the opera—people made fun of the opera. Today, I go to the Met in New York and it's revered. It's an experience shared by millions of people, now also in television. We get the productions of the Met in high-definition screens in Mexico, and thousands of people go to the national auditorium, which holds more than 12,000 people, to hear the representations of the Met.

   This means that high culture and low culture are difficult distinctions, because when opera—which used to be the very definition of "high"—becomes a part of the popular culture of a great mass of people, then how do you define it as high culture only? Mozart and Verdi, only for a few? Of course not. More and more people enter the realm of the opera as more and more people enter the realm of the arts, of literature as well. Even if literature is more difficult because it is written, and you need a book, and you're not passive. In literature, you must be very active. You see the film, theater, music, and the arts gaining public, not losing it.

MS: Do you think that there will be a point at which education returns the standards of literacy so that the novel has a rebirth?

CF: Yes, I think so. I think that education is the basis of everything. We are leaving many people outside the realm of education, and therefore out of the realm of the arts, out of the realm of reading, and seeing, and hearing, and arts in general. Let's look at the state of education in order to understand the state of culture and the state of a society.

MS: Now, give me a picture. A young person in Mexico, let's say Mexico City. When does he enter school, and what is the state of public education?

CF: Today we're 110 million. To bring education to all of these, it does reach a certain level. But listen, I go to Veracruz, which is my home state, and I see that kids have to go to school mounted on a donkey for a two-hour ride to school and a two-hour ride back to their homes. You have buses that teach people—they go from town to town—but only children and women attend—men do not—their basic teachings. This is a great challenge of our societies, because if we don't have education, we'll have nothing else.

MS: When I was in Paris, I discovered—to my surprise and delight—that young people were not particularly interested in Rimbaud. They said, "We learned him by heart in school. We're sick of Rimbaud." Who are the writers and poets in Mexico who a schoolchild would know?

CF: Very few of the ones that are in the curriculum. I have the fortune of being in the curriculum, so is Octavio Paz, Juan Rulfo, and a few older poets and writers, novelists. But not very many. If you're in the curriculum, you keep up your readership. It's a blessing.

MS: Which book of yours is most commonly read?

CF: I think *Aura*, because *Aura*, which is a ghost story, was banned by the minister of labor and the preceding government of Vicente Fox. He said that children, young people, should not read *Aura*—it was an immoral book, and the young woman who taught it was thrown out of her school, and my sales skyrocketed to 20,000 copies a week. So I said, "Should I give thanks to the minister?" But the question I asked was, "Why is the book being censored by the Catholics?" He said, "Because the couple makes love under crucifixes." I said, "But all Mexicans make love under crucifixes. What's the novelty in this?" [*laughter*]

MS: Now tell me, the Calderón government: Where do they stand on literature and the arts?

CF: I think they're sympathetic to it; it's just a center-right government. They wouldn't dare be against literature. They had a very meager celebration of the bicentennial of Mexican independence last September. The dictator, Porfirio Díaz, inaugurated monuments, books, anything. He did a grand celebration. The Calderón government made a very meager celebration, very small celebration of the bicentennial, which will now be a tricentennial a hundred years from now. But in the meantime, it showed us that Mexico is a country with so many problems, and the solutions—that would be good in Switzerland, mind you, in a country of that kind, well, okay, yes—but in a country like Mexico, you have to renew the policies in order to bring more and more people into education, into work, into health. You have to do a great job of this—really a crusade—and there are Mexicans aged thirty or less than thirty, who are going to expect this opportunity, who might go into crime. They are the *ninis*.

MS: What are *ninis*?

CF: They're neither—how do you say it in English? *Ni trabajo, ni educación.*

MS: Neither educated nor having jobs.

CF: They lack both. And what happens to them is what happens to the country. If they go on being *ninis*, or if they go to the drug bands, it's one thing. If we offer them a Mexican New Deal, to modernize the country, to build all that has not been built in the last thirty or forty years—ports, highways, health, education, et cetera, et cetera, the whole thing the New Deal did in this country, which is a revolution without blood being spilt, which is what I would like for my country—that the *ninis* would become a force for change in Mexico, and a change that is long overdue.

MS: You have, people estimate, between seven and eight million *ninis*.

CF: In two years, we have a renewal of powers, executive and legislative, and I think that we're going to have surprises. Right now, the three parties, the three major parties—left, center, and right—are fractured. They do not have majorities. But I think that eventually, if we're going to solve these problems, we're going to have to face a national movement for the solution of these problems. It might happen because of the elections in two years' time. It will start perhaps breeding right now. What shape it will take, how many people it will concern, is a mystery, of course. I'm not a reader of the future, but I think that it is in the cards in the country as it was in

1910. Violently in 1910. I think 2011, 2012, it should be peaceful, which is to have people say, "Hey, you're not doing enough for education. You're not doing enough for health. You're not doing enough for all of the things that matter in our life, but you think you're doing okay." You're doing okay if this were Switzerland, but it's Mexico, and it's Colombia, and it's Peru, and it's Bolivia, and it's Chile, and we have to do something more. And that is going to be a great jump. I hope it takes place peacefully, but there's going to be a surge of the younger people of Mexico to say, "Hey, we have this catalog of problems, let us hurry up and solve them. If not, we're going to go down and it's going to be dreadful." I think the government is not quite aware of this. I think the business class is not quite aware. I am sure that the cooperative system, the unions in Mexico, are not aware. They all have a mindset that comes from fifty years of so-called institutionalized revolution, which is very hard to change. But it must change if it's going to accept the new realities of the growing population of Mexico.

MS: How do you think the presence of narco violence will affect efforts like a New Deal or a new political amalgamation?

CF: The narco system in Mexico is really strange, because it's not evident. We know it's there. We know the damage it causes. It is not the totality of the country, of its economy, of its society. No way. It is part of it, and it's not visible. I have a couple of friends, intellectuals, Héctor Aguilar Camín and Jorge Castañeda, who do trips through all the states of Mexico. They give lectures everywhere. They're not bothered by any narco drug dealers or anybody. They don't even see them, because the magic of the drug dealer—if we call them that way—is that they're no different from you and me. They don't wear uniforms, they don't have badges. They look like civilians. So they hide in society very, very well. They fight amongst themselves and sometimes they fight the government, they fight the army. There are lots of dead people. But it's a very curious phenomenon. Who's the actual enemy—we do not know yet. What am I come to? We don't know. Whether for good or evil—we don't know where the future of this system will be. Because, Michael, this is a problem we share with the United States of America. And as long as there is no understanding that the problem will not be solved unless the United States accepts its responsibility in being the country of the demand of drugs. Drugs are produced and exported because American consumers want them. Who are these consumers? How will the drugs get to them? And besides, where do we get the arms? The drug dealers, where do they get the arms? They buy them from the United States. So there is a complicity here, and there is a common responsibility for both governments to attack this problem, which is not only a bilateral problem of Mexico and the United States. It's a worldwide problem.

I have joined a group—which is headed by former presidents Cardoso of Brazil, Gaviria of Colombia, and Zedillo of Mexico—in which we are saying, "Hey, the present policy has failed. Let us find further avenues to deal with this problem. Let us separate drug users—those who are criminals from those who are not. Don't send drug users who are not criminals to jail, send them to a hospital. And start thinking of legalizing drugs, of legitimizing the use of certain drugs. Let's have a whole new developing policy." This is the most we can do at this moment. I think it's a good thing.

MS: Now, that's the most we can do as humans. As a visionary novelist, would you tell me something of a story that will help me think about the border between Mexico and the United States? Not as a citizen, not as a former dignitary, as a visionary novelist.

CF: There is a new culture of being born in the border between the United States and Mexico. I would call it Mex-America. It partakes of both cultures, both countries. And there's a great influence of the United States and Mexico. It suffices to walk down any avenue to see the ads, American products. Very few Mexicans speak English, very few. We keep our traditions very much alive—culinary, love, ways of thinking, acting, speaking. We're very much in our mestizo traditions, Spanish and Indian, not that affected by American culture; whereas, I think, the Mexican presence in this country is very prominent and very much unto itself.

There is this secret consciousness in many of my compatriots in the

United States—they're in California, they're in Arizona, they're in New Mexico, they're in Texas—that, "This used to be our land, and it is no longer." Nobody says it out loud. It's a fact, but it's secondary. The fact is that all these people that are coming from Spanish-speaking America to the United States, they have to integrate into the United States. There has to be a policy in this country of yours that admits the diversity of these people. And the very interesting fact they're not coming across the ocean, like former immigrants used to—they are coming across our land border—that makes all the difference. How you integrate them into the culture is very important. Many have integrated. I know many people of Mexican descent in all the border states who are Americans—one hundred percent Americans, even in the worst sense of the word. But there should be a policy of integration with a humanitarian sense, with a humane sense that they're not a strange species, and that they do have very, very important relationships with their home country. I think the Poles, and the Italians, and the Germans did also in the past, yet they finally integrated into the great American society.

MS: Now, I want to ask a final question, and it does join geopolitics with literature. France, so dominant in the culture of the novel for so long, is now barely spoken of. They don't have a vital community of novelists who are doing accessible work. There is the art novel, and then there is the popular novel. Never the twain shall meet—and, it's over, in a sense. Now, in Mexico, I keep being exposed to a very vital, young writing community, both in the novel and culture. And certainly, Spanish became a dominant language and culture because of Neruda—before, Lorca, later, García Márquez, Carlos Fuentes, Jorge Luis Borges, Vargas Llosa won the Pulitzer Prize—and it seems to me that Spanish is part of living world culture. It's not like when I first went to college, speaking Spanish, and was told by the people that, no, no, no, Spanish was the language—if you were going to business, if you were going into the fashion dress business in New York, it would be helpful to speak Spanish. But now Spanish is the culture, and *Don Quixote* is the fount of the novel. Where does the future of the Mexican novel take us? What do you predict?

CF: Well, the Mexican novel—let me say, first of all—is part of the novel of the Spanish language. It is a novel that goes along with what is written in Chile, and Colombia, and Argentina, and Spain. So we have a community of Spanish-language writers, we have a community of Spanish-speaking peoples. We do not have an economic community, a political community, but at least you know when our heads of state meet, there are twenty heads of state who can understand each other in the same language. And when I meet a writer from Paraguay or Uruguay, I can understand him or her very well, and he or she, me. We have a community of language which is even more pronounced than in the Anglo-speaking world, where there are so many differences between what is spoken in Black African countries, or a country in the Pacific, Australia, New Zealand, or England, and the United States. As Bernard Shaw once said, the United States and England are two nations separated by a common language. It's a huge difference between the two cultures. We don't have that. We are very united in the sense of the language and the cultures. Then come the politics and the economics, and we're diverse. But at least we have that strength of identity given to us by the Spanish language, which was refused as a language of communication. When I was a young man in your country, and I asked people to speak in Spanish, they would refuse to. It would brand them as aliens, people who are not integrated into the United States. Now, a candidate for the presidency has to speak Spanish to get votes. It's a totally different picture from what happened twenty or thirty years ago. And it's all to the good because finally we are going towards a world community.

I think President Obama is doing very good in speaking, for the first time, of the globalization of work, which is a thing that affects us very much, because you have the globalization of finance—money travels easily, trade travels easily, but work does not. Work is impeded; work is subject to humiliations, to borders. Obama, when he speaks of the globalization of work, he is telling us what we like to hear in Mexico. So we're heading towards a full globalization in which everybody will contribute his or her culture, but no culture will be predominant, though the English language is very predominant as a way of communication, though the Spanish culture is very predominant as a way of feeling and expression. This won't matter because, after all, we will live together or we won't live at all. That is the question today. How can we live together? And what is the other option? It is not living differently—it is not living, period.

MS: And the novel.

CF: The novel is going to experience what cannot be said in any other way.

MS: Continue to express what cannot be said.

CF: Yes. What you can say in journalism, what you can say in movies or even in theater, philosophy, essays, is wonderful. But then there is what the novel can say, which is the contradiction of languages, the coexistence of diverse languages in one work. The possibility of having fiction, characters, plot, journalism, economy, philosophy—everything comes together in a great novel, as *Ulysses* proves. If we do away with that, we will be mutilating ourselves. We will have one less arm and maybe we'll lose both.

William H. Gass

1995: *The Tunnel*

MS: Today my guest is William H. Gass, the author of *The Tunnel*. This is a 653-page book composed over a period of thirty years. It's been being written since I was eight years old, and I feel like I've been reading it since virtually then.

But what I wanted to talk about is its structure. The narrator of this book, William Kohler, is a professor of history. He has studied modern Germany and sees in the rise of the Reich a model that is replicated in the arguments he's been having with his wife and his family, and he comes to understand what is referred to in the novel as the fascism of the heart. The book is a kind of domestic epic, and what we see in small is a kind of symbolic replication of the multiplication of angry cells, in a way.

How does one go about structuring such a book? The first thing, I know, is that once it used to be called *The Tunnel in 12 Philippics*.

WG: I took out the *Philippics* as being too pointed. Yeah. The book is trying to be a number of things, but one thing it's trying to be, and one of the reasons it's called *The Tunnel*, is the inside of history. I chose a historian who is just finishing a standard, objective kind of narration with the kind of expectation you get in history, where the arrangement of the narrative of events will be explanatory. When you come away from that text, you will presumably understand what went on and why in historical events.

Usually the things that get left out of history are the very things that tend to undermine it. Among other things, the first thing is the historian, himself: *his* nature, or *her* nature, and the kind of aims, ambitions, frustrations and problems he or she has. My metaphor for that was to have him hide the pages of this book between the pages of the objective history. But that's to symbolize the fact that inside those objective events are the private events. The objective things that are accounted for by historians do not account for the inner life, on the whole.

We have to remember also that while we're talking about the grand things, and historians love wars and changes of political regime and things of this sort, but even mass murderers have home lives. It's true that some people have blamed the German home family relationship, or the patriarchal father, et cetera, for the behavior of the people in the Third Reich. What I'm trying to do is not only reduce history to localism, particularly domestic, but also to put it inside the head where I think it belongs, anyway. Because really what counts in history, for me, is what happens to human consciousness and not just what happens, the piles of bodies. It's what was lost when you piled up bodies, what is gained when you decide not to.

MS: I wanted to discuss this tunnel, which as you suggest is the inside of a mind. But because the inside of the mind has its wrinkled passages, it too is replicated in the bowel. We've got in this book a tunnel under the house, a tunnel inside the head, and a digestive tunnel—

WG: That's right.

MS: —that's processing.

WG: Every tunnel, you've got that.

MS: As a result, everything is happening, every world: in the world, in the mind, and in the body.

WG: Yes. In other activities as well. That is, tunnels are not always escape tunnels or hiding tunnels. Sometimes you dig for ore. You dig for gold. Some of what presumably you might come out with is something rare and valuable as well. You have to add on all these different levels in the construction.

MS: What I'm trying to suggest is that in this book, at least structurally, metaphors—the head, heart, and bowel are tunnels—become superimposed, in a sense, on one another so that certain scenes of this book take place in three places at once.

WG: That's right. Yes. In quite a number of places, and this made the writing difficult in the way that you had to touch bases. It's unlike having what's called a conceit, an extended metaphor, which then grows and develops and has its sort of suburbs. You have to constantly be in touch with all of the elements of the image at one time, as it gets increasingly complex.

MS: The amazed reader of *The Tunnel* is going to find immediately fairly unusual things. There is on its title page a model of this tunnel itself. In other words, there's a structural model both of the plot of the book as well as the prose of the book and the shape of the book. The first thing that we notice is that there are three attempts to start the tunnel. *The Tunnel* begins with the attempt of the narrator to dig into earth. I guess it's too hard to be penetrated. The opening chapter is a starting over and over again and reaching impediment.

WG: Yes. Again, as in everything here, functioning in several ways. There are repeated attempts to get started and then finally the section that begins, "Today, I began today." Those repeated false starts also hide the beginning of the book the way a tunnel that's an escape tunnel would be hidden from the jailers, so that you don't start this book for some time any more than the narrator gets his tunnel started right away.

MS: Now, I want to ask you this because I think—and I've tested this—there are sections of this book that I've read aloud both to people who love literature but also to nonreaders. A very close friend read your description of Kohler's bringing together his soldiers and jars and toys to create an ultimate war with marbles rained from above, and he said, "I could read this forever." I think even for people who don't read, that it's absolutely true that its language—perhaps because representational, perhaps because it comes from childhood frustrations in this book—is very seductive. Then for readers of sophistication, by which I literally mean readers who jump to false conclusions, there are great enjoyable tracts of false logic in which undeniable and horrible conclusions are reached. And yet for all this, you've begun this book with ninety pages which will frustrate and baffle even your most persistent reader. When I came to the opening of this book, it stopped me three, four, five times.

WG: Yes, of course, I think this is a standard modernist thing. What it is, is to make sure that the person who gets into the book is ready and deserves to be there. It's a kind of test of competency. To discover the book is not only the narrator's problem; the writer's problem, as I'm trying to find out what the heck is going on too; but also the reader's problem. It's also essential to establish fairly early the kind of range of reference, of demand that the book is going to make of the reader. I think that's just fair. You could of course start out, "We're all going to see Grandmother in the woods with our basket," and suddenly alter the game down the road a piece. I think this would be more unfair than saying right from the start, "If you want to go on with this—"

MS: I see what you mean, because Kohler is in the tunnel even before he starts to dig.

WG: Oh, yes.

MS: The tunnel is everywhere.

WG: That's right. In one sense, the tunnel he's digging is to try and get out of the very mess he begins to be in. He never succeeds. He is trapped with, as the opening says, life in a chair. Here he is, stuck.

MS: That's the reason for the wheelchair, because it reminds him of an invalid. And that is another kind of life in a chair.

WG: Yes. It's the chair of history, it's the appointed, and he has had, of course, his professor who taught him in Germany. He's brought that swivel chair back with him, and he's now sitting in Magus Tabor's chair, and it's a chair in which Tabor says, "I can swivel and change my position any time I want."

MS: To go back to our amazed reader who is making his way into *The Tunnel*, he turns the page from this diagram of the tunnel—drawn, it seems, in chalk on a board—and finds, as always, a copyright page. But facing it immediately, after the black and white of this blackboard page, is a page of color. These are two "Pennants of Passive Attitudes and Emotions," but in fact, if he looks closely, he discovers it's the same pennant. The pennant's been turned like a page, and suddenly the black stripe which stood for bigotry now stands for vindictiveness; the red of long-suffering is, on its reverse side, pettiness. And it began to suggest to me that, as we turn the pages of this book, the meanings will change too, even though what look like oppositions finally amount to the same thing.

WG: Yes, that's of course a standard technique of modernism, too. It's the notion that as you proceed through a book, just as you proceed in a sentence from its subject to its conclusion, what you arrive at alters the meaning that you began with so that the whole text is constantly reverberating back on its beginning and altering the original. And then you start out over and over again, in a certain sense, in this circular, Joycean fashion, and these alternations, these oppositions begin to get cozier and cozier and more mixed, the way you get in a good stew. There's a flavor coming out of the interaction of the ingredients.

MS: Then, if that set of pennants stands for, in my sense, oppositions that are not in fact oppositions, in the next set of pages we get a page of acknowledgment which begins, "The author wishes to thank." But when we flip over the page we discover a picture drawn by hand, the first doodle, of a medal for ingratitude. Every thank you is matched by a "no thank you, I don't care."

WG: That's right. Yes. Isn't that like life now?

MS: That's what's exciting about this book. That people expect novels to be unitary and shudder when they start contradicting themselves. But we know that it's not just thinkers who are able to hold opposing thoughts in succeeding seconds. This is the nature of life. Every thought establishes its opposition, and what we love one moment we dread the next.

WG: That's right. Or simultaneously, eventually. Things that start out rather polar grow together until they're felt, as Freud often argued, with this the ambiguity, and that kind of thing then begins to generate its dialectical opposite as well.

MS: Now, I got a sense in this book at a certain point, and I remember when reading it I called you on the phone to say, "Time has started running backwards, hasn't it?" In this book, which seems to be shaped like an hourglass in a certain way, or at least like an X, suddenly time starts moving backward. We get these strange images, as if at the crook of the hourglass, or the hook of the X, time stopped and everything fused. Words are becoming the scenery. The ice that holds things together is part of the whole of things.

Then suddenly the book dives backward into childhood. Further and further back until the book seems to be saying that the very first disappointment in life was a birthday that didn't work, a Santa who wasn't, and how can you expect a life full of anything but disappointments when its ontological promises from the very beginning were of a creature, Santa, bearing gifts, who isn't real.

WG: Yes.

MS: The gifts are very quickly empty boxes under an aunt's bed. There's nothing inside them but other boxes and other boxes and other boxes and the terrible promise of a box that will someday have a gift brought by a Santa who isn't.

WG: Yes. It's based on the notion that earlier experiences are merely replicated, become model experiences, not only for failures, of course, or disappointments, but for successes as well. The idea is that all of the early experiences become archetypal and assume a kind of dominance that means that every, say, birthday party afterward is this same birthday party. And when one is in that mode, one tends to promote the event coming out that way.

MS: I must ask you, and it's external to the novel but I think in a way part of it: these sections in this book, which took over thirty years to write, originally appeared thirty years ago. Being a bookworm, I went and checked: there aren't very many changes in them.

WG: Some of the pieces that appeared originally in a sort of unitary thing have been cut up, but there aren't many changes otherwise, no.

MS: While, as some critics have pointed out, the thirty years of *The Tunnel* amounts to approximately two paragraphs a week, and this suggests great sedulousness, the things that appear, appear whole, like Athena from the brow of Zeus. There does seem to be an interesting collaboration between care and extreme intention on the one hand and inspiration on the other, as if truly the pulls of the novel were the years, on the one hand, that Joyce spent composing *Finnegans Wake*, and, on the other, the sudden appearance to Rilke of the late poems. He had been silent, and suddenly he tells us the angels arrived. I wondered if you can talk about that process of creation.

WG: Well, I'm not sure I'd call it inspiration. Might be just chaos. I think that what you're talking about is something very true in a way. Certainly, it was true in Rilke's case because when he wrote his first elegies, he didn't complete them for nearly twenty years. He knew they were the first of ten. He knew that he was writing fragments of the third and the fifth and so on without having them. There was somewhere in him a kind of frame, a structure, a kind of place where things could start filling in, in secret, without his knowing, and then coming forth eventually.

Of course, while I wouldn't compare my work at all to that, it is also true that, although it took all this time to write it, the last 600 pages of my manuscript—which was about 1,200 pages in typescript—were written in a year. You get the conclusion, the ending, and the finishing up of the book in a big hurry compared to the long gestational period. And it suggests to me that once you've set up this kind of obsession, everything that happens feeds into it and sticks there someplace, even when you're not thinking about it.

MS: For years I've asked you questions, and you've answered, "Well yes, you're right, but it's not as planned as that. It's much more intuitive. I didn't think that, but you are correct." What interests me is that people often accuse books like *The Tunnel* of being over-intellectualized and over-internalized.

These are, of course, in terms of the internality, the intentions of this particular book. But what fascinates me here is the sense of a writing athlete who has developed and trained for years so that at the moment of the prose—say, the last year of its composition—the very trained mind is prepared for a blinding process of intuition.

WG: Well, it just comes out. Partly that's due to my method of composition alone for a long work, which I should never embark on anyway. The work that I've done on it has to tell me what comes next. I don't know. I don't have any plan thrown out ahead. The organizations of the thing come later, when I begin to see what, in fact, is happening and then to tidy it up and fill it in a little bit. It took such a long time to figure out for myself *what* I was trying to do. Finally, I got to a point where the work I had already done simply wrote the rest of it. It's as if I had no blockages. I just went and wrote every day and it came out. And that's because the previous text was doing it.

Now, that means it's going to come out formed in a certain way because that's what's happening in the book. I'm a totally intuitive writer. I really don't know what I'm doing. I have to be told by what I've done, and I have to look in it. That means, of course, when I get blocked I have to rewrite until it tells me something.

MS: A final question or speculation or rant. I know that Gertrude Stein has been a big influence. When I think of Stein's essays, I think of these extraordinarily seminal things that, in any given sentence, really provide, up to a point, an explanation for the Stein text. And no surprise that she writes the essay "Composition as Explanation." At a certain point, she stops writing essays, and we get—to my mind—texts that are entirely strange. No more explanation. And we are going to have to regard them as hieroglyph and try to provide a codex or say, "No, there's no meaning. We just love the sound." But never again to know, to have the instruction of the author.

Now, you've been a writer who has composed essays hand-in-hand with fictions. In many cases, you've been the banister that I've held on to while wandering lost through *The Tunnel*. Is there a point at which explanation completely stops?

WG: Oh, yes. In fact, the explanations are merely aids for taking the trip. The trip is what counts, not a lot of explanations. Sometimes to take the trip, you have to know certain things in order to know how to read. Literature is made to be experienced. It helps to explain things sometimes in order to enable people to get the experience.

I have always been suspicious of theoretical explanations of passages and so on. And when I am tempted to do that in my own work, I know that my passage is no good and I am looking for rationalizations, which can always be found, for why it's okay and should be left there. Because if it doesn't move—if it doesn't, in Rilkean terminology, sing—if it hasn't got that kind of power, it's just not doing anything. When you get the power, as often happens when reading—let's say you read a poem by Paul Celan. You don't know what's going on, but you don't have to. You get punched. It hits you. You know you're dealing with greatness, and that's all you need to know.

MS: I did experience this book in a very physical way. There are certain physicalities that are always considered okay for novels. Crying, which along with protracted reading, results in red eyes. Laughter is thought to be okay. But I sneezed over this book and farted, and there are bits of food stain on it, and so the book, in its way, becomes a record for each reader of his passage through the tunnel. It seems like a book meant to be lived in and to invoke responses that are very visceral and nonliterary.

WG: Ideally, I would love to have it that way. Whether it succeeds in doing that, I don't know. Certainly one of the problems, as I was mentioning earlier, of literature in general is to *reach* the material, to be what we envy, as Rilke envied Rodin having his hands in it. Of course, then the painter or the sculptor says, "I want ideas. I want—" He has to reach out from the material to mind, and literature, which is so conceptual, has to reach for the world in the most immediate and telling way.

2004: *Reading Rilke: Reflections on the Problems of Translations*

MS: There has been inadequate talk about the content of your work, but I think still more inadequate talk about its influences and the way in which it developed as a literary style. In the last several years, you have been writing essays on the poet Rainer Maria Rilke, who began with the name René, sometimes called Sophia by his mother when he was good.

WG: Yes.

MS: Rilke was dressed as a girl when he was a child, and as a good girl he was Sophia. The forging of an identity as a poet seems to have depended upon his casting off identities put onto him by almost creating them as ghosts, writing elegies for versions of himself that were no longer supportable to him.

Your work on metaphor and image is profound, and seems to trace in Rilke a movement that takes a trajectory from voice to groove—the groove on a record, the reproduced voice when that groove is played becoming a ghost-like image. There is the sense that ghost and metaphor interpenetrate in their purpose, that people in fiction are not so much characters as traces, atmospheres, locations for the inter-surfacing of light. These, wonderfully and strangely, are found in Rilke and a few other places, and you name them from time to time—Valéry, Mallarmé—but the beautiful three-dimensional sense that we are witnessing events in the world that have been transformed into interpenetrating fields of language, metaphor, light, sensation, sound, this is the fascination of the work.

Most recently, one of your essays suggests that when you read Rilke's novel, you're reading a haunted house, you're reading a convocation of ghosts. I would like to propose that, in not too simple or obvious a way, this is the requirement for the house of fiction as imagined by James and revised and reimagined via Rilke by you, William Gass. I wanted to begin, after this enormous peroration, to ask when did this encounter with Rilke begin?

WG: I'm not good at telling dates, but I had gone as a visiting writer and teacher of philosophy from Purdue, where I was, to the University of Illinois in the '50s. It was at the university in Urbana that I started to read him. I don't remember in what way the books came into my hands, but I did begin with the poems, the elegies, and I was overwhelmed in a way that was rare for me. There are many, many, many poets whom I adore, but Rilke was different. It struck some sort of chord, and I spent a long time trying to find out what it had hit in me and whether it was a good thing or a bad thing.

It began to resonate, and although the individual poet in his life, as I began to read about it, was nothing like myself, I kept finding or feeling a sympathy, even in my antagonisms, because Rilke was, in many ways, a professional poseur. I think one of the things that struck me early on was that Rilke had this strange but very romantic notion that in order to be a poet and to write the great poems that he wanted to write, he had to be a great poet first. And once he was a great poet as a person, he would be able to write great poems. It wasn't the common sense view that you got to be a great poet by writing poems until they were great and then you were great because you'd written them. No, first, to be the great poet.

He worked very hard on his persona. That persona was not initially Rilke, and we could see that in the early work. One of the things that Rodin taught Rilke was how to cement this new persona into the greatness of stature of the individual that he needed to be.

MS: One of the things I love as I read, in order, your essays on Rilke—and you've been writing about him for years now—is that the sense of Rilke becomes profound. One of the newest essays accompanies a beautiful new book, a retranslation of the two monographs on Rodin, early and late, that Rilke wrote, published by Archipelago Books. They're a wonderful new press, and I want to commend them not only for doing this book but for making it so beautiful, for incorporating photographs of the Rodin sculptures by Michael Eastman, and for asking Gass for an introduction.

Now, the monograph is almost famous for its politeness. It's the part of Rilke that is courting. He wants, in a sense, to be accepted by Rodin and that group. What you find in the notebooks kept at the same time, is that another phase of Rilke is beginning, his response to the extraordinary poverty in Paris, and his sense then—this is the culminating thrill of the essay—that we see in the planes of Rodin's sculpture the formation in space of different planes of identity. The Rilke who is busy being polite, the Rilke who is being abraded by Paris, by Bohemian culture, these versions of himself are starting to be reflected in the planes of a statue, but more specifically in the planes of a different kind of sentence, a different kind of line of verse that's able to negotiate—as if it's an uncoiling dragon and all its scales catching light as it uncoils—a whole continuum of simultaneous emotion.

WG: Yes, I think he is changing. He is trying to do something in one sense impossible, and that is to make a verbal object into a *thing*. Rodin is teaching him not only to make works of art from the ontological point of view, from the point of view of creating being and placing it in the world as solidly as a statue, but also to give it the kind of almost impressionistic, multilayered, multi-*surfaced* effect that Rodin was getting in his sculpture. It is also, of course, for Rilke, an enormously important time psychologically. Because what he's doing when he begins to write *The Notebooks of Malte Laurids Brigge* is to write about a failed poet.

Rilke is seeing himself for the first time as a failure, as someone who is risking the failure. While he is courting—in order to stay alive, he is getting paid for this monograph on Rodin—he's courting genius, success, the overwhelming success that Rodin is enjoying at this time. Moreover, Rodin is—from Rilke's point of view—coarse, sexually on the rampage, causing models to pose erotically, naked. There is this Little Lord Fauntleroy type watching all this, who goes back to a little squalid room in Paris, can hardly make ends meet, and is also feeling an enormous amount of guilt because he has, in effect, left his wife and small child. It's a mess. That very mess is something that Rilke was able to make a capital of.

MS: We're speaking on the subject of Rodin and eventually the subject of how Rodin gives something to Rilke and Rilke gives something to you. We're going to be tracing a procedure. Now, at that time in his letters, he is writing descriptions of the Paris streets that will eventually secrete themselves into the sentences that begin *The Notebooks of Malte Laurids Brigge,* and it is in *Brigge* that you detect the broken surfaces that he is learning from Rodin. This book begins something in Rilke, which is—I would say it this way: that everything in the world is alive, is animistic. A woman weeping puts her hands to her face in a bowl. When she looks up, she has left her face in that bowl. In other words, the transposition between people and things, between an inert world and a living world. Image is making everything come alive, and it's as if the job of the writer is to take the dying world and not lie about the fact that it is a dying world but bring it to life in a constantly animating prose.

WG: Yes, I think that's a key thing with Rilke because in one sense, of course, he's not an animist. He knows that everything, in a sense, is *not* alive. What he wants to do is to invest the world with that necessary respect and to make it alive by inserting the poetic consciousness inside it. He's also working on a notion that pantheists have to work on and was developed even by such philosophers as Spinoza. Now, Rilke doesn't know he's using Spinoza, but he is, and without even getting permission.

What Spinoza suggests is that everything has its *conatus,* or its striving. It's a version of a self-preservation doctrine. Now, the problem for any great poem—for instance, Valéry expresses this beautifully too—is to create beautiful lines and beautiful imagery and beautiful ideas, each with their own integrity, each with their own life, which will nevertheless work in a community.

To get them to work in this community—how? To create a community in which a free spirit would choose freely to be. To put it at the sentential level, in the ideal sentence every word would have *chosen* to be in that sentence, not just picked up and used there.

Then he applies that to what he's learning from Rodin, and what he's learning from Rodin is the importance of light as a living principle in any surface. You break up the surface, you pick up the reflections, you make every part of that surface alive.

MS: This reminds me of a Gass sentence. The hero of *The Tunnel* is thinking about how he doesn't quite know what his wife will do when she discovers what he has been doing, which is digging an escape route from their house. At least he thinks he's doing that.

He says of her, "For she has more of passion's poses on the varnished wooden hangers that comprise her than the children have costumes for Halloween."

Suddenly, we have a woman who's made of a series of dresses, which are costumes, which are personalities, which this man will never be able to anticipate. She is the continuum that we're talking about. She is like a sentence that precedes plane after plane so that we never know in fact where the sentence (i.e., where the woman) will go. He doesn't know how to project her.

Now, I regard the consciousness revealed in your sentences as the product of a long, sometimes conscious, sometimes unconscious observation of the world and a question of how to represent it. In other words, we don't just want a cat, we want the cat at every moment: when it's doing its Halloween dance, arching its back, when it's playing the bass, licking itself below. How do we make something that is not single but many? How, in other words, do we stop the lie that's told by prose, stop-motion photography? I think, in part, you learn it from Rilke.

WG: Oh, yes, you learn the ideal. It was at the same time that Rilke was working that other people were teaching the same lessons in Paris. Cézanne was teaching. Gertrude Stein was learning this from Flaubert and Cézanne, and so was Rilke. The same material, all kinds of people doing it at the same time, and some of the same expression comes in someone like Henry James. In order to render any part of any, let's say, pose of the cat—this is what Rodin was teaching Rilke—in order to draw a person in a moment, you had to know the whole thing.

Now, the whole thing can't be crowded in, in every sentence, but the way you write has to be informed by knowing all these other things, which you do not explicitly put in. This, of course, is something that painters understand perfectly, and Rilke was finally understanding it.

MS: Now, a lot of Rilke's triumphs are also kind of trashy. There was a whole tendency in American poetry to make the inanimate come alive. It used to be called Midwestern surrealism, the bones and stones and feathers poetry. The movement beyond the misuse of metaphysical ideas, at what point can it become a triumphant art as it surely does in the case of Rilke?

WG: I think it does in most poets. I think that's what poetry is largely made up of: a misuse of ideas. If you took them out of the poetic realm and started to examine, they'd come apart in a minute. What makes them, I think, exemplary is that they catch, indeed, how we feel. How we often feel about things is the animistic way. Bachelard has, of course, written best about all of these in *The Poetics of Space* and *The Philosophy of No*. What Bachelard was dealing with was the sense that as we grow up we pass through an animistic period that stays with us. Of course, we have to pass it on from this.

In the poetic realm, this animistic part, Bachelard argues, is the supreme part. What we are in the scientific realm is constantly moving, stage after stage, into higher abstractions, more mathematical realizations, more complex and intellectual constructions, whereas in the poetic world we're moving always back to a sense of the world that is alive, makes sense because it has its wishes and desires just as we do, and with whom we can have a really intimate, warm, and angry relationship. There's something immensely comforting about that and about the sense of seeing everything—say, a glass—with the kind of respect that we reserve for people.

Now, when that glass becomes a work of art, we treat it better than we treat people. One of the reasons, I think, is that Rilke's arguing that the work of art has more being, and it has more being because the highest consciousness of *human beings* has been put in it in terms of the way it has been formed. So then, in that famous poem, "Torso of Archaic Apollo," the torso says, even though it's broken, has no head, no genitals, no legs, no arms, to the viewer, I'm more real than you are. "You must change your life."

MS: Now, at a certain point in the making or the concretizing of abstractions, you built a temple, *A Temple of Texts*. It was comprised of fifty pillars, and those fifty pillars were the works that had influenced you and hold up the temple of literature. In your holy of holies, the center of the temple, you put four Rilke pillars. The texts are *The Notebooks of Malte Laurids Brigge*,

Duino Elegies, *Sonnets to Orpheus*, and Rilke's letters. Each of these, in your temple, was accompanied by a paragraph of explanation. This is William H. Gass reading his description of the Rilke texts that are at the very center of the temple of his influences.

WG: Yes, this is about *The Notebooks of Malte Laurids Brigge*.

"There have been books that have struck me like lighting and left me riven, permanently scarred, perhaps burned out but picturesque; and there have been those that created complete countries with their citizens, their cows, their climate, where I could choose to live for long periods while enduring, defying, enjoying their scenery and seasons; but there have been one or two I came to love with a profounder and more enduring passion, not just because, somehow, they seemed to speak to the most intimate 'me' I knew but also because they embodied what I held to be humanly highest, and were therefore made of words which revealed a powerful desire moving with the rhythmic grace of Blake's Tyger; an awareness that was pitilessly unsentimental, yet receptive as sponge; feelings that were free and undeformed and unashamed; thought that looked at all its conclusions and didn't blink; as well as an imagination that could dance on the heads of all those angels dancing on that pin. I thought that the *Notebooks* were full of writing that met that tall order. Of the books I have loved (and there are so many, many more than I could have collected here), from the electrifying alliterations of *Piers Plowman* ('Cold care and cumbrance has come to us all') to the sea-girt singing of Derek Walcott's *Omeros*, there has been none that I would have wished more fervently to have written than this intensely personal poem in prose, this profound meditation on seeing and reading—on reading what one has seen, on seeing what one has read."

2012: *Life Sentences*

MS: Because you are an exquisite examiner of sentences, which are, after all, the unit out of which fiction, philosophy, even articulated thought itself is formed, I thought we would hear from an essay, "The Aesthetic Structure of the Sentence."

You've been writing essays so beautifully, so well, and for such a long time that these essays now have reached the point of abstract perfection that steps toward not only the beautiful and truthful, but the ecstatic and even blessed lunacy. "The Aesthetic Structure of the Sentence" asks us to think about a salesman at the door, nothing more than that. At the beginning of the essay, it's an encyclopedia salesman, so that sentence takes place in the Great Depression. This sentence is about a Fuller Brush man.

WG: Thank you, Michael. I'd just rather hear you say nice things about me.

MS: I love to.

WG: "'The shabby-suited fellow at the front door was a Fuller Brush salesman.' The rhythm of the sentence not only propels the sentence forward, it helps to organize its significant units—its phrases and clauses. The reader is made not merely to see the sentence, but to sound it, because it is now a small mouthful. These sounds are usually not those of ordinary speech, but the spectral mimicry of things that are said to the mind, heard only by the mind, in the arena of the mind—in the subvocal consciousness that exists during reading.

The salesman's sentence seems quite sure of itself. It is direct; it is definite; it has no room for reservations. Yet without altering a word, its epistemological and ontological status can be radically altered. That is why I call these verbal instruments *transformative operators*. For instance, we could lower the sentence's degree of assurance. '[I thought that] the fellow at the front door was a Fuller Brush salesman.' '[I guessed that] the shabby-suited fellow at the front door was a Fuller Brush salesman [but Gertrude was of quite a different opinion].' Amphibolously: '[Harold said that if] the shabby-suited fellow at the front door was a Fuller Brush salesman [he was a monkey's uncle].' Or change tone and attitude: '[I certainly hoped] the shabby-suited fellow at the front door was a Fuller Brush salesman [otherwise I've just now bought a cat's brush to comb my beard].' 'The shabby-suited fellow at the front door was a Fuller Brush salesman [but what if he were also the exhibitionist who has been frightening the neighborhood?]' More radically, we can put it in another realm of being. '[While seated before the fire in my dressing gown reading Descartes' *Meditations*, I dreamed I heard a knocking. Then a cuckoo popped out of its clockhouse to announce that] the shabby-suited fellow at the front door was a Fuller Brush salesman. [I realized, when I was awakened by my desire to answer his knocking, that I had been dreaming inside a dream not altogether mine.]'

Layers of reality, degrees of uncertainty, ranges of attitude, levels of society, depth of contextual connection, modulations of tone, the ramifications and complexities of concept, and, above all, the vocabulary of the denoted world must be taken into account, managed, and made the best of."

MS: Now, you're using that sentence as a toy the way you'd take a nickel—if there are still nickels—and spin one on its edge and watch it twirl. What I find fascinating is that, having used the sentence as a model, you then show us what it's like in the work of literature to see the master—and in this case, it's Henry James—twiddle with the basic unit until it becomes wondrous and full.

Now, we're going to hear William Gass reading a phenomenal sentence from the late Henry James's *The Wings of the Dove*.

WG: This passage occurs at a moment when the narrator, in effect, is sizing up the house he is about to enter the way we frequently do by measuring the language of the objects that are in there. That's one of the things that's interesting about this passage from *The Wings of the Dove*:

"It was the language of the house itself that spoke to him, writing out for him with surpassing breadth and freedom the associations and conceptions, the ideals and possibilities of the mistress. Never, he felt sure, had he seen so many things so unanimously ugly—operatively, ominously so cruel. . . . They constituted an order and abounded in rare material—precious woods, metals, stuffs, stones. He had never dreamed of anything so fringed and scalloped, so buttoned and corded, drawn everywhere so tight and curled everywhere so thick. He had never dreamed of so much gilt and glass, so much satin and plush, so much rosewood and marble and malachite. But it was above all the solid forms, the wasted finish, the misguided cost, the general attestation of morality and money, a good conscience and a big balance. These things finally represented for him a portentous negation of his own world of thought—of which, for that matter, in presence of them, he became as for the first time hopelessly aware. They revealed it to him by their merciless difference."

MS: What stuns me at the end of the passage is that the material world, the ugly and overstuffed furniture, reveals to this narrator the immaterial world that he has in mind, that thoughts have their place and that they flee from the material. Here's Gass with his commentary on the kind of passage this is.

WG: "There is no dimension of the sentence that is not operative here, from the upper class Latinate word choice, the steady interruption of qualifying phrases, the carefully constructed climax, the shocked tone, both dismayed and outraged, the repetitive encircling of *and* and *so*, and the helpful disclosure, as if for use in this essay, of the language—both in its syntax and lexicon—of the world of human things: the single teacup that speaks of former wealth and dashed hopes; for Henry James is as much a master of that language as he is of the urbane style of verbal social exchange with which he was daily engaged. There is no more attentive prose than one of the Master's sentences. The quality of what any one of them sees or feels is not only meticulously depicted, but placed in its proper sphere, and hefted for its proper weight, and seen through, realized, and measured as though each object were a little scene inside a glass globe, with snow that will obediently fall when its world is turned upside down.

I have suggested in other places that such sentences as these are containers of consciousness: a verbal consciousness, of course, one built of symbols, not sensations, yet one of perceptions all the same: perceptions followed by thoughts like tracking hounds, and infused throughout by the energies of memory and desire, the moods emotions foster, and the reach, through imagery and other juxtapositions, of imagination . . ."

MS: That's William Gass reading from the final essay in his book, *Life Sentences*, called "The Aesthetic Structure of the Sentence." A wonderful subject because, often, my friend Bill Gass is misunderstood by even make-believe friendly critics who want to say that his point of view is that the world is made of words: "This is the revelation of Gass. This doesn't surprise us."

Now, in fact, what I think he's saying is that the relationship between sentences within a paragraph, between that paragraph and its ideas, those ideas and the world, that world and the world of the story, the story and what it means, beyond what it's about, that the relationship among these things is what fiction is about. To talk about that relationship is to talk about fiction more clearly, more precisely, more meaningfully than to talk about morals and symbols and themes. Am I sort of in your realm, Bill?

WG: Yes, I think so. There are so many languages at once that one is trying to manipulate. There is a huge set of languages that we have outside our normal thinking selves: the world, and its activities, and its little intimations, its conversations, how one little thing will signify so much, other little things.

That part, on one hand, and then the constant travail and movement of thought through one's own head. And, in third place, the application of a language that has been built over centuries by the use of people in certain ways to bring all of those things together and make a vision of the world, which is going to be, in my sense, not direct as you might get in science—though even there you build a model—but sort of a metaphor for life.

James's world is not to be found anywhere in the world. It's too wonderful for that. It's too precise. It's too organized. It's the way it ought to be. To call my interest or thinking that the world is made of words is silly, but the world is made of words that we use to make it look that way. And then the novelist comes along and employs other things to build a model for it.

MS: Now, you once thrilled me by answering a question about how it was that you took thirty-five years to write your novel *The Tunnel*, by saying that you write very, very slowly and that you rewrite and rewrite and rewrite only to attain mediocrity. That's the way we should be reading too, isn't it?

WG: Well, yes, but I have to first say it wasn't thirty-five, it was only thirty.

MS: Thank you.

WG: It was probably not thirty, but only twenty-five, but it was a long time. We were always taught speed reading when I was a kid, and I was, one time, the speed reading champion of Ohio.

MS: No, not really. Truly?

WG: Yes. We used to have competitions, and you read as fast as you could and then you answered questions. And it was a kind of test I did very well at and was learning absolutely the wrong things. Unless you read junk all the time. Then the sooner you get through it, the better.

I had to relearn—and philosophy helped in this way—how to read slowly, not with difficulty, as if you couldn't read faster, but rather slowly to savor, to try to understand how out of all the choices that, say, James had in making a particular paragraph—so many words could have been used—every time he uses one he takes away these chances to use others, until finally he has a system of words put together there that is almost indestructible because you can't change anything without ruining everything.

The reader has to be counting the bricks because they weren't just hurled into the wall, they were fashioned and polished and assigned their position.

MS: You've spoken of how sometimes we can not only hear the word that's been chosen but the ghost of the words that haven't been chosen: in a good passage, those bricks may surround certain holes in the wall that represent choices we can feel but that the writer decided not to make.

WG: Yes. That's very much the case too. You can particularly notice this when you have a fairly well-defined environment. It's sort of evident that a certain number of terms would naturally fit into the situation, and then something comes along that is unexpected and transformative in terms of what your chances are, what you might decide to work over.

MS: We're always hearing ghosts when we're reading, not just the ghost of what the writer left out, but the ghost of what the writer heard, so that from time to time, when the writer is making an allusion to another work, it's the wall talking about part of another building.

WG: Yes. You're working with, in fact, if you're a writer who is well read—and not all of the good ones are—similar situations, similar maneuvers that have taken place. The ghost of Henry James, of course, is always with me saying, "Oh dear, that will never do," as I'm trying to write.

MS: I was thinking about the opening of *The Wings of the Dove*. I remember that it began: "She waited, Kate Croy, for her father to come in, but he kept her unconscionably. . . ." When we hear that, we know it's not "Kate Croy waited for her father to come," it's the first sentence of a novel. You can sing it. [*sings*] "She waited, Kate Croy, for her father to come in, but he kept her unconscionably," and it's because of you that I hear those hard Cs: "come in, but he kept her unconscionably." They're ascending Cs.

The 87-year-old William Gass, I'm happy to tell my listeners, has announced that a new novel will be published next year called *Middle C*. Here in this book, *Life Sentences*, you've got essays on Gertrude Stein; Proust; Nietzsche; Kafka; Lowry; Henry James, of course; John Gardner; Katherine Anne Porter; and Knut Hamsun.

There are writers who don't write with this degree of attention. Are they the writers we're meant to neglect? Do your insights not apply to them? Where is the rest of fiction in your view?

WG: I think much of a fine writer's attention is automatic. He just grew up that way. It's a part of being a writer, paying attention. One example, Katherine Anne Porter was writing brilliantly in her first story. I don't think she improved a whole lot as she went on, but she didn't need to. She was somehow unconsciously adapting and developing her work—sure, with difficulty, but not as if she weren't paying attention.

The same is true of a lot of other writers. Stanley Elkin wrote fast and furiously his first draft and then crawled back over it carefully. I can't write that way, that's all. That makes sense: to write, get it all down, see the whole. But I don't see anything but a hole if I'm trying to do that.

MS: Everyone is talking about how it's harder than ever to be published. I dare disagree. I've been being sent an unprecedented number of first novels that seem to have been written as quickly as possible and published as quickly as possible to get them out in the world before the end of the world occurs.

I feel sort of the way I felt when I read only yesterday that the Encyclopedia Britannica had announced that it couldn't compete with Wikipedia: there will be no more editions of the Encyclopedia Britannica, and I felt, "Well, yes, okay. I understand," but it's kind of the end of a world.

WG: Careless writing and careless books. You know, books are written to look careless too because the reader doesn't want to feel threatened by the difficulty. Glibness is good, it goes with "greed is good," I think.

MS: We've got another of your favorites, Gertrude Stein, in fact, about whom Katherine Anne Porter wrote some perfectly, brilliantly nasty essays.

WG: Absolutely wonderful. This proves a point though. I adore Gertrude, but she has her flaws. Katherine Anne Porter was all over them and wrote about it with such wit that you want her to be right for the moment. But, in fact, Gertrude is unharmed and goes on being obnoxiously in the way of tons of people. I like her for that, too.

Toni Morrison

1998: *Beloved*

MS: My guest Toni Morrison is, of course, the author of *Beloved* and more recently of *Jazz* and *Paradise*. She began publishing with *The Bluest Eye*, followed by *Sula*, *The Song of Solomon*, *Tar Baby*, and she really is one of my most admired American writers. I wrote her a letter two weeks ago knowing that the movie of *Beloved* would be coming out and wanting, not even having seen the film, to talk about the book because it's my sense that after a movie hits the public, a book is altered by it and that there are things that we find in language, in the shaping and writing of literature, that a movie cannot touch, not because it doesn't want to or because it's inadequate, but because they are different art forms, because it can't.

Now, it seems to me that at the center of *Beloved* is not the thing that people always talk about. They always talk about a story that happened in the days of slavery in which an actual woman killed her children rather than seeing them brought back and living the life that she had led on the plantation. But it seems to me that while this is the background of the book, what the writer has done is bring to it the question, which becomes the question in your following two books, *Jazz* and *Paradise*: What will you do? What kind of love is too much? And when does love of another eclipse the love of the self?

TM: The question is: How are we able to love under duress? And when we can, what distorts it for us? And how can we negotiate the various kinds of claims and loves that we choose in order to make it include ourselves, the love of self that is not narcissistic, not simply selfish, and also to love something bigger than ourselves that is not martyrdom, not setting oneself aside completely? Negotiating between those two extremes to get to someplace where the love is generous.

MS: Yes, it seems to me that, in the same way that one finds oneself afterward on a path without knowing when one has embarked, that the books, all of them, lead up to this. The first book, *The Bluest Eye*, is about the consequences of self-loathing, and the books that follow take the impaired self into the world where attempts at love are made. And in a sense, it's not until *Beloved* that the question of a transfiguring love, one that might destroy the self in the process of being enacted, becomes the central subject of the book. So in a way, all of the books have been a sequential path from the frightened self to the self that begins to risk in the world, and then the self that is taking grand and possibly disastrous strides.

TM: True. Yes. Because the frailty of the first book, of that child who is fairly doomed by things outside of her control and collapsing emotionally all the way to another kind of child, I suppose. And Beloved, whose hunger for disrupted love, lack of love, abandoned love, matching with the ferocity of mother love, which is on the one hand laudatory and on the other something that can actually condemn everybody, not just her child, but herself and her living child and make love impossible for her with a man. You know, all kinds of love, which is an exaggeration, of course, of parental love, but loving in an exaggerated, fierce, unhealthy, distorted way under circumstances that made such a love logical. I mean, she's not merely psychotic, she didn't just erupt into the world that way—I mean Sethe—but trying very hard as a writer to put into language the theatricality and the meaning of these kinds of distortions in order to reveal not only their consequences but what one should be warned against, what we should look out for, what we should be wary of.

And I thought Beloved's circumstances in the book were not limited in any way to 1873 or 1855. I think for those of us who live in 1998, male or female, the problem of trying to love oneself and another human being at the same time is a serious late twentieth-century problem. A very serious problem. And I thought, in particular, mother love is a very serious problem in the late twentieth century, because of the choices that women can make now. You don't really have to have children. And some women feel that not having children is the freedom they seek. And some women feel that having children is the fulfillment they seek. But in both cases things can go completely and terribly wrong if you don't understand—and no one does instantly—what that means.

It was interesting to me to write in 1984, I guess I started, about how one woman felt that she was only free and complete when she asserted herself as a mother as opposed to post-feminist notions of not having to be forced into motherhood as a way of completing, fulfilling the self and expressing one's freedom. So that it's not so much that they're contrary, it's just the same area, the same park in which I wanted to work and work out the problems of that kind of love as opposed to, say, the notions of romantic love and the so-called Jazz Age, compared to our notions of romantic love these days. I think I'm trying to stress the point that—I guess I'm echoing something you said earlier—which is, whatever the historical background, my hope, my earnest hope, was that the relevance of these people, whatever race, whatever region, whatever the historical circumstances were, resonate powerfully with contemporary difficulties.

MS: Years ago, you mentioned you brought the manuscript of *Beloved* to your editor, Robert Gottlieb, feeling that it was not complete, that it was one part of a trilogy of novels and you didn't even know if it could be published on its own.

TM: No, that's true.

MS: In each of these books though, a triangle or a configuration emerges, and it's as if the brilliance of the book is to rotate that configuration—which I see as a triangle—from every conceivable angle. In *Jazz*, because the metaphor is jazz, the characters at the vertices of these figures, they do their solos, they speak, they have arias. In *Beloved*, too, one senses that the whole novel has been directing itself toward a moment that, in my mind, a film can't possibly realize, a moment of locked gaze and psychic transfer, that seems at the heart of the narration of all of these books, that there be a moment when there is an exchange of eye and feeling, mind and touch, that allows people to know each other's stories without speaking them.

TM: Well, you have a major void in a movie: you don't have a reader, you have a viewer. And that is such a different experience. As subtle as a movie can be, as careful and artful as it can be, in the final analysis it's blatant because you see it. And you can translate certain things, make certain interpretations and wonder, and certainly there could be mystery, but the encounter with language is such a private exploration. The imagination works differently. The things that I can create and hint at via the structure, via the choice of words, via the silences are not the kinds of things that would be successful in any movie. And when it becomes sort of pointed and successful that way, it loses something. So for me, what you call the exchange of mind and touch, none of that they would even attempt, because that's not what movies do or do well.

And I had to realize, although I was not very interested in selling any book to the movies ever, and when I was persuaded to complete the sale of this one, I thought I would let them do what they do and I would go home and do what I do, and I had no further contact with it until, indeed, they were filming. And I went there to say certain things that I thought might be helpful and might be used but probably would never be. But I felt it important to simply say these things, and my judgments were powerfully structural: where to linger, where not to. And they were really unusable. They were literally unused by anybody because they were not cinematic.

MS: I want to explain the context here for my listeners. I think that trust and the agreement between a writer and a reader is very important to Toni Morrison. And so, when I wrote a letter to her several weeks ago, it was not only that we would talk but we would talk from her home because that was a decision not to be going out on the road again, to be making pronouncements or flacking for the movie, that the movie is a separate thing. And so we're talking from our studio to Toni Morrison's home, and the sounds that you hear are the sounds of intimacy, not of an accidental bad connection. It was out of respect for the writer that led to this particular circumstance.

It seems to me that your fiction does bring the reader to a space that cannot be defined, that must be, for lack of better terms, called the sacred or indeterminant space of the imaginative experience.

TM: Exactly.

MS: That words are the inadequate clothing of that experience when you're reaching the heart. Up until that point, the writer's choices, word by word, are immensely important. When you reach the heart, no word can be correct. You're talking about an experience that is close to a mystical experience.

TM: Wow! I wanted precisely that point to be rendered in a couple of occasions in *Beloved*, but particularly when the women are in front of Sethe's house, having been persuaded that enough is enough. And when they go there, they come with what they've got, whatever faith they've got, whatever superstition they've got, whatever religious iconography they have, using all the symbolic world. And then they pray and they do things, and then there's a moment when none of that works, not the symbol they hold in their hands, not the cross they may have around their necks, not the desire to have their will done. The only thing that works is to go very, very far back before language when there was only the sound. The sound is a kind of choral singing in this case, which works in terms of the folklore, in terms of who those people were. But it's another way of saying, of their saying and my saying: "I can't say what this is. There are no words to tell you how to get there from here."

MS: As opposed to that which can't be voiced, there is another kind of silencing that runs through the work that is not helpful to a writer, that a writer fights with every straining instinct against. That is the silence that fills the master's wife's throat. She can no longer speak. It is the silencer on the gun that kills Dorcas. She is silenced in *Jazz*. And I wondered if you could talk about the ways in which these books combat silence.

TM: Well, that's an interesting way to put it. I think the signal instrument of silence for me in *Beloved* was the bit, which was a kind of familiar and frequently used homemade instrument that you put into a person's mouth, which you could adjust, and there are quite a variety of them. And whatever other feature they had, they were not to keep you from working, because you worked with them, but they were to shut you up. So that you could not say, you could not talk back, you could not articulate a contrary position or do any violence with your tongue or your word. And that was a complete erasure of all language that the victim or the oppressed had.

So for me it was operating this way: I would try to say what they were prevented from saying.

MS: It seems to me that the writer's role in work of this kind is to save the characters from the silencing of society and bring them to that point that can only be quasi-articulate of the witnessing of the holy or the miraculous.

TM: Indeed, it is. It's bearing witness on the one hand. In a way—you mentioned it yourself—it's not quite secular. Let's put it that way. It's not quite secular work.

MS: Yes. Now, in that scene of the bit, there is what I consider to be one of the signatures and triumphs of your way of looking and writing. In the scene in which this brutal silencing occurs, several tortures and punishments are going on at once. Several witnessings without voicings. What we see instead is that rooster, and I wondered if you would tell me about him.

TM: You know, imagining it myself—What must it feel like? What must it look like?—this man, under those circumstances, being treated like a beast. So you're trying to not just re-emphasize that. But to have him look at something that is edible, something that he brought into the world. But nevertheless, roosters have a kind of royal way of behaving sometimes in the yard. And to have him compare himself to a creature so beneath him, but who visually—if you imagine, visualize a rooster—you see the crown, you see the beak, you see the eye, you see something close to an eagle, so you see something painterly that you recognize as having at least a certain kind of a visual authority. The rooster crows, et cetera. But you know, really, that it's just a little three or four pounds of nothing. And to have him feel less than that. And, more importantly, to know that rooster, he has a name, he remembers when it was born, he remembers helping it, and they named it Mister because he was so tough. So, here we have a man who will never be called Mister walking out of that yard, looking at a rooster that is already called Mister.

MS: And also participating in a flashback in a kind of ritual of male birth. He has, in some way, mothered this rooster. So amazing. Now, this of course is what a movie cannot do because it can only show you a rooster. It can't tell you where the rooster came from. It can't make the red of its comb pulsate the way yours does. It cannot enter the mind of the man who named it Mister, whose mouth is filled by a bit. These are those things that, in a book, last beyond the book. They are intersections that the author has structured that editing in movies can only rarely do—one needs an Eisenstein to think of a structure that would allow for so much association, so much fullness to go on in the midst of such devastation.

TM: They're so different. It's the most obvious thing to say, but I had no idea how very different the whole experience is, what you're being driven to. It's not even a reduction. It's just a powerful difference. First of all, it was important to me, at least on the paperback jacket, not to see Beloved's face, that she must be someone that the reader invents. Well, already when you're in a movie situation, you have a face that fixes it. So it moves from there to other kinds of scenes, gestures, voices, some of which enhance, I have to tell you, what the dialogue might be. You hear other things with very good actors, and they're very good in this movie. On the other hand, there are just whole areas that not only are not there, they're not gestured toward, but the mechanics of cinema doesn't work toward that anyway.

The part that you work so hard for is of no use whatsoever. They cannot use it and should not. I remember a scene in *Paradise* in which I worked a long time with a couple of scenes to make sure that the palette was right, that the same colors that were in this scene were also in another scene. And I don't expect a reader to necessarily know all of that, but I do believe that because I painted the scene the same colors, there is a sort of undertow or urtext where it may not look comparable in terms of the two scenes, but the reader may not even know that they're getting the nature of the comparison because I have painted them that way.

MS: It's very deeply embedded in the work, and what came to me in *Beloved* with Baby Suggs's quilt, in which there are two patches of orange and Baby Suggs is working on pink, is that what is going on in this book is that we are thinking about color in new ways.

TM: In a fresh way. I wanted it to be absolutely raw. And in the rest of the book, nobody mentions color. And then, when Sethe meets Paul D again and she thinks about maybe this can work, she thinks about color. Maybe she'll look at turnips; it's a pleasure. It's a deep, sensual, gratifying pleasure.

MS: And not only that, it's a way of making new. What is a Black writer supposed to do? He or she is supposed to think about color. And here it is. You've got it. I'm doing it right now.

TM: You've got it.

2004: *Love*

MS: I wanted to begin by saying that it struck me that people are needing several years to read *Jazz*, to read *Paradise*, and now *Love*, because the books seem to me to be extremely brilliant and complex in their organization. *Love* seems to be about time and place, the way in which—depending on who you are and when you are there—your experience changes who you are, what love is, and what you know.

The setting of this place has once been a resort. The people in the resort have moved into a home on Monarch Street. They are in an area that has been once an oceanside, but now there's a place called Oceanside, not by an ocean, with very cheap government housing. Other places that people remember are covered now by water. The place that we're hearing about so vibrantly does not exist except in memory, and the book seems to be about the way love is a collection of the pieces that people can assemble. Even when they can't speak to one another, the reader assembles love. Is that correct?

TM: Very, very close. What came to mind as you were talking was the idea I had of the way a crystal forms. You have a small piece and then it expands to another, and another layer comes on in a different shape, but it's all the same material. And when finished, it's different facets, different light, looking at one simple thing.

MS: I know that it is, in a sense, a presumptuous question because one never asks a magician about a particular trick, and it's even wrong to think of it as a trick, but the book seems to have been constructed in a very unusual way. That is to say—I don't know the words for it—but it seems that there are gists for each character, and in each section there's a passing of impulse so that one character reports on the previous one's experience and then extends it. Were there diagrams? How did you work?

TM: No, I had diagrams for groups of people in rooms and streets, but the structure basically was how to reveal this responsibility that this man Bill Cosey was given, all these roles. And how his life and his entrepreneurship affected, destroyed, helped, remade a set of people who lived in that community. So he is sort of not really on stage. Everything has to accrue around him. And in order to describe how and whether and what was possible in terms of the range of kinds of love in the book, I had this collection of people who knew him and each other in different ways and had a terrible time trying to articulate this.

MS: Now, you mentioned crystals, and I noticed that there were certain constellations that seemed permanent in the book, but from one group of characters to another group of characters. We have a couple who are raising their granddaughter, and also in the house we have a very similar situation with a granddaughter who has come—her grandfather is now dead, her mother has been put in a home—this sense of how generations mirror one another through layers of time and space.

TM: Well, it's true. It's that the past of one is very much connected to the past of the other, and across generational lines, at least in the book, I wanted to stress what happens when you can't talk between those lines. I'm thinking a lot in this book about the connection between love and language. And I wanted to have the narrator, that woman who opens and closes the book and intervenes in it, be a person who understands how precious language is. And it was interesting to me that she only says three or four things to the characters and styles herself as a woman who was always quiet, but she's talking constantly to the reader, constantly going on and on.

And for her, some things were unspeakable, I think. And for the others, theirs was not unspeakability, it's just a frozen language. They have no language to talk to one another. But the ability to speak—she says, "if they only understood how precious the tongue was"—to be able to say, or to reveal, or admit to, which is a way of knowing. And then never be able to do that until they get rid of the hovering excuse they had for not coming together, which was Bill Cosey.

MS: The book seems to be arranged so that Toni Morrison can be separate from several different narrators and that the structure should emerge almost on its own. The author is in charge of charting a crystal in growth, say, or an accumulation. For instance, we will watch a woman leave home on the way to her lawyer's office. She has an idea. By the time she reaches that office, a very brief scene, we've gone through several of her lives and marriages, and it's all been, in a sense, immaculately stage-managed.

The amount of background that gets compressed into each scene is not just a matter of linkages, it's a matter of knowing how to manage the house so that the hotel at the center of the book is something really for a novelist. In a hotel, many people are living, and it takes the efforts of an entire staff to chart who's on the dance floor, who's a performer, who's in the kitchen, who's cleaning, who's made up the menus for this day's special, who's hidden the will, who's hidden the deed, where will this all go? And it's almost as if the Toni Morrison implied by this book is a vast staff of arrangers whose job is to get everything immaculately in place and then disappear.

TM: I hope I disappeared. I hope I did. My feeling is that the lean plot is information: this is *what* happens. But the meaning of a novel is in the structure. The question of when the information is given, at what time, what you want the reader to not just know but feel about this character, and then to learn more, and that's when the crystal begins to take its shape. Just writing the beginning, the middle, the end is one way to do it. It's not very interesting to me because it is not really lifelike. I mean, we don't live lives in plots. We sometimes retell ourselves the narrative of our lives in a chronological way, but it doesn't happen to us that way.

We learn something today that clarifies something ten years ago. Or we think the most momentous thing that ever happened was something that happened yesterday, or twenty years ago, only to learn that it was part, really, of something else or that it wasn't momentous at all. So that the way in which the mind takes in the varieties of experiences of life and other people has to be reassembled for its meaning. And that's where the structure, at least, what I work very hard at is the sort of deep structure, what is there underneath this activity, and then you see it from another person's point of view, not just one character but another's. And how and when that information becomes available to the reader seems to me to be the real adventure.

MS: It seemed to me that we come to understand of this group, as several others in your books, that their identities are dependent upon their relations to one another.

TM: Absolutely.

MS: And that they may often, for private reasons, want to conceal those relationships. They may be the subjects of scandal. And so, truth is about what conceals identity in some strange way. And the working of this book is to watch—I thought of interconnected cogs like watch works—to watch these cogs turning until they turn so carefully, with such jewellike design, that their arrangement allows the reader to see a whole beyond the purview of any single figure.

TM: Right, exactly. If we're careful in the reading, you get the whole sort of back of the clock as well as the face, as it were, and you see them working and depending on one another so completely for almost every movement, every thought, whether it's back and forth or whirling or whatever. I like that notion of the cogs. It gives me another way to think and talk about it. There are no isolated people. They may feel separate, but everything they do and think is connected to the behavior, or what they think was the reason for the behavior, [of] somebody else.

MS: We get the sense that the only way to know, even within a single consciousness, is to assemble the whole. Now, would you be willing to tell me in what way you think of the whole in this book. What are they reaching toward?

TM: The title.

MS: Love.

TM: Love. Not just carnal, the way we normally talk about it, reduced to its lowest common denominator, but that human instinct to care for somebody else. Whether it comes from Romen as a teenager who doesn't even know that he wants to rescue but he can't help it and is ashamed of it. Or whether it's appetite; or parental love; or the love of a father as Cosey had for his son; or the love of a grandfather trying to explain in some comprehensible language, to give advice to his grandson. Or just that closeness of two children that is so close they're like invisible friends. And the sort of wide-spirited love that L has for them all, which is sort of unconditional but has some certain conditions, because she's perfectly willing to judge them very sternly, but she obviously is not going to abandon them. As a matter of fact, she takes steps to make sure that they are not abandoned, no matter how silly or stupid they may at some point appear to her to be.

MS: Now I'm beginning to understand this. Is it possible then, that for each of these characters there's a defining love? Cosey's for his son, perhaps, Billy.

TM: Then his mistress.

MS: And then his mistress. And then other simulacra, other mirages of love.

TM: All kinds. May is just terrified of the revolution coming. She will lose her place, the property, her move into another status. The girls are shattered. Not only because they've been separated, but they have been trained to hate one another, which is a little bit different from just being split apart. And then there is an abiding love of the L character, and then there is a nice sort of companionship of the grandparents who are Romen's grandparents. And then there is this little broken girl, Junior, who had no opportunities really to experience it except for one tiny moment when Romen lifts her broken foot up and caresses it. And she feels this strange alien thing that makes her giddy. She doesn't even know what it is. It's almost like trust, not big enough to be called love, but it's the beginning of something.

So that this urgency, this thing we want to be: someone should love us, and also we have to love somebody. And that's the simple way of saying it. But when you take it apart and look at it closely, that's what they were all yearning for and having difficulty achieving, responding to, and clarifying. I did run through that manuscript carefully after I finished it and knew what the title would be, and I removed every word, every time "love" appeared, so that it would be raw. The first time those women say it is the only time they could say it.

MS: Yes, yes. And what happens is ultimately there are replacements for love that they try to use, and love is a hugely uncomfortable thing. In one case that love between young girls becomes the hatred between those two women, and that hatred replaces their love but binds them together.

TM: Right, they're still there. Can't live without one another.

MS: In the same house. Oh my goodness. So in other words, there is, for each of these relationships, a spectrum of alternatives to love. In other words, they desert love.

TM: Exactly. They abandon it, and it morphs into this other thing. Junior, hers is hunger. She's just eating all the time, trying to fill up. Romen is embarrassed by the first one until he is able to claim himself with her. But it's something that doesn't go away. It might even be natural to him, so that it's true that appetite can take the place of that feeling he had when he was at that party. It's true for Junior, knowing that it was all her, the only one she can trust is herself, so she's constantly looking for more things to eat. And the women are there in this frozen clear silence together.

MS: The characters are going to replace love with something that feels stronger than it to them: envy, hatred, jealousy, wealth.

TM: Love is scary to them.

MS: Love is scary to them. What, in relation to this, is that empty resort?

TM: Well, it is, I suppose, the culmination of something that started out with a certain kind of love on the part of Bill Cosey, which was to have this fabulous place that was for good times. Good times.

MS: The best good times. That's right.

TM: The best good times this side of the law. And to see that slowly drain away for a number of reasons. You're right. It wasn't only that Black people didn't have to go there anymore. It wasn't only that he was distracted after his son died and married this little girl because he had the license to do it. He could act out a whim because his mistress left town. It wasn't only because May was so destructive in her terror. And it wasn't only because of his choice of a bride. It was a combination of things. But what sucked up all their ambition about loving one another was turning their attention to him.

He was the one who authenticated them. He was the one whose legacy they'd fight over. He was the one who ruined their lives beyond repair, and they lie about it to themselves all the time. He probably wasn't thinking about any of them, but the point is that they were complicit in that movement of constantly making him the big daddy, the one who did it all and everything was *his* fault. And, therefore, you did this and you did this and you did this until they finally exorcize him. But in any case, they're at the point now where nothing but language can save them, and that's when you can say "L-O-V-E."

MS: Yes. Now, to go back to my observation at the beginning that people are almost needing years to interrogate these more recent novels, it seems as if a novel was something like a haunted house in its relation to the present. That as we live with a novel longer, as it becomes older, as it is no longer new and populated with characters who are new to us, but rather, as time goes on, with ghosts, we start to know where the bodies are buried. We start to know what ghosts need attention, need to be balmed.

And it's almost as if the time spent by a novel in its culture is about healing that novel. In other words, the problems are not solved in the novel but are solved, in a sense, by time and the position of the reader who was asked to explore the haunted house until it can be freed of its ghosts and reinhabited. Yes?

TM: Yes. And then the epiphany. I mean, it's true. If you will just, as a reader, open the door or see an open door, step in, and look around. No, you don't know who this is right away. No, you don't know who that is. No, you may not know what that room is for. If you like it, you'll go further. If you're afraid of it, you'll step out. Maybe you go back in later at another time. And then maybe you run around the whole house and get the lay of the land. And then later you'll go back into that house, and now you can see something else, something different. Now you don't have to worry about what's going to happen. Now you can just enjoy the place where these things happened and understand far more than the characters ever did about what this place is. And the more familiar it becomes, my hope is that it doesn't become dross, that it's still interesting to look at these nooks and crannies. To have that visceral response as well as this sort of cognitive, intellectual response to how this whole thing is put to-gether.

MS: So in other words, for the book, as for some of these characters, clarity brings resonance.

TM: Absolutely. For me, that's the reason one reads again. I'm sure you have books that you read one year and later on you read them again and it's a different book, or it appears to be. It isn't. You've changed perhaps, or you know more now, or you're looking for something else other than the obvi-ous, other than what happens.

And the only other thing I know like that—well, I'm sure there are many other things—but the one that comes closest to mind is, in addition to becoming familiar with and interested in a house, is also music. In which you hear a song when you're seventeen and then you have powerful reaction in one way. You hear it later and you have another reaction. But what you're reacting to is the same piece of music, perhaps done in different hands, but your memories of it the first time you encountered it, as well as what you're thinking now. And so how it's worth listening to again.

MS: That is so interesting. Cause one of these characters thinks to herself that "Mood Indigo" will help someone swim.

TM: It's seductive, right?

MS: Yes, that it will take the rhythm. And one thinks of "Mood Indigo," if one's listening to its words, as words that would impede passage. "You ain't been blue, no, no, no." And so, yes, after you've lived with the words long enough, you hear the force and the structure.

TM: Right. Exactly so.

MS: Well, it's been a real pleasure to talk to you again. I've really enjoyed it.

TM: Oh, it's a delight talking to you. You are really such a first-rate reader. I mean, it's lovely.

MS: Well, I am grateful to have the work of a truly extraordinary novelist to read.

2009: *A Mercy* (Part 1)

MS: Today I am in a state of great—well, can I say it?—pleasure. Because my guest is Toni Morrison. It's been a long dream of mine to be able to talk to her face-to-face. We've spoken together in interview on the phone before this, but this is the first time we've met. Her new novel, *A Mercy*, has just been published by Knopf. It is, to my mind, an extraordinarily distilled work, one whose nature you can't begin to describe until you reach its final page. It's a novel that proceeds by an extraordinary design, and the design of this novel is to let itself be complete—and completion is a subject of the novel, as it is for people as well. It is not complete until you've witnessed the entire book.

Now, this book does seem to proceed to organize very rich historical and complex materials. Many people talk about American diversity as if it were invented in the last twenty-five years, but this novel takes us to our native soil beginning in around 1680; the present tense of the novel is in 1690, and we're seeing natives, slaves, free Black people, white people, traders, new landowners, indentured servants, and all of these types of people, of many different religions and nationalities, are finding a way into this novel to tell a story as another story, a story of love and its refusal, is being told centrally. Faulkner says, writing a novel is like building a chicken coop in a hurricane. What is it like to organize such diverse materials?

TM: It's exhilarating just to attempt to struggle with the enormity, the immensity, not just of the subject matter, but of the continent. Trying to look at this very strange, very bountiful, but also very dangerous place. Who were these people? And to try to shape a narrative, which I suppose is what Faulkner meant: making order, summoning order out of this chaos. And then, ultimately, finally, what you can only do with those twenty-six letters of the alphabet is to find meaning in that narrative and in that chaos and in the structure.

MS: Now, that concept of chaos recurs and recurs in different forms in the novel. The first time I notice it, we're told that in Maryland a set of laws has been created so that chaos will maintain order. They've created a chaos in order to protect the dominant order. While, several pages later, we're told that people are trying to build a life that they can live, a temperate life, out of raw life. So we have two things going on at once: chaos being invoked to protect the powers that be, and, at the same time, chaos being tamed, raw life being tamed, so that life is possible.

TM: That's true. One is ennobled, and the other one is destructive. Those people who instituted, created, and passed laws to underscore, solicit chaos—

which was a racial and racist division among people who were landed gentry, and indentured servants who were white, Native Americans, free Blacks, Black slaves. The point was, after Bacon's Rebellion in Virginia, where this people's army pulled itself together, some 400 people of all ranks, in order to overthrow the government. They were successful for a while, and then they were all hanged subsequently. When order was restored by the governors, they instituted certain laws to protect the landed gentry. And the most important of them said that any white could maim or kill any Black and would not be persecuted and would be protected in that act. So that set up a permanent, as it turned out, distinction between poor whites and Black slaves. Now, the poor whites were not white until they were deemed opposite of the slaves. They were Polish people, they were Irish people, they were Brits. So the process of becoming white depended completely on the process of solidifying a Black population that was understood to have no protection.

MS: I would say that if there is a paradigm running through the book, which is full of the stories of people, there's a journey and an animal.

TM: You're right about that. Yeah, I was even thinking about Rebekka's trip and there being horses right behind them in the stall next to where the lower-class passengers were, and of course Sorrow on her foundered ship and what she could find that was left from the animals that had left. Anyway, you're right. There's a lot of connection.

MS: When you're building that, does that become conscious? Because there are animal fables in the book about an eagle and her young. We've been told certain things early on in the book about bears. In fact, so furry that they look like they have no bones, and by the end of the book we're going to encounter a sow bear. There's the profile of a dog that appears in steam by a kettle, and we encounter that again and again. And we're told by the person who speaks most frequently and most steadily in the first person, Florens, that you must teach yourself to read, to read the signs, sometimes quickly, sometimes slowly, and sometimes they occur too rapidly to be read. But that's what this book is about, a reading of the signs.

TM: Oh, absolutely. I think we forget how intimate people were with animals. As food on the one hand, as dangerous threats on the other. Animals could be predators. They also had to be handled—cows, and sheep, and goats—and you had to slaughter them to eat. But even if they were not threats to human beings, they could destroy your whole farm. If you don't know where the foxes are, they eat the eggs. Animals come when you put certain kinds of dead fish for fertilizers down; that attracts all sorts of other animals who eat your crop. So that relationship of humans and animals is not, you know, now we have to protect wildlife in order to keep it wild, I guess. Otherwise, we shoot it or kill it, so we don't have quite the same relationship. Pets, of course, become our companions, not other workers the way they were. Even when I was a child, dogs were used for hunting in my family. But that relationship was not only close, but you could communicate with an animal, or you felt you could. And what animals did was as important as what humans did. Therefore, you had to read, find out what it meant if the hen did not brood and all of that.

MS: I'm very curious here, because this book begins in what's said to be, if not an Eden, the most bountiful place since Noah's flood. And the characters, in many ways, emerge from mists, and they gather names gradually. Some of them are never named. What does the act of naming your characters mean to you?

TM: Some of them just come with a name. Florens just appeared with that name. It worked because it had a hint of *florins*, Portuguese coins, because she was on a plantation run by a Portuguese slave owner. Others of them, I had to search. Jacob Vaark, for example. I looked in ships' manifests for names of people who had come to this country, and that struck me, that I just picked out of a list. It worked, the Vaark part, because I wanted him to have that kind of background—

MS: Dutch.

TM: Dutch, through England, and then willing—as an orphan, as many of these people are—to go to a new land but have a background that was that of a street child: an orphan who'd come up through the ranks, work for a company, get out on his own, inherit land, and he was a classic figure of the immigrant. And at the same time, he would have to be accompanied and surrounded by the other kinds of people whose help he needed and who needed him.

MS: But for instance, the blacksmith is not named, or at least I didn't pick up his name. Is that a choice, too?

TM: Very much. I wanted him just to be the smithy or the blacksmith. He's like canvas, and everybody in the book projects onto him their own hopes and fears. He's like a blank slate. In my mind I was calling him "the Magic Negro" because he was obviously beautiful, obviously skilled, obviously articulate, and had this other gift. Those things would make him an object of desire or someone that could be your friend, as Jacob and he become very close because they respect each other as craftspeople. The Native American, Lina, is terrified that he's free—he can do stuff—but she's not. So giving him a name meant giving him a specificity. I would have to identify his tribe, his country, his route, everything. But I wanted him to loom large in other people's imagination so that when the confrontation between him and Florens takes place, it's recognizable.

MS: Now, in addition to moving through history and geography, I think the novel is moving through literature as well, that there is a scene in which Florens enters a scene that resembles a story out of Hawthorne. She meets a widow, the Widow Ealing. The Widow Ealing has a daughter. The daughter, Jane, has been accused of witchcraft, and in fact, horribly, the mother, the widow, has been whipping the daughter's legs to prove that she bleeds. She can't be a witch because demons don't bleed. Interrupting this torture is the arrival of Florens, who is thought by the elders to indicate that the devil, the Black man, is present. And the signature is the signature of a Hawthorne allegory. Is that the case?

TM: There is an affinity with the Hawthorne and *Scarlet Letter* business and many of those other stories that he wrote, because he was writing a hundred years later than that period *about* that period. And I thought, you know, other than that and some James Fenimore Cooper things, there was really very little fiction recently about that period, which is so rich, virgin, untapped. Because in our minds what we have is precisely that story: Puritans, witchcraft, and then later on some clerics and so on. So that our history, our narrative of the early part of the construction of what was later to become the colonies and then the United States, is so narrow. And it's wider than that, it seemed to me. The stories are multiple. I wanted to put the religion in the margins and have this fresh entrance into this extraordinary place that was, as you suggested, terrifically bountiful. I mean, you could eat all winter. You could shoot a turkey, and the one next to it wouldn't even lift its head, so unused to being shot they were. There were coasts where the whole beach was full of oysters. You could reach your hand down and grab fish. All sorts of things like that, that I had to really work, read books on what it looked like. But at the same time, as you suggested, there was threat, there were bears who would tear your arm off.

MS: Now tell me, if an American were to want to know his or her history, what could he or she be reading that would give a picture of the place that would correct, as your novel does, the picture we receive?

TM: Well, the ones that were helpful to me started with *Changes in the Land*—the author's name is Cronon—which is the result of a lot of study by—I'm not even sure I know the right job they had there—archaeologists, botanists that go back and find what seeds, what grasses were there, how tall trees used to be, what happened—as he puts it in the book—to the land before the Europeans came, and what the European entrance did to the land in this area of New England.

I had to know what these people who came here were running from. So I read an extraordinary book called *Hubbub: Filth, Noise, and Stench in England, 1600-1770*. I needed to know what it was like to come to this place where the air was perfumed to them, where water was clear and not sewage, where there was space and not this closed-up city street full of, you know, garbage and pedestrians and peddlers. That made it just so wonderful. There was something of magic and magical about the letters people were sending back, and they were right about so much.

So, in looking at what the history was really like, the last one that was most interesting to me that I would recommend is a book called *White Cargo*, which is about indentured servants and where they came from. And what that meant. Because it wasn't our notion of somebody comes over, his passage is paid, he has a job for six or seven years, and then is let go. That was not typical. That was the so-called theory. But you could find indentured servants in people's wills, and their children could be assumed to have that debt, so that in effect they were slaves, and they were like the bound people of all countries we've ever known—Egypt and Athens and Russia. You called them different things, peons et cetera, but they're people who have no rights under the law. And at that time, that was very much what was true here. So that you found, and I found this in a number of books, Black slaves, white slaves, free people, poor people—particularly children—working together on these plantations.

MS: One of the things that is in the background of this book is a concept of freedom. We're told that there has been a suspension, at least in Maryland, of manumission, of setting free. And the signal act of freeing in the book—a book that's full of different forms of capture, and falling under the sway of, and being possessed by—this daughter, who's been thought to be a witch, tells Florens to be free, and she tells her to fly. We also notice that there are certain qualities that Florens is given, in addition to being told to fly, that have to do with birds. She brings her claws out from her feathers when she has to attack, and also she notices owls that are part of her love affair with the blacksmith. But I wanted to ask you about the idea of freedom in this book. What is it? People have already come to America claiming they're seeking at least freedom from religious persecution and other kinds, but what freedom can they find?

TM: They can find freedom from a certain kind of persecution, religious, and then reestablish a different kind of persecution on other people, which is often what they did. Most of them that were not involved in the religious communities were looking for license, not freedom. Freedom hadn't become a brand name quite as it is now and was later in the eighteenth century. Florens believes she's a throwaway and that fundamentally she's so needy. She craves connection and love. Any kind word is enough for her. So, obviously, when she falls in physical love she's taken over by it and has to be sort of instructed about freedom. The man says, "I have seen slaves freer than free men," so he believes freedom is an inside job, is the mental thing.

She evolves over time in the book. She is not the person at the end that she was at the beginning. And that journey, which is both physical as she goes to find him, is also her enlightenment bit by bit by bit, so that whatever happens to her, it's not a happily-ever-after status that she acquires, but she's an adult and she can make her own mistakes freely with consciousness. For the Native American, Lina, freedom is an entirely different thing. She's totally loyal, even when the person to whom she's being loyal turns out not to be what she was before. But her sense of herself, a kind of nobility of consistency. Because she had been thrown away, since all of her family and tribe were killed by pox. She's a survivor of that. So connection, being loyal, never letting anybody down, for her, is extremely important. And that's her liberation, as it were, even though it looks like a connection, to us, that she can't break. Then there are the indentured servants there. Well, I won't go on at great length about it. But your perception of the levels of freedom, what slave really means, legally as well as emotionally and in terms of the mind. When she says, "You own me, please, you own me." And the blacksmith says, "Woman, own yourself."

2009: *A Mercy* (**Part 2**)

MS: We've discussed the backgrounds to this novel—historical, some of them Biblical, some of them literary. But no matter how much you discuss background, what remains to discuss is the literary resonance of a book, how it's achieved, and what it comes to mean. Now, I believe that *A Mercy* is a very carefully shaped novel, a novel that does not give up its meanings and its secrets until you reach its final page. How was it shaped?

TM: Wanting to have a young Black girl, enslaved, on a journey, surrounding her with people upon whom she depended. But once I had her voice and I really heard how she sounded, the question was whether she should tell that whole story or not. And then I realized no, she wouldn't know. And also I couldn't have her evolve that way. Besides, she was talking in the first person and always she spoke in the present tense, and that I liked and shaped carefully to give the book that was taking place so long ago an immediacy. It was always now, now with her.

Then the question was: Who are the people that surround her? How shall they speak? How will we know? So then, I decided to have her interrupt each one of those characters who made up that put-together family until the end. That the story should move like a bullet. We really want to know if she gets there and what happens, but we really want to know who these other people are.

So their stories were difficult because they're third person. I had to tell their stories from their point of view, be very true to what they saw, but at the same time move the narrative along that was Florens's narrative, so that the momentum was never lost, even though we could stand and sort of watch one character at a time and get their feeling. It was always the movement, the movement, the journey, several journeys that were taking place at the same time.

MS: What I thought was its great originality of form was that, because of this first person narrative, which is a travel narrative, a journey, a quest narrative, it moves through the book and there are interrupting chapters about each of the people who have been on the tobacco farm. Is it a tobacco farm?

TM: Well, Jacob Vaark's is a normal, subsistence farm. They have cows, some crops, but there's no profit in it, which is why he's traveling around trying to make more.

MS: And what we see becomes a very unusually shaped picaresque narrative. She is moving forward on her quest, and each of these chapters takes the form, in a picaresque novel, of meeting a stranger, of being told the background of the person that you've met, except always these interruptions are interruptions of what she's known as home.

TM: That's right.

MS: She's moving to the blacksmith. She has a letter in her stocking giving her permission to travel. She is fetching the Black man with whom she has fallen passionately and helplessly in love because he is a healer. He has healed a woman on the farm, a woman named Sorrow. The master, Jacob Vaark, has died. His mistress is now beset by pox. She will die, too. Lina, the Native woman, awaits, and each of these characters, including two indentured servants, Will and Scully, will tell us the world to which Florens is bringing back the principle of healing.

TM: Yes.

MS: They believe in healing.

TM: Oh, yes.

MS: And this healing will precede the return of Florens. The strangeness and brilliance, I think, of the book is that there is a healing accomplished, but it alters things for the worse.

TM: Yes.

MS: In the book's climax, what we're going to see is that, although a superficial vision of healing has been visited and heals the pox, it leaves behind the brokenness of life and a broken community. Now returning is Florens, who during her journey has been set free several times, once by the daughter, Jane, suspected to be a witch, but most radically by the blacksmith, who essentially says to her, "Stop mythifying everything. I'm not mythic. I can't save you. Your mother who abandoned you, she will never be there to save you. You must return to wherever it is you come from and bring reality with you. You will be the principal of the real, and all of this insanity must find an adult form of solution rather than the mythic one."

TM: You nailed it, Michael.

MS: Thank you, I was hoping so.

TM: She says, "My feet are as hard as cypress now." You know, she comes with these little tender feet, because she loved to wear shoes, and she ends up barefoot but with soles as tough as the oldest wood, toughest wood you could find.

MS: She's been told something also about America, because everyone is always talking about the American wilderness and, in particular, its embodiment as the virgin land. And the book has a kind of, "Well, what is this about all these virgins?" And constant trauma about rape and sex and an awareness that nothing's virgin and what remains virgin is unknown. And so what happens is, in the climax, there's a new definition of wilderness, and the blacksmith essentially says, "Wilderness is what forms when a person is made a slave to no matter what." To no matter what: another man, to love, to nature, whatever it is that you have given yourself up to, that is your slavery. That is wilderness. And taming the wilderness means to become free.

TM: Exactly. And it's echoed by the mother at the end, her final words. There was a problem that I had to solve about whether or not Florens would ever know what her mother was thinking when she gave her away. And I decided not to let that happen because a) I wanted her to develop on her own, and b) that was the problem of enslavement, there was the separation of mothers and children and they may never know where they are, what happened to them, et cetera. So at the end, when the mother says what the mercy is, she says, "Well, there are certain kinds of things that are wrong, and there are certain kinds of things that are harmful. But giving your whole self, dominion of your whole self, to another is really wicked," which is exactly what the blacksmith was intimating.

MS: And more than that, that miracles come from God, but mercies come from man. And that what we have in this world is mercy. And therefore what are stories when they're not allegorical? Allegories can involve mystery and miracles, but human stories involve mercy, making do in a difficult situation with what kindness is available to us.

TM: Only humans can provide that. Only humans love like that. You don't get anything for an act of mercy. You don't feel good about it, it doesn't make you feel better. But she saw in Jacob Vaark someone who did not look at her daughter as though she were a product but looked at her as though she were a human being. And although the mother had been praying for a miracle, what she got was this almost accidental mercy of this man who permits her to get her children out of a situation, or her daughter out of a situation, that she thought would really destroy her.

MS: As we see Jacob Vaark arriving in his section of the novel, he's been let off of a boat and he's walking to the coast of Maryland where he does business. He does business there because, being owned by the King, it's open to foreign trade.

TM: Yes, yes.

MS: And the first thing we see him do is to save a young raccoon. Its bloodied leg has been caught in the split of a tree. And, you know, this is not an unfunny book. We're told his first act is to save a coon. The author is well aware of what's going on here and that the book is going to be investigating. Yes, it is a mercy. Yes, yes, he saves it, but no one can save someone else. Our character, Florens, who's going to be reflected not just by the animals in the book but by every other character.

TM: Well, he enters the chapter through gold, through this fog that's fired by the sun. And it's the dream part of America. You know, the American dream is through gold. It's happiness. He's on his way. He's tough. He's a good adventurer. He does stop. He's kind to animals. Later on, at the end, when he decides that he might get involved in rum, he washes his hand in the water at the beach and a little dried coon blood comes off.

MS: Yes, we've been watching him make the choice that a man will make in America to surrender perhaps his mercy and become an investor, an owner, a trader.

TM: This is America's origins, in that sense of the acquisition of property, and he wants this big house. I mean, all right, he's a consumer, but we can play with the consequences of that yearning, some of which is progress and some of which is excess. And it's the excess that drives him to figure out that it's okay to be involved in a business that is totally related to brutal slave labor so long as it's not something he has to actually himself protect and be intimately related to these bodies.

MS: As Florens says in her opening telling, it all begins with shoes. And Messalina, a fallen woman, is identified with high-heeled shoes, as is the Portuguese mistress. The minister, the Reverend Father, tells them that you'll be able to lead the good life after the difficult life here on earth when you get to heaven. And we're reminded: when I get to heaven, going to put on my shoes, going to walk all over God's heaven. But taking off the shoes and developing the tough sole that can deal with life is very much the end of what—what do you consider them to be? I call them symbol systems or nets of meaning, but when an image has a destination in a novel, how do you think about it?

TM: Well, it's never decorative, these metaphors that I am impressed with. It's partly the meeting of language and meaning. Obviously *sole* and *soul*. Obviously in other areas, like we were talking about coon, it has to be real, something somebody does. It has to have an allusive quantity. And then it has a meaning, and that is not always on top, and sometimes one searches for it, and sometimes it's just something that the reader absorbs without knowing that that is what is going on. You get the feeling of what it is.

MS: And sometimes you know something is resonant before you know what it means.

TM: Exactly.

MS: That when it's working you feel not just plot, which is what people like falling into place, but meanings arranging themselves sensibly so that they have been relayed by the narrative. The story has given you access to a realm of meaning that's higher than story.

TM: My trust in a reader, and the readers trusting me at some level, and that relationship between us, happens at that level. It's not only that one is a fastidious reader. It's that paying some attention the first or second time is rewarding because I don't have to say this means that. The reader can pick up his or her own meaning from this display that's available. The sexual scene that Sorrow witnesses between the blacksmith and Florens, she says it's like dancing. And she had never seen anybody make love that way. She wouldn't call it making love because her own experiences had been the passive young girl who is controlled by whomever likes her. Here is a man who kisses a woman on the mouth, and she hadn't ever seen that or felt it, so it moves her in another way. On the one hand, there's a sort of interesting passion, and I hope there's sensual language even that Florens uses about him. But then this is another person who knows about the act but sees it almost like a ballet, so that when she becomes pregnant, by probably the deacon, her response is quite different. She takes over because it's not about the act and the consequences. It's about her place in it.

MS: Now I want to turn in a slightly different direction. We've just said that a novel depends upon its achievement of resonance and meaning, and that along with the actual order of a book, there's its symbolic order. I think we've entered a time in America where an enormous symbolic act has occurred and we've yet to find out what its meaning will be. Since you gave, what was for me, the wittiest and most daring interpretation of President Clinton some years ago, what do you take to be the revelation we're encountering now that we've elected Barack Obama?

TM: Several things occur to me, most of them very, very positive. In a large sense, it feels brave, this choice. It's not just that we've been told to be frightened of everything and everybody, foreign and domestic, because somebody's going to get us. And somebody is going to get us, perhaps. They've already tried at 9/11. But the fear thing, there's something humiliating about that, to me, as a nation, because underneath it I keep saying it's a form of cowardice. Bad things happen. You have to be alert. You should be prepared, you should be tough, but not, "Oh my God, this." And that's part of what severe racism is to me. It's the bully's fear underneath, which is cowardice. The bully doesn't want to fight you because he might lose. He just wants to beat you up. That sort of feeling that I've had in many instances.

This election seems—now, I don't mean that it wiped all of that out—but the enormous thrill I felt in people's willingness to take it back, their own sense of what this country ought to mean or has meant, the myth of it, the reality of it, let's do it. And that is what the election revealed to me along with some other things. And it seemed to me that Barack Obama, with his myriad ethnicities—interestingly, he is African-American in a way that local African-Americans are not. This is a genuine Africa and American connection. But also that experience in other countries, not by flying over them or into their great hotels and protected by some diplomat, but living there, speaking that language.

So, these things make the identity game that we always play in this country moot. And the discourse is just how to say it. How do we say these things? And of course it's crude most of the time. It's obvious or overt the other times. But having this election, the discourse changes—not necessarily on television, but certainly among us, and the consequence was brave. I can only say it's courageous—about him and who we are.

MS: Well, much of your work, it seems to me, is about removing the bit and being given permission to speak. Florens, at the end of *A Mercy*, is down on the floor. It's literally a kneeling, but she is writing—

TM: Her story.

MS: Her story on the enormous floor of the room in which her master died, a room in a house that no one is allowed to go into. She's been given the ground to speak. One of the things that I thought was, for years now, all of us—as they say, white and Black, straight and gay, whoever we are—we've lost permission to speak. We lost the language to speak to others. All kinds of political correctness prevented us from having a direct and adult confrontation, and it felt to me like the return of language, that I was going to get a language that I didn't know yet how to speak, but that the next years would be a journey in searching for a language that we all can use to talk to one another again.

TM: Precisely, we can *really* talk to one another. I wrote an essay once called "Racial House"—and its confinement and its openness. When I saw her in there, first I had it with paper. And then I thought, no, that's too precious an item at those times, and nobody's going to have extra paper. But when I realized that she would be in that house, in the house that race built, writing her story with a nail, not even a pencil, and it would cover the whole place, that to me was an overwhelming image of her. Not only as the character tells her own story, but this particular person at this particular time in this particular house. It seemed to say something about journeys and language and what it's for.

Grace Paley

1996: *The Collected Stories*

MS: I can't tell you how many times I've read the stories of Grace Paley, but it begins in ignominy. When I was in college, Donald Barthelme said to me, "Have you read Grace Paley?" I said, "Ah, too many Jewish writers. It embarrasses me. It's where I come from. I know it all already." No, no. It's true.

GP: I believe you.

MS: I was afraid of it. And then one day I had a small paperback by Grace Paley, I started to read it, and my mouth fell open because in story after story she reinvents the language, she makes it possible to be whoever you are as an artist. The language, while taken from the street, is condensed in some unimaginable way, about which I mean to talk to her and figure out a little bit of how she did it. But these things, they seem simultaneously fragments of every day and built to last. And I wonder, does that have a special knowledge or forethought on your part?

GP: Well, it's a funny question. I can't even really answer it because when I began to write the stories I didn't even think anyone would read them. I didn't think they even had a present, let alone a future. So I'm surprised myself, in a lot of ways, with their longevity, so far anyway. But you know, when these stories came out everybody said, "You must not—you can't do short stories. It just can't be done." And it was done really by Doubleday as a kind of favor in the hopes that I would really eventually write a novel. And the same year, *Goodbye, Columbus* came out, and *Tell Me a Riddle* the next year. All these books of short stories, which the publishers said would never go, are still in print.

MS: Not only still in print, but still read, which is better still.

GP: Even better. Better to be read than in print. Yeah. We'll have to think that one through.

MS: Better read than dead.

GP: I was trying to do something with it.

MS: It won't happen.

GP: I know.

MS: There was this sense I always had, because Donald would tell me that you would gather things up and they would accrete slowly, and that you didn't want to publish them for the most part, and that he told you when you had a book ready. Is that true?

GP: Oh, yeah. Well, see, between the first book and the second book, there was the Vietnam War, in which I was very busy. But it wasn't only that, because I was writing the stories that became *Enormous Changes at the Last Minute*, and publishing some of them. It wasn't that they weren't published. People always ask you how you write a book. And I wasn't thinking a book, actually. I was writing as I lived along my life. And one day Don came to me—he lived across the street, so it was easy—he came over and we were leaning on the stoop and talking, as we often did. He said, "You know, you have enough stories for a book. What's the matter with you?" And I said I didn't think so. And he said, "Why don't you go upstairs and see if you do."

So I did that, and I began to get things together, and sure enough I did. And I probably would have eventually gotten them together, but it might have been another five years if it wasn't for Donald, really.

MS: He had told me when that story in *New American Review* came out. You see, I regarded Donald Barthelme as my literary father. He was someone who told you what to read and how to behave to another person. He would say if you were bad, "We were put here on earth to love one another," and he'd calm you down.

GP: That's right. No, he's right, absolutely right. I was going to say (to the audience): yes, you're right.

MS: He was the teacher of good literary manners. And when "Faith in a Tree" came out in *New American Review*, he said, "This is a permanent story." One, he meant, that would not only last forever, but every time you looked at it you would see something different. And he knew this, I think, the day it came out. The twenty-five years since has borne him out to be correct. Here is a little bit of Matisse in the sentence here and frilly greenery in a city and bits of Purcell—the whole thing a great collage of sound and ways of looking and feeling and seeing.

GP: Yeah. I think so. It's life in Washington Square Park.

MS: But tell me, how did that story in particular—because I love it so much—get written? What's the story?

GP: The first paragraph is really the story, is what the story's about. If you want me to read the first paragraph, then that might really save a lot of further conversation. Not that we want to do that.

MS: Here it is. The opening paragraph of "Faith in a Tree" by my guest Grace Paley.

GP: "Just when I most needed important conversation, a sniff of the man-wide world, that is, at least one brainy companion who could translate my friendly language into his tongue of undying carnal love, I was forced to lounge in our neighborhood park, surrounded by children."
So I sort of went on from there.

MS: There sometimes seems to be a crazy energy. Like in that paragraph, for me, there's a Grace Paley inevitability: brainy and carnal.

GP: I hope so.

MS: Right away. And then in that story I know there are words that I see that are Grace Paley words of a story moving on. "Curly" is one of them.

GP: Curly.

MS: Curly. Curly head. And "creepy." "I have seen you, creepy chief of the forest of four ginkgo trees."

GP: That's true. That's the little boy.

MS: There's a sense of words being like atoms. This extraordinary sense that everything is going to interact with everything else. This kind of pointillist—what is it?

GP: I can't really say. It's not for me to even think too hard about it. But I did enjoy writing those parts. I did love writing about the children.

MS: Were they your kids?

GP: Well, not really. I have a daughter and a son. And I lived with their father until my kids were about 18 years old. My life is not Faith's life at all. I lived a very, what one might call, a stable family life, if such a thing exists. And on and off it was stable.

MS: Faith and the two boys, Anthony (Tanto) and Richard, they're there.

GP: Well, we had kids; I had a feeling for children all the time, all my life, even from childhood. And I listen to them a lot. And my children's friends and so forth.

MS: You said one of the most important things for me. I found an interview somewhere, some book, one of those where authors say what's important. And you said something like, "I have one piece of advice for writers. Not many pieces of advice, but listen to your grandmother. She's probably too old to say anything unimportant." And that was really, for me, a big thing. Because I grew up with a grandmother. But the "listening to" seems nevertheless to be combined with the idea that every sentence is going to come out Grace Paley.

GP: I don't know if that's good.

MS: Well, that's pretty good to my mind. But where did that Grace Paley tone of voice come from?

GP: Where does it come from? I think this happens a lot in this country. It comes from home. So there are different tunes at home. There's a Yiddish tune, there's an English tune, and there's a Russian tune. And the Russian tune is very strong. A lot of Russian spoken, mostly. English spoken a lot. Yiddish, a little. Those tunes are there. I think that sort of has something to do with it. Plus loving English literature. I never didn't love that as well.

MS: I wanted to talk about one story in particular. And I thought I'd ask you to read "Wants." It is such a brief story and contains so many things that are simultaneously, individually beautiful and true. It's pretty odd. I guess this is, to my mind, the funny miracle of Grace Paley. That there are few writers more eccentric in their language, and yet most of the time eccentricity does not lend itself to truth. So eccentric and true.

GP: "Wants

I saw my ex-husband in the street. I was sitting on the steps of the new library.

Hello, my life, I said. We had once been married for twenty-seven years, so I felt justified.

He said, What? What life? No life of mine.

I said, O.K. I don't argue when there's real disagreement. I got up and went into the library to see how much I owed them.

The librarian said $32 even and you've owed it for eighteen years. I didn't deny anything. Because I don't understand how time passes. I have had those books. I have often thought of them. The library is only two blocks away.

My ex-husband followed me to the Books Returned desk. He interrupted the librarian, who had more to tell. In many ways, he said, as I look back, I attribute the dissolution of our marriage to the fact that you never invited the Bertrams to dinner.

That's possible, I said. But really, if you remember: first, my father was sick that Friday, then the children were born, then I had those Tuesday-night meetings, then the war began. Then we didn't seem to know them anymore. But you're right. I should have had them to dinner.

I gave the librarian a check for $32. Immediately she trusted me, put my past behind her, wiped the record clean, which is just what most other municipal and/or state bureaucracies will not do.

I checked out the two Edith Wharton books I had just returned because I'd read them so long ago and they are more apropos now than ever. They were *The House of Mirth* and *The Children*, which is about how life in the United States in New York changed in twenty-seven years fifty years ago.

A nice thing I do remember is breakfast, my ex-husband said. I was surprised. All we ever had was coffee. Then I remembered there was a hole in the back of the kitchen closet which opened into the apartment next door. There, they always ate sugar-cured smoked bacon. It gave us a very grand feeling about breakfast, but we never got stuffed and sluggish.

That was when we were poor, I said.

When were we ever rich? he asked.

Oh, as time went on, as our responsibilities increased, we didn't go in need. You took adequate financial care, I reminded him. The children went to camp four weeks a year and in decent ponchos with sleeping bags and boots, just like everyone else. They looked very nice. Our place was warm in winter, and we had nice red pillows and things.

I wanted a sailboat, he said. But you didn't want anything.

Don't be bitter, I said. It's never too late.

No, he said with a great deal of bitterness. I may get a sailboat. As a matter of fact I have money down on an eighteen-foot two-rigger. I'm doing well this year and can look forward to better. But as for you, it's too late. You'll always want nothing.

He had had a habit throughout the twenty-seven years of making a narrow remark which, like a plumber's snake, could work its way through the ear down the throat, halfway to my heart. He would then disappear, leaving me choking with equipment. What I mean is, I sat down on the library steps and he went away.

I looked through *The House of Mirth*, but lost interest. I felt extremely accused. Now, it's true, I'm short of requests and absolute requirements. But I do want *something*.

I want, for instance, to be a different person. I want to be the woman who brings these two books back in two weeks. I want to be the effective citizen who changes the school system and addresses the Board of Estimate on the troubles of this dear urban center.

I *had* promised my children to end the war before they grew up.

I wanted to have been married forever to one person, my ex-husband or my present one. Either has enough character for a whole life, which as it turns out is really not such a long time. You couldn't exhaust either man's qualities or get under the rock of his reasons in one short life.

Just this morning I looked out the window to watch the street for a while and saw that the little sycamores the city had dreamily planted a couple of years before the kids were born had come that day to the prime of their lives.

Well! I decided to bring those two books back to the library. Which proves that when a person or an event comes along to jolt or appraise me I *can* take some appropriate action, although I am better known for my hospitable remarks."

MS: Okay, will you hold my hand and let me talk honestly and directly?

GP: Yes. Now holding hands. Can't see it, but we're holding hands.

MS: We're holding hands, and I have a good magic trick, too. This story, the way it seems to work—like "Elsewhere," the story in the most recent book—there are two things that appear. In that story a man takes photographs in China and then takes photographs in the Bronx. And the difference between the way he's treated is sort of the difference in the way the story turns. Here, two things from the past appear—library books, the husband. She can return the library books, but in some sense the husband is still with her as a reprimand. I wonder, it's almost like the stanzas of a sonnet, the order, and then brilliant concealment in the surprising excitement of the language. So that the story should not tell itself too quickly or give itself away, and make itself utterly memorable in the process. Is this something like the composition?

GP: Well, I don't know. I always like demystifying things a little bit. But I will say that I was sitting on the steps of the library on 6th Avenue, and this guy passed who looked like my former husband. And that really is where the story started. And I had just given two books back after a long time. And I just sat and thought about it and thought about it. I think a short story like that does happen in a piece, almost. Once I get going. A longer story is another matter entirely and could take a whole year to just write twenty pages.

MS: But the compression is so enormous in it. A whole life is there.

GP: I believe in that, I do. I believe that most novels are far too long. And yet they're very interesting. It's not that I'm not interested in them; I read them just as much. But for me, I believe that that's part of my task I've assigned myself, although I didn't know it at first. I may not have known it for ten, fifteen years. Which is to tell as much about life and the world as I could in a short space, because I had been writing only poems until I wrote "Goodbye and Good Luck," and those stories.

And when I began to write stories, I tried to write a novel at one point, and I saw that it was disgusting, it was terrible. But I have all of these interests in the political world and in the historical world. Less in the psychological world, that interests me less. But in the historical and political world, I'm very interested in that. And it seemed to me that I had to, in some way, tell ordinary life within that complication and not leave it out.

It's more that I felt people, in writing a lot of domestic stories—which I believed in or I wouldn't have started writing them—but they were leaving out too much, or at least I missed it. And you put in what you miss.

MS: More and more as the stories go along, these stories of domestic and daily life contain in them criticisms of daily life. Capitalism, feminism, they enter too, as if life should not just be presented, it should also be commented upon by its livers.

GP: Right. I think in the first book I did that, maybe not for the first time in that story, but in "The Used-Boy Raisers," where they get into a long discussion about Newman and Catholicism. And then she throws in her Jewish two cents on the Diaspora. And I just felt that people really think about these things and talk about them and they're kind of left out.

MS: It's also as if thinking is part of who people are.

GP: Yeah, that's a good way to put it.

MS: So the characters seem to be named Darwin, Ricardo, Hegel-Shtein—thinkers. And then at the same time, in addition to the thinking, there's compassion. Faith and her sisters—Faith, Hope, and Charity. It's almost as if in the names there's this desire to have as much of life as possible jostling.

GP: But the funny thing is, I didn't think of it that way. Like when you just said to me "Hegel-Shtein," that's the first time I realized: Hegel.

MS: No, no you can't tell me that. I don't believe you.

GP: Yeah. I swear to God. I mean I may have known it then, but I forgot it ever since.

MS: Forgot it promptly.

GP: Because those names are common. I mean they're common sort of.

MS: Yes, but not when you have—

GP: Darwin, right?

MS: Come on.

GP: You're right. You're right. You're right. I guess I was fooling myself.

MS: I want to ask you, because for me the returning of library books is a very important thing. I have been grateful; I had read, of course, *The House of Mirth*, but I hadn't read *The Children*. And when I read that story I went and got *The Children*—

GP: You're wonderful.

MS: I also owe to Grace Paley a couple of writers that I want my listeners to hear a little bit about. Years ago you recommended a Russian writer, Konstantin Paustovsky, and the book I got was *The Story of a Life*. It's really an amazing book, and I wondered if you would tell about him?

GP: I think he's probably closer to you, you would probably tell about it more easily. But it's really about someone who was totally Russian and stayed there through the revolutions and tried to live his life there. If you think about what happened later, you really should read what happened earlier in him.

MS: But you mentioned him at one point as an influence.

GP: I did?

MS: Yeah. In an essay.

GP: If you live long enough, you know, you'll mention a lot of things.

MS: And then meet someone who will make you account for them.

GP: And then forget. I was just looking at a thing I wrote on teaching and what I told my class to read. I forget exactly what it was, but I told them to read a number of things that I really was astonished I hadn't read myself since then. I did tell them to make sure to the read *Memoirs of a Revolutionist* by Kropotkin. This was for a writing class.

MS: Well, it's important. You have to read everything. Isaac Babel will tell you that: "You must know everything."

GP: Right. You must know everything.

MS: You must know everything.

GP: Yeah.

MS: The story is very much about New York now and then. It comes up a lot. You've moved away from New York. To Vermont I think?

GP: Mm-hmm.

MS: Has that made a problem for your writing? Because it was so intimately connected with the circuits of the city.

GP: I don't know that it's made a problem for my writing because, really, what you write about and think about has been in your head a long time, at least in my head a long time before I write it and think about it. I was thinking about almost everything in each book for at least twenty years before that book came out. So I'm still thinking about a lot of New York things.

But I do miss New York very much. I miss all my old lady friends, and of course I miss Don who lived across the street and died, so he's not there. Anyway, he went and moved to Texas, so what good was he?

But I miss the city, and yet now that whole life of the city sort of scares me a little bit. And I don't mean the ordinary life of the street, the things that other people are afraid of. I mean the intensity of the literary life, that whole world that I had no knowledge of and no inkling of and no reason to be part of, so it never worried me. Now that I've gotten older and my books are out there, I would be afraid of that world a little bit.

MS: For me, at least, to have *The Collected Stories* of Grace Paley—I hope they are not the final collected stories—

GP: No. No. I'm working. I have a book of nonfiction that's going to come out next year called *Just as I Thought.* And it's a lot of stuff that I did during these years.

MS: Well, to have them together like that, to me, is a real occasion. Then, one by one, I said, "Oh, it will win the Pulitzer Prize." It didn't win the Pulitzer Prize. I said, "Oh, it will win the National Book Award." It didn't win the National Book Award. And something does happen. It's a strange thing. You start to think, well then there's something wrong with the world if the stories of Grace Paley come out and they don't win every major award there is.

Because I want to end by telling my listeners that really, in the time I have been doing this show, but really the time I've been reading, there aren't that many permanent books. And *The Collected Stories* of Grace Paley is several permanent books put into a more permanent book. So those of us who are interested, in some crazy way, in the middle of every kind of evanescence, impermanence, should get this book.

And thank you very much for joining me.

GP: Oh, thank you. Thank you so much.

W. G. Sebald

2001: *Austerlitz*

MS: I'm honored to have as my guest W. G. Sebald, the author of some of the most important prose writing of the century, including the novels *Vertigo*, *The Emigrants*, *The Rings of Saturn*, and now *Austerlitz*. The prose has the breaths and cadences of poetry, and I wanted to begin by asking, were you influenced by German poetry?

WGS: No, not at all by German poetry. The influence came, if from anywhere, from nineteenth-century German prose writing, which also has prosodic rhythms that are very pronounced, where prose is more important than, say, social background or plot in any manifest sense. And this nineteenth-century German prose writing even at the time was very provincial. It never was received outside Germany to any extent worth mentioning. But it's always been very close to me, not least because the writers all hailed from the periphery of the German-speaking lands, where I also come from. Adalbert Stifter in Austria. Gottfried Keller in Switzerland. They are both absolutely wonderful writers who achieved a very, very high intensity in their prose. One can see for them it's never a question of getting to the next phase of the plot, but that they devote a great deal of care and attention to each individual page, very much the way a poet has to do. What they all have in common is this precedence of the carefully composed page of prose over the mechanisms of the novel that dominated fiction writing elsewhere, in France and in England, notably, at the time.

MS: When I started reading *The Emigrants*, I was thrilled to encounter a kind of sentence that I had thought people had stopped being able to write, and I felt great relief at its gravity, its melancholy, but also its playfulness, its generosity. How did you find the way to reinvent such a sentence?

WGS: It's not of this time. There are hypotactic syntax forms in these sentences that have been abandoned by practically all the writers now for reasons of convenience. Also because simply they are no longer accustomed to it. But if you dip into any form of 18th- or 19th-century discursive prose—the

English essayists, for instance—these forms exist in previous ages of literature, and they simply have fallen into disrepair.

MS: The wandering that the prose does, both syntactically and in terms of subjects, reminds me a bit of my favorite of the English essayists, De Quincey: the need, in a sense, to almost sleepwalk, somnambulate from one center of attention to another, and a feeling in the reader that one has hallucinated the connection between the parts. This I think is among the loveliest qualities, especially in the new book, *Austerlitz*.

WGS: Well, certainly, moving from one subject, from one theme, from one concern to another always requires some kind of sleight of hand.

MS: I was struck in the opening of *Austerlitz* by the way in which the narrator moves from a zoo, from the—what is it called?

WGS: The Nocturama.

MS: The Nocturama. It's a structure for animals that are awake only at night. And before long the train station to which he returns becomes the double for the zoo. The eyes of certain thinkers become the doubles for the intense eyes of the nocturnal animals. Then the train station recalls a fortress, and there's a gradual opening out, an unfolding of structures and interpositions. The speaker might well be the person spoken to, by virtue of this logic. And it extends with, it seems to me, an invisible referent—as we go from the zoo to the train station, from the train station to the fortress, from the fortress to the jail to the insane asylum, the missing term is the concentration camp.

WGS: Yes.

MS: And always circling is this silent presence being left out but always gestured toward. Is that correct?

WGS: Yes. I mean, your description corresponds very much to my intentions.

I've always felt that it was necessary above all to write about the history of persecution, of vilification of minorities, the attempt, well-nigh achieved, to eradicate a whole people. And I was, in pursuing these ideas, at the same time conscious that it's practically impossible to do this; to write about concentration camps in my view is practically impossible. So you need to find ways of convincing the reader that this is something on your mind, but that you do not necessarily roll it out, you know, on every other page. The reader needs to be prompted that the narrator has a conscience—that he is and has been perhaps for a long time engaged with these questions. And this is why the main scenes of horror are never directly addressed. I think it is sufficient to remind people because we've all seen images, but these images militate against our capacity for discursive thinking, for reflecting upon these things. And also paralyze, as it were, our moral capacity. So the only way in which one can approach these things, in my view, is obliquely, tangentially, by reference rather than by direct confrontation.

MS: It seems to me, though, that, in addition, it is the invisible subject as one reads the book and one watches moths dying or many of the images. It's almost as if this has become a poem of the invisible subject, all of whose images refer back to it, a metaphor that has no statement of its ground, only of its vehicle, as they used to say.

WGS: Yes, precisely. You know, there is in Virginia Woolf this—probably known better to you than to me—wonderful example of her description of a moth coming to its end on a windowpane somewhere in Sussex. This is a passage of some two pages only, I think, and it's written somewhere, chronologically speaking, between the battlefields of the Somme and the concentration camps erected by my compatriots. There's no reference made to the battlefields of the Somme in this passage, but one knows, as a reader of Virginia Woolf, that she was greatly perturbed by the First World War, by its aftermath, by the damage it did to people's souls, the souls of those who got away, and naturally of those who perished. So I think that a subject which, at first glance, seems quite far removed from the undeclared concern of a book can encapsulate that concern.

MS: I notice in the work, in particular in *The Rings of Saturn* and *Austerlitz*, the tradition of the walker. I'm thinking of Rousseau's *Reveries of a Solitary Walker*, and thinking, too, that it was once beautifully common for a prose writer to write what he sees on his walk. In fact, the naturalist Louis Agassiz said that Thoreau used to bring things to him in the laboratory at Harvard and that the things Thoreau picked up by accident were never less than unique. It was necessary for a writer to develop an eye. And it seems to my ear that the rhythms here have to do a great deal with the writing of entomologists and naturalists.

WGS: Yes, the study of nature in all its forms. The walker's approach to viewing nature is a phenomenological one, and the scientist's approach is a much more incisive one, but they all belong together. And in my view, even today it is true that scientists very frequently write better than novelists. So I tend to read scientists by preference almost, and I've always found them a great source of inspiration. It doesn't matter particularly whether they are eighteenth-century scientists—Humboldt—or someone contemporary like Rupert Sheldrake. These are all very close to me and people without whom I couldn't pursue my work.

MS: It seems that in *Austerlitz*, even more so than in the other books, there is a ghostly prose. Dust-laden, mist-laden, penetrated by odd and misdirecting lights, as if the attempt here is really to become lost in a fog.

WGS: Yes, well, these kinds of natural phenomena like fog, like mist, which render the environment and one's ability to see it almost impossible, have always interested me greatly. One of the great strokes of genius in standard change to nineteenth-century fiction, I always thought, was the fog in *Bleak House*. This ability to make of one natural phenomenon a thread that runs through a whole text and then kind of upholds this extended metaphor is something that I find very, very attractive in a writer.

MS: It seems to me that this book is truly the first to pay extended stylistic respects to the writer who, it's been said, has been your mentor and model, Thomas Bernhard. I wondered, was it after three books that one felt com-

fortable in creating a work that could be compared to the writing of a
master and a mentor?

WGS: Yes, I was always, as it were, tempted to declare openly from quite early on
my great debt of gratitude to Thomas Bernhard. But I was also conscious
of the fact that one oughtn't do that too openly, because then immediately one gets put in a drawer which says Thomas Bernhard, a follower
of Thomas Bernhard, et cetera, and these labels never go away. Once one
has them, they stay with one. But nevertheless, it was necessary for me
eventually to acknowledge his constant presence, as it were, by my side.
What Thomas Bernhard did to postwar fiction writing in the German language was to bring to it a new radicality which didn't exist before, which
wasn't compromised in any sense. Much of German prose fiction writing,
of the '50s certainly, but of the '60s and '70s also, is severely compromised,
morally compromised, and because of that, aesthetically frequently insufficient. And Thomas Bernhard was in quite a different league because he
occupied a position which was absolute. Which had to do with the fact that
he was mortally ill since late adolescence and knew that any day the knock
could come at the door. And so he took the liberty which other writers
shied away from taking. And what he achieved, I think, was also to move
away from the standard pattern of the standard novel. He only tells you in
his books what he heard from others. So he invented, as it were, a kind of
periscopic form of narrative. You're always sure that what he tells you is
related at one remove, at two removes, at two or three. That appealed to
me very much, because this notion of the omniscient narrator who pushes
around the flats on the stage of the novel—you know, cranks things up
on page three and moves them along on page four, and one sees him constantly working behind the scenes—is something that I think one can't do
very easily any longer. So Bernhard, single-handedly, I think, invented a
new form of narrating which appealed to me from the start.

MS: It's not only a new form of narrating, it's a new form of making things
stop in space. Because the Bernhard works are often composed in one long
paragraph, sometimes in one long sentence, if I'm not mistaken. The effect
is of a dream, of being spoken to in a dream, and your attention can't help

but flicker in and out. You can move back a page or two and discover very careful links of the chain. But the intensity has been so nonstop that it's almost as if it breaks the mind's attempt to hold it in a chain.

WGS: Yes, it is that. Bernhard's mode of telling a tale is related to all manner of things, not least the theatrical monologue. In the early book that bears the English title *Gargoyles* and in German is called *Die Verstörung*, the whole of the second part is the monologue of the Prince of Salla, and it would make a wonderful piece on the stage. So it has the intensity, the presence that one can experience in the theater. He brings that to fiction.

MS: I've been very amused because critics of your work in America seem to be bewildered by its tone, and I don't, in fact, find its tone bewildering. I think they are unfamiliar with it because of its tenderness, a tenderness brought to bear on subjects that have usually compelled indignation, scorn, and, certainly in Beckett and in Bernhard, a huge and glittering kind of contempt and scorn. Here it really has the quality of—am I wrong here?—of infinite care taken in listening to speakers who are not being reviled in the slightest.

WGS: Yes. I don't know where it comes from, but I do like to listen to people who have been sidelined for one reason or another. Because in my experience, once they begin to talk, they have things to tell you that you won't be able to get from anywhere else. And I felt that need of being able to listen to people telling me things from very early on, not least, I think, because I grew up in postwar Germany where there was—I say this quite often—something like a conspiracy of silence (i.e., your parents never told you anything about their experiences because there was, at the very least, a great deal of shame attached to those experiences). So one kept them under lock and seal. And I, for one, doubt that my mother and father, even amongst themselves, ever broached any of these subjects. There wasn't a written or spoken agreement about these things. It was a tacit agreement. It was something that was never touched on. So I've always—I've grown up feeling that there is some sort of emptiness somewhere that needs to be filled by accounts from witnesses one can trust. And once I started—I would never have encountered these witnesses if I hadn't left my native country at the age of twenty, because the people who could tell you the truth, or something at least approximating the truth, did not exist in that country any longer. But one could find them in Manchester and in Leeds or in North London or in Paris, in various places, Belgium, and so on.

MS: I find it almost spooky how frequently these critics—I guess expecting the austerities and harshnesses of certain postwar prose—don't see that this is characterized by tenderness, bewilderment, horror, infinite pity, and a kind of almost willed self-mortification. That is, I am willing to hear and place great acts of attention on all things with the chance and hope that revelation will occur.

WGS: Well, I suppose if there is such a thing as a revelation, if there can be a moment in a text which is surrounded by something like *claritas, veritas,* and other facets that qualify epiphanies, then it can be achieved only by actually going to certain places, by looking, by expending great amounts of time in actually exposing oneself to places that no one else goes to. These can be backyards in cities; they can be places like that fortress of Breendonk in *Austerlitz.* I had read about Breendonk before, in connection with Jean Améry. But the difference is staggering, you know—whether you've just read about it or whether you actually go and spend several days in and around there to see what these things are actually like.

MS: It was once explained to me that there was in German prose something called *das Glück im Winkel,* "happiness in a corner." I think that your radical contribution to prose is to bring the sensibility of tininess, miniaturization, to the enormity of the post–concentration camp world. So that a completely or newly forgotten prose tone is being brought into the postmodern century, and the extraordinary echo, the almost immediate abyss that opens between the prose and the subject, is what results. Automatically, ghosts, echoes, trance states—it's almost as if you are allowing the world to howl into the seashell of this prose style.

WGS: Well, I think [Walter] Benjamin at one point says that there is no point in exaggerating that which is already horrific. And from that, by extrapolation, one could conclude that perhaps in order to get the full measure of the horrific, one needs to remind the reader of beatific moments in life, because if you existed solely with your imagination in *le monde concentrationnaire*, then you would somehow not be able to sense it. And so it requires that contrast. The old-fashionedness of the diction or of the narrative tone is therefore nothing to do with nostalgia for a better age that's gone past but is simply something that, as it were, heightens the awareness of that which we have managed to engineer in this century.

Stephen Sondheim

2009: *Road Show* with John Weidman (JW)

MS: I believe Stephen Sondheim and his collaborator, John Weidman, to have written a really great trilogy of musicals about America. Those three are *Pacific Overtures, Assassins,* and now, at last, in a final form, *Road Show. Road Show* began with a book about the Mizner brothers called *The Legendary Mizners.* It became a musical, which worked through in workshops, called *Wise Guys,* became a musical called *Bounce* when it was first recorded, and now it is *Road Show.* A recording of *Road Show* was recently released on Nonesuch PS Classics. And when I heard it, by the end of the record, I was kind of shivering. Now, this was in Los Angeles, so believe me, it wasn't cold out. It was that, somehow, they'd touched a certain thing about the nightmare of American optimism—what you might call American perpetual motion, the idea that it goes on and on, and that you can't change it, that not even death brings it to a close. Now, I'm curious, how did this start? I believe you had read *The Legendary Mizners,* Steve—and my guests, by the way, are Stephen Sondheim and John Weidman, the collaborators. And I'm very, very honored to have them here.

SS: Well, I read it when I was twenty-two years old. It was a couple of articles in *New Yorker* magazine, and then they were expanded by Alva Johnston, who wrote them into a book. And I read the book, and I thought it would make a terrific musical. I got fascinated by the character of Wilson Mizner, who was a jack-of-all-trades and perhaps a master of none, but the restlessness, and the fact that he never found a center for his energies and his talents fascinated me. And I wanted to buy an option on it, take an option on it. I was working in television, writing a series called *Topper* in California. And after five months, I had enough money to rent an apartment and some money left over to, I hoped, take an option. And I got back to New York and found out that an option had already been taken on it by, of all people, David Merrick, who was sort of the most notorious Broadway producer at the time. And it was to be written by S. N. Behrman, a very well-known playwright who had not written a musical before, and a score by Irving Berlin, and was to star Bob Hope. A number of years later, I was working on *Gypsy* and David Merrick was the producer. I asked him what had ever happened to that Mizner musical. And he said, "Oh, we gave it up. Behrman wrote about five scenes, and Berlin wrote half a dozen songs, and it just didn't work out." So, I thought, ooh. So I immediately looked into the rights again, and I tried to interest, over the years, a number of producers in it and couldn't, or rather didn't. And then many years passed, and I wrote two shows with John Weidman and mentioned it to him, and he got interested in it. But it was another aspect of the story that interested him. So he can tell you what interested him. It wasn't Wilson's character as much as it was Addison's.

JW: Steve called me, I guess right after he had written *Passion*. And he said he didn't want to write another gloomy musical, and had I ever heard of a guy named Wilson Mizner? And I said I hadn't, and Steve said, well, there's this book, would you be willing to? I said, yeah. So I got a copy of the book and read it. And my response to Wilson as he's characterized in the book was completely different from Steve's. He struck me as a selfish, self-involved, S.O.B. And at the same time I thought his relationship with his brother was interesting. He had a brother named Addison who took sort of a different path through life but one which kept him partnered with his brother much of the time. But Addison had very different ambitions and creative ambitions. He was a genuine artist. And in the end, his brother Wilson, after sort of bringing down everybody else he'd been involved with, looked around, and there was nobody else to bring down, and so he brought his brother down. That interested me. But, honestly, as much as anything else, it was the period of time against which these two guys lived their lives that I found fascinating. I mean, their lives, for all intents and purposes, began with gold rush in the Yukon in 1895 and ended with the land rush in Florida in the 1920s. The land rush had turned into a bust and really was a rehearsal for the market crash a few years later. In the meantime, they had sort of crisscrossed the country, always on the move, trying a variety of different things, Wilson more than Addison. But it seemed like—these seemed like two emblematic American lives. And if we could figure out what it was that was really emblematic about them, there was a great story there. And given what we finally figured out, and given where we landed on *Road Show*, I'm afraid that Steve's desire not to write another gloomy show went by the boards.

SS: Oh, I don't think it's gloomy.

JW: Well, it's, it's not exactly gloomy, but it is bleak.

SS: That's different, see, that's quite different.

MS: Fair enough.

SS: It's bright and bleak.

MS: Exactly. The thing that is amazing that makes *Road Show* a musical for our time, and maybe not the time when you discovered the book, is that, mysteriously, when you look at it carefully, the musical is structured as a series of very rapidly maneuvered, slippery pyramid or Ponzi schemes. So the mood of the musical is very much that of the dexterity, which we see today has not only destroyed our economy but destroyed our faith in one another, our ability to trust anything. Now, perhaps we needed to be a people whose gullibility got an overhaul, but somehow or other, this is the musical of our desperate times, it strikes me. The songs are shaped—I call them houses that Jack built—but they take a form that you've been work-ing on since "Pretty Little Picture." It's a growing crystal form.

SS: Old MacDonald.

MS: Yes. In the course of this, it seems that the material has been stripped down for ultimate swiftness so that we can watch the speed with which things self-destruct.

SS: That's very shrewd of you, because actually, I think it should be—I think I should say to the listeners that it took us, that we wrote this show over a period of fourteen years. We did not write steadily for fourteen years, but the first draft was finished in 1994, and the show didn't get produced until

2008. *Road Show*, that is to say. *Bounce* got produced a few years earlier. But the final shape—and the swiftness of the final shape is very much due to the influence of our director of *Road Show*, John Doyle, who, on reading the script, urged John and me to cut out as much extraneous material, including transitions between scenes, as possible, to give it exactly the spring-like tension and swiftness that you speak about. You agree, John?

JW: Yeah. And before John got his hands on it, it had wound up on the desk of Oskar Eustis at the Public Theater. And Oskar had really taken us through the first stage of refocusing the material. Oskar felt very strongly that the show still was a kind of a mix of tones and styles and that what we needed to do was to focus on the serious purpose that underlay the story. The three iterations of the show—the first one that we did downtown at the New York Theatre Workshop; then *Bounce*, which we did with Hal Prince at the Goodman in Chicago and at the Kennedy Center; and then *Road Show* at the Public—have a very similar structure in terms of the storytelling. The characters are the same, with the exception of a female character who was added to *Bounce*. But in terms of their intention, they are wildly different shows. And it was, as I said, first with the help of Oskar, and then John, we were nudged in the direction of finally creating a musical about the Mizners called *Road Show*, which, as you say, is a companion piece to *Pacific Overtures* and *Assassins*, and I think makes a collection of pieces about America that fit comfortably together, which would not have been true of any of the earlier versions of the show.

SS: It's true. By oversimplifying, I'll say: Oskar focused us on the subject matter and John on the style.

MS: Now, what I noticed was that *Wise Guys* began with a sort of medley of songs that Addison and Wilson sang together. *Bounce* began with one song that they sing together. *Road Show*, fascinatingly, comes to the understanding that these guys would never sing together, that their voices in harmony are an unimaginable thing. And, what's more, at the heart of the show, there is a song between Wilson and another man, not his brother. It's a love song between two men.

SS: You mean, Addison.

MS: Addison, excuse me, Addison. And what is his friend's name? Hollis. They're singing together—what I think is a first for a semitraditional Broadway musical—a love song between two men.

SS: Well, *La Cage* had that too, I think.

MS: But there, *La Cage*, that was the subject. This arrives at something with difficulty.

[Musical Excerpt: "The Best Thing That Ever Has Happened"]

MS: Well, you see, I think that this is one of the big discoveries of the Sondheim musical, and I don't think anyone has ever really pointed to it. The question being: Who sings? Who can sing with whom? For the beginning—I don't know how long—of *Gypsy*, except for the timid voices of two little girls, all you hear is Rose's voice. It's one monologue after another, and even in a duet with Herbie, she's drowning him out as he explains that he can neither sing nor dance, and she is saying, "You'll never get away from me," a terrifying impulse. The next indication that I had of this was when you said that *Do I Hear a Waltz?* shouldn't be a musical because you can't make a musical about a person whose essential nature—

SS: Well, no, actually, what I said was everybody should sing except Liana because it's about a woman who metaphorically can't sing until the very end of the show, at which point she would sing, and then you would understand what the—to use that dreadful word that's all too common these days, talking about her journey, as actors like to say—her journey would be towards the moment when she can sing. Then it would've made sense, and I would have loved to have done that, but Richard Rodgers would have none of it.

MS: And the discovery in *Sweeney Todd* that, although Sweeney and Mrs. Lovett will sing together, their harmonies are extremely bizarre and that they're always singing at something like cross purposes. Add to this the description of character in song, that complicated rhymes and multisyllabics are the province of intelligent—

SS: Or educated.

MS: Educated characters. You begin to get a whole sense of how to musicalize character. And I think that in *Road Show*, much of what's done in this show is done entirely in the choice of the kind of song: who's singing with whom; whether they sing together or apart; and who can, finally, even for a brief section of time, fit together. Because immediately after this love song, Wilson comes back and essentially seduces Hollis, and, suddenly, it's what we can do together.

SS: That's absolutely right.

JW: That's correct.

MS: This is, across the board, a lack of faith in human unions and continuities, yes?

SS: Well, I don't know about that. It's interesting, though, that at one point we had a trio between Wilson and Addison and Hollis, in which you actually saw what you just described happen. It was in our vaudeville days, you know, the original *Wise Guys* was conceived as a sort of Hope and Crosby road movie, a vaudeville, and partly justified by the fact that John discovered that vaudeville was born and died in the same years that the Mizners were born and died. Which turned out to be a very useful coincidence. And when you spoke about the medley of four songs, of course, they were done in vaudeville style. And that aspect played into a number of scenes that we would interrupt the story to have, these little vaudeville interludes. And one of them was a trio in which you saw Wilson seduce Hollis away from Addison. So, you know, that's a footnote to what you just said.

JW: I mean, it's an earmark of what we were struggling with, I think, in that first expression of the show that the first conversations we had started with a notion of a kind of a Hope-Crosby relationship between these two guys, which I thought was fascinating. And I thought if you could write a show, which felt like a Hope-Crosby musical, but which had a serious purpose of the "road to ruin," as opposed to the *Road to Morocco*, you'd have something extraordinary. As a practical matter, it turned out to be really undoable for all kinds of reasons that I could go—I can make a list. But that's one of the things we were discovering when we were down at the New York Theatre Workshop.

MS: Well, one of the things that I notice is that it's a peeling back of ingenuities. You know, the idea of doing the show as a vaudeville show, or as a "road-to" movie, it would have been ingenious. But what comes in *Road Show* is emotionally very intense. It's cloaked only by ambivalence, but it's a very dark interplay between characters. And it's made, it seems to me, brilliantly, out of the intersection of: where is song, where is dialogue.

SS: That was the essential change between *Bounce* and *Road Show*: what you call the darkening. *Bounce* was deliberately bouncy, and *Road Show* is deliberately more solid.

MS: Let's talk about that darkness. For one thing, musical comedy itself is thought, as an art form, to be involved in a war between commerce and art. Are those things necessarily at odds with one another?

JW: I think—and then Stephen, dive in here—I think they are more and more and more at odds with one another. And I think, really, the only home for musicals that have a serious artistic ambition at this point are not-for-profit theaters. And that, if something in that venue makes a splash, like *Spring Awakening*, then it may get picked up and may be moved and have some kind of a commercial life. But all these shows—except for *Pacific Overtures*, which is from a different era—began life at not-for-profits and have continued to have lives at not-for-profits.

SS: Not a coincidence.

MS: It seems to me that part of the ambivalence and bleakness is an interest in truth-telling, and that people don't feel very comfortable with the truth. They don't like it in songs, and musical comedy songs were, at one time, famous for asking you to look for the silver lining. And it was fairly deeply sophisticated people who were advising this search. So there's a tendency to like musicals for the shallow optimism of their prescription, of course.

SS: Of course. People look for truth—or used to anyway—in straight plays, and they still do in novels and things like that. They just have never looked for truth in musicals until—actually it started with—Oskar started to, with *Show Boat*, started to say, you know, a musical can actually be about something, and it can still be entertaining. And from then the history of musicals changed a bit, but sure, people essentially go to musicals—just the word itself suggests song and dance, suggests entertainment in its lightest and most mindless and soothing and exhilarating form.

2010: *Finishing the Hat*

MS: Today, the great Broadway songwriter Stephen Sondheim is my guest. His book, *Finishing the Hat*, is the first volume of his collected lyrics. It covers work from 1954 to 1981 and comes with attendant comments, principles, heresies, grudges, whines, and anecdotes. It's one I've been waiting for eagerly. From *West Side Story* to *Merrily We Roll Along*, *Finishing the Hat* is a book that puts on display the enormous amount of work that Stephen Sondheim puts into the writing of a theater song, down to tiny concerns about *a*'s and *ah*'s, *the*'s and *but*'s and *and*'s. It's an extraordinary process. I wonder: When you first began to hear lyrics—I know they were often Oscar Hammerstein's—had the difficulty occurred to you?

SS: No, I'd never thought about writing them. And I don't think Hammerstein's were the first I heard. In fact, they weren't. I grew up on—my father had records of people like Fats Waller and Rodgers and Hart. And so I heard a lot of songs long before I heard any of Hammerstein's, or even knowing, I should say, that I heard any of Hammerstein's—I probably heard some of the Hammerstein and Kern stuff, *Show Boat*, let's say, without knowing it. But, you know, it didn't particularly interest me. So, no, it didn't; nothing really occurred to me about the difficulties.

MS: When did they become apparent?

SS: Oh, after I submitted my fifteen-year-old show that—say, I was fifteen years old and submitted a school show that I'd written to Oscar in the surety that he was going to produce it, and asking to treat it as if he didn't know me. By that time, I was sort of a member of his family, sort of an orphan member of his family, and had been since the age of eleven. And I said, "Pretend you don't know me and it just crossed your desk." And he said, "Well, in that case, I have to tell you, it's the worst thing I ever read." And then he proceeded to tell me why it was the worst thing, but he treated me like an adult. And he did it as an encouragement because he said it's not that it's not talented, but let's just take a look at how the songs are structured, and how the rhymes are made, and how the scenes are constructed, and how the characters evolve, and the inconsistencies, and he went through it page by page. It was all in one afternoon, so he didn't get very far because there were so many errors on every page. But we got fifteen, twenty pages into my show. And I learned, as I've said many times, I probably learned more about song-writing for the theater in that afternoon than most writers learn in a lifetime.

MS: It must have been crushing. How quickly were you able to adapt?

SS: Oh, in five minutes, because it was so fascinating, listening to him talk about it. And he, you know, I knew he loved me, or at least liked me at the very least. It was a disappointment, not a hurt.

MS: Did he show you his worksheets? Because one of the fascinating things in *Finishing the Hat* is the opportunity to see many of them side by side, and to see the impulses that run into the making of a song.

SS: No, I never saw any of his worksheets. He didn't really share his work habits with me. Once, when he wrote *The King and I*, I remember he showed me the script. This was before it went into rehearsal. I'd had a bad time with my mother, who was a difficult woman. And so he asked me to come over to his house, and—I think in order to calm me down—he gave me a script of *The King and I* and said, "Why don't you—in your head—why don't you set some of these lyrics to music and then see what Dick Rodgers does with them and—

MS: Wow.

SS: So it was a way of diverting me, and it did, but otherwise I never saw any of his work in progress, no.

MS: That's extraordinary. Did you set them?

SS: I set "We Kiss in the Shadow," and I set it as a waltz because it seems to me so clear when you read the lyric that it's in three. And of course Dick Rodgers set it in four, which taught me a lot about how different composers think about different things. His is a much more original setting than mine was.

MS: When you got the opportunity to work with Rodgers—one of the sadder descriptions in *Finishing the Hat*—by that time, what did you think it would be like to have that opportunity?

SS: I didn't think one way or another. It was something that Arthur Laurents sort of talked me into. And Oscar had—when he was dying, and knew he was dying—he said to me, "You know, when I'm gone, Dick is gonna feel very bereft. And though I know you to write your own music, I wish you would consider writing something with him." And I said, "Of course I will." And over a period of a couple of years after Oscar did die, Dick kept sending me projects—or not *kept* sending me, sent me two, I think—and they didn't appeal to me. But because I'd had such a good time working with Arthur Laurents, when the opportunity came—it was actually Arthur's idea to adapt one of Arthur's plays, called *The Time of the Cuckoo*, into a musical—it seemed like a good way of killing two birds with one stone. And it was not.

MS: And in *Finishing the Hat* you demonstrate how sometimes the very best lyrics won't do. You talk about one of your own favorites, "Pretty Little Picture," as one that holds up the show. Is that what a lyricist has to expect in the process of working a show into place?

SS: You mean the business of cutting out songs or—

MS: Cutting out songs, finding that your favorites are somehow not going to make it.

SS: Yeah, well, "Pretty Little Picture"—actually, the reason—there was more than one reason for "Pretty Little Picture" being cut. First of all, *Forum* has numbers that hold up the action. That's part of what happens in the first act. *Forum* is not a show in which the songs carry the story forward, for the most part. And they are what Burt Shevelove, who co-wrote it with Larry Gelbart, described as "respites" in the action. He said, you know, they're different than the kinds of shows that Oscar writes and that you've been trained to write. And what he meant was, really, that it was more like the shows pre-Oscar—that is to say, pre-*Oklahoma*. The Rodgers and Hart shows and the Cole Porter shows were songs that were merely raisins in the cake. You know, it was comedy scene, and then a song, and a comedy scene, and then a song. And the songs were not meant to carry the story forward. That was a sort of, I won't say an *invention* of Oscar's, but that's what he developed in the musical theater. So "Pretty Little Picture"—the first act wasn't working anyway, the whole show wasn't working out of town. But more important: Zero [Mostel] was not a patter singer. You know, he had his speech patterns and his—in fact, all of his comedy had to do with bluster and not with patter. And the role was designed, when I wrote the song, the role was designed for a kind of terrier-like comic, not Zero. Zero was supposed to play the pimp, and Milton Berle was supposed to play—actually, we wrote it for Phil Silvers. And Phil Silvers, when Larry Burt brought him the script, he said, "Gosh, this is just like all the shtick I've been doing all my life," mean-ing Sergeant Bilko, which, of course, Sergeant Bilko is a form of Pseudolus. Plautus invented that character, and invented the sitcom, as a matter of fact. When you trace sitcoms back to where they really come from, they come from Plautus's plays. So Phil Silvers, I sort of designed it with that kind of fast-talking Sergeant Bilko mouth in mind. And then when he reneged, we got Milton Berle, and Milton Berle had a similar kind of thing. He could have done it, I think. But Zero was supposed to play the pimp, was sup-posed to be Lycus. And the irony was, of course, that he ended up playing Pseudolus. And the double irony was, in the movie, he ended up playing Pseudolus, and Phil Silvers ended up playing the pimp.

MS: So there, essentially, you are at that stage of your career—a show not pro-duced; *West Side Story*, but not with your music; *Gypsy* with Jule Styne's music; and *A Funny Thing, Anyone Can Whistle*, then *Do I Hear a Waltz?* And six years before the next show, which I think of as the time that you spent interrogating individual words in order to make crossword puz-zles—

SS: You're talking about the period between *Do I Hear a Waltz?* and *Company*?

MS: Yeah.

SS: Well, that was—first of all, it was only five years, it was '65 to '70. And secondly, James Coleman and I wrote the first few drafts of *The Girls Up-stairs*, which turned into *Follies* during those years. Then *Company* came along, and because George Furth's plays came along, and Hal said, "I'd love to do this as a musical," and I said, "Well, as soon as I finish *Follies* maybe we can talk about it." He said, "No, no, I want to do it first, and I'll tell you what, if you write *Company* first—if you write *Company*, and do it first, I'll do *Follies* second." And I said, "Okay, fine." So, no, those were not as fallow years as you think.

MS: Oh, so you were doing those while you were also—because I think of those puzzles as being like a full-time job—

SS: No, no, they were—well, it was—no, but I was fairly quick and glib about those puzzles. That was in 1969. That was the year just before *Company*. And I guess I was writing *Company* at the same time, and I quit the puzzles, simply—I did quit the puzzles after a year because I thought, "I got to get the show written." But no, it wasn't a full-time job. It was, I would say, it was probably a day a week.

MS: For listeners who are just coming in, I'm talking to Stephen Sondheim, and I'm talking about a little-known period of his life, but very well known to me, because every week in the *New York Magazine*, Sondheim was doing, really, an American version of the British cryptic crosswords. And these were so brilliantly done, and opened my eyes, really, to looking at single words and how they were composed, and how they could surprise and trick you. And then comes *Company*, a very original show where you begin to move beyond the Rodgers and Hammerstein show—

SS: Oh, indeed.

MS: —into a form that is, in a way, based on revue.

SS: It's a hybrid, it's a hybrid between revue and book, and as such, was a real, in its own way, an invention. But one of my principles, as I say in the book *Finishing the Hat*, is that content dictates form. And here the content was a cursory examination of five marriages and a single man who is contemplating marriage and observing the five married couples who are his closest friends. And how would you structure such a thing once you decide to do that? Well, you're not gonna try to—or you'd be foolish to try to weave the five into some kind of plotline story. And therefore what is suggested is individual scenes. But at the same time, you don't want to do just five little one-act musicals. And therefore it turned out to be exactly what it turned out to be, which is a combination of revue and what used to be called a book.

MS: You did, I think, three musicals with George Furth, who, here in LA, was beloved by many of us. If I'm not mistaken, *Company* was constructed from George's first plays?

SS: Yes, apparently he was in analysis, and the analyst suggested that he might write down some of the things he was feeling and some of the things he was observing in the form of, well—I think, write. I think he just said "write." I don't think he said play or short story, but "write." And so George indeed sat down and wrote, I think eleven—it may have been seven—little one-act plays that were his observations on emotional commitments.

MS: And then he's learning to put together a show with you and Hal Prince.

SS: Yeah. Well, the three of us talked at length, because Hal thought I—the plays came to Hal's attention because they were going to have a Broadway production and had fallen through, and George didn't know what to do. And he called me and he said, "I don't know what to do now that my production has fallen through." And I said, "Well, let me give them to Hal Prince, who's very savvy." And Hal at that point was a producer, had just begun directing. And I said he would really know what to do. Hal said he thought it could be a musical, which surprised both George and me, and he flew George in from the coast. And we just sat and talked about it a bit. And then George and I went home and gave it a big think and thought, you know, what could hold the play together was the fact that almost all of his little one-acts had a catalyst third character, and they were about a couple plus a third character. And the third character was different, of course, in each play. And not all the couples were married. Some of them were just living together or flirting, but whatever it was, there was a third character. And we thought the third character—because we had to have something to hold the evening together. And once we got the idea of Bobby as an observer of these marriages and somebody who was looking to make an emotional commitment or not, then the whole thing fell into place quite quickly.

MS: That's so interesting, because it's in the show *Company* where some of the songs are from the position of observers, too.

SS: They're all observational songs, really, unless they constitute a scene, like they do in "Barcelona," where the whole scene is a song.

MS: Now, those commentary songs become very much more complicated in the next show, *Follies*, when you are writing show songs that reveal moments in a major character's past, which we haven't seen—it's being reenacted as *Follies*. And we are in a kind of nightmare breakdown sequence, all of which is structured around a kind of, well, many of them are charm songs or novelty songs. There are even two counterpoint songs, four characters. I was there on the opening night of *Follies*, and I just about fell out of my seat with astonishment and admiration. But that kind of song, which is both a conventional song, a genre song, and a character song: How did that kind of song evolve?

SS: Well, you know, it's nice of you to say that. I'm not sure that's a character song. It certainly is a genre song that deals with a situation in which the four characters are finding themselves. So the notion of utilizing folly songs to reflect the states of mind of the four principals in a surreal setting, a surreal *Follies*.

MS: You've admired the lyrics of DuBose Heyward for their simplicity. And I wonder, when the lyrics become complicated, do you, consequently— your own lyrics—distrust them?

SS: I'm not sure what you mean.

MS: Well, when I got *Follies: The Complete Recording*, so-called, on two discs, and I heard for the first time a song, I guess, that was written for the London *Follies*, and there's a lyric—I think I'll have it right—"As changeable as a chameleon with all that entails, / But nobody saw what was really underneath all those veils." And, you know, that's the kind of thing you talk about, where writing a lyric is like dealing with flaming torches, juggling with them, torches and knives at the same time. And the lyric is so good that I wonder how you can distrust complexity and ingenuity in a lyric, or prefer the simple.

SS: It depends. First of all, that is a pastiche number, like these *Follies* numbers in the original. That number is a substitution for the number called "The

Story of Lucy and Jessie," and was written for Diana Rigg because she was not a dancer. And so I decided the only way to solve that was to write it for a singer. But it's the same thing. The complexity is a reflection of the complexity, and the wordplay, and the playfulness of the lyric writing of that generation, of the Cole Porter generation, of the Yip Harburg generation, where the songs did not have to do anything but be sources of enjoyment for the audience, and they didn't have to carry any kind of emotional weight at all, or certainly no story weight. And so you could afford to just play around with words, which I do in the first *Follies*, too, you know, the verses of "You're Gonna Love Tomorrow," or, you know, our playful puns and intricate inner rhymes and playing around with where—

MS: "Sally, dear, / Now that we're / Man and wife, / I will do / Wonders to / Make your life / Soul-stirring / And free of care." "If we fight / (And we might), / I'll concede. / Furthermore, / Dear, should your / Ego need / Bolstering, / I'll do my share." Yes, those verses.

SS: That's exactly the same kind of thing. It's the exact same thing. The complexity is—one of the things I liked about writing those pastiche songs was it allowed me to play with words and not be untrue to the characters.

MS: By the final shows in this book, which is just the first volume—and, really, so much happens afterwards—we've got, well, we've got *Sweeney Todd*, we've got *Merrily We Roll Along*, we've got *Pacific Overtures*. But it seems as if the subsequent musicals go so deep inside the form of what musical comedy can be. Does that become your goal?

SS: Oh, no, I never had a goal. No, each story, you know, generates its own style and all that. And I like stories, obviously, that offer chances to use music in unusual ways, or to use songs, I should say, in unusual ways. But no, I mean, it's nice that you think it gets deeper and maybe that's just me getting better as a writer.

MS: No, but I'm thinking of, say, *Pacific Overtures*. Now I may be quite wrong here, but one day I was sitting looking at it, and it seemed that the score was a big spiral, that the songs in the first part are repeated in a different form in the second part. And the complexity was so exciting to me. And if that's not getting deeper as you go along, I don't know what is.

SS: Well, okay. That's nice. And I take it as a compliment, but in fact, the only conscious effort to do that in *Pacific Overtures* is the opening number and the closing number, which echo each other, and that's because I wanted to show what had happened in a hundred years, 120 years. Otherwise the music does get more Western as it goes along, as the country becomes more Westernized. But no, it wasn't, I didn't conceive of it as, in any way, as a score with a shape. I wish I could say I did, but I didn't.

MS: Wow.

SS: But you know, the unconscious does that. If you're right—and I don't know that you're right and I don't know that you're wrong—but if you're right, then it's an unconscious thing. But I believe in that. I think the unconscious can very well shape something that you didn't know that you're not thinking of on the surface.

MS: It's very interesting that you say that because, you know, when I went through it and I think of you as someone—not exactly what people say about you—cerebral, but that it's a process of bringing to consciousness.

SS: Oh, it is indeed. But the unconscious is always there ready to spring forward when you least expect it, and you don't always recognize it. Nobody recognizes—nobody recognizes it all the time.

MS: The last show in this book is *Merrily We Roll Along*. It seems as if in the career of musical comedy writers, things falling apart is almost part of the story. And *Merrily We Roll Along* is not only about how things fall apart for the characters within the play, it will be the last time you work—well, it won't be the last time you work with Harold Prince, he comes in at a certain point to work on *Road Show*, called *Bounce* then—but it's an end.

It's a place where things are going to break up afterwards. I think we're going to, in the next volume, be looking at a new kind of show—

SS: Oh, absolutely.

MS: —a kind of show that's made in part out of collage with variable pieces. It's *Sunday in the Park with George*. Do you feel that there's an arc that ends with *Merrily We Roll Along*?

SS: Yeah. There's an arc that ends because I met somebody new. It's—you know, I remarried. And meeting [James] Lapine changed my life professionally in a very profound way, and changed the way I looked at the theater in a *certain* way, although I'd always been of an experimental nature, and Lapine was, but so was Hal. So there are similarities, but it was—as I will cover in the second book—after all, the first show that James and I did together was off-Broadway. I'd never done an off-Broadway show before, and that is a whole different set of principles and pressures or lacks of pressure, and related so much more to the kind of thing that Mickey and Judy did in the barn.

MS: Well, it's interesting. Because do you think, for instance—if *Anyone Can Whistle* had been an off-Broadway show, its future would've been different?

SS: It might have been. It might have been. I think at that point, off-Broadway wasn't quite as developed yet, but it might have been. That was the year of experiment—that was the *decade* of experimentation in plays. And many of them came from off-Broadway, you know, John Guare and Lanford Wilson, Albert Innaurato, that whole group of playwrights who were experimenting with the form. And most of those forms were not being experimented with on Broadway; these were off-Broadway playwrights. And Lapine was an off-Broadway playwright. So I became an off-Broadway playwright, and the freedom to experiment—*Sunday in the Park with George* is something no Broadway producer would have ever dreamed of producing. The thing is that, when I say no producer would've produced *Sunday in the Park with George*, there is one producer who would've, and that's Hal Prince. Hal Prince was the only producer who was constantly putting his own money, so to speak—and I don't mean out of his own pocket, I mean his own producing money—into experimental pieces. No other producer would ever have produced *Pacific Overtures*, and no other producer would have ever produced—I don't think maybe even *Merrily We Roll Along*. But, you know, *Follies*? I don't think any other producer would've done that. You know, an elaborate fantasy. So that's—I wanted to add that, because Hal, in a way, has the mentality of an off-Broadway playwright, but he just was born on Broadway, the way I was.

MS: *Finishing the Hat* is a combination of collected lyrics, attendant comments, principles, heresies, grudges, whines, and anecdotes. We haven't even begun to speak of the heresies, but we'll do that when the second volume comes out. It's been a great pleasure to be able to talk to you. Thank you for speaking.

SS: Oh, thank you, Michael, very much. I've enjoyed it.

Susan Sontag

1992: *The Volcano Lover*

MS: I wanted to begin by talking about what kind of book *The Volcano Lover* is because much of what I've been reading about it doesn't seem to correspond to my experience of it.

SS: It doesn't correspond with my experience either, Michael.

MS: I took it to be a kind of fantasia on received materials, that the romance of Emma, Lord Nelson, and Lord Hamilton is a kind of given around which many interpretations and styles are woven.

SS: Well, that's true for the way it started, but I have to admit that I did get caught up in the story. Maybe that's why it's reaching so many readers. I did get caught up in the story on a gut level. And maybe I started off by thinking I have to be very careful. After all, this was the subject of a famous film with Laurence Olivier and Vivien Leigh playing Lord Nelson and Emma Hamilton fifty years ago, and everybody's seen this movie in video or whatever. And it's a corny story, and it's history, and so what can I make of this story? How can I turn it into something else?

But then I did get caught up in the story itself. I have only my own sensibility and quirks to bring to it, but I really liked telling the story. And what I was terrified of, setting a novel in the past, two centuries ago, writing what's called—not a very prestigious label—a historical novel, actually was very liberating for me. It liberated a straightforward narrative gift, a storytelling gift that I didn't know I had. I thought precisely what you say now, that I would take the story for granted and it would be a fantasia, it would be all sorts of riffs on these people who are so well known and are sort of clichés. And it is full of riffs and stories within stories and fables and so on, but it also is the story. I found I was completely caught up in the story. I cried when I was writing some parts where terrible things happened to my characters, and I fell in love with them. There's a lot to be said against them, but I wanted to justify them and present them in their full humanity. I identified with them. I mean, this was nothing to do with any theory I had about what I was going to do. I found it was a big emotional blast to write the book. I didn't know it would be that. I started off more with the notion that the book would kind of float above the story. But the story is really there, and that's what I think makes it work for a lot of people. Because there's the other stuff too, of course, all the digressions and fantasies and fables and stories within stories.

MS: I guess what I mean is that it has the feeling of being a novel in a glass booth, that to some extent the characters are on display in it as characters, as representative figures. They're given not their own names, but representative names: the hero, the Cavaliere, the young woman.

SS: The young woman, the Cavaliere's wife, right.

MS: And there's a kind of ongoing commentary. Now, perhaps I'm quite wrong about this, but some of the themes on collecting and traveling seem to me to use the metaphor at the beginning, shopworn, as if the book is encased intentionally in a network of received ideas.

SS: Well, I don't know. That's interesting that you say that. The notions of collecting, tourism, exile, travel, passionate relationship to art—maybe they are shopworn, but they didn't seem shopworn to me. They're the kind of things that I'm drawn to. For instance, I had a period where I was mostly writing essays, and I think I was trying to carry this cargo of obsessions and passions through a very narrow door. The theme of collecting, for instance: the main character, the Volcano Lover, William Hamilton, he's a collector. And I know one of the things that got me interested in photography, apart from the fact that I'm a very visual person, is the notion that having photographs is collecting the world. And the notion of the photographic possession or appropriation of the world is a variant of the theme of collecting and the kind of dissociation that comes with the hyperdevelopment of the collecting instinct. So I could say, well, I've always been interested in the psychology of the collector and the phenomenon of collecting. And now I had the courage to work with the fictional character, based, as it happens, on a real person, of a collector, and I could bring ideas and fantasies and observations that I have about the psychology of collecting into an organic relationship with the story instead of segregating all this and making it sort of one-voiced in an essay form.

The thing about a novel is you can have many voices. This is a novel that addresses the reader in many voices. There's not only the different characters, but there's the many voices of the book, of all this commentary and digression and arias. So I don't know, I guess I don't agree with you in the sense that I don't think love, for instance, romantic passion, which is—I don't know what I'd call it—a theme or subject or something of the book; it's certainly shopworn, but it isn't any less interesting for that.

MS: Oh, no, no, no. I was not using shopworn as a pejorative. Rather, I felt as I was reading the book, and I could be quite wrong, that in the same way that Flaubert builds *Madame Bovary* out of used things that he has a certain amount of disdain for; nevertheless, he creates a passionate novel.

SS: Well, of course that's a very glorious comparison, and if that's what you meant, I couldn't agree with you more. But precisely what makes *Madame Bovary* so great is that he may have thought, and we know this from his letters to Maxime Du Camp, Louise Colet, and others, he said, "I'm writing this boring novel about this provincial doctor's wife who has a couple of disastrous love affairs and kills herself because she's basically a mediocre person." And then in the writing of the novel he really identified with her. You may start off with these sort of bracketing or condescending attitudes to your material because you want to be in control, you want to be superior to it. But fiction really works best when your sense of that material being used is completely transformed. I mean, I think it partly has to do with how you psych yourself up to write a very ambitious book. This is certainly the most ambitious book I've ever written. I think it's the best book I've ever written. First of all, to write it I had to give myself permission to fail. And maybe even to attempt it I had to say, "OK, everybody knows this, this is something we know about. We know about this famous triangle, the Hamiltons and Nelson, and the French Revolution and all of that. Now what can I do with this material?" I'm not disagreeing with you, I'm just saying that the other part of it is, yeah, used materials, even like the surreal. It's found objects.

MS: Exactly.

SS: Why, I'll tell you, if we have time I can tell you a little bit of some of my initial thinking about the book. I got interested in these people. And then I thought, why do I want to base it on these people? Why don't I just make it up? But it'll be for a few knowledgeable people. They'll say, oh yeah, that was based on the story of the Hamiltons and Nelson and that whole world. And I even had the idea, at one time, as if it would have been any easier to do, that I would make the main character—I'd have it take place now, and I'd have the main character an ambassador, the American ambassador to the Philippines. And he would be a collector of Chinese art, but he would also be fascinated by volcanoes, because that was the case for Hamilton as British ambassador to Naples in the late eighteenth century. But I have this, I can do it now in the 1980s or the 1990s—American ambassador to the Philippines, volcanic eruption, great collector—and do the whole thing as a sort of modern version of that story. And then a few people would say, "Wait a minute, this sort of reminds me of that old story." People say, "Oh, you've written a historical novel."

I remember one review—talking about the reviews not making sense to me—and as you know, the reviews have been mostly favorable, but they still don't make much sense. One reviewer said, "Well, this is a historical novel. That's very strange. Susan Sontag couldn't like historical novels." Of course I like historical novels, because an awful lot of novels are historical. I mean, *War and Peace* is a historical novel. Tolstoy wasn't writing about events in his own time, he was writing events that took place in his grandparents' time. And he had to do a lot of reading and working to know what was going on.

MS: And to some extent *The Benefactor* is a historical novel.

SS: Sure. The past is a big place, and that novel is such a sort of wonderful hybrid thing. People want to be moved. I, as a writer, want to move people. I was very moved, cried even, at a couple of passages that I was writing. Readers have told me that they cried, that they were moved to tears by some of the passages in the novel. It's also funny. I also laughed a lot of times at some things I was writing. There is information in this book. It's not *Moby-Dick*, I'm not trying to give an encyclopedia of whaling here or the equivalent about volcanoes or anything like that. But you can learn something from this book. That's a pleasure you get from novels. There's the education of the heart. There's getting information about interesting worlds that you don't know about, and actually we don't know anything, so we can always learn. There's speculation and there's fantasy. There are riffs, what I call riffs or arias. It can be a big feast.

MS: I have to tell you what I read, and we'll see whether it was in your heart or mind or both. You know, what I found very moving about the book was that it seemed to be a book about the death of everything, particularly about the death of love. It seemed to be about the process in which the things that one holds culturally dear are turned, after being lava, into hardened, petrified memories, memorials to an eruption that is now over and can be collected. But even the objects of the collection turn valueless. The heroes and heroines of the book end inevitably impoverished and dead. Life is like this, but novels not always. And so I took it as being a book about the death of culture and passion.

SS: You're right. You know, I'm probably not the best person to talk about this book, even though I wrote it and I didn't finish it so long ago. I only finished it about four or five months ago. It was published in record time. When you say that, it's actually convincing to me, and I can respond to that. I have those feelings.

There's one line that made me laugh grimly, where—I want to say "I say," but I don't feel it's me, I feel it's the book—the book says, "It was a time when knowledge was fashionable. Philistinism was unfashionable." And I wrote that line with a great deal of glee and grimness because the time we live in is a time in which knowledge is unfashionable and Philistinism is very fashionable. And I was thinking when I was writing it how, well, to take one of the great examples, think of James Joyce's *Ulysses*: it all takes place in twenty-four hours, all the stuff that he unfolds in that book. But the characters don't change. Leopold Bloom and Stephen Dedalus and Molly Bloom, they are what they are. And what makes the book is all the changes that Joyce rings on their identity, their characters, their sort of mythic prototypes from Ulysses's stories. But he's just got twenty-four hours. All that happens in *Ulysses* is some people meet and hang out together for twenty-four hours. I mean, literally nothing happens.

MS: They get more and more tired.

SS: More and more tired, yeah. And the book gets wilder and wilder. Here, this book has God, it has a lynching, a guillotining, it has a war, it has romance, it has childbirth, it has betrayal, it has adultery, it has life at court, it has music, it has all these elements. It doesn't have a horse race. I think of that because of Tolstoy. I read somewhere that Tolstoy, when he started *Anna Karenina*—I mentioned *War and Peace* before, but now I'm thinking of *Anna Karenina*—that he made a list of things that should go in a big novel, and one of them is a horse race. And sure enough, he does have Vronsky and Anna at the races at one moment. And *The Volcano Lover* is an expansive book. It has a shape. The shape was kind of hard to figure out, but I didn't start writing it until I had figured the shape out. Because you cover forty, fifty years and a bunch of celebrated people with a lot of public as well as private activity, and what do you tell? What do you leave out?

I had to have a form. But you're right, it follows that arc of a human life, which is, roughly speaking, they're full of beans at the beginning and they're down and out in one way or another at the end. I mean, of course, Lord Nelson dies in glory at the Battle of Trafalgar, but you know, he has suffered some tremendous blows, not only being mutilated but the end of his marriage and this very anguished, passionate relationship that he has with Emma Hamilton. Although there's no doubt that if he could have, he just would have come home and married her and settled down in the country. But that was not to be. And so they all, in fact, end very badly.

I think it was a big trip to do this. I liked writing it. I had no idea it would reach so many readers. I had no idea it was going to be a bestseller. Had somebody told me to look in a crystal ball and I had seen that piece of information, it wouldn't have helped me in the slightest. It couldn't possibly have influenced me because I'm going to write the way I do. Without even daring to think of how many would like it or not like it, I did have a feeling about a third of the way through that I was onto something much bigger than I had envisaged. And by the end of the book, before anybody had read it, I did think it was very original and the best thing I'd ever done. And that's the most I can ask of myself.

MS: I'll tell you, I thought early on, almost as soon as I'd heard about it, that it would be a bestseller. What came, partially because from *The French Lieutenant's Woman* on—

SS: But see, I never read *The French Lieutenant's Woman*.

MS: No, no, I'm not making a comparison.

SS: But I'm not even—I just say it in the sense that there are these books which are, quote, historical novels or romances like *The French Lieutenant's Woman* or *Possession* by A. S. Byatt. I know these books are out there. And I'm starting to sound like an awful snob, but I have never even looked at these books, much less read them.

MS: No, but they do tend, these anti-romantic romances, Darwinian, Victorian novels, to capture an audience. What impressed me about *The Volcano Lover* personally, because I'm indifferent to those books, too, was that I did think that it was a Sontag book.

SS: Good.

MS: I didn't find it to be disparate in theme from either the fiction or the essays. In fact, I liked it because it offered a continuity.

SS: Well, thank you for saying that, because now I know you really do understand the book, and that's not—I mean, that's exactly what I expect of you, being you—but it's not a satisfaction I have had very often since the book came out a few weeks ago. A lot of people, I don't know what they're reacting to, more an idea, I think, than any real knowledge of my work, have treated this book as if it's some kind of new phase and very different. I feel that everything I've ever done is in this book, and I don't know how to write differently. That's why I'm not jealous of other writers, and I'm not worried about other writers. I enjoy the success and accomplishment of other writers because I couldn't do what they do. And I know that nobody would want to do or could do what I do. I mean, what makes this book different is that it's freer, it's more expressive, and that I did find the right form that I could hook all these things. I'm coming back to your original idea of the used material.

MS: What I found was that—let me try and get this correctly—that if you took what they are calling nowadays the polyphonic novel, the novel by Hermann Broch or Kundera, the interpretations within, especially in Kundera, are set at a bizarre angle to the ongoing telling of the story. What fascinated me was that a certain kind of despair, a certain kind of world-weariness enters the book and begins almost to be a muse by itself. It knows that world-weariness has been around as long as its characters have. And so I found the book to be utterly original in its manipulation of emotions, events, received materials, and finally, a very almost celebrating mournfulness.

SS: Well, I think this is the smartest thing I've ever heard about the book. It certainly—yeah, I think you're right. I think you're right. I never thought of it, but absolutely. I think it's true. But still, I want to insist on the euphoria that there was in finding a voice for this because, well, we know from art you can present the most gruesome things but there's a kind of elation. I'm not saying this is all gruesome, but you know, there's gaiety in Beckett or Thomas Bernhard or the most pessimistic writers.

MS: The joy of wonderful prose is joy enough, don't you think?

SS: Yeah, but not just the prose. There's some pretty fancy prose in here. But just the sense of, I don't know, the kind of feeling you have. I'm using an Emersonian term. I'm thinking of one, and I can't remember the sentence. But the feeling of being a world devourer, that you actually can take it all in and give voice to it. My model, at times, was a musical model, or even more specifically an operatic model, that you could just stand, stage front and center, and belt it out and say: "I long, I love, I fear, I dread, I want to die, I want to live, I protest." And I mean, that's what, of course, it gets to at the end when I have the four monologues of the angry women. But they have to be earned. I have to tell the story and do all the variations on it. But it's interesting what you say. It's very interesting what you say. Our listeners should know, we haven't talked about this before. This is all just coming out spontaneously in this conversation.

I mean, you mentioned Hermann Broch. I always think I like Hermann Broch, but then when I read it—I love the idea of it, you know? And then when I read it, I think, "Where's the pep? Where's the energy? Where's the velocity?" It's turgid, and it needs more energy. It needs more euphoria. When I read Kundera, again, I love the idea of it. But for the most part I'm very dissatisfied. I think he's too in love with his own ideas. And a lot of the ideas aren't that interesting. They're sort of obvious. And he's too superior to his characters. I put a lot of myself in every single one of them, which is maybe why I brought in Baron Scarpia from *Tosca*, so I'd have one stage villain that I couldn't identify with. I don't feel superior to these people. I don't feel condescending. My beloved son, the author David Rieff, when I first told him about this book—and I probably described it very badly, I'm not good at describing my own work—when I told him what I was going to do or what I thought I was going to do— this was before I'd even started—he said, ever, ever witty, "Oh, I get it: Hermann Broch meets Barbara Cartland." I thought, oh God, is that true? Of course, I've actually never even seen a book by Barbara Cartland, but I sort of know what it is.

And then I used to tease myself and, in a way, almost egg myself on. Maybe it's why I put "A Romance" as a subtitle, as a kind of grin to myself. I said: "Okay, it is a romance. It's got a romance in it." And it floats, it floats. You talked before about the kind of generic names of the characters. It isn't just Horatio Nelson, Lord Nelson, Admiral Nelson. It's "the hero." They all have their names. Because I wanted it to have a kind of mythic character. What I guess I have to say, and it's very simple, is that the book, while it was planned out in a rough schematic way, did take off and got richer, and I gave more to the actual storytelling. I found myself moved to give more to the storytelling aspect, because it was so moving, more than I actually had expected.

Originally, I thought—again, here I'm betraying how little contemporary fiction I read—I've never read one line of John Fowles, but not only do I know he's written a book called *The French Lieutenant's Woman*, but I know he's written a book called *The Collector*, which I've never even seen or read. And when I started to look, I thought, oh God, what a pity *The Collector* is used as a title. Because this should be the title of my book. So, William Hamilton: collector and volcano lover. Unfortunately, I can't use *The Collector* because it's already been used by this famous novel, so I guess I have to call it *The Volcano Lover*. Of course, *The Volcano Lover* is a much better title, and had *The Collector* not been used, I still would have been well advised to call it *The Volcano Lover*. But I really thought it was about him, and then I thought, oh, that well-known, shopworn story of Emma and Lord Nelson, well, everybody knows that from the movie or from somewhere else. I can just allude to that. They'll be shadowy figures in the background. And then Emma comes along and kidnaps the book. And her vitality! I love self-made people, people who come out of nowhere and create themselves and rise out of their own fantasy and energy and wish not to be a victim. The book said, on her behalf, she didn't want to be a victim. She was not a victim. And of course she could have considered herself a victim, and Lord knows she was at the end. I love people who have this optimism of the will. And so I care about these people. And I wanted to tell their story, and I wanted to ride their story, to tell other stories as well.

2000: *In America*

MS: In this book, *In America*, Susan Sontag has taken the figure of a Polish actress who comes to America. What is the year?

SS: 1876.

MS: She is leaving her career and starting a collective enterprise, an experimental farm community modeled on the Fourier principles that give rise to Brook Farm. And one of the first things that we notice, if we're being very wary in reading this very ingenious book, is that there are, in fact, no principles on which this experimental community is based.

SS: That's right, Michael, you noticed. They keep talking about an ideal community. They want to form an ideal community. It's a community of an ideal way of living in which people will live ideally in an ideal way. I don't put it that way, of course. I'm making fun of it now, following your lead, but it's true. The idealism is both entirely sincere and entirely empty.

MS: In that way, it's a very devious book. I've said to friends again and again that I think its narrative strategies are as strange as those of *The Good Soldier* and more so. And the reader finds himself in a more and more artistically and ideologically depleted America as the new century of publicity and celebrity is dawning.

SS: It's true that the notion of the ideal is a kind of empty notion for these people, and yet at the same time it is connected with America as this big empty space. Of course, they land in New York—they come from Poland—but they head out for one of the emptiest parts of the country, which is, in fact, right here, Southern California. Anaheim, which is where they go, is a vineyard village of 2,000 people. Nearby, Los Angeles had about 10,000 people. And what's their idea? Their idea is to live the simple life, the pure life, the life after Europe, the life of virtue, the rural life. Of course, these are educated people. They didn't come here in steerage; they're educated, privileged people. And what do they do? Well, they try to be farmers. They eat communally. That seems to be about the only thing they do. Of course, they end up being lodged very uncomfortably, and so they have to build their little adobe houses so they can all, you know, have a little bit of privacy. They have their meals together. They try to do all the work together, but of course the work still gets very divided. Let's say the women are stuck with the kitchen work and then the milking and feeding the chickens, and the men are doing the so-called heavy-duty work. But mostly they like to sit in their hammocks and, dare I say it on this most wonderful of all book shows, they like to sit in their hammocks and read.

MS: When Maryna comes to America, she comes as an idealist but encounters the realities of people not even being willing or interested in learning to pronounce her Polish name. She is rather accommodating to change her name when she goes back on stage, but she will not change it to the Countess Zalenska of the Imperial Russian Theatre, which is what's wanted of her, because Russia has, in fact, occupied her country, and such a title would be an indication of terrible submission and defeat. But nevertheless, these are the compromises that the country wants. And everyone in America, in some way or another, in this book and I think in life, finds themselves changing their name. Is the very nature of being born into America a compromise?

SS: Well, it's a project. Let's put it that way, more neutrally. America is a project. Being a woman is a project. I'm very drawn, as a subject matter for fiction and for reflection and for storytelling in all forms, to ideas of self-transformation. And when I hit on this story of the Polish actress who thinks she's giving up the stage and bringing a group of people to start an ideal community in America and eventually goes back on the stage, I realized that in some way the two notions of being an immigrant, an immigrant to America, and being an actor, a performer, someone who goes on stage, sort of map on top of each other. That is to say, when you came to America, you were submitting to a real change of identity and a certain kind of self-evacuation, emptying out of the self. You had to get rid of whatever was encumbering in your old identity to adapt to the new. And after all, in a certain sense, that's what an actor does as well. An actor is engaged in or submitting to various projects of self-transformation as he or she plays this or that role. So I don't mean to say that being an immigrant is playing a role, but I do think in both cases it's committing yourself to being willing to sacrifice your attachment to any central core of identity.

MS: There are all kinds of reinventions in your work and in the narration of your work, and that emptying of identity, that vastation, seems to be very much the concern of the earlier novels, which are much more austere and involve complicated evacuations of selfhood in the interest, almost of a kind of empty self, an intellectually vacuumed self. These books, *The Volcano Lover* and *In America*, are very much more abundant, pregnant with incident, and the kind of austerity that informed the earlier work is almost not apparent. What happened? What changed?

SS: I'm not sure I really know. But you're absolutely right about the earlier projects of self-emptying or disburdenment, which was certainly a theme in the early fiction, in the first two novels, *The Benefactor* and *Death Kit*, in a lot of the essays as well, like "The Aesthetics of Silence," like the infamous—somewhat infamous—essay, "Against Interpretation." They were about emptying out and self-disburdenment in different registers. I was a very young writer then, talking about works that I did in the 1960s and 1970s. I was still enthralled by certain ascetic ideas, certain ideas of purity or self. I wasn't just interested in self-transformation or self-reinvention, I was interested in self-transcendence—if that doesn't sound too pretentious a term. I was very interested by certain religious ideas, gnostic ideas in particular. And in fact, *The Benefactor* is, in one respect, a kind of comic gnostic novel, using a sort of *Candide*-like story to express, again, in a comic register, certain gnostic ideals. What happened, how plenitude came to corrupt and transform asceticism—Michael, as always, you're kind of right on target—I really don't know. I got wiser, perhaps. I lived more, I understood more. I suffered. I sympathized with other people's suffering, which is more important than my own suffering. And I grew into, I came to inhabit a way of writing in which I didn't want to just empty out a world, I wanted to make a world, fill a world, educate and dilate other people's sympathies and capacity for compassion. And that's when I realized I could become a different kind of fiction writer.

MS: *Death Kit* famously has a rather frightening and recurrent train car. In *In America* we have a train car with a heroine in it, but by now it's a car of a different kind of shared communal consciousness. These are people who are referred to as her children. There's a much friendlier atmosphere, even when this car is derailed and off the tracks. It is in this peculiar sense an American home.

SS: That's quite wonderful. Yes. What's the difference? What made it possible for me to find more freedom as a writer? I don't know. These things are so mysterious I don't know that I could or ought to have any explanation. But I guess either you grow as a writer or you shrink as a writer, and I think I've done a lot of work on myself. Let me put it this way. I'm not reluctant to make that kind of effort and I make the, I think, not too immodest claim that I have become a better writer now—is because I've done a lot of work on myself to try not to shrivel and just stay with what I already know or live off my human capital, which is in a way what happens to most people. And quite understandably so. I mean, the truth is, Michael—and I wonder if you'll agree—that most, though not all, writers do their best work in probably not even the first half of their writing lives, more like the first third of their writing lives. And then, well, they become professional writers, and they don't do much living, and they don't take in very much. And I, for one reason or another, through destiny, through temperament, through appetite, have taken in a lot more than what I knew when I did that early work, even though I think that early work is good. And I suddenly realized I could talk about a lot more that I knew. It isn't that I know much more, but I have more access to what I know. And I can make a bigger world. And I don't just want to write about the commotion in one person's head. I want to make a world that has a lot of voices, in which people can express very different things. And as I said, I think of fiction as an education of the heart, an education of the sympathies. That's a moral question for me. That's why we need novels. That's why we go back and reread novels, to keep ourselves alive humanly and morally, so that we don't shrivel up.

MS: Well, I think you've also come through the other side of something. I won't try and characterize very much what it is, but the first two novels are both narrated by men. These new novels have at their center not only women but very strong, ambitious women who are influenced by the worlds around them and influence those worlds. These are women who are not the kind of women that feminism was bemoaning, robbed of power. This is the effect, in a sense, of power on women in a way very much like the latter half of Gertrude Stein's *The Mother of Us All*, where Susan B. Anthony realizes that, having crusaded for the vote for women, now women are more like men, and she has brought about the entrance of women into the illusion of parity.

SS: Well, both the main female character in *The Volcano Lover*, who is one of, though not the only protagonist, and, in *In America*, this Polish actress who comes to America, becomes American, are women with tremendous theatrical and performance skills. It's true that they're ambitious, they're clever, they're smart, they are not oppressed or downtrodden or mistreated in any of the conventional ways that the vast majority of women have been mistreated and condescended to and repressed throughout history. Nevertheless, they are far from feminist ideals. It's interesting, when you write two novels that are both set in the past. I don't think of these as "historical novels," because this is not some special category of novel, like a mystery novel or science fiction novel. These are novels. But it's true that both *The Volcano Lover* and the new novel, *In America*, are set in the past: *The Volcano Lover* in the late eighteenth century, *In America* in the late nineteenth century. Another thing that happened is I came awake or alive to, in the last fifteen years or so, history. Not that I'm a historian, and not that these are works of history—they're absolutely works of fiction, even in the sense that, yes, they're inspired by real stories, but totally reimagined, totally reinvented. But the reality of history, of the variety of life in the world, the influence of historical circumstances, the particular way in which you are, whether it's now or the late eighteenth century, the late nineteenth century, you are hinged to your time and saturated with various forms of collective imagination and happening. That just became a lot more real to me than when I was a young writer, when I thought I wanted to make a way through all that and find some essence of consciousness or despair or reflectiveness or struggle. I just opened out to something wider and more moving, actually, to me. I actually laugh sometimes when I'm writing what these characters do or say or feel, or I cry, as at the end of this novel when I was writing the final soliloquy.

MS: Now, you've done something very mischievous, I think, in this book. I think it's actually hilarious. After a prologue, the consciousness dawning in the book, which is about to begin or decides to begin a new life, that consciousness is virtually initiated by a slap, in the same way that a baby's bottom is slapped, and she comes to decide on a new life. And the novel ends similarly when that heroine, being confronted unkindly by a famous fellow actor, says, "Please stop." And the novel stops. This is consciousness as enunciation. She's born with a slap, she ends when she says she ends, and it's the second life.

SS: Absolutely. That's perfect. And it's funny—and excuse me for interrupting you—but that slap that the narrative part of the novel begins, that was in a way the biggest stretch I had in writing it. I wrote this prologue, which was a kind of a way of imagining how my characters would audition for their parts in my novel, and I—I the alter ego, not me, Susan Sontag, but somebody kind of lateral to me—a writer voice like a time traveler parachutes down into a party that's taking place in the second-floor private dining room of a hotel in the city of Krakow, and there's a party going on which this voice, this author consciousness, recognizes as probably being given in honor of this woman. And who is she? And then little by little, the characters are kind of teased out from different clues. I got to the end of this prologue, which I'm really proud of, and I thought, gosh, this is maybe the best thing I ever wrote. And then it ends with the sentence, finally, at the end of a very long evening, after many hours have passed, twenty-five pages into the book, the voice says, "I decided to follow them out into the world." And then I thought, now what do I do? And I puzzled and puzzled and puzzled over that. And I wrote the prologue, the zero chapter, very, very quickly, the first draft. I worked on it a long time, but then I had a hell of a time figuring out how to actually begin the narrative book properly. And in the meantime, this sort of amazing and very transforming alternate life reared its head for me, and I started spending a great deal of the time living and working in Sarajevo during the three-year siege of the city. And probably because I'm not just a writer and I wanted to do that, but partly, I have to admit, because I was so puzzled how to go on with the book, which was how to begin the book, really. I only had the prologue, the overture. And then it suddenly came to me, and I hope it wasn't all those shells and bombs going off in Sarajevo, that I would begin the book with a [*claps hands*] slap.

MS: Were you aware that is was a birth slap? Because it is.

SS: No, I wasn't. That's kind of wonderful. No, I never thought of that. You always come up with things, Michael. I thought, it has to be a slap, it has to be a slap. And the end, similarly, as you say, when this great actor who Maryna plays with tells her off and says, in effect, at the end of the book, "You think you've suffered. You don't know what suffering is." And then presents a self-portrait, as it were, of the unhappiest man on the planet. You do, I think, feel that he is the unhappiest man on the planet. And then what can she say at the end? You know, I puzzled a lot over that. I thought, I want to hear her voice just once more, even though we've heard his voice now for twenty-five pages. It's obviously the other monologue. There's the one that begins it, the alter ego voice, a kind of comic voice, and the tragic voice at the end. But I still want to hear her voice once more. I don't want to really give him absolutely the last word. And you know, for a long time, until I actually was writing the last pages of the last chapter—I write consecutively—in September of this past year, 1999, I was thinking, well, what could she say? What could she say? And I thought, the only thing I could think of that she could say would be, "yes." And of course I thought, I can't say that, that's what Molly Bloom says at the end of *Ulysses*. But I thought, what else could she say? She can't say, "Yes, you're right," or, my gosh, she can't say, "I agree." What could she say? And again I would come back to the fact that she could only say, "Yes. Yes, Edwin, yes." But I kept thinking I can't say that precisely, because Mr. Joyce has been there before me. Though that was the last word of his final monologue of *Ulysses*, Molly's words, not words that somebody else says to her, but nevertheless, can I end the book with "yes"? And then at four in the morning I woke up, I was staying at somebody's house in the country, and I knew what she says. She says, "Stop."

She says "stop" not just because I want to stop the book, which, of course you're absolutely right, starts with a slap, stops with a stop. But because it would be fatuous, inane, unsympathetic of her to say "yes."

He has just revealed an incredible state of suffering. And her "stop" is not "Stop, I don't want to hear this, you're making me feel bad." It's "Stop, don't torture yourself like that. Don't torture yourself." I think it's a compassionate stop. She wants him to stop bleeding in front of her because she sympathizes and feels so sorry for him. And I thought, that's the ending: "Stop." And the book stops.

MS: I have a final question. She is a very strong feminine presence, fully created. And throughout the book she really does not have an equal. Her husband is not—what would you call it?—a fully masculine presence. Her lover is a young man and just by nature kind of callow. And so, it's in the final chapter that a very masculine presence, in the form of Edwin Booth, who has been, in a sense, stalking the novel, a constantly present ghost, arises, and they have a scene in which, although Booth is really the only one who speaks, there are two very strong masculine and feminine roles present. And I wondered about that emergence, the emergence of an equal, as well as someone who is *more* suffering.

SS: Yes. He even describes himself, of course, in this endlessly self-execrating, self-excoriating way, as "your husband in art." He is her equal. He has been the actor, as you say beautifully, whose presence has been stalking her throughout the book in the sense that he's the actor she most admires, she dreams of playing opposite. Edwin Booth, the older brother, of course, of John Wilkes Booth, who assassinated President Lincoln, was the most famous American actor of the period in which this novel takes place. And it would be her dream, especially as she, in fact, becomes the most famous actress eventually, to play with Booth. So there's a kind of Booth-tease in every chapter, once they get to America, that she thinks about him, she dreams about him, people mention him, people tell stories about him. And then finally he's there in the last chapter to speak as her equal, and in a way to trump her, to top her. Because it's true, he has suffered more than she has.

She's a born winner. No matter what she has to do to her soul, she's going to make a terrific American. She's always going to land on her feet. She's always going to convert her defeats into victories. Booth knows that every victory is a defeat, and Booth has suffered unbelievable wounds. So that's the trajectory of the book. I think of a novel as a journey, and you should go a long distance from where you started from. By the time the reader comes to the end of this book, a big journey has been taken that's like the journey that the characters take from Europe to America.

2002: *Summer in Baden-Baden* by Leonid Tsypkin

MS: We call each other, Susan and I, and practically challenge each other to find books. I think there's been nothing on my side more difficult than Vigny's *Stello*. No, it wasn't *Stello*, it was—

SS: *The Military Necessity.*

MS: Yes. And Susan countered with a book called *Summer in Baden-Baden* by Leonid Tsypkin. The book had been published in London. I found it, and I said, "Yes, it is, it's a masterpiece." Do you know how rare it is now, with all of the excavation going on, to find an unknown, an absolutely unknown masterpiece? Here it is, three years later, and with the collaboration of New Directions, the publisher, the book is now available in America, thanks to Susan's efforts. Now I want to begin by saying that finding a great book is part of a life spent *looking* for great books. That this is an everyday occurrence, the search, and occasionally the find, and I wanted to begin by asking how you encountered *Summer in Baden-Baden*?

SS: I was in London and walking down a wonderful street in London that all of us who love books and have the habit of buying them know: Charing Cross Road. And outside one of the used book shops there was a barrel, and it was literally a barrel, about four feet high, filled with used paperbacks that were selling for the equivalent of twenty-five or fifty cents apiece. And I wasn't even in the store, I was coming down the street, and I remember very well because it was to my left. And I looked down, and just underneath the slightly exposed one on the top was a small paperback that had a photograph of Dostoevsky on the cover. So I stopped, and I picked it up. And this is, indeed, *Summer in Baden-Baden*, which is a novel fantasia, totally original work of fiction and meditation and ecstasy by this unknown Russian writer, which is, in part, an account of a certain period in Dostoevsky's life. So Dostoevsky's photograph was on the cover. And I stood there on the street, I remember it very well, and I opened it, and I read the first paragraph, and I thought, oh my God, this is a great book. This is a fantastic book. I just had to read the first page, and you knew you were in the presence of something truly wonderful. The prose was so original and strange. It was not normal, ordinary narrative prose. It was prose that was so over the top and yet completely lucid and not difficult to read. But it was the prose of ecstasy. An amazing, hectic energy. I bought the book for twenty-five or fifty cents in English money, went to the hotel, and read it right straight through. It's not very long, about 150 pages. I tried, in the next days before I left London, to find other copies but couldn't. It was clearly out of print. This was in the early '90s, and I could see from inside the book that it was published in 1987.

Over the years, I have managed to pick up two more copies—used copies, always in London—and given them away. Then I told you about it a couple of years ago. And then, the whole story is—I'll try to make it as brief as I can. About two years ago, Barnes & Noble was doing some sort of ad campaign where they were going to ask some well-known writers to list their ten favorite books, and they asked me. Well, I have so many books that are favorite books I couldn't begin to just pick ten. I thought, what, I'm going to say, I don't know, *The Brothers Karamazov* or *The Magic Mountain* or *The Portrait of a Lady*? It would seem too obvious. So I countered with a list of my ten favorite little-known books, and they said sure, because of course they didn't care. And one of the ten was *Summer in Baden-Baden*, which of course was by far the least known of the ten that I listed.

Shortly after that, I was in a Russian restaurant here in New York City called the Russian Samovar, and a man came up to me and, in a thick Russian accent, speaking English, said, "How you know this book by Leonid Tsypkin? No one knows this book." He had seen the ad. And I explained how. He didn't even know it had been published, ever translated or published in England, but it turned out he was the man who smuggled the manuscript out of the Soviet Union in 1981. And he said, "Oh, I must tell his son." I said, "His son? Where is his son?" Well, his son teaches at the Naval Postgraduate School in Monterey, California. He's a graduate of their Russian Studies program, has a PhD in Russian studies from Harvard University. At that moment, I thought, well, this is crazy. I'm going to try to get this book republished. And I gave it first to my own publisher, who wasn't interested, and then I took it to New Directions. They lingered a while before they gave a decision. I think, in fact, they just didn't get around to reading it. And then I got a call from an editor at New Directions that they loved it and they wanted to publish it. So now the book exists, and it's getting wonderful reviews, and it is, indeed, a masterpiece of twentieth-century literature. It's thrilling. This book would have been completely lost.

I think I have taken for granted and not yet explained that the book was written by a man who was a doctor and who never published a *line* in his own lifetime. He wrote for the drawer. He didn't even publish in samizdat. No one knew of his work except his wife and his son, who emigrated. He was not allowed to emigrate, although he wanted very much to. But his wife, Elena, and his son were allowed to come to the United States. He died without being published. Never a line. It was just the week of his death, the week he died of a heart attack, and he was on his 56th birthday in 1982, when he heard that the smuggled manuscript was going to appear serialized, in Russian, in a Russian émigré newspaper published in New York. That was the first time he even heard that a single line of his would be published. So this is really bringing back something that could have been lost forever. That's a great privilege.

MS: It seems to me, though, that the story as well is a story of how you intercept the world. By accident, in a barrel outside a bookstore, to read a book that I suspect, even when it was published in London, went unread. More than that, I think that when it was written, people—who always seem to need instruction about how to read—literally did not know how to read this book. That the door was opened, in a sense, by Thomas Bernhard and the meta-narrative that goes on there.

SS: Exactly. This Russian doctor, who could never have read Thomas Bernhard, obviously, he died in 1982, who could never have read Saramago, who has also very interesting long sentences. And yet he is, as a prose stylist, of the same family as Bernhard and Saramago. And he did it entirely out of his own head. He was not a reader, not a great reader. I mean, he was an intense reader, literary from the crown of his head to the toes of his feet, but he wasn't in any way a polymath or a great reader. And he concocted this all out of his own incredible sensibility, with just a couple of models. I would say the prose of Rilke, early Pasternak, and Kafka.

MS: In particular, what's thrilling is, at a time when the feverishness of Russian prose had subsided, in a sense, he creates the Dostoevsky fever, the air of infection, but surrounds it by the current antiseptic prose of a more observing sensibility, so that the novel is like a time machine. One experiences a revolution of consciousness and a devolution of consciousness within it.

SS: I think it belongs, as I suggested in my introduction, to a very special—what can I call it?—a kind of novel project. I don't think that people have this as an idea, and I can only think of a couple examples of it, where you're writing the book, but what gives the book—the narrative, rather—that you're writing a kind of ecstatic uplift, updraft, is a meditation that is interwoven *on* the writing of the book or the questioning of your ability to write the book and to understand the material that you are narrating. I know of only two other examples of that particular kind of novel. One of them is a novel by me, called *The Volcano Lover*, which has as an interwoven theme a narrative voice which questions the very telling of the story and the understanding of the story now because it is a story that takes place in the past, in the late eighteenth century. Out of modesty, I did not mention that in my introduction as another example of the kind of book that *Summer in Baden-Baden* is.

I preferred to mention another lost-cause book, which *is* printed in the United States but not known by anyone that I've ever met. An Italian novel that was written just after the Second World War called *Artemisia* by an Italian writer whose pen name was Anna Banti. And this book is, I believe, published by the University of Nebraska Press and came out some years ago to, as far as I know, no interest whatsoever. I read it in Italian, and it's an extraordinary novel, which is both a retelling of the life of one of the few important women painters from the past, Artemisia Gentileschi, and a meditation on the writing of the book because it was written by Anna Banti, who was in private life the wife, herself an art historian, of the leading art historian in mid-twentieth-century Italy, Roberto Longhi. Their apartment in Florence on the Arno was destroyed in the Allied bombing of Florence at the end of the war, and she lost the manuscript of her novel, and she rewrote it. And she rewrote it as she remembered it, interwoven with the meditation on the lost manuscript and what it was like to rewrite a book, which she had in fact just finished. I think it's one of the great Italian books of the twentieth century, one of the great European books of the twentieth century. It's completely unknown.

I grew up in the American—"in the sticks," as we say—the American provinces. But let's call it by its right name. I grew up in the sticks. And for me, the beginning of my mental life in a serious sense was discovering the Modern Library in the back of a stationery store in Tucson, Arizona, which was a very small town when I was growing up there and had, as far as I remember, no proper bookstore, at any rate, no bookstore with serious books, just maybe bestsellers or something like that. There was a stationery store, which for some reason carried the Modern Library. I don't know if it carried every single one, but I remember a whole wall, a narrow wall, at the end of the store that must have had two hundred books. And I can remember wandering down to the back of that stationery store and cocking my head to the right—and I think I spent a good part of my life with my head cocked to the right reading the titles on spines—and vaguely understanding, oh, these were the great books. And if you read these, you would be doing something wonderful. You would have pure pleasure, pure exaltation, and, dare I say it, real self-improvement, self-transformation, and self-transcendence. And so the notion of the list, my first list was the list in the back, in the inside of the jackets of the Modern Library. I like adding books to the list.

MS: Let me tell you my story because, you know, by the time I was reading, I had the Modern Library, and I had begun to discover literary magazines.

I think one of my most excited discoveries was the section in the back of many issues of *Antaeus*. It was published by Echo Press, and they had a section called "Neglected Books of the Twentieth Century." I didn't have friends as a child who would tell me about the secret books.

SS: I didn't have friends who read books.

MS: And there was, in the back of this literary magazine—

SS: I remember that series.

MS: Well, you were in it. And one of the things that I discovered back then, both you and John Ashbery had mentioned Laura Riding's *Progress of Stories*. And I thought, ah, Sontag and Ashbery. Because you see, in my mind another genealogy was forming of the special books, as opposed to the books that you were being lied to about by teachers who didn't know any better, that you had to read to discover what a real book was. They weren't offering it in high schools. I had to go fast and far to find these books because they were out of print then, many of them.

You know, you brought another book to my attention that was absolutely astonishing, as astonishing as *Summer in Baden-Baden*, and I wanted to mention it here because we have this unique forum. You called me to tell me about a book called *Fateless*.

SS: Yes. *Fateless* came, it's funny how you discover books, and I'm being a little bit indiscreet, but I will continue to be. I discovered *Fateless*, which is a novel by a Hungarian writer who is alive, though I think quite elderly. He must be close to eighty, if not over eighty. His name is Imre Kertész. Kertész, of course, is a very common Hungarian name. There's a great photographer by the name Kertész. I don't believe he's a relative, but he may very well be. Then it came about in the following way.

You know the old saying that if you have a Hungarian for a friend, you don't need an enemy? Well, I've had two great passions among European prose writers in the last five years or so. One is Sebald, all of whose work I'm intensely interested in and admiring of. The other is a more uneven writer, but I think at his best a great writer who has written one of the great novels of the twentieth century, written toward the end of the twentieth century, and that is a writer named Péter Nádas. It's a very long novel, just the opposite of *Summer in Baden-Baden*, a book called *A Book of Memories*. It is a classic European masterpiece. Not an eccentric book.

MS: And it is available; it's published in America by Farrar, Straus and Giroux.

SS: Exactly. I became intensely involved in my head with Nádas's work. I've now read a great deal of it in English translation and French translation also, because I can read French. I've come to know Nádas, and I think he's a great writer. I don't like everything he writes the way I like everything that Sebald writes. But he wrote, as I say, a great, great novel, and a lot of other wonderful stuff. I was mentioning my enthusiasm with Nádas to another Hungarian writer I know, who's a very good writer. And I saw that he was extremely annoyed and said, "Nádas, I don't think Nádas is so great. Nádas, what's so good about Nádas? All you foreigners are so interested in Nádas." One of those sorts of things. I said, uh oh, I should never have mentioned it; of course he's intensely jealous. And he said, "Have you ever read Imre Kertész?" So there was my tip, my lead. And I said, "No, I've never heard of him." He said, "You should try a book called *Fateless*."

The book is called *Fateless*, a novel. It's very short. And he said, "Oh, Kertész is five times better than Nádas." Well, this is a game I'm not interested in playing. I don't admire Nádas any less than I did before, but I did very quickly get hold of this book, which is published by Northwestern University Press. You have to hunt for it. I don't even think it's in their catalog for some reason. I think they're not even aware they publish it. And it is, indeed, a great book. It's very short. It is no less than a book about Auschwitz. Kertész himself, as a youngster, a teenager, I think fifteen, sixteen years old, was in Auschwitz and survived. And it is a novel about an adolescent in Auschwitz. I don't even want to try to describe it, but I will just praise it and say it is far and away the greatest fictional representation of the Holocaust, of the Shoah. The most moving, the most original, the most upsetting. Without anything gruesome, the angle of it is such that it's even more horrible, but without anything that is appallingly, gruesomely described. It is all refracted through the consciousness of a youngster, of an adolescent, who doesn't actually understand what's going on.

MS: Not only doesn't he understand, he has come to feel that he deserves what's going on and these goings on are more than he deserves, and they are, to some extent, mysterious and enjoyable. So he tells us about the world of Auschwitz from the point of view of someone who is *appreciating* the experience.

SS: Who is seriously defective, and yet, far from this limiting your understanding, it makes the whole thing more horrible.

MS: A risky final question. Because whereas I think it was once true and could be honestly said that there were so many great books to read of the nineteenth and early twentieth century that a life could be lived entirely in their company, why is it now that when we're talking about these great unknown books, we're talking about what should be the books of our time, the books of this century? They go unknown, they remain unknown, for the most part they are not reviewed. I think if the Tsypkin is getting reviewed, it's because it has your name coupled with it to draw attention to it. How has this happened?

SS: That's a question I think about and also *try* not to think about because it's so discouraging, so demoralizing. Every day of my life, I mean, I try not to think about whether literature, literature of the highest aspiration and the highest seriousness, still has an audience. I know it does. You and I are not alone, Michael, and there are a number of people listening to this program that I'm sure are sensitive readers who do, or would, care about the kind of books we're talking about.

But it's true that, generally speaking, this has lost prestige in the culture. There is not the support in literary magazines and in newspapers. You mentioned the reviews that are coming out now of *Summer in Baden-Baden* by Leonid Tsypkin. I'm sure it's true that my support of the book, my discovery and promotion of the book, is helping it to some extent, but I bet it isn't reviewed as widely as it might have been twenty years ago. There is only one newspaper book review in this country worth reading, and that is the *Los Angeles Times* book review, edited by Steve Wasserman and his team. The *New York Times* book review is now a disgrace—mediocre reviewers, conformist views, most good books neglected, not even reviewed. Really, there's only the *LA Times* right now where a certain literary standard is being maintained. That takes care of Sunday book reviews. And as for the magazines themselves, look at a magazine like *The New Yorker*, which used to carry very extensive, serious reviews in every single issue, as well as stories, *two* stories in every issue of the magazine. Now you might get one story every other issue and many issues of the magazine not containing any literary book review at all. In other words, I don't know what's cause and what's effect. The whole support system for spreading the news about books that are really valuable—and what do I mean by books that are "really valuable"? I mean the books you would want to reread. Ideally, I would never read a book that one wouldn't want to reread. And still, those books are being produced, and they are even in the bookstores, at least for a while. I mean the big chains of Barnes & Noble itself, for instance, will order these books. However, if they don't move off the shelves, they won't reorder. And if they're not supported by the whole infrastructure of reviewing, the news doesn't get out to people. And this is why we need bookstores, for people to browse. It's fine to order books online if you already know what you want, but you're never going to make any discoveries.

2003: *Where the Stress Falls*

MS: Now, the first thing that I want to talk about is the enormous resonance of the title. Stress, being simultaneously a term that poets are concerned with, the stress of a line; stress, being a term that cultures have been concerned with. And it seems to me, in particular, that this book represents a decision about how to live a life where the stress falls in a particular style of living. And that this collection of essays, which takes in literature, poetry, dance, photography, opera, travel, and matters of the intersection of letters and culture, tells us where the stress falls in your life.

SS: Well, I never like to talk about my work in relation to my life because I don't see it that way. I think it's not helpful for me to see it that way, and, more important, I'm not making a decision based on grounds of utility. It just doesn't come naturally to me. I don't think of the work as reflecting *me* any more than, more generally speaking, I think that I write to express myself. I don't think I'm writing to express myself or to define myself. I think of those as low, ignoble motives.

Now, of course, I'm sure I *do* express myself in my writing, and I'm sure I *do* define myself in my writing. But that's not the point, the purpose, the intention, the goal. If it were, it feels to me, I would be involved in a much more limiting and rather lowering project. I wouldn't have the inner freedom to do whatever I do if I thought that I was expressing myself or that I was talking about the choices that I've made. If the work were chapters in an autobiography—and yet, and yet Michael, of course I understand that it could look like that from the outside. So I think what I would want to start with is trying to explain, or really to formulate for myself, because I don't know if it's entirely clear to me either, that my work comes out of a tension or contradiction between what it might look like and what, maybe, it is, and the way I experience it and the way I keep it going.

By the way, the title, *Where the Stress Falls*: I was, of course, thinking of stress in the sense that poets speak of the stresses in a line. But of course, more generally, where the emphasis falls, where you put on the pedal, so to speak. I wasn't thinking of it as stress in the other meaning of anxiety or tension or pressure. It's true that as a person I am very committed to, by temperament, the project of self-improvement, of self-transformation, of self-reinvention, of self-transcendence. But I think of these essays and this thinking in public as being about "it" and not about me. It doesn't seem to me to be about me. It seems much more objective, even though I know from the outside it can't look like that, and it must be subjective. But I don't feel that that's true. I don't feel that it's a vehicle of me, of my ego, or my search for self-expression. I don't feel I'm searching at all for self-expression.

MS: Well, as someone who comes from the outside, I have to say that before I met you, the speaker of these books of essays meant something very deep to me. It was the knowledge that here was a person who was writing about movies, about literature, about so many things, who was not connected to a university, whose life had become concerned with, not whose profession, but whose passions were being expressed in these books. That they weren't being done for professional or academic reasons of advancement, that they were not the work of a specialist. In fact, the dazzling thing in the second section of *Where the Stress Falls* is that you watch Sontag teaching herself to write about art history, about dance. And you watch the forms of sentences being reshaped. Shaped, yes, by the history of criticism, but also by the sensibility that has made all these sentences on many subjects for many years, knowing that respect for dance would require a new dance sentence.

SS: Well, that's interesting that you put it like that. You see, I don't see it that way. But then I can't be outside myself. I can't step over my own feet. I don't feel I'm teaching myself how to write about these things because, for one thing, I never undertake to write anything where I don't feel I already know a lot more than I'm going to say. It's just like writing the last two novels, *The Volcano Lover* and *In America*. I did a vast amount of reading as I was writing the books—not before I was writing them, but as I was writing them—to get the period details correct. And I really wouldn't have been satisfied if it hadn't been something like a ratio of a hundred to one, in the sense that I know, or I did know—I'm a good student, so I can work it up—a vast amount about British naval history, because one of the characters in *The Volcano Lover* is none other than Lord Nelson. I probably used one percent or two percent of what I actually learned by reading a lot of books. I also, I hasten to add, have forgotten virtually all of it because I had to move on to other things. But working something up before you feel equipped to write about it, where you have much more at your disposal and then can be very, very selective about what you want to say, what you want to concentrate on. I wouldn't dare write about something that I didn't feel I already had thought about for a long time and knew a lot more than I was even going to show. Because that's the way I know what I should show or what's worth describing. Because obviously I want to describe some things that aren't described, and so I have to work through a lot of stuff. And I enjoy reading, and I enjoy learning. But the learning, I hope, is not something I'm doing in public. It's not as if, I think, when you're reading the essays, you're saying, "There she is teaching herself."

MS: Oh, no, I don't mean teaching herself about dance. I mean teaching herself to write a sentence that dances.

SS: Well, again, I think, maybe the reason that I see it this way, Michael, is because I'm a fanatic, self-tormenting rewriter. I deeply envy people who can pretty much get it right—I'm talking about the language, the level of the language, the eloquence, not just the ideas—pretty much the first time around in their early draft, and then they kind of fix it up. My essays, much more than my fiction, go through many, many, many drafts, in the course of which I change my mind, I have new ideas. I sometimes end up thinking quite the opposite from what I started out with. I have to think in stages, and in some funny way, I think the essays are a lot smarter than I am. I mean, I don't think I'm as smart, in real life—if I can put it so stupidly—as the essays, in the sense that I can't come up with this kind of stuff just like that, at the drop of a hat.

MS: As I was reading the title essay—you see, I suppose I have a very unusual point of view about this because I think that very little connects Elizabeth Hardwick's *Sleepless Nights*, Randall Jarrell's *Pictures at an Institution*—

SS: *Pictures from an Institution.* By the way, I made that same mistake throughout the essay. I only corrected it in the galleys. I think "Pictures at" is the normal way one would say it, but it is "Pictures from."

MS: —and Glenway Wescott's *The Pilgrim Hawk.* Now, what I enjoy this essay for as I read it is a spider-like activity in which a web is woven around these texts and that, as the web begins to consider itself in the course of the writing, more and more ideas, possibilities, ventures adhere in the web, like insects caught in it. And to my mind, this way of evolving—the essay as web—seems to me to be implicitly comic, you know. There's something delicious about the way in which ideas or themes are made to inhabit the essay. Slowly we discover a whole field of literature that no one talks about. One might say, the maiden aunt or uncle experience. Then it's noticed that, indeed, there is a tradition. Hawthorne has contributed to the tradition of the lonely observing bachelor. James. Bit by bit, how do these lonely sensoria know what they know and know what they report? And why is it that they seem simultaneously repressed and sexually immersed in a kind of hunger of observation? And so the essay discovers a way of billowing its subject into existence.

SS: That's so beautifully said. I resonate to every phrase that you used. The truth is, that essay, it's called "Where the Stress Falls," which gives the collection its title and has as a subject consideration of three relatively little-known American books—the Glenway Wescott novel, *The Pilgrim Hawk*, Randall Jarrell's novel, *Pictures from an Institution*, and Elizabeth Hardwick's novel, *Sleepless Nights*—came as a result of a kind of dare I gave to myself. I love all three of these books. You're absolutely right, they have virtually nothing to do with each other, at least, so it seemed to me when I first thought of it.

It began—Michael, you are the ideal person to say this to, and I have never said it to anyone—it began with an ambition, a conscious ambition to write an essay on something, it's a phrase that our beloved friend Donald Barthelme used to use: "art prose." I wanted to write an essay on American art prose. You know, there is this tradition of American prose that's exemplified by, the classic example of course is Hemingway, and then before him a lot of the naturalistic writers, of sort of artless prose. Of course, no prose is less than artful, but a prose which is stripped down, a prose which is not delicate, Mandarin, indirect, concerned with psychological subtleties and refinements. And I thought, well, there is an American tradition of art prose. I'm using Donald Barthelme's phrase, and, of course, his wonderful books—such as the many stories and his novel, *The Dead Father*—are marvelous examples of the most artful but still distinctively American prose.

So that was the original idea. I would write an essay on prose, on the Mandarin or art prose tradition in American literature. And then I looked around for three examples, and I thought of those three books. And if I had had a fourth, it would have been Donald Barthelme's *The Dead Father.*

And then the notion of stress, that I would find certain kinds of musical values in the prose, that's where I began to write the essay, and I realized that my books had nothing to do with each other, and that my concept was an empty concept. It was simply a concept of appreciation, if you will. I could say these are all wonderfully written books, and I love them, but there wasn't an idea there.

And then I began, as you put it, to weave my web, and I thought, if I weave a big enough web and I place my three little spiders in different parts of it, nobody will notice that they really don't have much to do with each other. And of course, in the end, I found that they did. I was able to make observations about a certain kind of first-person narrating voice, which has always fascinated me: the difference between first-person narration and third-person narration.

MS: These narrators have an inadvertent comic side, or in the case of the Jarrell narrator, an inadvertent serious side. And so comic and poignant is the necessary mixture for this kind of narrator: the man who sees exhaustively, tells what he sees or she sees, and has some area of the void that the seeing surrounds and that we read toward.

SS: But what interested me in these three books—see, I began, as you know, as a fiction writer, and my first novel, *The Benefactor*, has a first-person narrator. I was a young woman, I was in my twenties, and my narrator was a man in his sixties, which seemed about as old as anybody could possibly be on the planet. Now I'm in my sixties, of course, I don't think it's quite that old. But between a woman in her twenties and a man in his sixties, in other words, I was reaching beyond my own experience because I was writing the most anti-autobiographical novel you could imagine. And I had, as a very remote and intermittently conscious model, *Candide*. I was writing about somebody who would tell about his experiences, but the reader would understand that he didn't really understand what his experiences were worth. So you would both enjoy his narration and frame it with your own, you, the reader's, understanding of what was really going on. I like that book a lot, and I think there's a lot going for it.

MS: I do too. First-person fastidious to the task.

SS: They were again first-person narrations—the Glenway Wescott novel, the Randall Jarrell novel, the Elizabeth Hardwick novel. But what interested me in these three books is something very different. All three of these narrators are really smart, and they really do understand what is going on. Incredibly complex things are going on. The Jarrell novel, the middle one, published in the 1950s, is out-and-out a comic novel. It's probably, to my mind, the funniest American novel, just in terms of prose, wit, the funniest novel ever written in this country.

But you see, let me put it this way. I'm going to take a big jump now out of the essay and even a little bit out of the book. I really think that literature which does not embody or convey some wisdom is not worth reading. And that eliminates, of course, about ninety-nine percent of books that are published. I'm very devoted to, attracted to, in the thrall of, what I call—and that's the title of another of the essays—the wisdom project. That one should really understand something about human life and about feeling and about consciousness and about the complexity of reality. And literature is a vehicle for that. It is an education of the heart and of the consciousness. It's an enlarger of sympathies. It's a deepener of feeling. And I'm not interested in any literature that doesn't do that. I'm not interested in any art, I'm not interested in any movie that doesn't do that. And by which I don't mean everything has to be lachrymose and solemn. There are comic works which do this. It's a complex project. But I want books, or the work, whatever the work is, to know something and to be large. I'm not interested in work that's not ambitious in that way.

MS: And yet, I would like to say that this cover by the subject of one of the essays, Howard Hodgkin? Howard Hodgkins?

SS: Hodgkin, Hodgkin. His great uncle was a person who identified—or his great-great uncle—Hodgkin's disease. That's a form of lymphatic cancer. He comes from a scientific family. Hodgkin. Howard Hodgkin: great, great British painter.

MS: You see, it's a different kind of wisdom. The richness of these colors, the way in which they swamp over the frame, the depth of the greens, the yellows, the oranges, their contrast—

SS: The book is worth buying just for the cover.

MS: One wants the word *plumbago* to be used in the sentence about this painting.

SS: Well, you know, I had a feeling when I was putting this together—I like to contradict myself, but above all, not for the sake of contradiction, I like to think I'm going in the right direction. I always feel I'm just beginning now. Everything up to now is just juvenilia, and I'm really getting started. And I liked the way, inadvertently at first, this book felt like a step forward. Even though it is, in fact, a selection of work done in the '90s and a good deal part of the '80s, I felt there was a way—and you're right to focus on the cover—in which I could—even in the essays, which interest me less—show some evolution. The title doesn't sound like my kind of title, if you think of the other titles of my books. The cover certainly doesn't resemble the cover of any book of mine. I always do my own covers. I'm a visual freak, and I'm lucky enough to be able to choose my cover and my typography and the design of the book. And so, every cover that I've ever had on a book has been done by me, for better or for worse. And there was a great sense of liberation having something so flamboyantly colorful. I just felt, oh, what a relief.

MS: Well, what I have often said is that the books and the progress from book to book—this is tricky—have been in some sense about a flight from morbidity, that there were the grotesque narrators of the first and second novels, that this is not a flight toward frivolity or lightheartedness but to find the weight of pleasure. The book *Against Interpretation*, of course, called for an erotics of criticism, but in this later work, it seems to me, there is a responsible and responsive lulling into a pleasure state while waking in prose to recall consciousness. The essay takes place *after* the immersion in the work, and yet it is trying to recall, Hodgkin-like, an experience much denser and richer than normal intellection accounts for.

SS: Yes. And in some cases, just to describe what enthralls, what fascinates, what gives pleasure, what gives ecstasy is rather—well, I don't want to say it's hard. I mean, all writing is hard. It's hard to write well, especially if you're the product of the American public school system, as I am. I feel very much a self-taught writer. But it isn't just the writing itself, it's the right kind of platform to launch your spaceship. I want to take the reader on a ride, and I want there to be some kind of narrative or emotional or ethical climax in the essays. At the same time, I can't resist some sort of teacherly feeling that if I mention this, for instance, there's an essay, an utterly mindless essay I'm quite fond of on grottoes.

MS: Well, there are digressions into the toasting of marshmallows in the midst of an essay on a collaboration between Jasper Johns, John Cage, and Merce Cunningham. It's almost as if the essay is daydreaming, and the texture between these sensibilities, these three unusual sensibilities, becomes the subject of the essay, including the impossibility of writing an essay about three such unlikely participants.

SS: And my own sense of discretion, since at one time I knew all three of these people extremely well. So I have to tell you, one of the guiding principles in the writing of that essay was not in any way to betray any personal confidence or anything that I knew about them personally. Because I am not only an anti-autobiographical writer, although that's weakening slightly, but I'm very interested in protecting the privacy of my friends, unlike most writers.

David Foster Wallace

1996: *Infinite Jest*

MS: I don't know how exactly to talk about this book, so I'm going to be reliant upon you to kind of guide me. But something came into my head that may be entirely imaginary, which seemed to be that the book was written in fractals?

DFW: Expand on that.

MS: It occurred to me that the way in which the material is presented allows for a subject to be announced in a small form. Then there seems to be a fan of subject matter, other subjects, and then it comes back in a second form containing the other subjects in small and then comes back again, as if what were being described were, and I don't know this kind of science, but it just—I said to myself, "This must be fractals."

DFW: I've heard you were an acute reader. That's one of the things, structurally, that's going on. It's actually structured like something called a Sierpiński Gasket, which is a very primitive kind of pyramidical fractal. Although what was structured as a Sierpiński Gasket was the draft that I delivered to Michael in '94, and it went through some, I think, mercy cuts. So it's probably kind of a lopsided Sierpiński Gasket now. But it's interesting, that's one of the structural ways that it's supposed to kind of come together.

MS: "Michael" is Michael Pietsch, the editor at Little, Brown. What is a Sierpiński Gasket?

DFW: I would almost have to show you. It's kind of a design that a man named Sierpiński, I believe, developed. It was quite a bit before the introduction of fractals and before any of the kind of technologies that fractals are a real useful metaphor for. But it looks basically like a pyramid on acid with certain interconnections between parts of them that are visually kind of astonishing, and then the mathematical explanations of them are interesting.

MS: All I really know about fractals comes from an essay by Hugh Kenner, who leapt up and said, "Oh, Pound did this!" And he was trying to suggest that the ways in which material is organized in poetry and elsewhere is extremely unsophisticated, that the patterns of disorder are much more beautiful than the patterns of order and equally discoverable. When you structure a book in this way, do you mean it to be discovered?

DFW: Yeah, that's a very tricky question because I know that when I was a young writer I would play endless sort of structural games that I think, in retrospect, were mostly for myself alone. I didn't much care. I mean, *Infinite Jest* is trying to do a whole bunch of different things at once, and it doesn't make much difference to me whether somebody—I mean, I would expect that somebody who's a mathematician or a logician or an ACS guy might be interested in some of the fractal structures of it. For me, I mean, a lot of the motivation had to do with, it seems to me, so much of pre-millennial life in America consists of enormous amounts of what seem like discrete bits of information coming and that the real kind of intellectual adventure is finding ways to relate them to each other and to find larger patterns and meanings, which of course is essentially narrative, but structurally it's a bit different. And since fractals are a more—oh Lord—since its chaos is more on the surface, its bones are its beauty a little bit more. I thought that would be a more interesting way to structure the thing.

I—okay, now I'm meandering—but I know that doing something this long, a fair amount of the structural stuff is for me because it's kind of like pitons in the mountainside. I mean, it's ways for me to stay oriented and engaged and get through it. I don't think I would impose weird structures on the reader the way I would have, say, ten years ago. Does that make any sense?

MS: Yes, it does.

DFW: Okay.

MS: But I wanted to suggest, at least for me, that the organization of the material, whether or not someone leaps up and says, "Fractal!" or even has heard of fractals, seemed to me to be necessary and beautiful because we're entering a world that needs to be made strange before it becomes familiar. And so it seemed to me that in this book, which contains both the banality and extraordinariness of various kinds of experience and the banality of extraordinary experience as well, that—

DFW: And the extraordinariness of banal experience.

MS: Yeah—that a way needed to be found, and it thrilled me that it seemed to be structural, that the book found a way to arrange itself so that one knew. For the longest time you would be faced with these analogies: when *Ulysses* came out, people talked about its musical structures; when Dos Passos's books came out, people talked about film editing. It seems very hard, in the last period of years, to find a new way to structure a book. The only thing that I know is Barth working with logarithmic spirals to deal with the unfoldings of memory and of seeing things from new perspectives at later dates.

DFW: You gotta realize, though, when you're talking to somebody who's actually written the thing, there's this weird Monday-morning quarterbacking thing about it. Because I know that, at least for me, I mean, I don't sit down and say, "Oh, let's see. How can I find a suitable structural synecdoche for experience right now?" It's more a matter of kind of whether it tastes true or not. And I know that this is the first thing I ever did, that I took money for before it was done—because I just didn't have any money, and I wanted to finish it—and Michael Pietsch, the editor, said—I think that he got like the first four hundred pages—and he said it seemed to him like a piece of glass that had been dropped from a great height. And that was the first time that anybody had ever conceptualized what was to me just a certain structural representation of the way the world kind of operated on my nerve endings, which was as a bunch of discrete, random bits, but which contained within them—not always all that blatantly—very interesting connections. And it wasn't clear whether the connections were my own imagination—were crazy—or whether they were real, and which were important and which weren't. And so, I mean, a lot of the structure in there is kind of seat-of-the-pants, what kind of felt true to me and what didn't. I did not sit down with, you know, I'm gonna do a fractal structure or something. I don't think I'm that kind of writer.

MS: So there aren't diagrams? Or the diagrams emerged as you went along?

DFW: Well, I've got a poster of a Sierpiński Gasket that I've had since I was a little boy that I like just because it's pretty. But it's real weird. I think writing is a big blend of—there's a lot of sophistication, and there's a lot of kind of idiocy about it. And so much of it is gut and saying, "This feels true, this doesn't feel true; this tastes right, this doesn't." And it's only when you get about halfway through that I think you start to see any sort of structure emerging at all. Then, of course, the great nightmare is that you alone see the structure and it's going to be a mess for everyone else.

MS: Well, what thrilled me about the book is that around two hundred pages in it just began to get better and better and better. I started to like it more and more and look forward to going back to reading it, and I felt a kind of, I don't know, tenderness toward it, toward both its characters and its narrator, because of the extraordinary effort that was going into writing it. It didn't seem like difficulty for difficulty's sake; it seemed like immense difficulty being expended because something important about how difficult it has become to be human needed to be said and there weren't other ways to say that.

DFW: I feel like I wanna ask you to adopt me.

Because, yeah, I mean, this is the great nightmare, when you're doing something long and hard, you're terrified it will be perceived as gratuitously hard and difficult—that this is some avant-garde, for-its-own-sake sort of exercise. And having done some of that stuff, I think, earlier in my career, I was really scared about it. The trick of this—I've got this whole rant about how I think a lot of avant-garde fiction and serious literary fiction that bitches and moans about readers' defection and blames it all on TV is, to a certain extent, bullshit. I think a lot of the avant-garde has forgotten that part of its job is to seduce the reader into being willing to do the hard work.

And so doing something like this, there were a lot of fears, and one of them was: "Oh no, this doesn't make any sense." Another was: "Oh no, this is going to come off as gratuitously long or gratuitously hard," and, I don't know—it makes me happy you said that because, yeah, I worked harder on this than anything I've ever done in my life, and there's nothing in there by accident. And there've already been some readers and reviewers that see it as kind of a mess and as kind of random, and I just have to sort of shrug my shoulders.

MS: Well, it does seem to me that, unfortunately, if you haven't encountered, if you can't look at a jellyfish and see how miraculously complex it is—I don't know why it is, but people seem to look at, say, a computer and say, "Well, that's the computer. I don't know how it works, but it does the silly job I give to it." And so they don't know how to look at prose—something man-made or something natural—and see that its beauty is in resolving complexity into a kind of organism, order.

DFW: And part of that is maybe the fault of some sort of reading culture or something, but part of it is that fiction has got a very weird and complicated job. Because part of its job is to teach the reader, communicate with the reader, establish some sort of relationship with the reader where the reader is willing, on a neurological level, to expend effort to look hard enough at the jellyfish to see that it's pretty. And that kind of effort is very hard to talk about, and it's real scary because you can't be sure whether you've done it or not, and it's what makes you sort of clutch your heart when somebody says, "I really like this; it didn't strike me as gratuitous." Because that's, of course, your great hope when you're doing it.

MS: Well—

DFW: Does that make any sense?

MS: Absolutely. Doubly so because I have to explain: I first met John Barth when *Lost in the Funhouse* had just come out. I was a student at Buffalo; *Chimera* was about to appear. There were—between the *Lost in the Fun-*

house publication and *Chimera*—many, many years of confusion and indecision. And to some extent—although there will never be an influence as great on my life as to be in the presence of that man—I feel, in many ways, he took a wrong turning, you know? And that what we see now is two things: a squirming, the feeling that the turning was so narrowly wrong that it can be rectified, so you see, almost, books being written again and again in the attempt not exactly to get them right but to find out where they went wrong. And the other is the strange quality—and you find it in your books as well—that he's solved certain of life's problems in ways that he thought that life couldn't be solved: he's become happy, he's become uxorious, and he truly loves someone. And this is something that seems to be difficult for fiction that began with a nihilist bent to reconcile.

DFW: Yeah, one of the things—now I'm not going to be able to remember the titles—but there have been short pieces that have appeared recently. There was one in *Harper's*, and there were three in *Conjunctions*. And it's very interesting to watch this. You're right, the vibe is discomfort at being happy, discomfort about how to write about heart-craft and the kind of stuff that in the '60s, I think, would have seemed real cheesy and cliché and sentimental, through the kind of filter that he's so very carefully built.

The thing—when you were talking—the thing that amuses me is the stuff that he's going back and rewriting is, for me, the stuff that's alive. I mean, for me, all the way, I think, through parts of *Lost in the Funhouse*, I'm with him, and it's starting with *Chimera* that I think he becomes this sort of Clang Bird that flies in ever-diminishing circles, although gorgeously—and, I mean, he writes some of the best prose in America. But he was a very big deal for me because I sort of broke—I think I really saw myself as coming out of that tradition, and then in the late '80s I worked on the real long story that's sort of a reworking of *Lost in the Funhouse*. And really, I think that I came to see that there was nothing but involution and basically masturbation—for me, anyway—in that kind of game-playing, meta-move, intertextual stuff. And I, too, had a number of years where I didn't write any fiction and really had no idea where to go after doing "Westward," which was the long story.

MS: This may be hard to do, but can you find a way of saying what the difference is between that kind of involution and the complexities of this novel?

DFW: Boy. I probably can't do it and sound very smart or coherent. I know that, I guess when I was in my twenties—like deep down, underneath all the bullshit—what I really believed was that the point of fiction was to show that the writer was really smart. And that sounds terrible to say, but I think, looking back, that's what was going on. And I don't think I really understood what loneliness was when I was a young man. And now I've got a much less clear idea about what the point of art is, but I think it's got something to do with loneliness and something to do with setting up a conversation between human beings.

I know that when I started this book I had very vague and not very ambitious ambitions, and one was I wanted to do something really sad. I'd done comedy before. I wanted to do just something really sad, and I wanted to do something about what was sad about America. And there's a fair amount of weird and hard technical stuff going on in this book, but, I mean, one reason that I'm willing to go around and talk to people about it and that I'm sort of proud of it in a way I haven't been about earlier stuff, is that I feel like whatever's hard in the book is in service of something that, at least for me, is good and important. And it's embarrassing to talk about because I think it sounds kind of cheesy. I sort of think, like, all the way down kind of to my butthole, I was a different person coming up with this book than I was about my earlier stuff. And I'm not saying my earlier stuff was all crap, you know? But it's just it seems like—I think when you're very young and until you've sort of faced various darknesses, it's very difficult to understand how precious and rare the sort of thing that art can do is. You're welcome to cut all this out if this just sounds like, you know, a craft product or something.

MS: No, no, no. It seems to me—this is what I noticed, and maybe it's not there—that on the one hand, in *Infinite Jest*, there's a very high-tech tennis academy bent on training prodigies. And prodigies can be trained, and one might say that the result of such a training in the novel might be a novel like *LETTERS*, by John Barth. That there's a lot of internal structure, a lot of complicated, intertextual exchange, that brilliance is, in a way, the subject of that novel, even while it attempts to blow itself up. It's like the mad scientist who says, "I'm going to take everyone and all of my characters with me!" And then there's another kind of school. It seems to me that maybe up until around 1973 it was perhaps important to be smart, but then suddenly you looked outside the universities and you said, "Well, these people in the university are not all that interesting, and these people outside the university speak an entirely different language, value entirely different things, and are being blown to bits not by the training to be prodigies but by the hopelessness of having nothing but addictions to erect structures upon." And so what goes on in this book seems to be that there's a second world, almost like a second chance. That one can be that kind of high-performing tennis acrobat, or you can completely fall apart and become someone who enters a different set of metaphors that all have to do with something called recovery, in which the book seems, in some sense, to believe. Am I way off here?

DFW: Yeah, although—I mean, the thing that makes me nervous talking about this is so far it seems as if people think it really is sort of a book about drug addiction and recovery, and, you know, intentional fallacies notwithstanding, what was really going on in my head was something more general, like what you were talking about before. That some of the sadness that, it seems to me, kind of infuses the culture right now has to do with this loss of a sense of purpose or organizing principles, something you're willing to give yourself away to, basically. And the addictive impulse, which is very much kind of in the cultural air right now, is interesting and powerful only because it's a kind of obvious distortion of a religious impulse or an impulse to be part of something bigger. And the stuff at the academy is kind of weird because, yeah, it's very high-tech and it's very, "Become technically better so that you can achieve X, Y, and Z," but also the guy who essentially runs the academy now is a fascist, and, whether it comes out or not, he's really the only one there who, to me, is saying anything that's even remotely non-horrifying. Except it is horrifying, because he's a fascist. And part of the stuff that was rattling around in my head when I was doing this, is that it seems to me that one of the scary things about the nihilism of contemporary culture is that we're really setting ourselves up for fascism. Because as we empty more and more values, motivating principles—spiritual principles, almost—out of the culture, we're creating a hunger that eventually is going to drive us to the state where we may accept fascism just because, you know, the nice thing about fascists is they'll *tell* you what to think, they'll *tell* you what to do, they'll *tell* you what's important. And we as a culture aren't doing that for ourselves yet.

I know this is somewhat digressive. But that was the only thing that it seemed to me you were missing in the thing about the academy, is there's an embedded fascist whose status is really ambivalent because he's a horrifying figure but he's also, to me, the only figure there who isn't completely insane in terms of his approach to, at least, sports.

MS: Now, when I first got this—

DFW: I am not Wyndham Lewis, by the way. It's not a pro-fascist book.

MS: Although it may look like *The Apes of God* in its size and length, it isn't *The Apes of God*. I did want to say that when I first got the book in the mail from its editor, I got it as a bound typescript, and I immediately then—to jump to the other side of the metaphor of this book, or at least the metaphor I'm suggesting in this book—I was immediately upset because the author begins by announcing that AA meetings are open to the public, and that he's grateful for the people who've shared their experience, strength, and hope with him, and that he tells some of their stories in this book. And at first I found myself thinking, "Oh, this is real trouble; he's going to be in real trouble here," and then thinking, "Yes, but it's absolutely necessary to tell these stories." That the culture that insists on anonymity and silence is one in which the spiritual principles you're talking about being emptied out of life are being sort of hidden underground, and this book seemed to want to find a trapdoor through which those things could be incorporated again without embarrassment.

DFW: I think that puts it very well. I think one of the great ironies is—I mean, I've been to a few different churches, I've been to a few different things.

The one place, when I was researching this book, the one place where I saw the kind of stuff that seemed to me—at the time, anyway—to be important talked about was AA. The great irony is that AA's got this thing called the Twelve Traditions, the eleventh of which is that any member of AA can't identify themselves on the level of press, radio, and film. Which means, really, technically, to write a book like this that's got a lot of AA in it, you can't be an AA member, which is one reason why it was very lucky that the city that I was doing the research in, Boston, like seventy-five percent of its meetings were open. So you could just totter in off the street, fork over a buck, and kinda settle back.

MS: But I'm curious. This begins to describe one of those double binds that this book seems to like to structure around its characters, that the only way that you can be part of a spiritual community is not to be part of it. There's a very funny one, I think the first one where I began to put an exclamation point: a teacher is giving a class an exam in dysfunctional double binds and tells the class to imagine that they are on the one hand kleptomaniacs and have as a *raison d'être* the need to get out and steal, steal, steal. But, on the other hand, they're agoraphobics and are afraid to go out and steal, steal, steal. And you think, "Oh, what a great double bind!" And the person beginning to answer this essay question, in gender-neutral terms, is starting to write about mail fraud, and you just rub your hands together and say, "This is the kind of delicious complexity and comedy the book is capable of." But why the double binds?

DFW: I think it's hard to talk smartly about. It seems to me that most of the stuff in my own life and in my friends' lives that's interesting and true involves double binds or setups where you're given two alternatives which are mutually exclusive, and the sacrifices involved in either seem unacceptable. I mean, one of the big ones is the culture places a huge premium on achievement. And I went to this real hoity-toity college, and everybody's now a millionaire on Wall Street. Anyway, how both to work hard enough and invest enough of yourself, really to achieve something and yet retain the sort of integrity so that you've got a self apart from your achievement? I mean, even something as banal as "the modern woman can have it all," she can have a family and a deep, fulfilling relationship with her children while being a CEO of a successful company. I mean, it's as if the culture is some Zen teacher whacking us no matter what we do. It's very interesting. I'm not really quite sure why we set it up that way. I'm also—I gotta tell you—I'm worried that these answers are just sounding totally insane. They're great questions, but it just seems to me like a lot of this is stuff that we could talk about for three hours.

MS: Well, the pleasure about *Infinite Jest* is that it does feel like a book that invites the beginning of a conversation, that the book is long enough, involved enough, rich enough, deep enough, and moving enough to begin to feel like a dialogue. That you could go back and talk to the book in the form of reading it again, because I did, I'm halfway through it a second time. And, of course, the second time round you know things that you couldn't have known the first time through. And so the book is like getting to know someone well.

DFW: That—I mean, yeah, it's designed to be a book—I mean this is probably a little pretentious, to write a book this long and have it be designed to be read more than once. That for me wasn't the thing that was really hard and really scary. The really hard and really scary thing was trying to make it fun enough so somebody would want to. And also how to have it be fun without having it be reductive or pandering or get co-opted by the very principles of commercialism and, you know, "like me, like me, like me," that the book is partly about. And that stuff was real migraine-producing.

1997: *A Supposedly Fun Thing I'll Never Do Again*

MS: Listeners to *Bookworm* know that I consider David to be the rare thing: someone who knows how to build something new that's complicated and rich, and maybe among the last who knows how to create technologies that result in these kinds of structure.

I noticed when I was reading the essays in *A Supposedly Fun Thing I'll Never Do Again* that, at a certain point, most of the things that you are looking at yield an addictiveness quotient: the tennis gets to a point where the volley turns into a trance; the pampering on board the cruise, in the final essay, becomes something that yields a desire for still more mega-pampering. And I wanted to ask you to address this. I found, as I was reading the essays, that I was growing addicted to them, that the essays themselves, in their length, in their repetitions, were forming a counter-trancelike addiction. And I wondered if you could talk about that.

DFW: I think the oldest essay in that collection was written in 1990, which is when I was making the first stab at *Infinite Jest*. There's a lot of addiction stuff in *Infinite Jest*, and it's odd—I mean, I went to a lot of open AA meetings, and I'd read a lot of sort of addictionology books, and it does become a kind of model or lattice through which you end up seeing a lot of stuff, particularly American stuff, like advertising as seduction. I mean, the ultimate in elastic demand is an addict, which is, you know, terrific for commercial interests.

I'm not sure about addiction so much. I know that a lot of the essays ended up being about certain kinds of seduction. And seduction can, on one hand, be a neat thing, it can make us feel alive, but, on another hand, seduction is literally promising more than you can deliver. And there seems to me to be something particularly American about that experience.

It's also true that I'm not a journalist, and a lot of these pieces came about because *Harper's* commissioned one thing and other magazine editors liked it and commissioned me to do other stuff. So, I don't think it's all that surprising that a fair amount of the sort of theory behind *Infinite Jest* comes out in the essays, because I didn't really have any idea how to write nonfiction. I was basically walking around paying as close attention as I could and then trying to form it into something.

MS: Well, one of the things that interests me here is that it reminded me a good deal, as I went along in it, of James Thurber. And I thought the James Thurber technique of humor is to find a way for the person narrating the events to be exactly the wrong person to be participating in the events. In other words, the thing that the humorist must first do is disqualify himself, at which point, having become Charlie Chaplin, everything that happens to him is hilarious.

DFW: Interesting. I hadn't thought of it that way, and I don't know that much about Thurber. I know that, particularly starting with about the third essay, the state fair thing, there was a certain persona that I found to do these things. A great deal of it was that I was petrified because I feel like I know a certain amount about writing fiction but didn't know anything about writing nonfiction. I am just now teaching a class at ISU in nonfiction, and I'm realizing how illiterate in the genre I am. I hit on a tactic fairly early on of simply being candid about that and actually developing a persona who came out in the essay and said, "I'm not a journalist. I'm petrified. The terror is making me pay a whole lot of attention." And then it becomes, yeah, kind of lovable schmuck. One guy in New York kept asking if I'd gotten it from Woody Allen, and there is a kind of Woody Allen—it's another reason why I wanted to collect them all together in the book and then not do any more for a while, because by the last one I was finding that it was a particular kind of narrator.

MS: Yes, and yet the reason I think of Thurber is that he's from the Midwest, Columbus, that he famously looks into a microscope in university days to examine his own eye—

DFW: Mm.

MS: And that—

DFW: That's the stuff about Ohio State? Yeah, okay, I've read some of that.

MS: But there's the endearing tone of a man, who, in your case, will find himself in the beautiful legs contest, in Thurber's case, is a man who by the end of his life is blind and is drawing cartoons.

DFW: Uh-huh. Well, I actually would—I would claim that I belonged in the best legs contest. I actually have—I'm not the best-looking guy in the world, but I have been complimented on my legs more than once.

It's weird, and since I'm on a coast this might be news to somebody: there is a kind of Midwestern persona that's very useful to use, particularly in New York, which is just shy of the "Golly, the buildings are so tall!" thing, where I think people from the Midwest are expected to be not only non-hip but several IQ points slower, and it can be extremely useful. People will reveal themselves to you in ways that they wouldn't to another East Coaster. And I think a lot of these were complex because, not only was I dealing with topics that I didn't know all that well, but I was also doing them for East Coaster magazines. I'm not used to being edited very closely. I was very anxious, and I think there's a certain amount of construction of the kind of—and it is, it's somewhat of an ironic pose 'cause I'm bright and I'm a good writer, so it's not like I'm shaking the straw out of my hair as I'm going to these things. But there was this kind of extremely anxious, compulsive, agoraphobic person, who—I guess part of it, too, was the danger of a lot of these seem like they were setups to just sneer at stuff. The East Coaster guy returns home and sneers at the state fair; the egghead goes on a cruise and sneers at the gross consumption. And that setting myself up as sort of vulnerable and neurotic and in-bent was a way to have at least a lot of the humor directed at myself rather than them. I don't know if that makes any sense, but I didn't just want to do literate *Spy* magazine parodies of things.

MS: But the effect that is most visible here has something to do with the information-gathering in the essays. The writing is presented as a kind of hunger. In fact, I think one of the book's funniest moments is when you have the historian of the Illinois State Fair give a whole set of very hard to remember facts that are recited dutifully in prose in the paragraph, and you say, "I wish I had a pen." There's a certain aggressiveness about the amount of information and how to parse it out, which is also true of *Infinite Jest*. The situating of the reader in *Infinite Jest* comes around a third of the way into the book when we find out what year we are in fact in—what is past, what is present, what is future—and how you take in new information and arrange it seems to be part of your subject.

DFW: See, this is one of the things that's neat about coming on this show is you will point out stuff to me that I haven't realized. I know that with the nonfiction book, particularly the first few essays were extraordinarily stressful to me because, number one, you can't lie. Fact-checkers call you up, and they get very nervous. And number two, nonfiction is incredibly different because what's real is just—I mean, we could spend three hours describing the inside of this room, which is not very lavishly decorated. And I had a tremendously difficult time knowing what was important and what wasn't, and I was myself overwhelmed. And I did—it was a rhetorical strategy I hit on, simply to be utterly candid about it and invite the reader to kind of empathize both with my anxiety and with the overload.

MS: Now, some of the overload effect takes the form, at least visually, spatially, reader consciousness–wise, of footnotes: having to go to the bottom of the page, the information not fitting on the page, itself. And it began to make me think of something you say about television: that the television effect depends upon a splitting of the word, the image, and what you hear about the image. This seems to be a kind of tennis game that goes on in these footnotes as well, a whole resetting, actually. The footnote form has become yours. You're using it now, it seems, virtually for everything.

DFW: Well, you get—no. In the later essays, which I wrote when I was typing *Infinite Jest*—I mean, the footnotes get, dare I say, addictive. Somehow there's a certain way that a kind of call-and-response thing gets set up in your head. They're a terrific way to sort of drop back a dimension or do a meta-comment on the thing that you're doing. In the essays, since I decided there was no way I could pass myself off as a journalist and was, in fact, going to do these as kind of meta-essays and have part of the essay be about the anxiety of producing the essays, the footnotes were great places to do that.

The way that the editor of the book helped me is that the footnotes can become, for me, very compulsive. What will happen is there's an anxiety that I haven't made something entirely clear or that, "Oh dear, an element of reality has escaped my ken," and so what I'll do is drop it down at the bottom of the page. And Michael Pietsch, the editor, pointed out to me that it seems—about a third of the footnotes, particularly in the Lynch thing and in the cruise thing, were cut out because he can nail when I have forgotten that the footnotes have to be read exactly the same way the text does. To me they have become sort of corollaries or afterthoughts, but for the reader, actually, they're even more demanding, because the reader has to stop, hold his or her place in the text, go down, read the interpolation, and then return to the text. And so, the reason why I was lucky Michael Pietsch was a really good editor of both these books is that he was able—he gets it, and he sees some of the virtues of the footnotes—but he was very good at figuring out where I had just kind of lost it, was ceasing to identify with the reader in any way, which is kind of working out this weird, kind of addictive quality that footnotes have.

I have, by the way—I'm in cold turkey from footnotes. I am not doing them anymore.

MS: I want to talk to you about style. You are the inventor, as far as I know, of the compound conjunction: paragraphs beginning "And but now." I've never seen them before, and I wanted to ask you about them. You do it ferociously, and so I assume not unconsciously.

DFW: What I'm interested in more than style is just pace, and it's one reason why these tours are hard for me, because I don't think my stuff's meant to be read out loud, and I get terrible breathing problems—it's like the text's revenge.

I just have a lot of friends, and I myself, when I get—when somebody's talking and they get on a roll and they start talking faster and faster and they don't breathe and one of the things they'll do is have compound conjunctions because you're really wanting that sentence to serve a number of things: it's both a contrast and a continuation, and it's also an extrapolation. And it's, I think, a little unconscious clue to the reader that he's more listening than reading now, that we're in a speed, we're at a pace now that's supposed to be far more sound and pace and breath than it is these short, contained sentences.

MS: Well, when I was in college, I knew a girl who, speaking so fast and furiously as she would, at the point where she would want to say, "You know like," she would say, "Y'n'ike." And we used to write it on walls with spray paint. It was like a motto—

DFW: The other thing that's annoying is when people say "like" in speech, you know, "I'm like thirty-five years old." There's never a comma, and I would always read this stuff where writers trying to be hip would have like, "I'm," comma, "like," comma, "thirty-five," which is just absolutely wrong. It makes it easier to read, but it doesn't sound—it doesn't make your brain-voice mimic the sound of somebody actually saying it, which is one reason why, I guess, when I'm writing stuff that's meant to be read very fast there's not much punctuation and there's a lot of stuff that's, strictly speaking, ungrammatical, although the syntax is kind of strategic.

MS: Well, I'm glad you used the phrase because I was about to use it, and in fact I thought I had invented it. I would say that these things, at least these books that I know, are written in the brain-voice.

DFW: To an extent. I think—I don't know whether anybody else sees this— there's a real progression. I mean, the first two things in here were done before I wrote *Infinite Jest*, and *Infinite Jest* is the first thing that I wrote where it's supposed to sound like the narrator's talking to you. The first few pieces of fiction that I wrote were very what I thought was literary: they were very written and very kind of distant and contained. And I think, as the essays in the book go on—they're in roughly chronological order—more and more of that voice kind of creeps into the voice of the essays. I'm not sure that it's entirely intentional, although I'd be happy to pretend that it was if it would make me sound more impressive.

MS: Well, what's nice, I guess, is that as impressive as these books are, there's also a contravening desire not to sound impressive. In other words, from time to time the essayist who's writing *A Supposedly Fun Thing I'll Never Do Again*, calls himself a weenie. The world of *Infinite Jest* is also full of people who are saying brilliant things to you and apologizing for saying them, apologizing for being the kind of people who think these things and think them at this rate and express them at this length. And that's what I mean, I guess, by the brain-voice, that somehow or other there is that self-interrupting capacity.

Everything that a writer does is not peculiar to a writer, it's something that he's located somewhere in the culture or in his head that, finally, put onto the page, people stop and say, "Yes, people *do* that!" And your work seems to be the result of something that developed in America when everyone started going to college. They read things that their parents hadn't read—maybe not your parents, but mine—and suddenly all sorts of locutions entered speech that previously had only been on the page.

DFW: For example?

MS: The "inasmuch as" stuff. Meta-language. Little bits of apologies for being smart.

DFW: Or for looking as if you're trying to sound smart. For me, I find what you're saying flattering, but I think you're overestimating some of the reasons—like this thing about the constant self-consciousness and apology. Somebody at the reading in San Francisco last night was very acute and made me very uncomfortable because she talked about the second essay in the book, which is this big thing about writing fiction when you've watched a lot of TV and you live in this kind of very hip ironic culture and how hip irony can become toxic and blah-blah-blah—I won't rehash the argument. But she pointed out that this essay makes that argument and then a great deal of the rest of the essays in the book employ a certain kind of hip, ironic self-consciousness that, to me, isn't that attractive. And the apologizing for being smart, I think, can very easily become trying to head off potential criticism by acknowledging that I can get there first and deprecate myself so that you don't get a chance to do it, and it's very much of a piece with a certain kind of insecurity, what to me seems like a very American insecurity that I have fully internalized, where I am so terrified of your judgment that if I can show some kind of hip, self-aware, self-conscious judgment of myself first, I somehow am defended against your ridiculing me or parodying me, or something like that, to the extent that I don't think I'm the only person who suffers from that. It may be effective, but a great deal of it, I think, is—that's expressive stuff that I'm not comfortable with. I think a lot of that's just a tic about my own psychology. I think my work would be better if there wasn't quite so much of that in there. Because it really is manipulative. I mean, it is acting out of terror of another's judgment and so trying to look as if he can't possibly come up with a criticism of you, having to do with how you appear, that you haven't gotten there first.

MS: Well, one of my favorite things to talk to you about follows from this. We both share an admiration for a barely known book called *Wittgenstein's Mistress* by David Markson, which is published by Dalkey Archive Press. The books by David Foster Wallace, *A Supposedly Fun Thing I'll Never Do Again* and *Infinite Jest* are published by Little, Brown—

DFW: Nice of you to insert the plug. *Wittgenstein's Mistress* now, by the way, available in paperback for, I think, only eight dollars from Dalkey Archive Press.

MS: But what we like about it is its mixture of extraordinary intelligence and, at the same time, sadness. And the intelligence in it is really swallowed by a narrative situation that wants to compress it and make it nearly impossible to express, so that the book alternates between weeping, really, and extraordinary observation—

DFW: Or both at the same time.

MS: And we talked about that kind of book—I say that Rilke and Kafka do it—that manages to be extremely self-conscious and yet to attain some kind of sanctity or purity or holiness or humanness or all at the same time, that I sense is the alternative to the massive book of *Infinite Jest* and the massive self-consciousnesses and paralyses that this kind of book involves. I wanted to talk about that a bit.

DFW: I think—I mean, I agree with you, and I think *Wittgenstein's Mistress* is a magical book, not because it alternates between incredible intellectual stunt-pilotry and pathos but because it manages to marry the two in a way that—I mean, that's what my dream is, to someday be able to do something like that.

I think there's a difference, though, between the kind of self-consciousness that you're talking about in *Wittgenstein's Mistress* or *Notebooks of Malte Laurids Brigge* or "A Hunger Artist," from the *Metamorphosis*. The self-consciousness there is a far sort of deeper, wiser—it's a more autonomous, almost solipsistic self-consciousness. The kind that I'm talking about is far more concerned with the perception by others, what others' judgments are of you. It's a way of positioning oneself to prevent something terrible happening that only you think is going to happen, or something. And it's—I think we need more words for self-consciousness the way Eskimos have for snow, because I think, you're right, there are some kinds of self-consciousness that are much more like self-awareness or a kind of deep, a very involved, sophisticated acceptance of human limitation, versus: I want to make a certain kind of impression. I want to show you, number one, I'm very smart, but, number two, I'm not pretentious at all, I'm not hung-up on myself, so I will therefore, every time I say something erudite, make very clear to you that I'm not all puffed up because if, for a moment, I show myself as puffed up, well, we know from watching American sitcoms what happens to the character who shows himself as puffed up or pretentious. I mean, the analogy is somewhat forced, but I think there are moments in some of my later stuff where I've managed to hit a note of that kind of self-consciousness that, for me, is wise and timeless, but there are also times when I know that I get scared and I'm positioning myself a certain way, particularly in the nonfiction, that I don't think is interesting or productive self-consciousness. In a perverse way, though, I think it's mimetic of a very kind of late twentieth-century American experience, which is—I think this is a time when we're terribly afraid of one another, and there seem to be very few venues for talking about it. And so, if betraying some of that neurosis in these essays is at least a way of inviting some kind of conversation between me and the reader about it, that's one thing. But I also know that I'm very bright, but I'm also terrified of coming off as somebody who thinks he's very bright because people who think they're very bright are buttholes.

MS: After around—what was it?—fifteen years of waiting for William H. Gass to finish *The Tunnel*, I said to myself, "Wouldn't it be wonderful if, after all this time, during which time we know that he's been working like a dog, he published a book, and it was seventy-seven pages long." For me, that would have been extremely heroic because it wouldn't have been one of those little, tiny apéritif-and-toothpick kind of books. It would have been the exudation—

DFW: It would've been the *Philosophical Investigations*, is what you're talking about.

MS: Exactly. And I'm very curious about that ability to heroically throw away what might be brilliant stand-up stuff, set pieces, wit, extravagance, and to have the essence. It seems to me that a lot of the questions that get asked in *A Supposedly Fun Thing I'll Never Do Again*—that is to say, how do you get out of the loop of addiction and consumerism and everything else—is to tell not the truth but the essence of truth, to get past the process of truth-telling and go to the truth itself.

DFW: I agree with ninety percent of what you're saying, in principle. The problem is in practice. What you're talking about is a very condensed, aphoristic—you're talking about *Thus Spake Zarathustra* or the *Philosophical Investigations* or the *Tao Te Ching* or something. Or really, really good poetry. And the problem with doing something like that in nonfiction is that, I think, then you're setting yourself up as a teacher rather than as a companion. And I think part of it—I agree with a lot of what you're saying, and in fact even though *Infinite Jest* is really long, the thing I'm most proud of is that, for once, I did not reptilianly fight and hang on to every single page that I did. I allowed myself to have faith in a really smart editor and cut some of it. And that, for me, was what was valuable about that process. But I am not yet good and smart enough to be able to do what you're talking about. I agree with you about what would be magical about that, and I think one of the most toxic things about the movement called minimalism in the 1980s was that it aped the form of that without any of its spirit or any of what would truly be magical about it—moments in Carver, maybe the end of "So Much Water So Close to Home"—but for the most part it got Americanized, it got reduced to a set of formal schticks, an appearance, a persona.

   For now, given my limitations—at least, like in the nonfiction book—I wanted much more to set myself up as the sort of companion whom the reader could tell might be somewhat annoying but was not going to BS the reader and was not going to adopt a certain kind of posture where I'm up here and the reader's down there or I'm up here and the other cruisers are down there, who was going to be a kind of companion or tour guide who was very observant but was also every bit as bound up and Americanized and self-conscious and insecure as the reader. Now, I realize what I'm giving you is a literary defense for a kind of literature that is inferior to the kind you're talking about, but I don't think it's without value.

MS: Well, no, you're very present, and I guess what I'm talking about is a literature that implicitly takes to heart the Zen maxim, "Live as if you were already dead."

DFW: Oh, yeah. Well, you're talking about an effaced narrator where it's not a literary choice, but it's, in fact, a truth. And except for very rare, transcendent pieces of fiction, I haven't seen that done anywhere except spiritual and religious literature. Or at the end of Wittgenstein's *Tractatus*. I mean, you're talking about the sort of thing that an absolute genius—I mean, a *Mozart* of living—comes up with after decades of effort. And I'm comfortable—I'm comfortable saying I'm not there yet.

MS: I've been speaking to David Foster Wallace—

DFW: Good grief!

MS: —on the occasion of the publication of *A Supposedly Fun Thing I'll Never Do Again*. Thank you, David, for joining me.

DFW: Thank you. [*laughter*] I'm now going to beat my head against the wall for thirty seconds.

MS: [*laughter*] I'm Michael Silverblatt. Join me again—No, he actually is. Stop!—on *Bookworm*.

1999: *Brief Interviews with Hideous Men*

MS: Now, the book's title, in a sense, tells you what it is, but at the same time a bag is over a gentleman's head, on the cover, and while the title describes the contents, it's sort of like the contents of the bag. The book itself seems very different—rather, its inner subject is different, it seems to me, than its ostensible subject. Is this true?

DFW: Oy. Hmm. Other than liking the color of the cover, I have nothing to do with the cover. The book has the title it does because I like that title, and the greatest number of pages of the book are given over to things called "Brief Interviews with Hideous Men," and then, at a certain level, the interviews begin playing off of and stitching together various other elements in the book.

I get to ramble on this answer because the question was very hard. Part of the book consists of short stuff that I had written kind of independently of anything else and then wanted to collect, and another part of the book is supposed to dwell in that weird area between novel and short-story collection. And it really wasn't until fairly late in the game, when the editor—this is the third book that Michael Pietsch has been the editor on with me, and he's got a lot of credibility with me—when he started working on order and what to take out and what to put in.

MS: I sense, though, that there's a philosophical procedure going on in the book, not in the pieces themselves but in the space between them, in the area they structure around them. And unless I was hallucinating, I began to feel that, I don't know, a post–something or other—postpersonal, postapocalyptic—philosophy or psychology was evolving in this book.

DFW: Golly. Four different sections of the book consist of long compilations of these interviews, and the interviews are conducted by a female whom you never see and you never hear. When she asks questions, it's represented just by a journalistic capital Q. And it's primarily the interviews that were written with an eye toward making a book out of them. And the thing that I was most interested in was—I mean, I was far more interested in the interlocutor than in the people who were speaking. I don't know that I expect a reader to be, because the ways in which the interlocutor is developed are very oblique and very—I mean, she's defined almost exclusively through what she, in her transcription process, allows men to direct toward her, and so it all gets very sort of complicated. But meanwhile, while I was concentrating on this woman, this sort of fairly dark and, in some instances, predatory and evil collection of male voices and male attitudes and male dimensions and meta-dimensions of self-consciousness—in the stuff they were saying to her—started coming out, and by the second and third drafts I was also getting interested in those voices.

I don't know that I intend the book to have a psychology. It certainly doesn't have an ideology, which is something that I've started to get nailed for in interviews a little bit. Yeah, it has a fair amount to do with sex; it has a fair amount to do with heterosexual, male attitudes and orientations toward heterosexual females. But as far as I can tell, that's just kind of a unifying principle for something that's just sort of about loneliness, which is, as far as I can see—everything that I write ends up being about that. So that's my attempt at an answer to that question.

MS: The subject, though, of the absence of a mirror comes into the book, partially because the interviewer is not present. We just see her letter, Q, and you get these answers. And this subject of interpersonality or reflection: there's a retelling of Narcissus and Echo in the book. There's a terrifying twin moment at the end of the book, where, Samson-like, hair is being shorn not by Delilah but by a boy's mother, and the boy sees his face replicated by his twin brother, who's grimacing in imitation of the boy's fear and pain. And it's very much a complicated picture of the book itself because fear and pain *and* parody exist, hand in hand, in the book itself. So I wanted to ask you about this mirror theme.

DFW: I can give you a couple ideas that occur to me about the subject. I'm not certain of the extent to which they apply to the book. I'm a heterosexual male who's never been married but has been in one of these serial-monogamy-type things. I'm thirty-seven—I've been out there, alright, and I know men and I know women and I know myself, and I'm interested. I'm interested in—in misogyny, and I'm interested in hostilities both political and sort of emotional between males and females. I don't know that I'm interested in them for the reasons that a whole lot of other people are interested in them—I mean, it's a huge sort of cultural locus right now. For instance, I found really interesting stuff in *Men Are from Mars, Women Are from Venus*, which is a very pop book and which like—anyway. My guess is that a certain amount of misogyny—and I'm just talking about straight, white, male, sneery objectification of women, your classic pre-feminist Neanderthal, knuckle-dragging male thing—is rooted almost a hundred percent in fear but it's a weird kind of fear. It's got something to do with, I think, American male self-definition being very precarious, being extraordinarily focused on sex and sex stuff. And I think, for all the talk in our culture about women being objectified, being the object of a certain kind of gaze, I don't think very much gets talked about in terms of—of men's terror of women's judgment of them, and not just judgment of them sexually but judgment of them existentially, humanistically. And in a whole lot of cases the reason it's very tempting to objectify women, or to use any of the very standard, unoriginal, male, withdraw-and-don't-deal-with-women tactics, is that the idea of being perceived and judged by the Other—by another's subjectivity—is incredibly horrifying. I'm not pretending that any of this is original, and you can read really interesting descriptions of the kind of anti-Semitism that led to the Holocaust in sort of the same terms. I mean, the instinct to dehumanize the Other, the instinct to turn the Other into a means rather than an end, is—I can't defend it, but for me it seems like what a tremendous amount of our cultural flux and our cultural pain is about.

I should say, I'm not describing to you stuff that was in my head when I was doing this. This is kind of the postgame; you're asking interesting questions, and I'm answering them. It's—It's very much I just sort of heard these guys, and I heard these guys through the sensibility of a particular kind of woman, who was very real to me but didn't exist, and I couldn't see her, and I couldn't hear her, and it was very strange, and that's really much more the truth. It's just that's not an interesting answer.

MS: Well, when I say that the book is, in a way, postpersonal, I do feel that this character and all the characters exist and don't exist. And their talk is both an accurate depiction of a kind of talk and an abstraction of that kind of talk *and* a parody of that kind of talk. And the virtue of the book seems to be that in tickling the funny bone, as they say, it arouses pain or avoidance anxiety or a kind of need—out of repulsion—to get away from the tickler, that there's a complicated kind of reader response being called forth by the book.

DFW: It's even more complicated than I was just rambling about before because, of course, these guys are speaking to a woman whom they give every indication of knowing is a kind of feminist journalist or essayist, and so they're very rhetorically self-conscious, too.

I wanted to do a book that was sad, and I wanted to do a book that had more to do with the kind of conventional love-story-ish, male-female, parent-child stuff. It's something I'd tried to do on *Infinite Jest*, and everybody thought that book was very funny, which was of course nice, but it was also kind of frustrating, and I designed this one so that nobody is going to escape the fact that this is sad.

MS: But there is, in this book, a kind of personal sadness that's constantly afraid of being accused of pretentiousness. In fact, it seems that in a particular story, which I liked very much, called "Church Not Made with Hands," that there's a deliberate goad to the reader: a presentation of a writing that is simultaneously very poetic and at the same time intentionally pretentious, or portentous. Feeling it's being recognized, is being reached by risking or enduring or even floating past portentousness, and that poetry doesn't matter, really, either. There's some kind of liquid emotion in this story that the space between its styles and its dangers is trying to evoke.

DFW: I doubt, I doubt that any period of writing fiction is any harder or less hard than any other, but it feels, of course, because I'm writing now, it feels like this is an unprecedentedly hard time to do this. And it's particularly hard, at least for me, as I get older and I get far less interested in intellectual stuff and far more interested in precisely the kind of stuff that I have a horror of and I've been trained to have a horror of, and that's sentimentality, and that's strong emotion, and that's didacticism, pretentiousness—

MS: Commercialism?

DFW: Commercialism—I mean, commercialism, I think, is the initial bite of the apple that pollutes it, but I think it's now become a cultural engine. I'm trying to think of an example of—for instance, imagine that I'm home and I'm listening to the radio, and maybe I'm listening to your show, and maybe I'm listening to an author who I think is just being a raging a–hole and a pretentious, you know, whatever, and I'm thinking how self-centered he is and how much he's trying to impose a vision of himself on the listener. Well, here's the 1999 element of this for me: really, if I stop and am honest with myself for a moment, the only difference between—hopefully—hopefully, the only difference between me and that author is that I am somewhat more cunning. That is, for instance, in a story I'm so horrified, I think, of the reader having certain reactions that I regard as prima facie, just intolerable. If the guy thinks I'm an obtuse, pretentious dweeb, I'm dead, the story's dead, any possibility of interaction between the two of us is dead. But also, on a less romantic level, I myself, Dave, personally am dead. And so, there's a certain amount of—I think some of what's uncomfortable for people about my stuff the last couple of years has been that it's very much like watching somebody kind of reach out for and recoil from something at the same time. I *do* want to do stuff that's moving, and I want to do stuff that feels important—and that feels important to me—and on the other hand, I am scared poopless of it. I'm assuming I can't say four-letter words on radio?

MS: Better not to.

DFW: Okay, *poopless* then, scared poopless. And in my own defense, I think it's a very tricky rhetorical time for any but the most either commercially manipulative writer, on one hand, or the most pointy-headed, brilliant, temporal-lobed, intellectual writer, on the other. Because I'm not any different from anybody else, and I think it's a time in America when we're intensely self-conscious, in terms of our presentation, and in terms of other people's analysis of us and the sophistication of that, and *our* awareness of *their* awareness of *our* awareness that they're interpreting, and, yeah, it can all get kind of Clang-Bird-ish, but it's also—it also seems to me to be very sad.

MS: Well, for me, at the beginning there was the sense of stories beginning because they can, and we'll see where they go, almost like an improvisation—

DFW: Like, what ones start like that?

MS: Well, the first story or the diving-board story, and then these stories start to revolve. Styles accrete around them. There are tones within tones, and what seems complicated—it reminds me: I remember saying to you about *Infinite Jest* that there, in the middle of that hilarious game-of-worlds war game at the boys' school, there's a child tasting snow on his tongue, and there's something heartfelt and achieved because what surrounds it has become so complicated. Here it felt as if, in reading these stories with eyes wide open, I was being asked to revolve so much that I would get dizzy, and in the fall, in the dizziness, was a kind of compelling sadness, itself formed by the obligation to have no stable position, that everything has to spin on itself until a kind of weariness, attrition, ecstasy, exhilaration, humor, terror become *compounded*. And the emotion bomb, as the therapists say, is left in the reader.

DFW: Well, you're giving—I mean, this is why I look forward to coming to LA, is you tend to give interpretations of the stuff that's real close to, you know, to what I want. For me, the great fantasy wish is that, in complication and in layer upon layer of sort of excruciatingly detailed, jot-and-tittle, psychological, mirrors-staring-at-each-other stuff, within all that stuff there's the possibility for great and profound emotional and spiritual and existential affect. I worry, as a fiction writer, I worry sometimes that there isn't, that I'm just kidding myself and that, in fact, what it is, is that I'm wedded to a certain style that allows me to use certain things I'm good at and to play a whole lot of games. So it's nice to hear you say that. I'm also aware that there are readers who are not going to have that reaction, that there are readers who are going to see this as a book by a technician, and a cold book, and a book that's being mean to just about everybody that it's possible to be mean to. And one of the weirdnesses about coming out here and—coming out of the burrow and talking to people about this is—I could fairly well predict how this would go 'cause I know you read stuff a bunch of times, and you're a good reader and our tastes are similar. This I wasn't too worried about, but I'm going to have to talk to people who don't have that reaction at all, and I'm not, deep down, sure which one is right.

MS: Now, that is a question that I wanted to talk to you about because something happened between my generation and yours. I remember, back when, stories that seemed to goad a deliberate hate response from me, which were usually called "black humor" and were usually written by people like Terry Southern, Bruce Jay Friedman, a kind of celebration of obviously hideous values meant to make the reader, usually, sneer in complicity with the writer. Here, the complicity has become very complicated, because—it's so interesting!—as I was reading I was saying, "Okay, who's speaking here? Who has made this person speak? And why would a writer want to give voice to so many anathematic attitudes, given that the world is full of them, given that these are all attitudes that exist? The author is choosing to populate a book with attitudes that any sane person would hate." Why?

DFW: Most of the voices, at least for me, even the most misogynistic ones, have elements of fear and insecurity and loneliness that I identify with. I mean, a couple of these are very close to some stuff that I have done and said in my career. Particularly, there are some really craven breakup monologues, where, you know, "Baby, your quitting your job and moving out here has put so much pressure on me that I can't stand it, and now I need you to move back out"—kind of charming stuff I did in my twenties. But those guys are the small potatoes. I mean, it gets very, very dark. If it works at all, these guys are not freaks, and the show isn't *Real People*, and they're not monsters for me to set up and the reader and I join in pointing at them and going, "Ugh, we're so glad we're not like that!" I mean, that stuff's dead. I recognize myself in almost every speaker in there, and that doesn't mean that that speaker's beliefs are mine or that the speaker's way of representing himself is mine, but—the last interview in there is the longest one, and it's by a guy kind of having to confront his views about a New Age person who tells him a story about avoiding getting killed by a serial killer. That, for me, was the most upsetting part of the book to write. I think it's the best of the interviews, but it's very upsetting because I realized that, even though I would disavow, proposition by proposition, everything this guy says, I also identify an enormous amount with the guy. And so, a certain amount of the interviews—and, this will horrify some readers if they've read the interviews—a certain amount of the interviews is really kind of stuff about me. My hope, and I think Little, Brown's hope, is that there's sufficient loci of identification on the part of the reader that it won't just be Dave doing some veiled confession and seeing if he can gross people out.

MS: It's a very complicated effect, and I can only describe its effect on me. Almost all of those speakers were emanations of a spirit that I don't want to be but have tendencies in common with. As a result, as they accumulate—and in addition to the interviews there are short stories that sort of reflect the interviews, conceptualize upon views offered by them, bring them to logical or preposterous extremes—and the feeling was that in this tornado country there is no stable way to live. So I found myself feeling that every person becomes like a one-person ghost town. The reader is kind of put in this really unstable position. Not just, "We have not lived the right life, and there is no right life to live," but some other kind of realization that there is no moral underground and that identification has become, in complicated ways, impossible.

DFW: I don't think the book has an ideology, but I think there are things about the book that are symptomatic of a particular kind of complication that's potentially pernicious, which is—when you talk about "there's no moral underpinning right now," I guess I would respond that, particularly in male-female relationships where very often you get the richest and darkest psychic truths delivered through jokes or very loutish stuff that you almost see on cable TV, the big thing is how to appear sensitive in the '90s, you know? The '90s skirt-chaser now has to affect the kind of Alan Alda-ish sensitivity and almost androgyny as opposed to the machismo of fifteen years ago. This idea, not that there's no moral underpinning, but that everything is rhetoricized. Everything has an element of presentation and interpretation and sales pitch and this mental chess where before I say the thing, I already scan and triage your possible responses to it, and my responses to that response, and the portraits we're going to get of each other from what we're going to say, such that one reason why I, who have reasonably strong moral beliefs, would never, in a radio show like this, promulgate them is because half of me is split off and floating and is appallingly aware of what I am going to come off to your listeners as looking like should I promulgate moral beliefs. Which I do not think vacuums our universe out of the possibility of moral belief, but it puts a spin on things that I—I'm not a great historian, but as far as I can see, not since the Sophists in Athens has there been this rapacious and affective and widespread rhetoricizing and performance and review and me-watching-you-watching-me-watching-you-type metastasis in a vibrant culture. And that, I think, in a small way is interesting, and in a large way is a tremendous engine of loneliness and is something that, I think, we as a culture are going to have to find a way to deal with.

There. That was almost an earnest moral statement, and I feel better for having made it.

2000: "A Heartbreaking Group of Staggering Geniuses"

MS: Today you're going to hear the last installment in our series "A Heartbreaking Group of Staggering Geniuses." You've heard, in no particular order, Dave Eggers, Donald Antrim, George Saunders, Mark Z. Danielewski, Dennis Cooper, and Bret Easton Ellis, and today we're talking to David Foster Wallace. David Foster Wallace is the author, most recently, of *Brief Interviews with Hideous Men*, which has come out in paperback from Back Bay Books. He is the author as well—I want to say "of course" here, and I think it should be "of course"—of *Infinite Jest, A Supposedly Fun Thing I'll Never Do Again, Girl with Curious Hair,* and *The Broom of the System*. He is, if you've been listening, the writer that most of our writers have most frequently referred to as an inspiration, as a breakthrough point, as a level against which they aspire. So in this interview, I'm going to be asking David about his own work and about some of the questions that have been coming up again and again during the series.

I caution listeners: I am talking to David in his home in Illinois. It is an outpost of Illinois, and we are at the mercy of the sounds of the telephone and the background sounds of human life. [*Dog barks*] Like that.

DFW: Not rigged. As long as he does that elsewhere in the house, we'll be all right.

MS: What is his name?

DFW: That dog is named Jeeves. He heard about this and was actually looking forward to sitting in, but apparently he's being called away.

MS: I wanted to begin by talking to you about the difficulty of some of these books and certainly about *Infinite Jest.* It was only a couple of weeks ago, at an ongoing reading of *Gravity's Rainbow* at UCLA, that a very triumphant-sounding graduate student told me that they'd lobbied, and *Infinite Jest* had been put on as a required book under the category "Postmodern Novel" in the UCLA graduate oral exams. But at the same time, some of the writers have spoken about how dazzled they were by the book—so impressed and even bewildered by it—that they're only now coming to a sense of how great it is. And I wanted to ask, because I've never asked anyone before: Do you see that book itself as a challenge for you? Are you trying to match its difficulty? Does trying to do that, even in prospect, fatigue or inspire you?

DFW: I guess what interests me is just like what interests everybody else. It's just sort of what feels real, and a lot of what feels real to me or resonates with my own life in fiction involves digesting and handling a large volume of information and also having the real problem being not how to resolve certain stuff, but the question of whether certain stuff can be resolved or not. I don't know whether that makes any sense.

I get a little puzzled when people talk about the difficulty of *Infinite Jest*, because to the best of my recollection, it's not that complicated. I mean, there are a couple of things sort of toward the end that can go one way or the other, but for the most part I just remember it as being kind of sad.

MS: Irresolvability does seem extremely important in my sense of your work. When I read, and in this case reread, and in this case, more so, not only reread but heard a two-volume tape you did for Time Warner Audiobooks of unexpurgated stories from *Brief Interviews with Hideous Men*, my sense was that, like the ending of *Infinite Jest*, what qualifies a subject for you is that it be irresolvable.

DFW: Well, I guess I would just come back to what kind of feels real, quote-unquote, in our tummy. And your classic sort of commercial art, of which the easiest example would be the detective genre—the whole thing is about establishing a puzzle and then resolving it somehow, and it's not hard to make the argument that a lot of sort of more mainstream-y or re-alist fiction works the same way. But I don't think irresolvability is really what feels real to me, because once you've determined that something is in fact irresolvable, well, it sounds like I'm just playing with words, but you've really resolved it. Unsolvable.

I don't know about you, but it just seems to me that, in all kinds of situations, some of which are very important, most of the energy goes into trying to decide whether it's worth spending energy trying to resolve it or not, you know?

MS: There's a test, I think, given the students in *Infinite Jest*. They're asked to resolve an apparent irresolvable situation: there is a kleptomaniac who has developed agoraphobia, so he can't go to the places that he richly yearns to steal from. And eventually—it seems like a classical joke, and it's so funny that I always tell about it—someone comes up with the solution of mail fraud for that hapless young kleptomaniac. But in *Brief Interviews with Hideous Men*, double binds of that sort are discovered and magnified so that a woman, for instance, who has a kind of perfection mania wants to be a perfect mother, feels very critical of her imperfect son, but, wanting to be a perfect mother, she can't criticize him, so she continues to praise him. And eventually, as a kind of gift—the title of that story suggests—the son commits suicide. And I wondered about the double bind as the inspiration point for a lot of these fictions.

DFW: The *Brief Interviews* book, if it was unified by anything, it had to do with loneliness, and loneliness particularly in the context of relationships between people. And I guess it emerged that, at least for me, double binds or that kind of W. Somerset Maugham, *Appointment in Samarra*—I'm running from death, and death is actually waiting for me in the city that I'm running off to—it's like a little fable from Iraq or something. That those sorts of, you'd call it a "cosmic irony," I guess, in a lit class, have a certain kind of weird resonance for me. I don't think they're entirely an intellectual resonance; it just sort of seems to me to be the way things are.

MS: What amazes me when I'm reading these books is that previous writers, the writers that an earlier generation worshipped—those would include, I think, Vladimir Nabokov, Thomas Mann, James Joyce—had a kind of standard of prose beauty or excellence that could be, I think, referred to as a belletristic tradition, the tradition of beautiful letters. The writing that I've been talking about is less interested in consistency of style or the forging of a high style than, it occurs to me, in making a kind of beautiful mess, risking throwing all kinds of things into the soup in order to make the situation more complex. And when you think of the person who kept putting oddments and bits of the culture's effluvia into the work, you think of Donald Barthelme and that generation, and even he, or perhaps especially he, was interested in a kind of consistent, no-mess, stylist's prose. I wondered if you could talk about the kind of prose that's getting written now, the kind of prose that you write.

DFW: I guess maybe I'd say this, which I'm not sure is true, but I think it's at least interesting, is that—and now what am I thinking of? There was a thing that hardly anybody talks about anymore called "Within the Context of No Context" by George W. S. Trow. Now, this is a little toss-off, and I think it's in the second part about music, where he talks about awkwardness versus smoothness. And he's talking about a certain moment in blues and in the evolution of popular music out of blues. And his basic point was that, transferring it to this, call this my generation—yeah, I was born in '62, so call it those people who were born then or after—I think smoothness and prettiness might have a slightly different connotation for us than it did, say, for the earlier generation. For the earlier generation it was probably associated with education and refinement, sort of good manners. And I think, for my generation, smoothness—whether it be kind of the effortless prose or the smooth, seamless document where no question is brought up that isn't resolved and no gun is shown that isn't fired in the third act and all that stuff—I think we equate that kind of sophistication more with not smoothness but slickness and a certain kind of—I mean, you might even say it's the difference between a top-forty song and a kind of more alternative or garage song. That there is something in people of around my generation, and I don't know whether it's right or not, but I think a certain kind of awkwardness or lack of the traditional patrician refinement we associate not with naïveté or clumsiness, so much as with sincerity and being heartfelt, being real/homemade versus being slick, seamless, more like a corporate product.

And I don't know whether that makes any sense, but when I think, for instance, of Gaddis, some of his stuff is very messy and very, very hard to read, but, of course, most of what he's writing about are corporations and sort of fake institutions and forgeries and lawsuits and all the kind of smooth, sleek, basically lies, stylistically, that we kind of live and move in. And I would say that if I had a stylistic influence it would be more Gaddis than anything else.

MS: In some way, for the writer, who, for better or worse, we're characterizing as a John Updike–John Barth pretty writer, the ability to locate a problem itself had something to do with solving the problem. You could write a seamless kind of prose. For this subsequent generation—and perhaps we have to throw out lists or generations because what you say *is* true of Gaddis as well, especially in the later books when he's following more the syntax of the spoken voice than he is the syntax of beautiful writing—to name the problem does not put the writer above the problem, it locates the writer *in* the problem. The problem becomes something like the tar baby: the writer gets caught both outside and inside, or more inside than outside, and the book seems like the recording of the process of trying to find an extrication point while suspecting that there is none. This may be what I'm describing as "mess" or "beautiful mess."

DFW: There's been some sort of change, I think, where—and I don't know enough sociology—but I think issues that were fundamentally issues of class for perhaps some older writers—that is, it was okay to be a rebel and an experimentalist, but one, in a certain sense, had to establish one's class credentials in order to do so, right? So that while one could subvert certain ideas of fiction, it was certainly going to be pretty, and it was going to be able to do all the sort of sensuously gratifying things that the more quote-unquote naïve fiction could do. And in that sense, you had kind of dukes and earls rebelling, sort of, instead of the rabble.

Somewhere along the line—and I may be talking more about myself than anybody else—I think what for a long time were issues of class and kind of upper and educated class versus uneducated or more blue-collar class—and these are fluctuations that I think you can see even in the movement from the quote-unquote founding postmodernists to the '80s minimalists with the kind of short sentences and downtrodden characters and trailer-park and duplex settings. I think somewhere in the late '80s, or at some point when that sort of minimalist fiction began to pass from vogue, it wasn't that the class questions changed, it was that the class questions disappeared, and issues that were fundamentally about class and inclusion became more, for people maybe my age and a little younger, questions of corporations and consumers and consuming models versus alternative, homemade, quote-unquote noncorporate transactions. I don't know if this makes any sort of sense. I know, for me, a certain kind of smoothness that you can identify with resolution, easily identified black-

and-white heroes and villains, standardly satisfying endings involving the gratification of romance or epistemological problems, I associate with corporate entertainment, whose agenda is fundamentally financial. And some of it's quite good, but its fundamental orientation is—there's no warmth in it toward the reader or no attempt to involve the reader or the audience in a kind of relationship or interaction. It's a transaction of a certain kind of gratification in exchange for money.

MS: You know, you've just filled me with ideas that I want to express some of, and this is why I prefer to work without questions, because I never thought this before, but I'm responding to you. I think that, when you think about it, Barth, Updike: these are not patrician people. These are people whose acceptance at Harvard, in Updike's case, or at Johns Hopkins in Barth's, came as something of a surprise, but college was going to be, for them, this friendly place that raised them out of the squalor of, in Barth's case, the corner-sandwich-shop father he had, in Updike's case, I don't remember the particular circumstance—

DFW: His dad was a high school teacher.

MS: Yeah. And so, it was at a time when entering the corporation, as represented by the status college, in this case, seemed like a good, ennobling, friendly thing to do. By countering it, by writing fictions that pointed out the cracks in the system, they were even further experiencing what a writer has to experience: you have to be against what spawned you. But they were not against it to the extent that it didn't seem, at that time, inimical. We're at a point now I don't think we anymore know, offhand, what college Bill Vollmann or David Foster Wallace or Dennis Cooper went to. We do know where Bret went, but maybe he's part of an earlier minimalist generation there, because it doesn't matter anymore. The college did not ennoble you or raise you out of any muck or change your language into the language of the ruling class. And I think you're absolutely right. What's happening here, in a lot of work I'm caring about right now, is—what I'm calling "the mess"—is looking for a language that one can use without deception. And you're trying not to use the corporate voices because they've revealed themselves too clearly as not our friends but the voices of a kind of patristic culture or a numbing culture or an anesthetizing culture.

DFW: Yeah, I don't know. I would just use *cold* or *warm*.

MS: This may be generational. For me, the "warm" business—happiness was a warm puppy or happiness was a warm gun. But "warm" started to seem like something that was too gooey and sweet, and a whole generation of writers turned, as an antidote, to coldness, feeling that it wouldn't be sloppily used against one, that the ability to melt a heart, the consequence of warmth, would not be—the heart-melting quality was always the artillery of what we used to consider to be the corporate logo. So, why warm-cold as poles here?

DFW: Yeah, we're using them in different ways. When I was a dutiful little student in my writing classes, I do know that the great odium, the great thing that you didn't do was melodrama or tear-jerker stuff; and so, to that extent, I get what you're talking about. I guess I mean cold in terms of whether the fundamental transaction is an artistic transaction, which I think involves a gift, or fundamentally an economic transaction, which I regard as cold. I think television, commercial films, commercial top-forty music, some of which, make no mistake, I put in my time watching, these are all very cold media, even though they're probably the only place in any kind of art where melodrama is still extensively used. The coldness I'm talking is not—none of this is *for* you. I mean, what it is, is to get you to like it enough so that certain rewards accrue to the producers and sponsors of these things. Very easy to say, right? Because now I'm going to contrast my own work with this, although both books that you've talked about in this half hour are published by Little, Brown, which is owned by Time Warner, which is now, I guess, owned by AOL. One of the reasons why people, I think, react to certain things like alternative music or poetry slams or kind of makeshift art that you see in parks and stuff—some of which is kind of ugly, but it's warm. One senses that the transaction is, for lack of a better term, spiritual, and it's between people, and economics and sales are not at the absolute fundament of it.

MS: What occurs to me as you speak is that, in a way, that I didn't know when I started this, when I got Dave Eggers's book *A Heartbreaking Work of Staggering Genius*, I didn't isolate that phrase "staggering genius." But you're helping me to do so, because it occurs to me that for a whole period in fiction a thing that we didn't want was genius. Genius belonged to the Nabokov-Joyce and then, by extension, Barth-Pynchon category, and suddenly, during the years of minimalism, we had Carver and others, who, no matter how human an artist we talk of them as, didn't have genius in that encyclopedia's-worth-of-knowledge sense. Now, suddenly, there's the emergence, I think, with a lot of people's work—your own among them—but with Vollmann and Danielewski and all sorts, of the return of this genius writer, but the emphasis on, say, "staggering genius." In other words, as opposed to "perfect genius," or "inviolable genius," or "heartless genius"—that maybe the staggering part is what re-establishes it as human, as noncorporate, as opposed to the corporate. Can you comment?

DFW: Yeah—I guess the thing that occurs to me is that talking about quote-unquote the genius writer and the non—I would say that Carver's a genius but his persona was anti-genius, I agree. But what about readers? I think—this may be goopy of me—but I think most of the writers I really respect and know and whose work is important to me seem to have a very high estimation of the reader and to require genius as a criterion for good reading as well as for good writing. And this may be part of this mess that you're talking about, but it also may be that the kind of genius we're talking about here is the genius of negotiating the mess, and putting the things together, and being able to decide whether something resolves or not. And it just doesn't seem to me—You're right, there's a certain imperial quality to some of the quote-unquote geniuses you mentioned before that I myself just don't associate with any of the writers who are doing powerful work today. Some of them are, I think, involved in transactions requiring genius, but it seems to me to be sort of required on both sides. And the thing I like about that is that one of the things, for me, that distinguishes the smooth and the facile and the corporate is that it feels to me, despite melodrama and despite good comedy, that there's a kind of cool contempt for the reader or the audience or a low estimation of the reader and the audience's willingness to do any sort of work or withstand any sort of discomfort. And some of the fiction I'm familiar with on the list that you prepared seems to me to be operating in a very different way.

MS: Thank you for joining me, David.

DFW: Thank you. Now what should I say in response?

MS: [*laughter*]

DFW: No, no, no, I mean like, "Thank *you?*" Or something droll? I don't know.

MS: Well, you know, I think this is perfect.

DFW: What about something collegial like, "A pleasure, as always"?

MS: [*laughter*] Perfect.

DFW: A pleasure, as always.

2006: *Consider the Lobster*

MS: We haven't seen each other face-to-face in a couple of years, and it's been a while since David has been on the show, but he's been on the show from the very beginning. I'm particularly happy because this book, *Consider the Lobster*, reprints some of the essays that had been excluded from earlier books, like an essay on Dostoevsky and a lecture on Kafka, but also a fabulous and scabrous essay on the pornography business and one of its conventions called "Big Red Son." It's got the famous review of John Updike. It's got a long report on the debate about American usage in grammar and vocabulary, "Authority and American Usage"; an essay on 9/11, "The View from Mrs. Thompson's"; an essay on sports biography, "How Tracy Austin Broke My Heart." David followed the McCain campaign, but *Roll-*

ing Stone only printed a sliver of his essay—here it is, in full—called "Up, Simba"; a *Gourmet* magazine essay, "Consider the Lobster"; and a very, I think, brilliant and moving essay called "Host," on political talk radio.

Now, as I was reading, it seemed to me that these essays really have a deep logic to them, that—I'm going to start with that essay "Host"—that they begin by correcting the premises of previous commentators. That essay "Host," on American political talk radio, begins by saying that many of the liberals who've criticized these stations do so from a false perspective. They consider this as political commentary and journalism when in fact, at the stations, these are considered entertainment, and therefore the arguments, which are largely political in nature, are irrelevant to the concerns of these stations, which are about how to use forms of anger and stimulation as entertainment. Facts, correct facts, are not the bases here. It seems to be the organizing point for how to consider this phenomenon of right-wing radio, and the essay seems to be about reaching conclusions based on correct and corrected premises.

DFW: Well, if there's a thing that a lot of the long pieces in this book have in common, it's that, to a large extent, they're about ideology. And I don't know—I do know that in doing some of the research reading for the talk radio piece there was a sort of paradox or trap that I'm sure you're aware of, which is that things divide very neatly into two camps: there are apologists and opponents. And so, most articles about talk radio that run in organs like *The Nation*, *Dissent*, *Harper's* are blistering attacks focused almost entirely on what's pernicious and/or wrong. The rather loose relationship with facts is made much of. And if you read the *American Standard*, or some of the more conservative organs, they're very different, and their arguments have to do more with the fact that radio, including talk radio, was for many years guided by ideology without anybody ever having said so and that now, suddenly, there are voices on the right that are in some ways correcting or balancing the liberal media bias. Now, all of a sudden, people on the left are all worried, right? And so it's almost like listening to an old married couple argue with each other, where pretty much everybody has a point, but it's clear that there's a larger problem, which is that these are two sides that are not having any kind of meaningful conversation with each other. To the extent that there was a project in the talk radio piece, it was to try to do just about the only different thing I could think of to do, which was, rhetorically, to do a piece where there was certainly the appearance of trying to be a great deal more fair and broad-minded to right-wing talk radio than right-wing talk radio itself was to its opponents and to try, to an extent, to look at or balance both sides.

MS: Now, in the essay about Tracy Austin, you come to an interesting conclusion, and I think of it as being sort of a paradigm for the way these essays find themselves thinking.

First, let me say that the essays are what I truly enjoy: thought in action. That in reading them you're going to be following certain lines of argument, suspending them for a consideration of an opposite. That there's a kind of muscular activity of mind going on here, in addition to a lot of fun and a lot of moral consideration.

You say about the Tracy Austin book, that it breaks your heart because you've loved watching her, she's a tragic figure in the sports community, the autobiography comes out, and it contains none of the understanding of what it might feel like to be on the playing field, making any number of immediate, instinctual decisions—what that feels like, what it's like to be wired in that way, what it's like to be a genius of that sort. And then the essay concludes with the idea that, perhaps, being a genius of that sort precludes being able to voice distinctions and careful choices, that the immediacy of the sport is born out of a body's immediate response without intervention of the mind. This seemed to me to be a very generous way of saying that the verbal art operates independently of the trained body, and that these books are striving toward something that a sports person can't even be expected to start to do.

DFW: See, you do a way better job of describing these things than I would. I know whatever muscularity there is in a piece like the Tracy Austin or the lobster one had to do with the fact that some of these start out as sort of magazine assignments, and they end up—oh, I don't know how to explain this.

I don't know a whole lot about nonfiction, journalism, all this sort of stuff—the way that I think about these things, in terms of what I can do, is I almost think of this as kind of a service industry and that essays like this are occasions to watch somebody reasonably bright, but also reasonably average, pay far closer attention and think at far more length about all sorts of different stuff than most of us have a chance to in our daily lives. I mean, to the extent to which I understand what I'm trying to do in these pieces, it's that. So—and I'm remembering the word because it's a compliment—what you're referring to as this "muscularity"—some pieces that have a certain problem end up being good enough that I'll put them in a book. The problem will be: I did a review of the Tracy Austin autobiography, which maybe now is somewhat dated. I know people under thirty who don't even know who Tracy Austin was, but she was kind of the first great nymphet prodigy of the female tennis world in the '70s and '80s and someone who I grew up watching. Well, the problem is that—and I mean this with no offense—from any kind of literary point of view, the book's a train wreck. It's banal, it's insipid, in places it's incoherent. And the problem with—I'm sure you've written book reviews too. One can really make the point and back it up with examples in like two paragraphs, and then what is there to say that makes this an interesting piece of writing? In the Tracy Austin thing, the thing that the piece ended up being about was I decided to pay attention to something rather different, which is: Why did I expect this to be better?

The genre of sports autobiographies happens to be one of the subgenres that I have this kind of guilty addiction to. I, at least, did read huge numbers of them, and almost every one involved this sense of kind of angry betrayal or disappointment because they were never as interesting as I was sure they were going to be. And so, really, to the extent that it's an essay, it ends up being about 1) why would a more or less averagely intelligent person like these things when they're so dreadful and b) what is it about them—I guess you don't say "one" and "B." One, why would I like them? Two, what exactly is it that makes them so bitterly disappointing for somebody who, say, played sports as a kid? And so that ends up being what it's about. The same way that the lobster essay—I mean, nothing personal, but the Maine Lobster Festival was really kind of boring, and there wasn't very much to write about. The only thing that was interesting was that it was this entire thing devoted to the pleasures of boiling alive and eating lobster, and on the fringes you had people from PETA (People for the Ethical Treatment of Animals) who were offering a very different template through which to look at the experience of eating lobster. And so that's what the piece ended up being about.

MS: The lobster essay comes to a kind of breaking point at which it addresses its reader and says, "You, reader of *Gourmet Magazine*, don't want to be told about the potential pain of the lobster, but, on the other hand, who would be more appropriate to tell?" And so, the essay takes on a kind of sense of its place and form, a sense of direct, logical address to its audience, telling its audience why they need to be addressed this way, because, in fact, who would care more, or could be expected to care more, than the readers of *Gourmet Magazine*, if these readers, in fact, want to be informed and are thinking deeply about lobster?

DFW: Well, but it depends—I mean, it's predicated on my admitting that there are certain gustatory things I don't know. One of the things that was interesting about that piece is the subtitle of *Gourmet Magazine* is "The Magazine of Good Living," right? When you start looking at a phrase like "Good Living," obviously there are all kinds of different ways that you can interpret it.

Here's another weird thing about this book: there are three or four of the pieces in here that are nearly, to me, inexplicable unless frequent acknowledgment is made, in the piece, that they are appearing in a certain organ—*Rolling Stone*, in the McCain piece, is another example I can think of. What was interesting to me is that at the time that the magazines were chopping them up and deciding to run them, they seemed somehow allergic to the idea of the article talking about the organ in which it was appearing and what certain demographic or rhetorical considerations followed from that, so the only place that I really have space and permission to talk in detail about that is in the book. But of course, now that it's in the book, it's, in fact, not in that organ. And so, it all ends up being extremely strange.

MS: But in relation, for instance, to the lobster essay, that idea about "Good Living" being a widely definable concept, which would include living in conscious awareness of one's environment and what one does to it. These essays often unfold gradually into subjects, I would say, larger than their occasions, often the subject of morality in what might be considered a largely post-moral age. And what becomes very interesting to me is that, as a young writer, you might be considered an avatar or spokesperson for the post-moral age. So watching David Wallace in these essays parsing moral distinctions and insisting, "No, I don't feel comfortable doing the humor piece on the Maine Lobster Festival. What's more, occasioned by the festival, I've been approached by people with pamphlets who've told me about what animals suffer, but I still want to continue eating certain things." So the essay becomes an attempt by the author to demonstrate a kind of moral relativism for his reader. That's what thrilled me about it.

DFW: Other than arguing with you about whether I'm in any way a "young writer" anymore, I'm just curious: Avatar of the post-moral age, how? Like, what do you mean by "moral" and "post-moral"?

MS: I think that, until I read this book of essays, for many reasons, I didn't know where you stood politically. I had certain assumptions. When in the course of the 9/11 essay you visit a neighbor of yours who attends the same church you go to, I say to myself, "Gee, I didn't know David Foster Wallace goes to church. That's interesting." I think of the apocalyptic complexity of the fiction as being not necessarily the work of someone I expect going to church and visiting neighbors to watch their TV. That kind of thing.

DFW: Hmmm. You know more about this than I. My sense is that somehow, around the time of modernism, literary stuff, meaning not mass-market—I mean, the kind of stuff you talk about on your show—has become almost exclusively an aesthetic enterprise. Um, I don't—moral? I guess I associate the word *moral* with self-righteousness and judgment, and so it makes me—

MS: Oh, not at all!

DFW: But, then, I don't like *post-moral* either because it sounds amoral. All I can tell you is that—as I'm driving on the terrifying freeways down here, I'm thinking, "Okay, so what general thing to say about these kind of nonfiction pieces?"—a lot of it involves, as far as I can see, just a service. The ordinary person is going to the Maine Lobster Festival in order to rest and escape from complicated, stressful, unpleasant parts of their lives. Between that and little kids tugging at your pant cuff, you don't have time really to sit and noodle—the average person—for long periods of time about what this experience is like, what assumptions you bring to bear to it, what conclusions are to be reached. And for the very few Americans who have a taste for that sort of thing, I think these essays simply provide: here's somebody who really went absolutely to the wall, dropping all the attention filters, trying to pay attention to absolutely everything, including his own responses and his own ideological templates, and trying his very best to figure out what the truth is.

MS: One of the reasons I liked seeing the Dostoevsky essay reprinted—although my sense is that it's slightly older than some of the other pieces—was that it ends on a question of how a novelist today might aspire toward the ethical, moral, spiritual authority that Dostoevsky attained and wonders whether that's even possible. But in the course of wondering, the essay identifies you, David Wallace, as someone who likes to write fiction, who regards fiction considered from a solely aesthetic standpoint as being insufficient, but who finds the big questions hard to address, and sometimes ridiculous to consider addressing, in the direct and extreme ways that Dostoevsky found. So maybe the word *moral* should be *ethical*, but, at any rate, putting this, rather than solely aesthetic dimensions at the center of the piece, or amusement—"This'd better be funny, or I'm outta here!"—but to find a way to bring these pieces to a concern with the ethics of the community seemed to me to be heroic and beautiful.

DFW: Do I possibly want to argue with that?

MS: [*laughter*]

DFW: I mean—the Dostoevsky thing, which is older, is in there partly because, as with the last four or five books, I have a really good editor. And so, the things that are in here are in here in an order that's meant to establish connections that may not be—you know what? They may not be obvious to anybody but me and him, but one of them has to do with—boy, see, some of this stuff's so complicated, it's hard even to talk about—ideology, or what Stanley Cavell would call it, "Conditions that have to do with an audience's willingness to be pleased." So that when you use words like *moral* or *ethical*, those, to me, connote a situation that's really good for the kind of era in which Dostoevsky, or in Europe maybe the Romantics were writing, and this involves the "artist" as this kind of solitary, heroic figure, wrestling with his own soul and finding a way to turn that struggle into art for the reader.

Maybe what I would say about that just makes me sound like an avatar of some kind of post-moral thing, but it seems to me, having being born in 1962 and having grown up without any memory of a life without television, for example, is that, in fact, what we have when you talk about stuff like the Dostoevsky, or ethical or moral dimensions to art, is we really have what appear to me to be two different problems, which are related in complicated ways. One is the classic one of: the writer decides—the way all of us have to decide—what is it to be a human being, what is it to find some way to make an accommodation with being an individual and being self-centered but also being part of a larger group and loving some people and not—all that stuff, all the old romantic stuff. But the other concerns appear to me to be more rhetorical or technical. Something that doesn't get talked about very much in any era I know of up till maybe the postmodern era, is that these are also public documents and works of art that are not meant simply to be expressive. They're not meant simply to be spontaneous effusions from an individual soul. They are also communications and pieces of art that are designed to please, gratify, edify, whatever, other human beings. So that you've got not just what's true for me as a person, but what's going to sound true, what's going to hit readers or music listeners or whatever, what's going to hit their nerve-endings as true in 2006, or 2000, or 1995. And it seems to me—I mean, I may have kind of a pessimistic view of it—but it seems to me that the situation, the environment in which nervous systems receive these communications is vastly more complicated, difficult, cynical, and overhyped than it used to be. The easy example, and one that I go through over and over with students in writing classes, is that these students are far more afraid of coming off as sentimental than they are of coming off twisted, obscene, gross—any of the things that used to be the really horrible things that you didn't want to betray about yourself. And it would appear that the great danger of appearing sentimental is that sentimentality is mainly now used in what appear to be very cynical marketing or mass-entertainment devices that are meant to sort of manhandle the emotions of large numbers of people who aren't paying very close attention. So that some of the most urgent themes or issues—how to deal with mourning the loss of somebody you love very much—have been so adulterated by sort of treacly, cynical commercial art that it becomes very, very, very difficult to think about how to talk about it in a way that's not just more of that crap.

Acknowledgments

Very special thanks to the Lannan Foundation for its generous longtime support and stewardship of KCRW's *Bookworm*, especially Patrick Lannan, along with John Lannan, Martha Jessup, and the staff at the Foundation.

A few years after moving to Los Angeles, Michael attended a dinner where he met Ruth Seymour, then General Manager of KCRW. They spoke for hours about Russian literature. Recognizing his gifts, Ruth asked him if he'd like to host a radio show about books. At first, Michael didn't believe in interviewing writers; he didn't want to do it. He thought it was "a violation of the essential privacy of the imagination." But what if it could be done with tenderness and enchantment? He agreed to do the show and continued to do so without pay for years. Many thanks are due to Ruth Seymour for her vision.

We're grateful to the entire staff of KCRW. Special thanks to KCRW President Jennifer Ferro; Producers Melinda Siegel, Connie Alvarez, and Shawn Sullivan; Producer/Editor Alan Howard; Engineers Mario Diaz, PJ Shahamat, and JC Swiatek; Content Director Anyel Fields; and Assistants Rob Sullivan, Anthony Miller, Jane Parshall, Robert Dewhurst, David Sobel, Linda Toderof, and Kraig Thein.

Thank you to our copyeditors James Longley and Anya Szykitka, and to early readers of these transcripts for their helpful suggestions: Leon Pan, Thomas Dolan, Dobby Gibson, Mary Gossy, Sam Grossman, and Jesse Arnholz. Extra special thanks to Chris Via for his attention and insight.

Thank you to the many people who gave permissions for the excerpts that appear in these transcripts: David Kermani, Jeffrey Lependorf, the John Ashbery Estate, Ron Padgett, the John Berger Estate, Mary Gass, and the Estate of William H. Gass.

We're extremely grateful to Art Spiegelman for making the wonderful cover for this book.

And thank you to all the listeners of *Bookworm* around the world!

Permissions

Grateful acknowledgment is made for permission to reprint excerpts from these copyrighted works:

"A Worldly Country" from *A Worldly Country* by John Ashbery, © John Ashbery and John Ashbery Estate, 2007. All material by John Ashbery is used by arrangement with Georges Borchardt, Inc. for John Ashbery's estate.

"Episode" and "Planisphere" and "Zero Percentage" from *Planisphere* by John Ashbery, © John Ashbery and John Ashbery Estate, 2009. All material by John Ashbery is used by arrangement with Georges Borchardt, Inc. for John Ashbery's estate.

"Words" and "Self-portrait 1914-18" from *Collected Poems* by John Berger. © John Berger and John Berger Estate, 2014, Smokestack collection. Used by permission of the John Berger Estate.

Excerpts from *Blue Nights* by Joan Didion, 2011 by Joan Didion. Used by permission of Alfred A. Knopf, an imprint of the Knopf Doubleday Publishing Group, a division of Penguin Random House LLC. All rights reserved.

Excerpts from *Life Sentences* by William H. Gass, 2012. Used by permission of the Estate of William H. Gass.

OTHER TITLES FROM THE SONG CAVE: